A GUIDE TO COLLEGES
FOR LEARNING DISABLED STUDENTS

A GUIDE TO COLLEGES FOR LEARNING DISABLED STUDENTS

Edited by

MARY ANN LISCIO

Future Search, Inc.
Nyack, New York

AN ACADEMIC PRESS PROFESSIONAL/TECHNICAL BOOK

1984

ACADEMIC PRESS, INC.
(Harcourt Brace Jovanovich, Publishers)
ORLANDO   SAN DIEGO   NEW YORK   LONDON
TORONTO   MONTREAL   SYDNEY   TOKYO

ACADEMIC PRESS, INC.
Orlando, Florida 32887 → 407-345-4100 (Orlando)

→ 800-321-5068   → 314-528-8110

United Kingdom Edition published by
ACADEMIC PRESS, INC. (LONDON) LTD.
24/28 Oval Road, London NW1 7DX

Library of Congress Cataloging in Publication Data

Main entry under title:

A Guide to colleges for learning disabled students.

    1. Universities and colleges--United States--
Directories. 2. Learning disabilities--United States.
I. Liscio, Mary Ann.
L901.G843 1984   378.73   84-45683
ISBN 0-12-452240-8

PRINTED IN THE UNITED STATES OF AMERICA

84 85 86 87   9 8 7 6 5 4 3 2 1

PREFACE

This first edition of "A Guide to Colleges for Learning Disabled Students" has been written to fill the gap in the college selection process for learning disabled students. Current college guides rarely mention the availability of services for learning disabled students. Learning disabled students are faced with the burdensome task of determining, without adequate information and guidance, which schools they should consider. This guide is especially valuable as it contains the name of the "Key Contact Persons" at each school. These Key Contact Persons can give immeasurable assistance, support, and encouragement to potential college students.

This guide was prepared to provide an overview of 2- and 4-year accredited colleges in the United States that have indicated specific services and arrangements for learning disabled students. The guide does not attempt to recommend schools but rather gives students and their parents an opportunity to review each school's offerings and recommends the procedure to follow in applying for admission.

Determination as to which programs will best suit a particular person with particular disabilities must be made by carefully reviewing the student's disability, accumulating data relevant to each school's program, analyzing the data in cooperation with the Key Contact Person at each school, and selecting those schools that meet the needs of the individual student. Parents, LD teachers, and guidance professionals must work together to assure the best choices for learning disabled students. We make no attempt in this guide to evaluate individual programs but rather to provide the learning disabled student with information about schools with varying services.

Colleges listed in this guide may or may not offer specific programs for learning disabled students. Further discussion with Key Contact Persons on each campus will give better understanding of the depth of individual programs.

As many schools will have expanded or added programs during the time that this guide was being published, some information may be outdated or incomplete. We welcome updated information and individual comments that will help to make this a more complete guide in future publications.

ACKNOWLEDGMENTS

Future Search Inc. was formed in 1983 as a college placement service, counseling local college-bound students of all ages in proper college selection. As more and more learning disabled students sought help in college selection through Future Search, the need for a college selection guide specific to learning disabled students became apparent. The Future Search College Planning Center franchise concept is being developed in order to provide college placement services nationwide.

As a concept develops and grows, many individuals lend support, inspiration, consultation, and labor to its completion. Thanks to SAT English skills tutor, Hilary Silver of Rye Brook, New York, for her inspiration and belief in the need for such a guide. Thanks also to Roslyn Myerowitz, special education teacher and Learning Disabilities Specialist at Ramapo High School in Spring Valley, New York, for making materials available and for her support throughout this project.

And finally special applause to Kevin Derella of Future Search who carefully collected and formatted all data for this guide and utilized his knowledge of microcomputers to specialize the data to its maximum usefulness. Without his diligence and dedication this guide could not have been written.

HOW TO USE THIS GUIDE

INFORMATION ARRANGEMENT

Colleges are grouped by 4-year and 2-year accredited programs in the United States. Colleges are then alphabetized by state and information on each college is then listed in outline form for briefness and clarity so that the user can easily discern specific data and compare schools.

DESCRIPTION OF DATA

College Identification Data

College name
College address
Telephone number

Key Contact Person

The name of the person or department on campus responsible for disabled student services

Size of School

Small = up to 2999 students enrolled, all programs
Medium = 3000 to 9999 students enrolled, all programs
Large = 10,000 or more students enrolled, all programs

Applications Deadline

The date by which incoming freshman must apply. The application deadline may not be same date for transfer students.

Approximate Tuition

Required college costs including fees required of all students

Approximate Room and Board

Cost of residential facilities including the dining program

Requirements for Admission

Lists standards each school requires in order to consider students for admission and other requirements such as tests, essays, interviews, etc. In some cases requirements for learning disabled students are the same as for all other students. In many cases certain requirements are modified or waived.

Additional Services Offered

Facilities on and off campus which enable learning disabled students to deal more effectively with college academic life and requirements.

Modifications to Traditional Learning Environment

Variations in traditional classwork requirements which make it easier for learning disabled students to accumulate lecture data and other classroom information.

Majors Offered

Majors are fields of specialized study leading to a degree. Majors are listed by broad groups into which many programs are included. In order to have a more detailed description of individual programs and courses, college catalogues should be acquired and studied.

GETTING STARTED

A wide variety of options in post secondary education are offered to learning disabled students. Generally programs are one of two different types.

1. Separate admissions and standards are offered to learning disabled students. The goal of special programs is to teach learning disabled students to manage their disability through special support services so that they may eventually function successfully in regular college programs. Some classes may be specifically for learning disabled students. These colleges put emphasis on developing study habits and skills based on individual strengths and learning styles. Normally an LD specialist in a learning lab works with students in individual counseling.

2. No special admissions policies for LD students are followed, however LD students able to meet college standards are provided with various modifications to traditional classroom learning environments as well as on campus remedial and tutorial help so that they may adjust to college academic work.

START EARLY

LD students should begin college planning at the end of the 11th year of high school or early in the 12th year.

Start early to accumulate necessary evaluations and test results that you will need to do intelligent planning for college. Contact your high school guidance counselor to obtain the following records:

1. High school transcripts
2. Written evaluations from LD teachers
3. Recommendations from regular classroom teachers
4. Test results—SAT, ACT, WAIS, etc.
5. Medical reports relevant to your learning disability

Outline your priorities for attending a post secondary institution. Things to be considered are as follows:

1. Two-year or four-year program
2. College or University

3. Majors offered
4. Facilities for LD students
5. Location
6. Size
7. Tuition
8. Clubs and Athletics offered
9. Other needs

Once priorities have been established consult this guide and choose those colleges which best meet your needs. Try to find 6 to 10 colleges with potential. Compare each school based on your priorities. Eliminate those schools that do not meet your requirements.

Send for college catalogues and program of study brochures. Write or call the Key Contact Person at each school (listed in each college description). Where an actual name is not listed contact the Handicapped Student Services Office directly. Allow one week to ten days for your letter to be received. Telephone the Key Contact Person to arrange an appointment to discuss their program. Where a face to face meeting is not possible you will need to spend time on the telephone or through a letter to get answers to some relevant questions.

WHAT TO ASK[1]

1. Is there a special program for LD students?
2. How many full-time LD students are enrolled in the program?
3. Is there a brochure or written description of the program available?
4. Do LD students in special programs take regular college courses?
5. Are special courses required of LD students? Do they carry college credit? Can credit be used toward graduation?
6. Are there additional tuition or fee requirements for LD students?
7. Are there special admission procedures for LD students?

8. NOTE: Refer to the listing provided in this guide on each college and question the Key Contact Person on each specific point so that you have a full understanding of their program and procedures. Take notes on all questions so that you may later compare schools.

It is strongly recommended that you visit each school if at all possible. Call to arrange a campus visit and a personal interview with the Key Contact Person listed in this guide and/or the Director of Admissions.

Apply to those colleges meeting your requirements and where you had a favorable campus visit.

As acceptances are received, read each carefully to determine latest response date, enrollment requirements, and tuition and aid responsibilities.

Good Luck.

[1] Taken from the Association for Children and Adults with Learning Disabilities. 1983 Internal Conference, Washington, D.C., "College Night" Presentation. Published in *Learning Disabilities in Adults: Educational Principles and Practices* (Doris Johnson and June Blalock, eds.) with permission of the publisher (Grune & Stratton, Orlando, in press).

TWO-YEAR COLLEGES

```
JOHN C. CALHOUN STATE COMMUNITY COLLEGE
P.O. BOX 2216
DECATUR, AL 35602
205-353-3102
```

KEY CONTACT: Attn: Handicapped Student Services

SIZE OF SCHOOL: MEDIUM

APPLICATION DEADLINE: NONE

	APPROXIMATE TUITION	ROOM AND BOARD
IN DISTRICT	$ 600	$NOT OFFERED
IN STATE	$ 600	$NOT OFFERED
OUT-OF-STATE	$1200	$NOT OFFERED

REQUIREMENTS FOR ADMISSIONS:
   High school equivalency diploma
   High school diploma
   Placement tests

ADDITIONAL SERVICES OFFERED:
   Diagnostic testing services on campus
   Remedial and/or tutorial help available

MODIFICATIONS TO TRADITIONAL LEARNING ENVIRONMENT:
   Use of calculator for all math courses
   Someone else may take class notes
   Extended time limits for graduation
   Physical education may be waived

MAJORS OFFERED:

   BIOLOGICAL SCIENCES
   BUSINESS AND MANAGEMENT
   COMMUNICATIONS
   COMPUTER SCIENCES
   EDUCATION
   ENGINEERING TECHNOLOGIES
   FINE AND APPLIED ARTS
   HEALTH
   MATHEMATICS
   PHYSICAL SCIENCES
   PUBLIC SERVICES
   GENERAL LIBERAL ARTS

===

SNEAD STATE JUNIOR COLLEGE
200 WALNUT STREET
BOAZ, AL 35957
205-593-5120

KEY CONTACT: Attn: A.L. LAMBERT
                      DEAN OF STUDENT SERVICES

SIZE OF SCHOOL: SMALL

APPLICATION DEADLINE: NONE

	APPROXIMATE TUITION	ROOM AND BOARD
IN DISTRICT	$ 375	$1780
IN STATE	$ 375	$1780
OUT-OF-STATE	$ 750	$1780

REQUIREMENTS FOR ADMISSIONS:
  High school equivalency diploma
  High school diploma
  Untimed or oral ACT Scores accepted
  University or College sponsored tests
  State/District residency

ADDITIONAL SERVICES OFFERED:
  Learning Lab
  Diagnostic testing services on campus
  Remedial and/or tutorial help available
  Reader services for the blind available for LD
  Handicapped student services works with LD

MODIFICATIONS TO TRADITIONAL LEARNING ENVIRONMENT:
  Oral presentation in lieu of written exams
  Use of calculator for all math courses
  Tape recorders to record class lectures
  Someone else may take class notes
  Longer time allowed to complete exams
  Extended time limits for graduation
  Physical education may be waived

MAJORS OFFERED:

  AGRICULTURE
  BUSINESS AND MANAGEMENT
  COMMUNICATIONS
  COMPUTER SCIENCES
  EDUCATION
  ENGINEERING TECHNOLOGIES
  FINE AND APPLIED ARTS
  HEALTH

HUMANITIES
LIBRARY SCIENCE
THEOLOGY
GENERAL LIBERAL ARTS

==

GLENDALE COMMUNITY COLLEGE
6000 WEST OLIVE AVENUE
GLENDALE, AZ 85302
602-934-2211

KEY CONTACT: Attn: MARK FERRIS
                    DISABLED STUDENT COUNSELOR

SIZE OF SCHOOL: SMALL

APPLICATION DEADLINE: NONE

         APPROXIMATE TUITION   ROOM AND BOARD

IN DISTRICT $ 340 $NOT OFFERED
IN STATE $ 340 $NOT OFFERED
OUT-OF-STATE $2500 $NOT OFFERED

REQUIREMENTS FOR ADMISSIONS:
    21 years of age or older, with or without a
      high school diploma or equivalency
    Untimed or oral ACT Scores accepted
    Untimed or oral SAT Scores accepted
    University or College sponsored tests
    Personal interview
    Placement tests
    Recommendations

ADDITIONAL SERVICES OFFERED:
    Learning Lab
    Diagnostic testing services off campus
    Remedial and/or tutorial help available
    Reader services for the blind available for LD
      students
    Handicapped student services works with LD
    Vocational Rehabilitation can provide diagnostic
      testing off campus

MODIFICATIONS TO TRADITIONAL LEARNING ENVIRONMENT:
    Has an adaptive physical education program
    Tape recorders to record class lectures
    Someone else may take class notes
    Take limited course load and graduate within time
      required

```
    Extended time limits for graduation
    Physical education may be waived
    All other modifications are possible but depend on
      instructor
```

MAJORS OFFERED:

```
    AGRICULTURE
    ARCHITECTURE
    AREA STUDIES
    BIOLOGICAL SCIENCES
    BUSINESS AND MANAGEMENT
    COMMUNICATIONS
    COMPUTER SCIENCES
    EDUCATION
    ENGINEERING TECHNOLOGIES
    FINE AND APPLIED ARTS
    FOREIGN LANGUAGES
    HEALTH
    HOME ECONOMICS
    HUMANITIES
    LIBRARY SCIENCE
    MATHEMATICS
    MILITARY SCIENCES
    PHYSICAL SCIENCES
    PSYCHOLOGY
    PUBLIC SERVICES
    SOCIAL SCIENCES
    GENERAL LIBERAL ARTS
```

==

```
MESA COMMUNITY COLLEGE
1833 WEST SOUTHERN AVENUE
MESA, AZ 85202
602-833-1261

KEY CONTACT: Attn:  MARLENE DENNER
                    HANDICAPPED PROGRAM COORDINATOR

SIZE OF SCHOOL: LARGE

APPLICATION DEADLINE: NONE

        APPROXIMATE TUITION    ROOM AND BOARD

IN DISTRICT      $ 250         $NOT OFFERED
IN STATE         $1800         $NOT OFFERED
OUT-OF-STATE     $2300         $NOT OFFERED
```

REQUIREMENTS FOR ADMISSIONS:
  High school equivalency diploma
  High school diploma
  21 years of age or older, with or without a
    high school diploma or equivalency
  Untimed or oral ACT Scores accepted
  Untimed or oral SAT Scores accepted
  Placement tests

ADDITIONAL SERVICES OFFERED:
  Remedial and/or tutorial help available
  Reader services for the blind available for LD
    students
  Handicapped student services works with LD

MODIFICATIONS TO TRADITIONAL LEARNING ENVIRONMENT:
  Has an adaptive physical education program
  Tape recorders to record class lectures
  Someone else may take class notes
  Students have exams read to them
  Longer time allowed to complete exams
  Extended time limits for graduation
  Physical education may be waived

MAJORS OFFERED:

  AGRICULTURE
  BIOLOGICAL SCIENCES
  BUSINESS AND MANAGEMENT
  COMMUNICATIONS
  COMPUTER SCIENCES
  EDUCATION
  ENGINEERING TECHNOLOGIES
  FINE AND APPLIED ARTS
  FOREIGN LANGUAGES
  HEALTH
  HOME ECONOMICS
  HUMANITIES
  MATHEMATICS
  PHYSICAL SCIENCES
  PSYCHOLOGY
  PUBLIC SERVICES
  SOCIAL SCIENCES
  GENERAL LIBERAL ARTS

==

PIMA COMMUNITY COLLEGE
2202 WEST ANKLAM ROAD
TUCSON, AZ 85709
602-884-6640

KEY CONTACT: Attn: CHERYL HIPSKIND
                     SPECIAL EDUCATION COORDINATOR

SIZE OF SCHOOL: LARGE

APPLICATION DEADLINE: NONE

         APPROXIMATE TUITION   ROOM AND BOARD

IN DISTRICT $ 360 $NOT OFFERED
IN STATE $1800 $NOT OFFERED
OUT-OF-STATE $2400 $NOT OFFERED

REQUIREMENTS FOR ADMISSIONS:
  Placement tests
  Open door policy

ADDITIONAL SERVICES OFFERED:
  Diagnostic testing services on campus
  Remedial and/or tutorial help available
  Reader services for the blind available for LD
     students
  Handicapped student services works with LD

MODIFICATIONS TO TRADITIONAL LEARNING ENVIRONMENT:
  Oral presentation in lieu of written exams
     (sometimes)
  Tape recorders to record class lectures
  Someone else may take class notes
  Student takes exams in separate rooms (sometimes)
  Students have exams read to them (sometimes)
  Students take typewritten exams
  Longer time allowed to complete exams (sometimes)
  Submit papers on cassette tape (sometimes)
  Extended time limits for graduation

MAJORS OFFERED:

  AGRICULTURE
  AREA STUDIES
  BIOLOGICAL SCIENCES
  BUSINESS AND MANAGEMENT
  COMMUNICATIONS
  EDUCATION
  ENGINEERING TECHNOLOGIES
  FINE AND APPLIED ARTS
  HEALTH
  HOME ECONOMICS
  MATHEMATICS
  PHYSICAL SCIENCES

```
PUBLIC SERVICES
SOCIAL SCIENCES
GENERAL LIBERAL ARTS
```

===

```
MISSISSIPPI COUNTY COMMUNITY COLLEGE
P.O. DRAWER 1109
BLYTHEVILLE, AR 72315
501-762-1020
```

KEY CONTACT: Attn: Handicapped Student Services

SIZE OF SCHOOL: SMALL

APPLICATION DEADLINE: NONE

	APPROXIMATE TUITION	ROOM AND BOARD
IN DISTRICT	$ 600	$NOT OFFERED
IN STATE	$ 900	$NOT OFFERED
OUT-OF-STATE	$1800	$NOT OFFERED

REQUIREMENTS FOR ADMISSIONS:
  21 years of age or older, with or without a
    high school diploma or equivalency
  Untimed or oral ACT Scores accepted
  Untimed or oral SAT Scores accepted
  Open admission

ADDITIONAL SERVICES OFFERED:
  Learning Lab
  Learning Lab has a specialist with a masters degree
    or above in Learning Disabilities
  Diagnostic testing services on campus
  Special Education department

MODIFICATIONS TO TRADITIONAL LEARNING ENVIRONMENT:
  Oral presentation in lieu of written exams
  Tape recorders to record class lectures
  Someone else may take class notes
  Longer time allowed to complete exams
  Extended time limits for graduation
  Physical education may be waived

MAJORS OFFERED:

  GENERAL LIBERAL ARTS

===

NORTH ARKANSAS COMMUNITY COLLEGE
PIONEER RIDGE
HARRISON, AR 72601
501-743-3000

KEY CONTACT: Attn: Handicapped Student Services

SIZE OF SCHOOL: SMALL

APPLICATION DEADLINE: NONE

	APPROXIMATE TUITION	ROOM AND BOARD
IN DISTRICT	$ 455	$NOT OFFERED
IN STATE	$ 555	$NOT OFFERED
OUT-OF-STATE	$ 855	$NOT OFFERED

REQUIREMENTS FOR ADMISSIONS:
  High school equivalency diploma
  21 years of age or older, with or without a
    high school diploma or equivalency
  ACT Scores required
  Admission requirements modified
  Placement tests

ADDITIONAL SERVICES OFFERED:
  Learning Lab
  Learning Lab has a specialist with a masters degree
    or above in Learning Disabilities
  Remedial and/or tutorial help available

MODIFICATIONS TO TRADITIONAL LEARNING ENVIRONMENT:
  Oral presentation in lieu of written exams
  Use of calculator for all math courses
  Has an adaptive physical education program
  Tape recorders to record class lectures
  Someone else may take class notes
  Student takes exams in separate rooms
  Students have exams read to them
  Students take typewritten exams
  Longer time allowed to complete exams
  Submit papers on cassette tape
  Take limited course load and graduate within time
    required
  Extended time limits for graduation
  Physical education may be waived

MAJORS OFFERED:

  AGRICULTURE
  AREA STUDIES

```
BIOLOGICAL SCIENCES
BUSINESS AND MANAGEMENT
COMMUNICATIONS
COMPUTER SCIENCES
EDUCATION
ENGINEERING TECHNOLOGIES
FINE AND APPLIED ARTS
HEALTH
MATHEMATICS
PHYSICAL SCIENCES
PSYCHOLOGY
PUBLIC SERVICES
SOCIAL SCIENCES
GENERAL LIBERAL ARTS
```

===

```
PHILLIPS COUNTY COMMUNITY COLLEGE
P.O. BOX 785
HELENA, AR 72342
501-338-6474
```

KEY CONTACT: Attn: Handicapped Student Services

SIZE OF SCHOOL: SMALL

APPLICATION DEADLINE: AUGUST 20

	APPROXIMATE TUITION	ROOM AND BOARD
IN DISTRICT	$ 465	$NOT OFFERED
IN STATE	$ 590	$NOT OFFERED
OUT-OF-STATE	$ 875	$NOT OFFERED

REQUIREMENTS FOR ADMISSIONS:
  High school equivalency diploma
  High school diploma
  21 years of age or older, with or without a
    high school diploma or equivalency
  Untimed or oral ACT Scores accepted
  Untimed or oral SAT Scores accepted
  Admission requirements modified

ADDITIONAL SERVICES OFFERED:
  Learning Lab
  Learning Lab has a specialist with a masters degree
    or above in Learning Disabilities
  Diagnostic testing services on campus
  Remedial and/or tutorial help available

MODIFICATIONS TO TRADITIONAL LEARNING ENVIRONMENT:
    Use of calculator for all math courses
    Tape recorders to record class lectures
    Someone else may take class notes
    Student takes exams in separate rooms
    Students have exams read to them
    Students take typewritten exams
    Longer time allowed to complete exams
    Extended time limits for graduation
    Physical education may be waived

MAJORS OFFERED:

    BIOLOGICAL SCIENCES
    BUSINESS AND MANAGEMENT
    COMPUTER SCIENCES
    EDUCATION
    ENGINEERING TECHNOLOGIES
    FINE AND APPLIED ARTS
    HEALTH
    HUMANITIES
    MATHEMATICS
    PHYSICAL SCIENCES
    SOCIAL SCIENCES
    GENERAL LIBERAL ARTS

==

ALLAN HANCOCK COLLEGE
800 SOUTH COLLEGE DRIVE
SANTA MARIA, CA 93454
805-922-6966

KEY CONTACT: Attn: MICHAEL MCMAHON, LD SPECIALIST

SIZE OF SCHOOL: MEDIUM

APPLICATION DEADLINE: AUGUST 14

           APPROXIMATE TUITION   ROOM AND BOARD

IN DISTRICT $ 15 $NOT OFFERED
IN STATE $ 15 $NOT OFFERED
OUT-OF-STATE $1800 $NOT OFFERED

REQUIREMENTS FOR ADMISSIONS:
    Untimed or oral ACT Scores accepted
    Untimed or oral SAT Scores accepted
    Placement tests
    Recommendations
    Essay

ADDITIONAL SERVICES OFFERED:
  Learning Lab
  Learning Lab has a specialist with a masters degree
    or above in Learning Disabilities
  Diagnostic testing services on campus
  Remedial and/or tutorial help available
  Reader services for the blind available for LD
    students
  Handicapped student services works with LD

MODIFICATIONS TO TRADITIONAL LEARNING ENVIRONMENT:
  Oral presentation in lieu of written exams
  Use of calculator for all math courses
  Has an adaptive physical education program
  Tape recorders to record class lectures
  Someone else may take class notes
  Multiple choice exams only
  Essay exams only
  Student takes exams in separate rooms
  Students have exams read to them
  Students take typewritten exams
  Longer time allowed to complete exams
  Submit papers on cassette tape
  Take limited course load and graduate within time
    required
  Extended time limits for graduation
  Physical education may be waived
  Modifications depend on instructor and individual
    need

MAJORS OFFERED:

  AGRICULTURE
  ARCHITECTURE
  AREA STUDIES
  BIOLOGICAL SCIENCES
  BUSINESS AND MANAGEMENT
  COMMUNICATIONS
  COMPUTER SCIENCES
  ENGINEERING TECHNOLOGIES
  FINE AND APPLIED ARTS
  FOREIGN LANGUAGES
  HEALTH
  HOME ECONOMICS
  HUMANITIES
  MATHEMATICS
  MILITARY SCIENCES
  PHYSICAL SCIENCES
  PSYCHOLOGY
  SOCIAL SCIENCES
  GENERAL LIBERAL ARTS

AMERICAN RIVER COLLEGE - SACRAMENTO
4700 COLLEGE OAK DRIVE
SACRAMENTO, CA 95841
916-484-8171

KEY CONTACT: Attn: ENABLING CENTER

SIZE OF SCHOOL: LARGE

APPLICATION DEADLINE: AUGUST 4

        APPROXIMATE TUITION   ROOM AND BOARD

IN DISTRICT $ 0 $NOT OFFERED
IN STATE $ 0 $NOT OFFERED
OUT-OF-STATE $1728 $NOT OFFERED

REQUIREMENTS FOR ADMISSIONS:
  High school equivalency diploma
  High school diploma
  21 years of age or older, with or without a
    high school diploma or equivalency

ADDITIONAL SERVICES OFFERED:
  Learning Lab
  Diagnostic testing services off campus
  Remedial and/or tutorial help available
  Reader services for the blind available for LD
    students
  Special Education department
  Handicapped student services works with LD

MODIFICATIONS TO TRADITIONAL LEARNING ENVIRONMENT:
  Oral presentation in lieu of written exams
  Use of calculator for all math courses
  Tape recorders to record class lectures
  Someone else may take class notes
  Multiple choice exams only
  Essay exams only
  Student takes exams in separate rooms
  Students have exams read to them
  Students take typewritten exams
  Longer time allowed to complete exams
  Submit papers on cassette tape
  Take limited course load and graduate within time
    required
  Extended time limits for graduation
  Physical education may be waived

MAJORS OFFERED:

    AGRICULTURE
    BIOLOGICAL SCIENCES
    BUSINESS AND MANAGEMENT
    COMMUNICATIONS
    COMPUTER SCIENCES
    ENGINEERING TECHNOLOGIES
    FINE AND APPLIED ARTS
    FOREIGN LANGUAGES
    HEALTH
    HOME ECONOMICS
    HUMANITIES
    MATHEMATICS
    PHYSICAL SCIENCES
    PSYCHOLOGY
    PUBLIC SERVICES
    SOCIAL SCIENCES
    GENERAL LIBERAL ARTS

===

ANTELOPE VALLEY COLLEGE
3041 WEST AVENUE K
LANCASTER, CA 93534
805-943-3241

KEY CONTACT: Attn: JOY MCCASLIN, PROGRAM MANAGER

SIZE OF SCHOOL: MEDIUM

APPLICATION DEADLINE: NONE

          APPROXIMATE TUITION   ROOM AND BOARD

IN DISTRICT $ 5 $NOT OFFERED
IN STATE $ 5 $NOT OFFERED
OUT-OF-STATE $2010 $NOT OFFERED

ADDITIONAL SERVICES OFFERED:
    Learning Lab
    Learning Lab has a specialist with a masters degree
      or above in Learning Disabilities
    Diagnostic testing services on campus
    Diagnostic testing services off campus
    Remedial and/or tutorial help available
    Reader services for the blind available for LD
      students
    Special Education department
    Handicapped student services works with LD

MODIFICATIONS TO TRADITIONAL LEARNING ENVIRONMENT:
  Oral presentation in lieu of written exams
  Has an adaptive physical education program
  Tape recorders to record class lectures
  Someone else may take class notes
  Student takes exams in separate rooms
  Students have exams read to them
  Students take typewritten exams
  Longer time allowed to complete exams
  Physical education may be waived

MAJORS OFFERED:

  AGRICULTURE
  BIOLOGICAL SCIENCES
  BUSINESS AND MANAGEMENT
  COMMUNICATIONS
  COMPUTER SCIENCES
  ENGINEERING TECHNOLOGIES
  FINE AND APPLIED ARTS
  FOREIGN LANGUAGES
  HEALTH
  HOME ECONOMICS
  HUMANITIES
  MATHEMATICS
  PHYSICAL SCIENCES
  PSYCHOLOGY
  SOCIAL SCIENCES
  GENERAL LIBERAL ARTS

===

BAKERSFIELD COLLEGE
1801 PANORAMA DRIVE
BAKERSFIELD, CA 93305
805-395-4301

KEY CONTACT: Attn: JERRY LUDEKE, LD SPECIALIST

SIZE OF SCHOOL: MEDIUM

APPLICATION DEADLINE: NONE

          APPROXIMATE TUITION   ROOM AND BOARD

IN DISTRICT $ 30 $2405
IN STATE $ 30 $2405
OUT-OF-STATE $1800 $2405

REQUIREMENTS FOR ADMISSIONS:
  High school equivalency diploma
  High school diploma
  21 years of age or older, with or without a
    high school diploma or equivalency
  Untimed or oral ACT Scores accepted
  Untimed or oral SAT Scores accepted
  University or College sponsored tests
  Admission requirements modified
  Personal interview
  Placement tests
  Essay

ADDITIONAL SERVICES OFFERED:
  Learning Lab
  Diagnostic testing services on campus
  Remedial and/or tutorial help available
  Reader services for the blind available for LD
    students
  Handicapped student services works with LD
  Special LD section of Learning Skills Class

MODIFICATIONS TO TRADITIONAL LEARNING ENVIRONMENT:
  Oral presentation in lieu of written exams
  Use of calculator for all math courses
  Has an adaptive physical education program
  Tape recorders to record class lectures
  Someone else may take class notes
  Multiple choice exams only
  Essay exams only
  Student takes exams in separate rooms
  Students have exams read to them
  Students take typewritten exams
  Longer time allowed to complete exams
  Submit papers on cassette tape
  Extended time limits for graduation
  Physical education may be waived
  All of the above modifications may and have been
    permitted by specific teachers in specific courses
    at the request of the LD specialist

MAJORS OFFERED:

  AGRICULTURE
  ARCHITECTURE
  BIOLOGICAL SCIENCES
  BUSINESS AND MANAGEMENT
  COMMUNICATIONS
  COMPUTER SCIENCES
  ENGINEERING TECHNOLOGIES
  FINE AND APPLIED ARTS

```
FOREIGN LANGUAGES
HEALTH
HOME ECONOMICS
HUMANITIES
MATHEMATICS
PHYSICAL SCIENCES
PSYCHOLOGY
PUBLIC SERVICES
SOCIAL SCIENCES
GENERAL LIBERAL ARTS
```

==

```
BUTTE COMMUNITY COLLEGE
3536 BUTTE CAMPUS DRIVE
OROVILLE, CA 95965
916-895-2561
```

KEY CONTACT: Attn: Handicapped Student Services

SIZE OF SCHOOL: MEDIUM

APPLICATION DEADLINE: NONE

	APPROXIMATE TUITION	ROOM AND BOARD
IN DISTRICT	$ 55	$NOT OFFERED
IN STATE	$ 55	$NOT OFFERED
OUT-OF-STATE	$2700	$NOT OFFERED

REQUIREMENTS FOR ADMISSIONS:
  High school equivalency diploma
  High school diploma
  21 years of age or older, with or without a
    high school diploma or equivalency
  State/District residency (for tuition)

ADDITIONAL SERVICES OFFERED:
  Learning Lab
  Learning Lab has a specialist with a masters degree
    or above in Learning Disabilities
  Diagnostic testing services on campus
  Diagnostic testing services off campus
  Remedial and/or tutorial help available
  Reader services for the blind available for LD
    students
  Handicapped student services works with LD

MODIFICATIONS TO TRADITIONAL LEARNING ENVIRONMENT:
  Oral presentation in lieu of written exams
  Has an adaptive physical education program

Tape recorders to record class lectures
Someone else may take class notes
Students have exams read to them
Students take typewritten exams
Longer time allowed to complete exams
Submit papers on cassette tape
Physical education may be waived

MAJORS OFFERED:

AGRICULTURE
BIOLOGICAL SCIENCES
BUSINESS AND MANAGEMENT
COMMUNICATIONS
COMPUTER SCIENCES
ENGINEERING TECHNOLOGIES
FINE AND APPLIED ARTS
FOREIGN LANGUAGES
HEALTH
HOME ECONOMICS
HUMANITIES
MATHEMATICS
PHYSICAL SCIENCES
PSYCHOLOGY
PUBLIC SERVICES
SOCIAL SCIENCES
GENERAL LIBERAL ARTS

==

CABRILLO COLLEGE
6500 SOQUEL DRIVE
APTOS, CA 95003
408-425-6201

KEY CONTACT: Attn: Handicapped Student Services

SIZE OF SCHOOL: MEDIUM

APPLICATION DEADLINE: NONE

          APPROXIMATE TUITION   ROOM AND BOARD

IN DISTRICT $ 30 $NOT OFFERED
IN STATE $ 30 $NOT OFFERED
OUT-OF-STATE $2300 $NOT OFFERED

REQUIREMENTS FOR ADMISSIONS:
  High school equivalency diploma
  High school diploma

21 years of age or older, with or without a
high school diploma or equivalency

ADDITIONAL SERVICES OFFERED:
Learning Lab
Learning Lab has a specialist with a masters degree
or above in Learning Disabilities
Diagnostic testing services on campus
Remedial and/or tutorial help available
Reader services for the blind available for LD
students
Handicapped student services works with LD

MODIFICATIONS TO TRADITIONAL LEARNING ENVIRONMENT:
Oral presentation in lieu of written exams
Tape recorders to record class lectures
Someone else may take class notes
Student takes exams in seperate rooms
Students have exams read to them
Students take typewritten exams
Longer time allowed to complete exams
Submit papers on cassette tape
Extended time limits for graduation
Physical education may be waived

MAJORS OFFERED:

AGRICULTURE
ARCHITECTURE
AREA STUDIES
BIOLOGICAL SCIENCES
BUSINESS AND MANAGEMENT
COMMUNICATIONS
EDUCATION
ENGINEERING TECHNOLOGIES
FINE AND APPLIED ARTS
FOREIGN LANGUAGES
HEALTH
HOME ECONOMICS
HUMANITIES
LIBRARY SCIENCE
MATHEMATICS
PHYSICAL SCIENCES
PSYCHOLOGY
SOCIAL SCIENCES
GENERAL LIBERAL ARTS

==

```
CERRITOS COLLEGE
11110 EAST ALONDRA BLVD
NORWALK, CA 90650
213-860-2451
```

KEY CONTACT: Attn: Handicapped Student Services

SIZE OF SCHOOL: LARGE

APPLICATION DEADLINE: NONE

APPROXIMATE TUITION   ROOM AND BOARD

IN DISTRICT	$ 0	$NOT OFFERED
IN STATE	$ 0	$NOT OFFERED
OUT-OF-STATE	$1650	$NOT OFFERED

REQUIREMENTS FOR ADMISSIONS:
  ACT Scores required
  Untimed or oral ACT Scores accepted
  SAT Scores required
  Untimed or oral SAT Scores accepted
  Placement tests
  State/District residency

ADDITIONAL SERVICES OFFERED:
  Learning Lab
  Learning Lab has a specialist with a masters degree
    or above in Learning Disabilities
  Diagnostic testing services on campus
  Diagnostic testing services off campus
  Remedial and/or tutorial help available
  Reader services for the blind available for LD
    students
  Special Education department
  Handicapped student services works with LD

MODIFICATIONS TO TRADITIONAL LEARNING ENVIRONMENT:
  Oral presentation in lieu of written exams
  Use of calculator for all math courses
  Tape recorders to record class lectures
  Someone else may take class notes
  Student takes exams in separate rooms
  Students have exams read to them
  Students take typewritten exams
  Longer time allowed to complete exams
  Submit papers on cassette tape
  Extended time limits for graduation
  Physical education may be waived

MAJORS OFFERED:

    AGRICULTURE
    ARCHITECTURE
    AREA STUDIES
    BIOLOGICAL SCIENCES
    BUSINESS AND MANAGEMENT
    COMMUNICATIONS
    COMPUTER SCIENCES
    ENGINEERING TECHNOLOGIES
    FINE AND APPLIED ARTS
    FOREIGN LANGUAGES
    HEALTH
    HOME ECONOMICS
    HUMANITIES
    MATHEMATICS
    MILITARY SCIENCES
    PHYSICAL SCIENCES
    PSYCHOLOGY
    PUBLIC SERVICES
    SOCIAL SCIENCES
    GENERAL LIBERAL ARTS

===

CERRO COSO COMMUNITY COLLEGE
3000 COLLEGE HEIGHTS BLVD
RIDGECREST, CA 93555
619-375-5001

KEY CONTACT: Attn: Handicapped Student Services

SIZE OF SCHOOL: MEDIUM

APPLICATION DEADLINE: NONE

        APPROXIMATE TUITION   ROOM AND BOARD

IN DISTRICT $ 20 $NOT OFFERED
IN STATE $ 20 $NOT OFFERED
OUT-OF-STATE $2160 $NOT OFFERED

REQUIREMENTS FOR ADMISSIONS:
    High school equivalency diploma
    High school diploma
    21 years of age or older, with or without a
        high school diploma or equivalency

ADDITIONAL SERVICES OFFERED:
    Learning Lab

Learning Lab has a specialist with a masters degree
   or above in Learning Disabilities
Remedial and/or tutorial help available
Reader services for the blind available for LD
   students
Handicapped student services works with LD

MODIFICATIONS TO TRADITIONAL LEARNING ENVIRONMENT:
   Oral presentation in lieu of written exams
   Use of calculator for all math courses
   Tape recorders to record class lectures
   Someone else may take class notes
   Student takes exams in separate rooms
   Students have exams read to them
   Students take typewritten exams
   Longer time allowed to complete exams
   Submit papers on cassette tape
   Take limited course load and graduate within time
      required
   Extended time limits for graduation
   Physical education may be waived

MAJORS OFFERED:

   GENERAL LIBERAL ARTS

===

CHABOT COLLEGE
25555 HESPERIAN BLVD
HAYWARD, CA 94545
415-786-6600

KEY CONTACT: Attn: CATHY NOBLE, COORDINATOR
                     SERVICES FOR DISABLED STUDENTS

SIZE OF SCHOOL: LARGE

APPLICATION DEADLINE: NONE

        APPROXIMATE TUITION   ROOM AND BOARD

IN DISTRICT	$ 0	$NOT OFFERED
IN STATE	$ 0	$NOT OFFERED
OUT-OF-STATE	$1800	$NOT OFFERED

REQUIREMENTS FOR ADMISSIONS:
   18 years of age or older, with or without a
      high school diploma or equivalency
   University or College sponsored tests
   Admission requirements modified

Personal interview
Placement tests
State/District residency

ADDITIONAL SERVICES OFFERED:
  Learning Lab
  Learning Lab has a specialist with a masters degree
    or above in Learning Disabilities
  Diagnostic testing services on campus
  Remedial and/or tutorial help available
  Reader services for the blind available for LD
    students
  Special Education department
  Handicapped student services works with LD

MODIFICATIONS TO TRADITIONAL LEARNING ENVIRONMENT:
  Oral presentation in lieu of written exams
  Use of calculator for all math courses
  Has an adaptive physical education program
  Tape recorders to record class lectures
  Someone else may take class notes
  Student takes exams in separate rooms
  Students have exams read to them
  Students take typewritten exams
  Longer time allowed to complete exams
  Supportive services staff will type papers
  Extended time limits for graduation
  Physical education may be waived

MAJORS OFFERED:

  ARCHITECTURE
  BIOLOGICAL SCIENCES
  BUSINESS AND MANAGEMENT
  COMMUNICATIONS
  COMPUTER SCIENCES
  EDUCATION
  ENGINEERING TECHNOLOGIES
  FINE AND APPLIED ARTS
  FOREIGN LANGUAGES
  HEALTH
  HUMANITIES
  LIBRARY SCIENCE
  MATHEMATICS
  MILITARY SCIENCES
  PHYSICAL SCIENCES
  PSYCHOLOGY
  PUBLIC SERVICES
  SOCIAL SCIENCES
  GENERAL LIBERAL ARTS

CHAFFEY COLLEGE
5885 HAVEN AVENUE
ALTA LOMA, CA 91701
714-987-1737

KEY CONTACT: Attn: DR. ROBERT HARRIS

SIZE OF SCHOOL: LARGE

APPLICATION DEADLINE: NONE

        APPROXIMATE TUITION   ROOM AND BOARD

IN DISTRICT $ 45 $NOT OFFERED
IN STATE $ 45 $NOT OFFERED
OUT-OF-STATE $3690 $NOT OFFERED

REQUIREMENTS FOR ADMISSIONS:
  High school equivalency diploma
  High school diploma
  21 years of age or older, with or without a
    high school diploma or equivalency
  Admission requirements modified
  State/District residency

ADDITIONAL SERVICES OFFERED:
  Learning Lab
  Learning Lab has a specialist with a masters degree
    or above in Learning Disabilities
  Diagnostic testing services on campus
  Diagnostic testing services off campus
  Remedial and/or tutorial help available
  Reader services for the blind available for LD
    students
  Special Education department
  Handicapped student services works with LD

MODIFICATIONS TO TRADITIONAL LEARNING ENVIRONMENT:
  Oral presentation in lieu of written exams
  Tape recorders to record class lectures
  Someone else may take class notes
  Multiple choice exams only
  Student takes exams in separate rooms
  Students have exams read to them
  Students take typewritten exams
  Longer time allowed to complete exams
  Submit papers on cassette tape
  Extended time limits for graduation
  Physical education may be waived

MAJORS OFFERED:

    BIOLOGICAL SCIENCES
    BUSINESS AND MANAGEMENT
    COMMUNICATIONS
    COMPUTER SCIENCES
    EDUCATION
    ENGINEERING TECHNOLOGIES
    FINE AND APPLIED ARTS
    FOREIGN LANGUAGES
    HEALTH
    HOME ECONOMICS
    HUMANITIES
    LIBRARY SCIENCE
    MATHEMATICS
    PHYSICAL SCIENCES
    PSYCHOLOGY
    PUBLIC SERVICES
    SOCIAL SCIENCES
    THEOLOGY
    GENERAL LIBERAL ARTS

==

CITRUS COLLEGE
18824 EAST FOOTHILL
AZUSA, CA 91702
213-335-0521

KEY CONTACT: Attn: Handicapped Student Services

SIZE OF SCHOOL: MEDIUM

APPLICATION DEADLINE: NONE

            APPROXIMATE TUITION   ROOM AND BOARD

IN DISTRICT $ 50 $NOT OFFERED
IN STATE $ 50 $NOT OFFERED
OUT-OF-STATE $2140 $NOT OFFERED

REQUIREMENTS FOR ADMISSIONS:
    18 years of age or older, with or without a
        high school diploma or equivalency
    Personal interview
    Recommendations
    State/District residency

ADDITIONAL SERVICES OFFERED:
    Learning Lab

Learning Lab has a specialist with a masters degree
  or above in Learning Disabilities
Diagnostic testing services on campus
Diagnostic testing services off campus
Remedial and/or tutorial help available
Reader services for the blind available for LD
Handicapped student services works with LD

MODIFICATIONS TO TRADITIONAL LEARNING ENVIRONMENT:
  Oral presentation in lieu of written exams
  Use of calculator for all math courses
  Has an adaptive physical education program
  Tape recorders to record class lectures
  Someone else may take class notes
  Student takes exams in separate rooms
  Students have exams read to them
  Students take typewritten exams
  Longer time allowed to complete exams
  Submit papers on cassette tape
  Extended time limits for graduation
  Physical education may be waived

MAJORS OFFERED:

  GENERAL LIBERAL ARTS
  BUSINESS AND MANAGEMENT
  COMPUTER SCIENCES
  HEALTH
  ENGINEERING TECHNOLOGIES
  NATURAL SCIENCE
  PUBLIC SERVICES

==

CITY COLLEGE OF SAN FRANCISCO
50 PHELAN AVENUE
SAN FRANCISCO, CA 94112
415-239-3285

KEY CONTACT: Attn: REBECCA REILLY, COORDINATOR
                    Handicapped Student Services

SIZE OF SCHOOL: LARGE

APPLICATION DEADLINE: JULY 23

        APPROXIMATE TUITION   ROOM AND BOARD

IN DISTRICT $ 0 $NOT OFFERED
IN STATE $ 0 $NOT OFFERED
OUT-OF-STATE $2280 $NOT OFFERED

REQUIREMENTS FOR ADMISSIONS:
  High school equivalency diploma
  High school diploma
  21 years of age or older, with or without a
    high school diploma or equivalency

ADDITIONAL SERVICES OFFERED:
  Learning Lab
  Learning Lab has a specialist with a masters degree
    or above in Learning Disabilities
  Diagnostic testing services on campus
  Remedial and/or tutorial help available
  Reader services for the blind available for LD
    students
  Handicapped student services works with LD

MODIFICATIONS TO TRADITIONAL LEARNING ENVIRONMENT:
  Oral presentation in lieu of written exams
  Use of calculator for all math courses
  Has an adaptive physical education program
  Tape recorders to record class lectures
  Someone else may take class notes
  Multiple choice exams only
  Essay exams only
  Student takes exams in separate rooms
  Students have exams read to them
  Students take typewritten exams
  Longer time allowed to complete exams
  Submit papers on cassette tape
  Physical education may be waived

MAJORS OFFERED:

  AGRICULTURE
  BUSINESS AND MANAGEMENT
  COMPUTER SCIENCES
  ENGINEERING TECHNOLOGIES
  HEALTH
  PUBLIC SERVICES
  FINE AND APPLIED ARTS
  GENERAL LIBERAL ARTS

==

COASTLINE COMMUNITY COLLEGE
10231 SLATER AVENUE
FOUNTAIN VALLEY, CA 92708
714-963-0811

KEY CONTACT: Attn: Handicapped Student Services

SIZE OF SCHOOL: LARGE

APPLICATION DEADLINE: SEPTEMBER 7

```
        APPROXIMATE TUITION    ROOM AND BOARD

IN DISTRICT       $   0       $NOT OFFERED
IN STATE          $   0       $NOT OFFERED
OUT-OF-STATE      $2190       $NOT OFFERED
```

REQUIREMENTS FOR ADMISSIONS:
  High school equivalency diploma
  High school diploma
  21 years of age or older, with or without a
    high school diploma or equivalency
  Admission requirements modified

ADDITIONAL SERVICES OFFERED:
  Learning Lab
  Learning Lab has a specialist with a masters degree
    or above in Learning Disabilities
  Diagnostic testing services off campus
  Remedial and/or tutorial help available
  Reader services for the blind available for LD
    students
  Handicapped student services works with LD

MODIFICATIONS TO TRADITIONAL LEARNING ENVIRONMENT:
  Oral presentation in lieu of written exams
  Use of calculator for all math courses
  Tape recorders to record class lectures
  Someone else may take class notes
  Multiple choice exams only
  Essay exams only
  Student takes exams in separate rooms
  Students take typewritten exams
  Longer time allowed to complete exams
  Submit papers on cassette tape
  Take limited course load and graduate within time
    required
  Physical education may be waived

MAJORS OFFERED:

  AGRICULTURE
  BUSINESS AND MANAGEMENT
  PUBLIC SERVICES
  ENGINEERING TECHNOLOGIES
  GENERAL LIBERAL ARTS

==

COLLEGE OF THE CANYONS
26455 NORTH ROCKWELL CANYON ROAD
VALENCIA, CA 91355
805-259-7800

KEY CONTACT: Attn: FRANCIS B. WAKEFIELD
                     SUPPORT SERVICES SPECIALIST

SIZE OF SCHOOL: MEDIUM

APPLICATION DEADLINE: NONE

         APPROXIMATE TUITION   ROOM AND BOARD

IN DISTRICT $ 0 $NOT OFFERED
IN STATE $ 0 $NOT OFFERED
OUT-OF-STATE $2200 $NOT OFFERED

REQUIREMENTS FOR ADMISSIONS:
  High school equivalency diploma
  High school diploma
  21 years of age or older, with or without a
    high school diploma or equivalency
  Untimed or oral ACT Scores accepted
  Untimed or oral SAT Scores accepted
  Placement tests

ADDITIONAL SERVICES OFFERED:
  Learning Lab
  Learning Lab has a specialist with a masters degree
    or above in Learning Disabilities
  Diagnostic testing services on campus
  Diagnostic testing services off campus
  Remedial and/or tutorial help available
  Reader services for the blind available for LD
    students
  Special Education department
  Handicapped student services works with LD

MODIFICATIONS TO TRADITIONAL LEARNING ENVIRONMENT:
  Oral presentation in lieu of written exams
  Use of calculator for all math courses
  Tape recorders to record class lectures
  Someone else may take class notes
  Multiple choice exams only
  Essay exams only
  Student takes exams in separate rooms
  Students have exams read to them
  Students take typewritten exams
  Longer time allowed to complete exams
  Submit papers on cassette tape

    Extended time limits for graduation
    Physical education may be waived

MAJORS OFFERED:

    BIOLOGICAL SCIENCES
    BUSINESS AND MANAGEMENT
    COMMUNICATIONS
    COMPUTER SCIENCES
    EDUCATION
    ENGINEERING TECHNOLOGIES
    FINE AND APPLIED ARTS
    FOREIGN LANGUAGES
    HEALTH
    HUMANITIES
    MATHEMATICS
    PHYSICAL SCIENCES
    PSYCHOLOGY
    SOCIAL SCIENCES
    GENERAL LIBERAL ARTS

==

COLLEGE OF THE DESERT
43500 MONTEREY AVENUE
PALM DESERT, CA 92260
619-346-8041

KEY CONTACT: Attn: DIANE RAMIREZ, DIRECTOR
                    HANDICAP PROGRAMS AND SERVICES

SIZE OF SCHOOL: MEDIUM

APPLICATION DEADLINE: NONE

        APPROXIMATE TUITION   ROOM AND BOARD

IN DISTRICT $ 0 $NOT OFFERED
IN STATE $ 0 $NOT OFFERED
OUT-OF-STATE $2520 $NOT OFFERED

REQUIREMENTS FOR ADMISSIONS:
    18 years of age or older, with or without a
       high school diploma or equivalency
    University or College sponsored tests
    Personal interview
    Placement tests
    Recommendations
    Essay

ADDITIONAL SERVICES OFFERED:
  Learning Lab
  Learning Lab has a specialist with a masters degree
    or above in Learning Disabilities
  Diagnostic testing services on campus
  Diagnostic testing services off campus
  Remedial and/or tutorial help available
  Reader services for the blind available for LD
    students
  Handicapped student services works with LD

MODIFICATIONS TO TRADITIONAL LEARNING ENVIRONMENT:
  Oral presentation in lieu of written exams
  Has an adaptive physical education program
  Tape recorders to record class lectures
  Someone else may take class notes
  Student takes exams in separate rooms
  Students have exams read to them
  Students take typewritten exams
  Longer time allowed to complete exams
  Submit papers on cassette tape
  Physical education may be waived

MAJORS OFFERED:

  AGRICULTURE
  ARCHITECTURE
  BIOLOGICAL SCIENCES
  BUSINESS AND MANAGEMENT
  COMMUNICATIONS
  COMPUTER SCIENCES
  EDUCATION
  ENGINEERING TECHNOLOGIES
  FOREIGN LANGUAGES
  HEALTH
  HOME ECONOMICS
  MATHEMATICS
  PHYSICAL SCIENCES
  PSYCHOLOGY
  SOCIAL SCIENCES
  GENERAL LIBERAL ARTS

===

COLLEGE OF THE REDWOODS
7351 TOMPKINS HILL ROAD
EUREKA, CA 95501
707-443-8411

KEY CONTACT: Attn: MR. BEACHAMP
                     LD SPECIALIST

SIZE OF SCHOOL: MEDIUM

APPLICATION DEADLINE: NONE

	APPROXIMATE TUITION	ROOM AND BOARD
IN DISTRICT	$ 0	$2670
IN STATE	$ 0	$2670
OUT-OF-STATE	$2250	$2670

REQUIREMENTS FOR ADMISSIONS:
  High school equivalency diploma
  High school diploma
  21 years of age or older, with or without a
    high school diploma or equivalency
  University or College sponsored tests
  Personal interview
  Recommendations
  State/District residency

ADDITIONAL SERVICES OFFERED:
  Learning Lab
  Learning Lab has a specialist with a masters degree
    or above in Learning Disabilities
  Diagnostic testing services on campus
  Remedial and/or tutorial help available
  Reader services for the blind available for LD
    students
  Special Education department
  Handicapped student services works with LD

MODIFICATIONS TO TRADITIONAL LEARNING ENVIRONMENT:
  Oral presentation in lieu of written exams
  Use of calculator for all math courses
  Has an adaptive physical education program
  Tape recorders to record class lectures
  Someone else may take class notes
  Student takes exams in separate rooms
  Students have exams read to them
  Longer time allowed to complete exams
  Submit papers on cassette tape

MAJORS OFFERED:

  AGRICULTURE
  BIOLOGICAL SCIENCES
  BUSINESS AND MANAGEMENT
  COMPUTER SCIENCES
  ENGINEERING TECHNOLOGIES
  FINE AND APPLIED ARTS
  FOREIGN LANGUAGES

```
HEALTH
HOME ECONOMICS
HUMANITIES
MATHEMATICS
PHYSICAL SCIENCES
PSYCHOLOGY
SOCIAL SCIENCES
GENERAL LIBERAL ARTS
```

==

```
COLLEGE OF THE SISKIYOUS
800 COLLEGE AVENUE
WEED, CA 96094
916-938-4462
```

KEY CONTACT: Attn: C.D. ABEL
                     LD SPECIALIST

SIZE OF SCHOOL: SMALL

APPLICATION DEADLINE: NONE

          APPROXIMATE TUITION   ROOM AND BOARD

	APPROXIMATE TUITION	ROOM AND BOARD
IN DISTRICT	$ 35	$2185
IN STATE	$ 35	$2185
OUT-OF-STATE	$2130	$2185

REQUIREMENTS FOR ADMISSIONS:
  18 years of age or older, with or without a
    high school diploma or equivalency

ADDITIONAL SERVICES OFFERED:
  Learning Lab
  Learning Lab has a specialist with a masters degree
    or above in Learning Disabilities
  Diagnostic testing services on campus
  Remedial and/or tutorial help available
  Reader services for the blind available for LD
    students
  Handicapped student services works with LD

MODIFICATIONS TO TRADITIONAL LEARNING ENVIRONMENT:
  Oral presentation in lieu of written exams
  Has an adaptive physical education program
  Tape recorders to record class lectures
  Someone else may take class notes
  Student takes exams in separate rooms
  Students have exams read to them
  Students take typewritten exams

```
      Longer time allowed to complete exams
      Submit papers on cassette tape
      Extended time limits for graduation
      Physical education may be waived

MAJORS OFFERED:

      AGRICULTURE
      BIOLOGICAL SCIENCES
      BUSINESS AND MANAGEMENT
      COMPUTER SCIENCES
      ENGINEERING TECHNOLOGIES
      FINE AND APPLIED ARTS
      MATHEMATICS
      PHYSICAL SCIENCES
      PUBLIC SERVICES
      SOCIAL SCIENCES
      GENERAL LIBERAL ARTS


===========================================================

COMPTON COMMUNITY COLLEGE
1111 EAST ARTESIA BLVD
COMPTON, CA 90221
213-637-2660

KEY CONTACT: Attn:  Handicapped Student Services

SIZE OF SCHOOL: MEDIUM

APPLICATION DEADLINE: NONE

          APPROXIMATE TUITION    ROOM AND BOARD

IN DISTRICT        $  20         $NOT OFFERED
IN STATE           $  20         $NOT OFFERED
OUT-OF-STATE       $1800         $NOT OFFERED

ADDITIONAL SERVICES OFFERED:
   Learning Lab
   Learning Lab has a specialist with a masters degree
     or above in Learning Disabilities
   Diagnostic testing services on campus
   Remedial and/or tutorial help available
   Special Education department
   Handicapped student services works with LD

MODIFICATIONS TO TRADITIONAL LEARNING ENVIRONMENT:
   Tape recorders to record class lectures
   Someone else may take class notes
   Student takes exams in separate rooms
```

Students have exams read to them

MAJORS OFFERED:

    ARCHITECTURE
    BIOLOGICAL SCIENCES
    BUSINESS AND MANAGEMENT
    COMMUNICATIONS
    COMPUTER SCIENCES
    EDUCATION
    ENGINEERING TECHNOLOGIES
    FINE AND APPLIED ARTS
    FOREIGN LANGUAGES
    HEALTH
    HOME ECONOMICS
    HUMANITIES
    MATHEMATICS
    PHYSICAL SCIENCES
    PSYCHOLOGY
    PUBLIC SERVICES
    SOCIAL SCIENCES
    GENERAL LIBERAL ARTS

==

CONTRA COSTA COLLEGE
2600 MISSION BELL DRIVE
SAN PUEBLO, CA 94806
415-235-7800

KEY CONTACT: Attn: MRS. PEGGY FELMINE
                     LEARNING SPECIALIST

SIZE OF SCHOOL: MEDIUM

APPLICATION DEADLINE: NONE

         APPROXIMATE TUITION   ROOM AND BOARD

IN DISTRICT $ 0 $NOT OFFERED
IN STATE $ 0 $NOT OFFERED
OUT-OF-STATE $1824 $NOT OFFERED

REQUIREMENTS FOR ADMISSIONS:
   18 years of age or older, with or without a
      high school diploma or equivalency
   WAIS scores required
   University or College sponsored tests
   Personal interview
   Placement tests
   Recommendations

ADDITIONAL SERVICES OFFERED:
  Learning Lab
  Learning Lab has a specialist with a masters degree
    or above in Learning Disabilities
  Diagnostic testing services on campus
  Remedial and/or tutorial help available
  Reader services for the blind available for LD
    students
  Handicapped student services works with LD

MODIFICATIONS TO TRADITIONAL LEARNING ENVIRONMENT:
  Has an adaptive physical education program
  Tape recorders to record class lectures
  Someone else may take class notes
  Student takes exams in separate rooms
  Students have exams read to them
  Longer time allowed to complete exams
  Extended time limits for graduation

MAJORS OFFERED:

  ARCHITECTURE
  AREA STUDIES
  BIOLOGICAL SCIENCES
  BUSINESS AND MANAGEMENT
  COMMUNICATIONS
  COMPUTER SCIENCES
  ENGINEERING TECHNOLOGIES
  FINE AND APPLIED ARTS
  FOREIGN LANGUAGES
  HEALTH
  HOME ECONOMICS
  HUMANITIES
  MATHEMATICS
  PHYSICAL SCIENCES
  PSYCHOLOGY
  SOCIAL SCIENCES
  GENERAL LIBERAL ARTS

==

CONSUMNES RIVER COLLEGE
8401 CENTER PARKWAY
SACRAMENTO, CA 95823
916-689-1000

KEY CONTACT: Attn: Handicapped Student Services

SIZE OF SCHOOL: MEDIUM

APPLICATION DEADLINE: AUGUST 1

```
        APPROXIMATE TUITION    ROOM AND BOARD

IN DISTRICT        $   0        $NOT OFFERED
IN STATE           $   0        $NOT OFFERED
OUT-OF-STATE       $2160        $NOT OFFERED
```

REQUIREMENTS FOR ADMISSIONS:
  High school equivalency diploma
  High school diploma
  21 years of age or older, with or without a
    high school diploma or equivalency
  State/District residency

ADDITIONAL SERVICES OFFERED:
  Learning Lab
  Diagnostic testing services off campus
  Remedial and/or tutorial help available
  Reader services for the blind available for LD
    students
  Handicapped student services works with LD

MODIFICATIONS TO TRADITIONAL LEARNING ENVIRONMENT:
  Oral presentation in lieu of written exams
  Use of calculator for all math courses
  Has an adaptive physical education program
  Tape recorders to record class lectures
  Someone else may take class notes
  Student takes exams in separate rooms
  Students have exams read to them
  Students take typewritten exams
  Longer time allowed to complete exams
  Submit papers on cassette tape
  Take limited course load and graduate within time
    required
  Extended time limits for graduation
  Physical education may be waived

MAJORS OFFERED:

  AGRICULTURE
  ARCHITECTURE
  BUSINESS AND MANAGEMENT
  COMMUNICATIONS
  FINE AND APPLIED ARTS
  SOCIAL SCIENCES
  GENERAL LIBERAL ARTS

===

CRAFTON HILLS COLLEGE
11711 SAND CANYON ROAD
YUCAIPA, CA 92399
714-794-2161

KEY CONTACT: Attn: Handicapped Student Services

SIZE OF SCHOOL: SMALL

APPLICATION DEADLINE: NONE

	APPROXIMATE TUITION	ROOM AND BOARD
IN DISTRICT	$ 0	$NOT OFFERED
IN STATE	$ 0	$NOT OFFERED
OUT-OF-STATE	$2250	$NOT OFFERED

REQUIREMENTS FOR ADMISSIONS:
  Admission requirements modified

ADDITIONAL SERVICES OFFERED:
  Learning Lab
  Learning Lab has a specialist with a masters degree
    or above in Learning Disabilities
  Diagnostic testing services off campus
  Remedial and/or tutorial help available
  Reader services for the blind available for LD
  Handicapped student services works with LD

MODIFICATIONS TO TRADITIONAL LEARNING ENVIRONMENT:
  Oral presentation in lieu of written exams
  Use of calculator for all math courses
  Tape recorders to record class lectures
  Someone else may take class notes
  Multiple choice exams only
  Essay exams only
  Student takes exams in separate rooms
  Students have exams read to them
  Students take typewritten exams
  Longer time allowed to complete exams
  Submit papers on cassette tape
  Take limited course load and graduate within time
    required
  Extended time limits for graduation
  Physical education may be waived

MAJORS OFFERED:

  AGRICULTURE
  BIOLOGICAL SCIENCES
  BUSINESS AND MANAGEMENT

EDUCATION
FINE AND APPLIED ARTS
FOREIGN LANGUAGES
HEALTH
HUMANITIES
MATHEMATICS
PHYSICAL SCIENCES
PSYCHOLOGY
PUBLIC SERVICES
SOCIAL SCIENCES
THEOLOGY
GENERAL LIBERAL ARTS

==

CUYAMACA COLLEGE
2950 JAMACHA BLVD
EL CAJON, CA 92020
619-464-1980

KEY CONTACT: Attn: MARSHA FRALICK, COUNSELOR

SIZE OF SCHOOL: SMALL

APPLICATION DEADLINE: AUGUST 12

	APPROXIMATE TUITION	ROOM AND BOARD
IN DISTRICT	$ 10	$NOT OFFERED
IN STATE	$ 10	$NOT OFFERED
OUT-OF-STATE	$2250	$NOT OFFERED

REQUIREMENTS FOR ADMISSIONS:
  WAIS scores required

ADDITIONAL SERVICES OFFERED:
  Learning Lab
  Learning Lab has a specialist with a masters degree
    or above in Learning Disabilities
  Diagnostic testing services on campus
  Diagnostic testing services off campus
  Remedial and/or tutorial help available
  Reader services for the blind available for LD
  Special Education department
  Handicapped student services works with LD

MODIFICATIONS TO TRADITIONAL LEARNING ENVIRONMENT:
  Oral presentation in lieu of written exams
  Tape recorders to record class lectures
  Someone else may take class notes
  Student takes exams in separate rooms

```
Students have exams read to them
Students take typewritten exams
Longer time allowed to complete exams
Submit papers on cassette tape
Extended time limits for graduation
Physical education may be waived
```

MAJORS OFFERED:

```
AGRICULTURE
ARCHITECTURE
COMPUTER SCIENCES
ENGINEERING TECHNOLOGIES
```

===

```
CYPRESS COLLEGE
9200 VALLEY VIEW
CYPRESS, CA 90630
714-826-2220
```

KEY CONTACT: Attn: Handicapped Student Services

SIZE OF SCHOOL: LARGE

APPLICATION DEADLINE: SEPTEMBER 16

	APPROXIMATE TUITION	ROOM AND BOARD
IN DISTRICT	$ 15	$NOT OFFERED
IN STATE	$ 15	$NOT OFFERED
OUT-OF-STATE	$1730	$NOT OFFERED

REQUIREMENTS FOR ADMISSIONS:
    18 years of age or older, with or without a
       high school diploma or equivalency
    WAIS scores helpful but not required
    High school grade point average (not specified)
    Personal interview

ADDITIONAL SERVICES OFFERED:
    Learning Lab has a specialist with a masters degree
       or above in Learning Disabilities
    Diagnostic testing services on campus
    Reader services for the blind available for LD
    Special Education department
    Handicapped student services works with LD

MODIFICATIONS TO TRADITIONAL LEARNING ENVIRONMENT:
    Oral presentation in lieu of written exams
    Use of calculator for all math courses

```
    Tape recorders to record class lectures
    Someone else may take class notes
    Multiple choice exams only
    Essay exams only
    Student takes exams in separate rooms
    Students take typewritten exams
    Longer time allowed to complete exams
    Submit papers on cassette tape
    Most modifications depend on teacher
```

MAJORS OFFERED:

```
    BIOLOGICAL SCIENCES
    BUSINESS AND MANAGEMENT
    CQMMUNICATIONS
    COMPUTER SCIENCES
    EDUCATION
    ENGINEERING TECHNOLOGIES
    FINE AND APPLIED ARTS
    FOREIGN LANGUAGES
    HEALTH
    HUMANITIES
    MATHEMATICS
    PHYSICAL SCIENCES
    PSYCHOLOGY
    PUBLIC SERVICES
    SOCIAL SCIENCES
    GENERAL LIBERAL ARTS
```

==

DE ANZA COLLEGE
21250 STEVENS CREEK BLVD
CUPERTINO, CA 95014
408-996-4419

KEY CONTACT: Attn: Handicapped Student Services
SIZE OF SCHOOL: LARGE

APPLICATION DEADLINE: NONE

	APPROXIMATE TUITION	ROOM AND BOARD
IN DISTRICT	$ 30	$NOT OFFERED
IN STATE	$ 30	$NOT OFFERED
OUT-OF-STATE	$2190	$NOT OFFERED

REQUIREMENTS FOR ADMISSIONS:
  Placement tests

ADDITIONAL SERVICES OFFERED:
  Learning Lab
  Learning Lab has a specialist with a masters degree
    or above in Learning Disabilities
  Diagnostic testing services on campus
  Remedial and/or tutorial help available
  Reader services for the blind available for LD
  Special Education department
  Handicapped student services works with LD

MODIFICATIONS TO TRADITIONAL LEARNING ENVIRONMENT:
  Oral presentation in lieu of written exams
  Has an adaptive physical education program
  Tape recorders to record class lectures
  Someone else may take class notes
  Student takes exams in separate rooms
  Students have exams read to them
  Students take typewritten exams
  Longer time allowed to complete exams
  Extended time limits for graduation

MAJORS OFFERED:

  BIOLOGICAL SCIENCES
  BUSINESS AND MANAGEMENT
  COMPUTER SCIENCES
  ENGINEERING TECHNOLOGIES
  FINE AND APPLIED ARTS
  FOREIGN LANGUAGES
  HEALTH
  HOME ECONOMICS
  HUMANITIES
  MATHEMATICS
  MILITARY SCIENCES
  PHYSICAL SCIENCES
  PSYCHOLOGY
  PUBLIC SERVICES
  SOCIAL SCIENCES
  GENERAL LIBERAL ARTS

==

EVERGREEN VALLEY COLLEGE
3095 YERBA BUENA ROAD
SAN JOSE, CA 95135
408-270-6447

KEY CONTACT: Attn: WILLIAM H. COOKSLEY
                    COUNSELOR - SPECIALIST

SIZE OF SCHOOL: MEDIUM

APPLICATION DEADLINE: AUGUST 3

    APPROXIMATE TUITION   ROOM AND BOARD

	APPROXIMATE TUITION	ROOM AND BOARD
IN DISTRICT	$ 10	$NOT OFFERED
IN STATE	$ 10	$NOT OFFERED
OUT-OF-STATE	$2580	$NOT OFFERED

REQUIREMENTS FOR ADMISSIONS:
  18 years of age or older, with or without a
    high school diploma or equivalency
  University or College sponsored tests
  Open door policy

ADDITIONAL SERVICES OFFERED:
  Learning Lab
  Learning Lab has a specialist with a masters degree
    or above in Learning Disabilities
  Diagnostic testing services on campus
  Remedial and/or tutorial help available
  Reader services for the blind available for LD
  Special Education department
  Handicapped student services works with LD

MODIFICATIONS TO TRADITIONAL LEARNING ENVIRONMENT:
  Oral presentation in lieu of written exams
  Use of calculator for all math courses
  Has an adaptive physical education program
  Tape recorders to record class lectures
  Someone else may take class notes
  Multiple choice exams only
  Essay exams only
  Student takes exams in separate rooms
  Students have exams read to them
  Students take typewritten exams
  Longer time allowed to complete exams
  Submit papers on cassette tape

MAJORS OFFERED:

  BIOLOGICAL SCIENCES
  BUSINESS AND MANAGEMENT
  COMMUNICATIONS
  COMPUTER SCIENCES
  ENGINEERING TECHNOLOGIES
  FINE AND APPLIED ARTS
  FOREIGN LANGUAGES
  HEALTH
  HOME ECONOMICS
  HUMANITIES

```
MATHEMATICS
PHYSICAL SCIENCES
PSYCHOLOGY
SOCIAL SCIENCES
GENERAL LIBERAL ARTS
```

===

```
FEATHER RIVER COLLEGE
P.O. BOX 1110
QUINCY, CA 95971
916-283-0202
```

KEY CONTACT: Attn: DONNA MARIE FERRO
                    ENABLER - VOCATIONAL COUNSELOR

SIZE OF SCHOOL: SMALL

APPLICATION DEADLINE: AUGUST 31

	APPROXIMATE TUITION	ROOM AND BOARD
IN DISTRICT	$ 20	$NOT OFFERED
IN STATE	$ 20	$NOT OFFERED
OUT-OF-STATE	$1560	$NOT OFFERED

REQUIREMENTS FOR ADMISSIONS:
  18 years of age or older, with or without a
    high school diploma or equivalency
  Or can benefit from the instruction offered

ADDITIONAL SERVICES OFFERED:
  Diagnostic testing services off campus
  Remedial and/or tutorial help available
  Handicapped student services works with LD

MODIFICATIONS TO TRADITIONAL LEARNING ENVIRONMENT:
  Oral presentation in lieu of written exams
  Use of calculator for all math courses
  Has an adaptive physical education program
  Tape recorders to record class lectures
  Someone else may take class notes
  Student takes exams in separate rooms
  Students have exams read to them
  Longer time allowed to complete exams

MAJORS OFFERED:

  AGRICULTURE
  BUSINESS AND MANAGEMENT
  ENGINEERING TECHNOLOGIES

PUBLIC SERVICES
GENERAL LIBERAL ARTS

==

FOOTHILL COLLEGE
12345 EL MONTE ROAD
LOS ALTOS, CA 94022
415-948-8590

KEY CONTACT: Attn: PATRICK MOONEY - COUNSELOR

SIZE OF SCHOOL: LARGE

APPLICATION DEADLINE: NONE

            APPROXIMATE TUITION   ROOM AND BOARD

IN DISTRICT $ 25 $NOT OFFERED
IN STATE $ 25 $NOT OFFERED
OUT-OF-STATE $2250 $NOT OFFERED

REQUIREMENTS FOR ADMISSIONS:
   18 years of age or older, with or without a
      high school diploma or equivalency

ADDITIONAL SERVICES OFFERED:
   Learning Lab
   Learning Lab has a specialist with a masters degree
      or above in Learning Disabilities
   Remedial and/or tutorial help available
   Reader services for the blind available for LD
   Special Education department
   Handicapped student services works with LD

MODIFICATIONS TO TRADITIONAL LEARNING ENVIRONMENT:
   Has an adaptive physical education program
   Tape recorders to record class lectures
   Someone else may take class notes
   Take limited course load and graduate within time
      required
   Extended time limits for graduation
   All modifications are possible at the discretion of
      the instructor

MAJORS OFFERED:

   ARCHITECTURE
   AREA STUDIES
   BIOLOGICAL SCIENCES
   BUSINESS AND MANAGEMENT

```
COMMUNICATIONS
COMPUTER SCIENCES
ENGINEERING TECHNOLOGIES
FINE AND APPLIED ARTS
FOREIGN LANGUAGES
HEALTH
HUMANITIES
LIBRARY SCIENCE
MATHEMATICS
PHYSICAL SCIENCES
PSYCHOLOGY
SOCIAL SCIENCES
GENERAL LIBERAL ARTS
```

==

```
FRESNO CITY COLLEGE
1101 EAST UNIVERSITY AVENUE
FRESNO, CA 93741
209-442-8241
```

KEY CONTACT: Attn: JEANETTE IMPERATRICE
                     LD SPECIALIST

SIZE OF SCHOOL: LARGE

APPLICATION DEADLINE: NONE

	APPROXIMATE TUITION	ROOM AND BOARD
IN DISTRICT	$ 20	$NOT OFFERED
IN STATE	$ 20	$NOT OFFERED
OUT-OF-STATE	$1800	$NOT OFFERED

REQUIREMENTS FOR ADMISSIONS:
  Personal interview
  Placement tests
  Recommendations

ADDITIONAL SERVICES OFFERED:
  Learning Lab
  Learning Lab has a specialist with a masters degree
    or above in Learning Disabilities
  Diagnostic testing services on campus
  Diagnostic testing services off campus
  Remedial and/or tutorial help available
  Reader services for the blind available for LD
  Special Education department
  Handicapped student services works with LD

MODIFICATIONS TO TRADITIONAL LEARNING ENVIRONMENT:
  Oral presentation in lieu of written exams
  Use of calculator for all math courses
  Has an adaptive physical education program
  Tape recorders to record class lectures
  Someone else may take class notes
  Student takes exams in separate rooms
  Students have exams read to them
  Students take typewritten exams
  Longer time allowed to complete exams
  Submit papers on cassette tape
  Extended time limits for graduation
  Physical education may be waived

MAJORS OFFERED:

  ARCHITECTURE
  AREA STUDIES
  BUSINESS AND MANAGEMENT
  EDUCATION
  ENGINEERING TECHNOLOGIES
  FINE AND APPLIED ARTS
  HEALTH
  HOME ECONOMICS
  MATHEMATICS
  SOCIAL SCIENCES
  GENERAL LIBERAL ARTS

==

GAVILAN COMMUNITY COLLEGE
5055 SANTA TERESA BLVD
GILROY, CA 95020
408-847-1400

KEY CONTACT: Attn: SUSAN BUNCH - LD SPECIALIST

SIZE OF SCHOOL: SMALL

APPLICATION DEADLINE: NONE

        APPROXIMATE TUITION   ROOM AND BOARD

IN DISTRICT $ 20 $NOT OFFERED
IN STATE $ 20 $NOT OFFERED
OUT-OF-STATE $2088 $NOT OFFERED

REQUIREMENTS FOR ADMISSIONS:
  Personal interview
  Battery of L.D. asssesment tests required before
    admitting student to program

ADDITIONAL SERVICES OFFERED:
  Learning Lab
  Learning Lab has a specialist with a masters degree
    or above in Learning Disabilities
  Diagnostic testing services on campus
  Remedial and/or tutorial help available
  Reader services for the blind available for LD
  Special Education department
  Handicapped student services works with LD

MODIFICATIONS TO TRADITIONAL LEARNING ENVIRONMENT:
  Oral presentation in lieu of written exams
  Use of calculator for all math courses
  Has an adaptive physical education program
  Tape recorders to record class lectures
  Someone else may take class notes
  Multiple choice exams only
  Essay exams only
  Student takes exams in separate rooms
  Students have exams read to them
  Students take typewritten exams
  Longer time allowed to complete exams
  Submit papers on cassette tape
  Extended time limits for graduation
  All of the above modifications permitted at
    discretion of individual instructor

MAJORS OFFERED:

  BIOLOGICAL SCIENCES
  BUSINESS AND MANAGEMENT
  COMPUTER SCIENCES
  EDUCATION
  ENGINEERING TECHNOLOGIES
  FINE AND APPLIED ARTS
  HUMANITIES
  MATHEMATICS
  PHYSICAL SCIENCES
  PSYCHOLOGY
  PUBLIC SERVICES
  SOCIAL SCIENCES
  GENERAL LIBERAL ARTS

===

GLENDALE COMMUNITY COLLEGE
1500 NORTH VERDUGO ROAD
GLENDALE, CA 91208
213-240-1000

KEY CONTACT: Attn: Handicapped Student Services

SIZE OF SCHOOL: LARGE

APPLICATION DEADLINE: NONE

```
        APPROXIMATE TUITION    ROOM AND BOARD

IN DISTRICT       $    0      $NOT OFFERED
IN STATE          $    0      $NOT OFFERED
OUT-OF-STATE      $2150       $NOT OFFERED
```

REQUIREMENTS FOR ADMISSIONS:
  High school equivalency diploma
  High school diploma
  21 years of age or older, with or without a
    high school diploma or equivalency
  Admission requirements modified

ADDITIONAL SERVICES OFFERED:
  Learning Lab
  Learning Lab has a specialist with a masters degree
    or above in Learning Disabilities
  Diagnostic testing services off campus
  Remedial and/or tutorial help available
  Reader services for the blind available for LD
  Special Education department
  Handicapped student services works with LD

MODIFICATIONS TO TRADITIONAL LEARNING ENVIRONMENT:
  Tape recorders to record class lectures
  Someone else may take class notes
  Student takes exams in separate rooms
  Students have exams read to them
  Students take typewritten exams
  Longer time allowed to complete exams
  Submit papers on cassette tape
  Extended time limits for graduation
  Physical education may be waived

MAJORS OFFERED:

  AGRICULTURE
  ARCHITECTURE
  BIOLOGICAL SCIENCES
  BUSINESS AND MANAGEMENT
  COMPUTER SCIENCES
  ENGINEERING TECHNOLOGIES
  FINE AND APPLIED ARTS
  FOREIGN LANGUAGES
  HEALTH
  HUMANITIES

```
LIBRARY SCIENCE
MATHEMATICS
PHYSICAL SCIENCES
PSYCHOLOGY
SOCIAL SCIENCES
GENERAL LIBERAL ARTS
```

==

```
GROSSMONT COLLEGE
8800 GROSSMONT COLLEGE DRIVE
EL CAJON, CA 92020
714-465-1700
```

KEY CONTACT: Attn: MIMI LEE
                    LEARNING DISABILITIES SPECIALIST

SIZE OF SCHOOL: LARGE

APPLICATION DEADLINE: AUGUST 12

	APPROXIMATE TUITION	ROOM AND BOARD
IN DISTRICT	$ 10	$NOT OFFERED
IN STATE	$ 10	$NOT OFFERED
OUT-OF-STATE	$2250	$NOT OFFERED

REQUIREMENTS FOR ADMISSIONS:
  18 years of age or older, with or without a
    high school diploma or equivalency
  University or College sponsored tests
  Personal interview
  Placement tests

ADDITIONAL SERVICES OFFERED:
  Learning Lab
  Learning Lab has a specialist with a masters degree
    or above in Learning Disabilities
  Diagnostic testing services on campus
  Remedial and/or tutorial help available
  Reader services for the blind available for LD
  Special Education department
  Handicapped student services works with LD

MODIFICATIONS TO TRADITIONAL LEARNING ENVIRONMENT:
  Oral presentation in lieu of written exams
  Has an adaptive physical education program
  Tape recorders to record class lectures
  Someone else may take class notes
  Student takes exams in separate rooms
  Students have exams read to them

Longer time allowed to complete exams
Submit papers on cassette tape

MAJORS OFFERED:

BUSINESS AND MANAGEMENT
COMMUNICATIONS
COMPUTER SCIENCES
FINE AND APPLIED ARTS
HEALTH
HOME ECONOMICS
LIBRARY SCIENCE
PUBLIC SERVICES
GENERAL LIBERAL ARTS

==

IMPERIAL VALLEY COLLEGE
P.O. BOX 158
IMPERIAL, CA 92251
714-352-8320

KEY CONTACT: Attn: MELVIN WENDRICK

SIZE OF SCHOOL: MEDIUM

APPLICATION DEADLINE: NONE

	APPROXIMATE TUITION	ROOM AND BOARD
IN DISTRICT	$ 15	$NOT OFFERED
IN STATE	$ 15	$NOT OFFERED
OUT-OF-STATE	$2250	$NOT OFFERED

REQUIREMENTS FOR ADMISSIONS:
  High school equivalency diploma
  High school diploma
  21 years of age or older, with or without a
    high school diploma or equivalency
  Untimed or oral ACT Scores accepted
  Untimed or oral SAT Scores accepted
  Admission requirements modified
  Placement tests

ADDITIONAL SERVICES OFFERED:
  Learning Lab
  Learning Lab has a specialist with a masters degree
    or above in Learning Disabilities
  Diagnostic testing services on campus
  Diagnostic testing services off campus
  Remedial and/or tutorial help available

Reader services for the blind available for LD
Handicapped student services works with LD

MODIFICATIONS TO TRADITIONAL LEARNING ENVIRONMENT:
   Oral presentation in lieu of written exams
   Has an adaptive physical education program
   Tape recorders to record class lectures
   Someone else may take class notes
   Student takes exams in separate rooms
   Students have exams read to them
   Students take typewritten exams
   Longer time allowed to complete exams
   Submit papers on cassette tape
   Extended time limits for graduation
   Physical education may be waived

MAJORS OFFERED:

   AGRICULTURE
   AREA STUDIES
   BIOLOGICAL SCIENCES
   BUSINESS AND MANAGEMENT
   COMMUNICATIONS
   COMPUTER SCIENCES
   EDUCATION
   ENGINEERING TECHNOLOGIES
   FINE AND APPLIED ARTS
   FOREIGN LANGUAGES
   HUMANITIES
   MATHEMATICS
   PHYSICAL SCIENCES
   PSYCHOLOGY
   PUBLIC SERVICES
   SOCIAL SCIENCES
   GENERAL LIBERAL ARTS

==

LAKE TAHOE COMMUNITY COLLEGE
P.O. BOX 1445
SOUTH LAKE TAHOE, CA 95702
916-541-4660

KEY CONTACT: Attn: Handicapped Student Services

SIZE OF SCHOOL: SMALL

APPLICATION DEADLINE: NONE

```
      APPROXIMATE TUITION    ROOM AND BOARD

IN DISTRICT        $  50      $NOT OFFERED
IN STATE           $  50      $NOT OFFERED
OUT-OF-STATE       $2700      $NOT OFFERED
```

REQUIREMENTS FOR ADMISSIONS:
  High school equivalency diploma
  High school diploma
  21 years of age or older, with or without a
    high school diploma or equivalency
  Untimed or oral ACT Scores accepted
  Untimed or oral SAT Scores accepted
  Admission requirements modified
  Placement tests

ADDITIONAL SERVICES OFFERED:
  Learning Lab
  Learning Lab has a specialist with a masters degree
    or above in Learning Disabilities
  Diagnostic testing services on campus
  Diagnostic testing services off campus
  Remedial and/or tutorial help available
  Reader services for the blind available for LD
  Handicapped student services works with LD

MODIFICATIONS TO TRADITIONAL LEARNING ENVIRONMENT:
  Oral presentation in lieu of written exams
  Use of calculator for all math courses
  Tape recorders to record class lectures
  Someone else may take class notes
  Multiple choice exams only
  Essay exams only
  Student takes exams in separate rooms
  Students have exams read to them
  Students take typewritten exams
  Longer time allowed to complete exams
  Submit papers on cassette tape
  Physical education may be waived

MAJORS OFFERED:

  BUSINESS AND MANAGEMENT
  FINE AND APPLIED ARTS
  HEALTH
  HUMANITIES
  PHYSICAL SCIENCES
  PUBLIC SERVICES
  SOCIAL SCIENCES
  GENERAL LIBERAL ARTS

```
LASSEN COLLEGE
P.O. BOX 3000
SUSANVILLE, CA 96130
916-257-6181
```

KEY CONTACT: Attn: CHRISTINE O'DELL or
                     RICHARD SPRINGER

SIZE OF SCHOOL: SMALL

APPLICATION DEADLINE: NONE

	APPROXIMATE TUITION	ROOM AND BOARD
IN DISTRICT	$ 15	$1995
IN STATE	$ 15	$1995
OUT-OF-STATE	$ 75	$1995

REQUIREMENTS FOR ADMISSIONS:
  18 years of age or older, with or without a
    high school diploma or equivalency
  Untimed or oral ACT Scores accepted
  Untimed or oral SAT Scores accepted
  University or College sponsored tests
  Admission requirements modified
  Placement tests

ADDITIONAL SERVICES OFFERED:
  Learning Lab
  Learning Lab has a specialist with a masters degree
    or above in Learning Disabilities
  Diagnostic testing services on campus
  Diagnostic testing services off campus
  Remedial and/or tutorial help available
  Reader services for the blind available for LD
  Handicapped student services works with LD

MODIFICATIONS TO TRADITIONAL LEARNING ENVIRONMENT:
  Oral presentation in lieu of written exams
  Use of calculator for all math courses
  Has an adaptive physical education program
  Tape recorders to record class lectures
  Someone else may take class notes
  Multiple choice exams only
  Essay exams only
  Student takes exams in separate rooms
  Students have exams read to them
  Students take typewritten exams
  Longer time allowed to complete exams
  Submit papers on cassette tape
  Extended time limits for graduation

Physical education may be waived
All modifications with instructors approval

MAJORS OFFERED:

    AGRICULTURE
    ARCHITECTURE
    BIOLOGICAL SCIENCES
    BUSINESS AND MANAGEMENT
    COMMUNICATIONS
    COMPUTER SCIENCES
    ENGINEERING TECHNOLOGIES
    FINE AND APPLIED ARTS
    HEALTH
    HOME ECONOMICS
    HUMANITIES
    MATHEMATICS
    PHYSICAL SCIENCES
    PSYCHOLOGY
    PUBLIC SERVICES
    SOCIAL SCIENCES
    GENERAL LIBERAL ARTS

==

LONG BEACH CITY COLLEGE
4901 EAST CARSON STREET
LONG BEACH, CA 90808

KEY CONTACT: Attn: D.E. SCHMALZRIED, COORDINATOR
                    SPECIAL EDUCATION

SIZE OF SCHOOL: LARGE

APPLICATION DEADLINE: NONE

        APPROXIMATE TUITION   ROOM AND BOARD

IN DISTRICT $ 10 $NOT OFFERED
IN STATE $ 10 $NOT OFFERED
OUT-OF-STATE $2160 $NOT OFFERED

REQUIREMENTS FOR ADMISSIONS:
  High school equivalency diploma
  High school diploma
  21 years of age or older, with or without a
    high school diploma or equivalency
  Placement tests

ADDITIONAL SERVICES OFFERED:
  Learning Lab

Learning Lab has a specialist with a masters degree
   or above in Learning Disabilities
Diagnostic testing services on campus
Remedial and/or tutorial help available
Reader services for the blind available for LD
Special Education department
Handicapped student services works with LD

MODIFICATIONS TO TRADITIONAL LEARNING ENVIRONMENT:
   Oral presentation in lieu of written exams
   Use of calculator for all math courses
   Has an adaptive physical education program
   Tape recorders to record class lectures
   Someone else may take class notes
   Students have exams read to them
   Longer time allowed to complete exams

MAJORS OFFERED:

   AGRICULTURE
   BUSINESS AND MANAGEMENT
   COMPUTER SCIENCES
   ENGINEERING TECHNOLOGIES
   HEALTH
   PUBLIC SERVICES
   GENERAL LIBERAL ARTS

==

LOS ANGELES CITY COLLEGE
855 NORTH VERMONT AVENUE
LOS ANGELES, CA 90029
213-669-4385

KEY CONTACT: Attn: Handicapped Student Services

SIZE OF SCHOOL: LARGE

APPLICATION DEADLINE: AUGUST 26

         APPROXIMATE TUITION   ROOM AND BOARD

IN DISTRICT $ 0 $NOT OFFERED
IN STATE $ 0 $NOT OFFERED
OUT-OF-STATE $2940 $NOT OFFERED

REQUIREMENTS FOR ADMISSIONS:
   High school equivalency diploma
   High school diploma
   21 years of age or older, with or without a
      high school diploma or equivalency

ADDITIONAL SERVICES OFFERED:
  Learning Lab
  Learning Lab has a specialist with a masters degree
    or above in Learning Disabilities
  Diagnostic testing services on campus
  Remedial and/or tutorial help available
  Reader services for the blind available for LD
    students
  Handicapped student services works with LD

MODIFICATIONS TO TRADITIONAL LEARNING ENVIRONMENT:
  Oral presentation in lieu of written exams
  Tape recorders to record class lectures
  Someone else may take class notes
  Multiple choice exams only
  Student takes exams in separate rooms
  Students have exams read to them
  Students take typewritten exams
  Longer time allowed to complete exams
  Submit papers on cassette tape
  Extended time limits for graduation
  Physical education may be waived

MAJORS OFFERED:

  ARCHITECTURE
  BIOLOGICAL SCIENCES
  BUSINESS AND MANAGEMENT
  COMMUNICATIONS
  COMPUTER SCIENCES
  ENGINEERING TECHNOLOGIES
  FINE AND APPLIED ARTS
  FOREIGN LANGUAGES
  HEALTH
  HOME ECONOMICS
  MATHEMATICS
  PHYSICAL SCIENCES
  PUBLIC SERVICES
  PSYCHOLOGY
  SOCIAL SCIENCES
  GENERAL LIBERAL ARTS

==

LOS ANGELES HARBOR COLLEGE
1111 FIGUEROA PLACE
WILMINGTON, CA 90744
213-518-1000

KEY CONTACT: Attn: SALLEY SMITH FASTEAU
                     LEARNING DISABILITIES SPECIALIST

SIZE OF SCHOOL: LARGE

APPLICATION DEADLINE: NONE

	APPROXIMATE TUITION	ROOM AND BOARD
IN DISTRICT	$ 0	$NOT OFFERED
IN STATE	$ 0	$NOT OFFERED
OUT-OF-STATE	$2355	$NOT OFFERED

REQUIREMENTS FOR ADMISSIONS:
   18 years of age or older, with or without a
      high school diploma or equivalency

ADDITIONAL SERVICES OFFERED:
   Learning Lab
   Learning Lab has a specialist with a masters degree
      or above in Learning Disabilities
   Diagnostic testing services on campus
   Remedial and/or tutorial help available
   Reader services for the blind available for LD
      students
   Special Education department
   Handicapped student services works with LD

MODIFICATIONS TO TRADITIONAL LEARNING ENVIRONMENT:
   Oral presentation in lieu of written exams
   Use of calculator for all math courses (except
      remedial math class0
   Tape recorders to record class lectures
   Someone else may take class notes
   Student takes exams in separate rooms
   Students have exams read to them
   Students take typewritten exams
   Longer time allowed to complete exams
   Submit papers on cassette tape

MAJORS OFFERED:

   BIOLOGICAL SCIENCES
   BUSINESS AND MANAGEMENT
   COMMUNICATIONS
   COMPUTER SCIENCES
   ENGINEERING TECHNOLOGIES
   FINE AND APPLIED ARTS
   FOREIGN LANGUAGES
   HEALTH
   HOME ECONOMICS
   MATHEMATICS
   PHYSICAL SCIENCES
   PSYCHOLOGY

```
SOCIAL SCIENCES
GENERAL LIBERAL ARTS
```

==

```
LOS ANGELES MISSION COLLEGE
1212 SAN FERNANDO ROAD
SAN FERNANDO, CA 91340
213-365-8271

KEY CONTACT: Attn:  JACK OLIVER, ASSISTANT DEAN

SIZE OF SCHOOL: MEDIUM

APPLICATION DEADLINE: SEPTEMBER 18

      APPROXIMATE TUITION    ROOM AND BOARD

IN DISTRICT        $   0        $NOT OFFERED
IN STATE           $   0        $NOT OFFERED
OUT-OF-STATE       $2355        $NOT OFFERED
```

REQUIREMENTS FOR ADMISSIONS:
  Untimed or oral ACT Scores accepted
  Untimed or oral SAT Scores accepted
  University or College sponsored tests
  Placement tests
  Recommendations

ADDITIONAL SERVICES OFFERED:
  Learning Lab
  Learning Lab has a specialist with a masters degree
    or above in Learning Disabilities
  Diagnostic testing services on campus
  Remedial and/or tutorial help available
  Reader services for the blind available for LD
    students
  Special Education department
  Handicapped student services works with LD

MODIFICATIONS TO TRADITIONAL LEARNING ENVIRONMENT:
  Oral presentation in lieu of written exams
  Use of calculator for all math courses
  Has an adaptive physical education program
  Tape recorders to record class lectures
  Someone else may take class notes
  Student takes exams in separate rooms
  Students have exams read to them
  Students take typewritten exams
  Longer time allowed to complete exams
  Submit papers on cassette tape

Take limited course load and graduate within time
  required
Extended time limits for graduation

MAJORS OFFERED:

BIOLOGICAL SCIENCES
BUSINESS AND MANAGEMENT
COMPUTER SCIENCES
EDUCATION
ENGINEERING TECHNOLOGIES
FOREIGN LANGUAGES
HOME ECONOMICS
HUMANITIES
MATHEMATICS
PHYSICAL SCIENCES
PSYCHOLOGY
SOCIAL SCIENCES
GENERAL LIBERAL ARTS

===

MENDOCINO COLLEGE
P.O. BOX 3000
UKIAH, CA 95482
707-468-0406

KEY CONTACT: Attn: NANCY PROTO - ROBINSON
                    SPECIALIST, DISABLED STUDENTS

SIZE OF SCHOOL: MEDIUM

APPLICATION DEADLINE: NONE

           APPROXIMATE TUITION   ROOM AND BOARD

IN DISTRICT $ 5 $NOT OFFERED
IN STATE $ 5 $NOT OFFERED
OUT-OF-STATE $2430 $NOT OFFERED

REQUIREMENTS FOR ADMISSIONS:
  Personal interview
  Placement tests

ADDITIONAL SERVICES OFFERED:
  Learning Lab
  Learning Lab has a specialist with a masters degree
    or above in Learning Disabilities
  Diagnostic testing services on campus
  Remedial and/or tutorial help available
  Reader services for the blind available for LD

    Handicapped student services works with LD

MODIFICATIONS TO TRADITIONAL LEARNING ENVIRONMENT:
    Oral presentation in lieu of written exams
    Use of calculator for all math courses
    Has an adaptive physical education program
    Tape recorders to record class lectures
    Someone else may take class notes
    Student takes exams in separate rooms
    Students have exams read to them
    Students take typewritten exams
    Longer time allowed to complete exams
    Submit papers on cassette tape
    Extended time limits for graduation

MAJORS OFFERED:

    AGRICULTURE
    BIOLOGICAL SCIENCES
    BUSINESS AND MANAGEMENT
    COMPUTER SCIENCES
    EDUCATION
    FINE AND APPLIED ARTS
    FOREIGN LANGUAGES
    HEALTH
    HUMANITIES
    MATHEMATICS
    PHYSICAL SCIENCES
    SOCIAL SCIENCES
    GENERAL LIBERAL ARTS

===

MERCED COLLEGE
3600 M STREET
MERCED, CA 95340
209-384-6000

KEY CONTACT: Attn: Handicapped Student Services

SIZE OF SCHOOL: MEDIUM

APPLICATION DEADLINE: NONE

        APPROXIMATE TUITION   ROOM AND BOARD

IN DISTRICT $ 10 $NOT OFFERED
IN STATE $ 10 $NOT OFFERED
OUT-OF-STATE $1800 $NOT OFFERED

REQUIREMENTS FOR ADMISSIONS:
  High school equivalency diploma
  High school diploma
  21 years of age or older, with or without a
    high school diploma or equivalency
  Untimed or oral ACT Scores accepted
  Untimed or oral SAT Scores accepted
  Admission requirements modified
  Placement tests

ADDITIONAL SERVICES OFFERED:
  Learning Lab
  Learning Lab has a specialist with a masters degree
    or above in Learning Disabilities
  Diagnostic testing services off campus
  Remedial and/or tutorial help available
  Reader services for the blind available for LD
    students
  Handicapped student services works with LD

MODIFICATIONS TO TRADITIONAL LEARNING ENVIRONMENT:
  Oral presentation in lieu of written exams
  Use of calculator for all math courses
  Has an adaptive physical education program
  Tape recorders to record class lectures
  Someone else may take class notes
  Multiple choice exams only
  Essay exams only
  Student takes exams in separate rooms
  Students have exams read to them
  Students take typewritten exams
  Longer time allowed to complete exams
  Submit papers on cassette tape
  Extended time limits for graduation
  Physical education may be waived

MAJORS OFFERED:

  AGRICULTURE
  BIOLOGICAL SCIENCES
  BUSINESS AND MANAGEMENT
  COMPUTER SCIENCES
  ENGINEERING TECHNOLOGIES
  FINE AND APPLIED ARTS
  HEALTH
  HOME ECONOMICS
  HUMANITIES
  MATHEMATICS
  PHYSICAL SCIENCES
  SOCIAL SCIENCES
  GENERAL LIBERAL ARTS

```
MERRITT COLLEGE
12500 CAMPUS DRIVE
OAKLAND, CA 94619
415-531-4911
```

KEY CONTACT: Attn: ANNE LONG, LD SPECIALIST

SIZE OF SCHOOL: MEDIUM

APPLICATION DEADLINE: NONE

	APPROXIMATE TUITION	ROOM AND BOARD
IN DISTRICT	$ 0	$NOT OFFERED
IN STATE	$ 0	$NOT OFFERED
OUT-OF-STATE	$2340	$NOT OFFERED

REQUIREMENTS FOR ADMISSIONS:
  Untimed or oral ACT Scores accepted
  Untimed or oral SAT Scores accepted
  Admission requirements modified

ADDITIONAL SERVICES OFFERED:
  Learning Lab
  Learning Lab has a specialist with a masters degree
    or above in Learning Disabilities
  Diagnostic testing services on campus
  Remedial and/or tutorial help available
  Reader services for the blind available for LD
    students
  Special Education department
  Handicapped student services works with LD

MODIFICATIONS TO TRADITIONAL LEARNING ENVIRONMENT:
  Oral presentation in lieu of written exams
  Use of calculator for all math courses
  Tape recorders to record class lectures
  Someone else may take class notes
  Student takes exams in separate rooms
  Students have exams read to them
  Students take typewritten exams
  Longer time allowed to complete exams
  Submit papers on cassette tape
  Extended time limits for graduation
  Physical education may be waived

MAJORS OFFERED:

  AREA STUDIES
  BIOLOGICAL SCIENCES
  BUSINESS AND MANAGEMENT

```
COMPUTER SCIENCES
EDUCATION
ENGINEERING TECHNOLOGIES
FINE AND APPLIED ARTS
FOREIGN LANGUAGES
HEALTH
HOME ECONOMICS
HUMANITIES
LIBRARY SCIENCE
MATHEMATICS
PHYSICAL SCIENCES
PSYCHOLOGY
PUBLIC SERVICES
SOCIAL SCIENCES
GENERAL LIBERAL ARTS
```

==

MIRACOSTA COLLEGE
ONE BARNARD DRIVE
OCEANSIDE, CA 92056
619-757-2121

KEY CONTACT: Attn: Handicapped Student Services

SIZE OF SCHOOL: MEDIUM

APPLICATION DEADLINE: NONE

	APPROXIMATE TUITION	ROOM AND BOARD
IN DISTRICT	$ 0	$NOT OFFERED
IN STATE	$ 0	$NOT OFFERED
OUT-OF-STATE	$2185	$NOT OFFERED

REQUIREMENTS FOR ADMISSIONS:
  High school equivalency diploma
  High school diploma
  21 years of age or older, with or without a
    high school diploma or equivalency

ADDITIONAL SERVICES OFFERED:
  Learning Lab
  Learning Lab has a specialist with a masters degree
    or above in Learning Disabilities
  Remedial and/or tutorial help available
  Reader services for the blind available for LD
    students
  Handicapped student services works with LD

MODIFICATIONS TO TRADITIONAL LEARNING ENVIRONMENT:
  Has an adaptive physical education program
  Tape recorders to record class lectures
  Someone else may take class notes
  Multiple choice exams only
  Essay exams only
  Student takes exams in separate rooms
  Students have exams read to them
  Students take typewritten exams
  Longer time allowed to complete exams
  Submit papers on cassette tape
  Physical education may be waived

MAJORS OFFERED:

  AGRICULTURE
  BIOLOGICAL SCIENCES
  BUSINESS AND MANAGEMENT
  COMMUNICATIONS
  COMPUTER SCIENCES
  EDUCATION
  ENGINEERING TECHNOLOGIES
  FINE AND APPLIED ARTS
  FOREIGN LANGUAGES
  HUMANITIES
  MATHEMATICS
  PHYSICAL SCIENCES
  PSYCHOLOGY
  SOCIAL SCIENCES
  GENERAL LIBERAL ARTS

==

MISSION COLLEGE
3000 MISSION COLLEGE BLVD
SANTA CLARA, CA 95054
408-988-2200

KEY CONTACT: Attn: CAROL D. TOPPEL, COORDINATOR
                     DISABLED STUDENTS PROGRAM

SIZE OF SCHOOL: MEDIUM

APPLICATION DEADLINE: NONE

        APPROXIMATE TUITION   ROOM AND BOARD

IN DISTRICT $ 0 $NOT OFFERED
IN STATE $ 0 $NOT OFFERED
OUT-OF-STATE $2190 $NOT OFFERED

REQUIREMENTS FOR ADMISSIONS:
   Untimed or oral ACT Scores accepted
   Untimed or oral SAT Scores accepted
   Placement tests

ADDITIONAL SERVICES OFFERED:
   Learning Lab
   Learning Lab has a specialist with a masters degree
      or above in Learning Disabilities
   Diagnostic testing services on campus
   Remedial and/or tutorial help available
   Reader services for the blind available for LD
      students

MODIFICATIONS TO TRADITIONAL LEARNING ENVIRONMENT:
   Oral presentation in lieu of written exams
   Has an adaptive physical education program
   Tape recorders to record class lectures
   Someone else may take class notes
   Student takes exams in separate rooms
   Students have exams read to them
   Students take typewritten exams
   Longer time allowed to complete exams
   Extended time limits for graduation
   Physical education may be waived

MAJORS OFFERED:

   BIOLOGICAL SCIENCES
   BUSINESS AND MANAGEMENT
   COMPUTER SCIENCES
   ENGINEERING TECHNOLOGIES
   FINE AND APPLIED ARTS
   FOREIGN LANGUAGES
   HEALTH
   HUMANITIES
   MATHEMATICS
   PHYSICAL SCIENCES
   PSYCHOLOGY
   SOCIAL SCIENCES
   GENERAL LIBERAL ARTS

==

MODESTO JUNIOR COLLEGE
COLLEGE AVENU
MODEST, CA 95350
209-575-6013

KEY CONTACT: Attn: MARILYN STERN

SIZE OF SCHOOL: LARGE

APPLICATION DEADLINE: AUGUST 12

	APPROXIMATE TUITION	ROOM AND BOARD
IN DISTRICT	$ 0	$NOT OFFERED
IN STATE	$ 0	$NOT OFFERED
OUT-OF-STATE	$2370	$NOT OFFERED

REQUIREMENTS FOR ADMISSIONS:
  High school equivalency diploma
  High school diploma
  21 years of age or older, with or without a
    high school diploma or equivalency

ADDITIONAL SERVICES OFFERED:
  Learning Lab
  Learning Lab has a specialist with a masters degree
    or above in Learning Disabilities
  Diagnostic testing services on campus
  Remedial and/or tutorial help available
  Reader services for the blind available for LD
    students
  Handicapped student services works with LD

MODIFICATIONS TO TRADITIONAL LEARNING ENVIRONMENT:
  Oral presentation in lieu of written exams
  Tape recorders to record class lectures
  Someone else may take class notes
  Multiple choice exams only
  Essay exams only
  Student takes exams in separate rooms
  Students have exams read to them
  Students take typewritten exams
  Longer time allowed to complete exams
  Submit papers on cassette tape
  Extended time limits for graduation
  Physical education may be waived

MAJORS OFFERED:

  AGRICULTURE
  ARCHITECTURE
  BIOLOGICAL SCIENCES
  BUSINESS AND MANAGEMENT
  COMMUNICATIONS
  COMPUTER SCIENCES
  EDUCATION
  ENGINEERING TECHNOLOGIES
  FINE AND APPLIED ARTS

```
FOREIGN LANGUAGES
HEALTH
HOME ECONOMICS
HUMANITIES
LIBRARY SCIENCE
MATHEMATICS
PHYSICAL SCIENCES
PSYCHOLOGY
PUBLIC SERVICES
SOCIAL SCIENCES
GENERAL LIBERAL ARTS
```

==

```
MOORPARK COLLEGE
7075 CAMPUS ROAD
MOORPARK, CA 93021
805-529-2321
```

KEY CONTACT: Attn: J. DILLON, LD SPECIALIST

SIZE OF SCHOOL: MEDIUM

APPLICATION DEADLINE: NONE

	APPROXIMATE TUITION	ROOM AND BOARD
IN DISTRICT	$ 15	$NOT OFFERED
IN STATE	$ 15	$NOT OFFERED
OUT-OF-STATE	$2265	$NOT OFFERED

REQUIREMENTS FOR ADMISSIONS:
  High school equivalency diploma
  High school diploma
  21 years of age or older, with or without a
    high school diploma or equivalency

ADDITIONAL SERVICES OFFERED:
  Learning Lab
  Remedial and/or tutorial help available
  Reader services for the blind available for LD
    students
  Special Education department
  Handicapped student services works with LD

MODIFICATIONS TO TRADITIONAL LEARNING ENVIRONMENT:
  Oral presentation in lieu of written exams
  Use of calculator for all math courses
  Has an adaptive physical education program
  Tape recorders to record class lectures
  Someone else may take class notes

Multiple choice exams only
Essay exams only
Student takes exams in separate rooms
Students have exams read to them
Students take typewritten exams
Longer time allowed to complete exams
Submit papers on cassette tape
Physical education may be waived

MAJORS OFFERED:

AGRICULTURE
BIOLOGICAL SCIENCES
BUSINESS AND MANAGEMENT
COMMUNICATIONS
COMPUTER SCIENCES
ENGINEERING TECHNOLOGIES
FINE AND APPLIED ARTS
FOREIGN LANGUAGES
HOME ECONOMICS
MATHEMATICS
PHYSICAL SCIENCES
PSYCHOLOGY
SOCIAL SCIENCES
GENERAL LIBERAL ARTS

===

MOUNT SAN ANTONIO COLLEGE
1100 NORTH GRAND AVENUE
WALNUT, CA 91789
714-594-5611

KEY CONTACT: Attn: Handicapped Student Services

SIZE OF SCHOOL: LARGE

APPLICATION DEADLINE: NONE

	APPROXIMATE TUITION	ROOM AND BOARD
IN DISTRICT	$ 35	$NOT OFFERED
IN STATE	$ 35	$NOT OFFERED
OUT-OF-STATE	$2370	$NOT OFFERED

REQUIREMENTS FOR ADMISSIONS:
  High school equivalency diploma
  High school diploma
  21 years of age or older, with or without a
    high school diploma or equivalency

ADDITIONAL SERVICES OFFERED:
  Learning Lab
  Learning Lab has a specialist with a masters degree
    or above in Learning Disabilities
  Diagnostic testing services off campus
  Remedial and/or tutorial help available
  Reader services for the blind available for LD
    students
  Handicapped student services works with LD

MODIFICATIONS TO TRADITIONAL LEARNING ENVIRONMENT:
  Oral presentation in lieu of written exams
  Tape recorders to record class lectures
  Someone else may take class notes
  Student takes exams in separate rooms
  Students have exams read to them
  Students take typewritten exams
  Longer time allowed to complete exams
  Physical education may be waived

MAJORS OFFERED:

  AGRICULTURE
  BUSINESS AND MANAGEMENT
  COMPUTER SCIENCES
  ENGINEERING TECHNOLOGIES
  HEALTH
  PUBLIC SERVICES
  GENERAL LIBERAL ARTS

===

MOUNT SAN JACINTO COLLEGE
21-400 HIGHWAY 79
SAN JACINTO, CA 92383
714-654-8011

KEY CONTACT: Attn: M. HIGHT

SIZE OF SCHOOL: MEDIUM

APPLICATION DEADLINE: SEPTEMBER 7

	APPROXIMATE TUITION	ROOM AND BOARD
IN DISTRICT	$ 0	$NOT OFFERED
IN STATE	$ 0	$NOT OFFERED
OUT-OF-STATE	$2280	$NOT OFFERED

REQUIREMENTS FOR ADMISSIONS:
  High school equivalency diploma
  High school diploma
  21 years of age or older, with or without a
    high school diploma or equivalency
  Admission requirements modified
  Placement tests

ADDITIONAL SERVICES OFFERED:
  Learning Lab
  Learning Lab has a specialist with a masters degree
    or above in Learning Disabilities
  Remedial and/or tutorial help available
  Reader services for the blind available for LD
    students
  Handicapped student services works with LD

MODIFICATIONS TO TRADITIONAL LEARNING ENVIRONMENT:
  Use of calculator for all math courses
  Tape recorders to record class lectures
  Someone else may take class notes
  Student takes exams in separate rooms
  Students have exams read to them
  Students take typewritten exams
  Longer time allowed to complete exams
  Submit papers on cassette tape
  Extended time limits for graduation
  Physical education may be waived

MAJORS OFFERED:

  AGRICULTURE
  BIOLOGICAL SCIENCES
  BUSINESS AND MANAGEMENT
  COMMUNICATIONS
  COMPUTER SCIENCES
  EDUCATION
  FINE AND APPLIED ARTS
  HEALTH
  HUMANITIES
  LIBRARY SCIENCE
  MATHEMATICS
  PHYSICAL SCIENCES
  PSYCHOLOGY
  SOCIAL SCIENCES
  GENERAL LIBERAL ARTS

==

```
NAPA COLLEGE
2277 NAPA-VALLEJO HIGHWAY
NAPA, CA 94558
707-255-2100
```

KEY CONTACT: Attn: DOUG DIBBLE

SIZE OF SCHOOL: MEDIUM

APPLICATION DEADLINE: NONE

	APPROXIMATE TUITION	ROOM AND BOARD
IN DISTRICT	$ 0	$NOT OFFERED
IN STATE	$ 0	$NOT OFFERED
OUT-OF-STATE	$2200	$NOT OFFERED

REQUIREMENTS FOR ADMISSIONS:
  High school equivalency diploma
  High school diploma
  21 years of age or older, with or without a
    high school diploma or equivalency

ADDITIONAL SERVICES OFFERED:
  Learning Lab
  Learning Lab has a specialist with a masters degree
    or above in Learning Disabilities
  Diagnostic testing services on campus
  Remedial and/or tutorial help available
  Reader services for the blind available for LD
    students
  Special Education department
  Handicapped student services works with LD

MODIFICATIONS TO TRADITIONAL LEARNING ENVIRONMENT:
  Tape recorders to record class lectures
  Someone else may take class notes
  Student takes exams in separate rooms
  Students have exams read to them
  Students take typewritten exams
  Longer time allowed to complete exams
  Submit papers on cassette tape
  Extended time limits for graduation
  Physical education may be waived

MAJORS OFFERED:

  AGRICULTURE
  BIOLOGICAL SCIENCES
  BUSINESS AND MANAGEMENT
  COMMUNICATIONS

```
COMPUTER SCIENCES
ENGINEERING TECHNOLOGIES
FINE AND APPLIED ARTS
FOREIGN LANGUAGES
HEALTH
HUMANITIES
MATHEMATICS
PHYSICAL SCIENCES
PSYCHOLOGY
SOCIAL SCIENCES
```

==

OHLONE COLLEGE
43600 MISSION BLVD
FREMONT, CA 94538
415-657-2100

KEY CONTACT: Attn: Handicapped Student Services

SIZE OF SCHOOL: MEDIUM

APPLICATION DEADLINE: NONE

	APPROXIMATE TUITION	ROOM AND BOARD
IN DISTRICT	$ 0	$NOT OFFERED
IN STATE	$ 0	$NOT OFFERED
OUT-OF-STATE	$1875	$NOT OFFERED

REQUIREMENTS FOR ADMISSIONS:
  18 years of age or older, with or without a
    high school diploma or equivalency
  ACT Scores required
  Untimed or oral ACT Scores accepted
  SAT Scores required
  Untimed or oral SAT Scores accepted

ADDITIONAL SERVICES OFFERED:
  Remedial and/or tutorial help available
  Reader services for the blind available for LD
    students
  Special Education department
  Handicapped student services works with LD

MODIFICATIONS TO TRADITIONAL LEARNING ENVIRONMENT:
  Oral presentation in lieu of written exams (possibly)
  Use of calculator for all math courses
  Has an adaptive physical education program
  Tape recorders to record class lectures
  Someone else may take class notes

```
Student takes exams in separate rooms (possibly)
Students have exams read to them (possibly)
Students take typewritten exams  (possibly)
Longer time allowed to complete exams (possibly)
Submit papers on cassette tape (possibly)
Extended time limits for graduation
Physical education may be waived
```

MAJORS OFFERED:

```
BIOLOGICAL SCIENCES
BUSINESS AND MANAGEMENT
COMPUTER SCIENCES
ENGINEERING TECHNOLOGIES
FINE AND APPLIED ARTS
FOREIGN LANGUAGES
HEALTH
HOME ECONOMICS
HUMANITIES
MATHEMATICS
PHYSICAL SCIENCES
PSYCHOLOGY
SOCIAL SCIENCES
GENERAL LIBERAL ARTS
```

===

```
ORANGE COAST COLLEGE
2701 FAIRVIEW ROAD
COSTA MESA, CA 92626
714-556-5735
```

KEY CONTACT: Attn: Handicapped Student Services

SIZE OF SCHOOL: LARGE

APPLICATION DEADLINE: NONE

	APPROXIMATE TUITION	ROOM AND BOARD
IN DISTRICT	$ 25	$NOT OFFERED
IN STATE	$ 25	$NOT OFFERED
OUT-OF-STATE	$1728	$NOT OFFERED

REQUIREMENTS FOR ADMISSIONS:
  High school equivalency diploma
  High school diploma
  21 years of age or older, with or without a
    high school diploma or equivalency

ADDITIONAL SERVICES OFFERED:
  Learning Lab
  Learning Lab has a specialist with a masters degree
    or above in Learning Disabilities
  Diagnostic testing services on campus
  Remedial and/or tutorial help available
  Reader services for the blind available for LD
  Handicapped student services works with LD

MODIFICATIONS TO TRADITIONAL LEARNING ENVIRONMENT:
  Oral presentation in lieu of written exams
  Use of calculator for all math courses
  Tape recorders to record class lectures
  Someone else may take class notes
  Multiple choice exams only
  Student takes exams in separate rooms
  Students have exams read to them
  Students take typewritten exams
  Longer time allowed to complete exams
  Submit papers on cassette tape
  Extended time limits for graduation
  Physical education may be waived

MAJORS OFFERED:

  AGRICULTURE
  ARCHITECTURE
  BIOLOGICAL SCIENCES
  BUSINESS AND MANAGEMENT
  COMMUNICATIONS
  COMPUTER SCIENCES
  EDUCATION
  ENGINEERING TECHNOLOGIES
  FINE AND APPLIED ARTS
  FOREIGN LANGUAGES
  HEALTH
  HOME ECONOMICS
  HUMANITIES
  MATHEMATICS
  PHYSICAL SCIENCES
  PSYCHOLOGY
  SOCIAL SCIENCES

==

OXNARD COLLEGE
4000 SOUTH ROSE AVENUE
OXNARD, CA 93033
805-488-0911

KEY CONTACT: Attn: Handicapped Student Services

SIZE OF SCHOOL: MEDIUM

APPLICATION DEADLINE: NONE

	APPROXIMATE TUITION	ROOM AND BOARD
IN DISTRICT	$ 0	$NOT OFFERED
IN STATE	$ 0	$NOT OFFERED
OUT-OF-STATE	$1800	$NOT OFFERED

REQUIREMENTS FOR ADMISSIONS:
  High school equivalency diploma
  High school diploma
  21 years of age or older, with or without a
    high school diploma or equivalency
  Admission requirements modified

ADDITIONAL SERVICES OFFERED:
  Learning Lab
  Learning Lab has a specialist with a masters degree
    or above in Learning Disabilities
  Diagnostic testing services on campus
  Diagnostic testing services off campus
  Remedial and/or tutorial help available
  Reader services for the blind available for LD
  Special Education department
  Handicapped student services works with LD

MODIFICATIONS TO TRADITIONAL LEARNING ENVIRONMENT:
  Oral presentation in lieu of written exams
  Use of calculator for all math courses
  Has an adaptive physical education program
  Tape recorders to record class lectures
  Someone else may take class notes
  Student takes exams in separate rooms
  Students have exams read to them
  Students take typewritten exams
  Longer time allowed to complete exams
  Submit papers on cassette tape
  Extended time limits for graduation
  Physical education may be waived

MAJORS OFFERED:

  AGRICULTURE
  BUSINESS AND MANAGEMENT
  ENGINEERING TECHNOLOGIES
  HEALTH
  PUBLIC SERVICES
  GENERAL LIBERAL ARTS

```
PASADENA CITY COLLEGE
1570 EAST COLORADO BLVD
PASADENA, CA 91106
213-578-7391
```

KEY CONTACT: Attn: E. WELLER
                    LEARNING DISABILITY SPECIALIST

SIZE OF SCHOOL: LARGE

APPLICATION DEADLINE: NONE

	APPROXIMATE TUITION	ROOM AND BOARD
IN DISTRICT	$ 0	$NOT OFFERED
IN STATE	$ 0	$NOT OFFERED
OUT-OF-STATE	$2250	$NOT OFFERED

REQUIREMENTS FOR ADMISSIONS:
  High school equivalency diploma
  High school diploma
  21 years of age or older, with or without a
     high school diploma or equivalency

ADDITIONAL SERVICES OFFERED:
  Learning Lab
  Learning Lab has a specialist with a masters degree
     or above in Learning Disabilities
  Diagnostic testing services on campus
  Diagnostic testing services off campus
  Remedial and/or tutorial help available
  Reader services for the blind available for LD
  Handicapped student services works with LD

MODIFICATIONS TO TRADITIONAL LEARNING ENVIRONMENT:
  Use of calculator for all math courses
  Tape recorders to record class lectures
  Someone else may take class notes
  Multiple choice exams only
  Essay exams only
  Student takes exams in seperate rooms
  Students have exams read to them
  Students take typewritten exams
  Longer time allowed to complete exams
  Submit papers on cassette tape
  Extended time limits for graduation
  Physical education may be waived

MAJORS OFFERED:

    AGRICULTURE
    ARCHITECTURE
    AREA STUDIES
    BIOLOGICAL SCIENCES
    BUSINESS AND MANAGEMENT
    COMMUNICATIONS
    COMPUTER SCIENCES
    EDUCATION
    ENGINEERING TECHNOLOGIES
    FINE AND APPLIED ARTS
    FOREIGN LANGUAGES
    HEALTH
    HOME ECONOMICS
    HUMANITIES
    LIBRARY SCIENCE
    MATHEMATICS
    PHYSICAL SCIENCES
    PSYCHOLOGY
    PUBLIC SERVICES
    SOCIAL SCIENCES
    GENERAL LIBERAL ARTS

===

RIVERSIDE CITY COLLEGE
4800 MAGNOLIA AVENUE
RIVERSIDE, CA 92506
714-684-3240

KEY CONTACT: Attn: Handicapped Student Services

SIZE OF SCHOOL: LARGE

APPLICATION DEADLINE: NONE

          APPROXIMATE TUITION   ROOM AND BOARD

IN DISTRICT $ 10 $NOT OFFERED
IN STATE $ 10 $NOT OFFERED
OUT-OF-STATE $1095 $NOT OFFERED

REQUIREMENTS FOR ADMISSIONS:
    18 years of age or older, with or without a
      high school diploma or equivalency
    University or College sponsored tests (recommended)
    Personal interview
    Placement tests
    Recommendations

ADDITIONAL SERVICES OFFERED:
  Learning Lab
  Learning Lab has a specialist with a masters degree
    or above in Learning Disabilities
  Diagnostic testing services on campus
  Remedial and/or tutorial help available
  Reader services for the blind available for LD
  Handicapped student services works with LD

MODIFICATIONS TO TRADITIONAL LEARNING ENVIRONMENT:
  Use of calculator for all math courses
  Has an adaptive physical education program
  Tape recorders to record class lectures
  Someone else may take class notes
  Students have exams read to them
  Longer time allowed to complete exams
  Physical education may be waived
  All other modifications depend on instructor

MAJORS OFFERED:

  AGRICULTURE
  BUSINESS AND MANAGEMENT
  COMPUTER SCIENCES
  ENGINEERING TECHNOLOGIES
  HEALTH
  PUBLIC SERVICES
  GENERAL LIBERAL ARTS

==

SADDLEBACK COLLEGE
28000 MARQUERITE PARKWAY
MISSION VIEJO, CA 92691
714-831-4500

KEY CONTACT: Attn: PAULA JACOBS
                    LEARNING SPECIALIST

SIZE OF SCHOOL: LARGE

APPLICATION DEADLINE: NONE

        APPROXIMATE TUITION   ROOM AND BOARD

IN DISTRICT $ 5 $NOT OFFERED
IN STATE $ 5 $NOT OFFERED
OUT-OF-STATE $2190 $NOT OFFERED

REQUIREMENTS FOR ADMISSIONS:
  University or College sponsored tests
  Personal interview
  Placement tests
  Institution operates on open access basis

ADDITIONAL SERVICES OFFERED:
  Learning Lab
  Learning Lab has a specialist with a masters degree
    or above in Learning Disabilities
  Diagnostic testing services on campus
  Remedial and/or tutorial help available
  Reader services for the blind available for LD
  Special Education department
  Handicapped student services works with LD

MODIFICATIONS TO TRADITIONAL LEARNING ENVIRONMENT:
  Oral presentation in lieu of written exams
  Use of calculator for all math courses
  Has an adaptive physical education program
  Tape recorders to record class lectures
  Someone else may take class notes
  Student takes exams in separate rooms
  Students have exams read to them
  Students take typewritten exams
  Longer time allowed to complete exams
  Submit papers on cassette tape

MAJORS OFFERED:

  AGRICULTURE
  ARCHITECTURE
  AREA STUDIES
  BIOLOGICAL SCIENCES
  BUSINESS AND MANAGEMENT
  COMMUNICATIONS
  COMPUTER SCIENCES
  EDUCATION
  ENGINEERING TECHNOLOGIES
  FINE AND APPLIED ARTS
  FOREIGN LANGUAGES
  HEALTH
  HOME ECONOMICS
  HUMANITIES
  MATHEMATICS
  PHYSICAL SCIENCES
  PSYCHOLOGY
  PUBLIC SERVICES
  SOCIAL SCIENCES
  GENERAL LIBERAL ARTS

SAN BERNADINO VALLEY COLLEGE
701 SOUTH MOUNT VERNON AVENUE
SAN BERNADINO, CA 92410
714-888-6511

KEY CONTACT: Attn: Handicapped Student Services

SIZE OF SCHOOL: LARGE

APPLICATION DEADLINE: NONE

        APPROXIMATE TUITION   ROOM AND BOARD

IN DISTRICT $ 0 $NOT OFFERED
IN STATE $ 0 $NOT OFFERED
OUT-OF-STATE $1125 $NOT OFFERED

REQUIREMENTS FOR ADMISSIONS:
  High school equivalency diploma
  High school diploma
  21 years of age or older, with or without a
    high school diploma or equivalency

ADDITIONAL SERVICES OFFERED:
  Learning Lab
  Learning Lab has a specialist with a masters degree
    or above in Learning Disabilities
  Diagnostic testing services on campus
  Remedial and/or tutorial help available
  Reader services for the blind available for LD
  Special Education department
  Handicapped student services works with LD

MODIFICATIONS TO TRADITIONAL LEARNING ENVIRONMENT:
  Oral presentation in lieu of written exams
  Use of calculator for all math courses
  Tape recorders to record class lectures
  Someone else may take class notes
  Multiple choice exams only
  Essay exams only
  Student takes exams in separate rooms
  Students have exams read to them
  Students take typewritten exams
  Longer time allowed to complete exams
  Submit papers on cassette tape
  Take limited course load and graduate within time
    required
  Extended time limits for graduation
  Physical education may be waived

MAJORS OFFERED:

    ARCHITECTURE
    BIOLOGICAL SCIENCES
    COMMUNICATIONS
    COMPUTER SCIENCES
    ENGINEERING TECHNOLOGIES
    FINE AND APPLIED ARTS
    HEALTH
    HOME ECONOMICS
    MATHEMATICS
    PHYSICAL SCIENCES
    PSYCHOLOGY
    PUBLIC SERVICES
    GENERAL LIBERAL ARTS

==

SAN DIEGO CITY COLLEGE
1313 TWELFTH STREET
SAN DIEGO, CA 92101
714-230-2400

KEY CONTACT: Attn: K. MAYER

SIZE OF SCHOOL: LARGE

APPLICATION DEADLINE: AUGUST 12

	APPROXIMATE TUITION	ROOM AND BOARD
IN DISTRICT	$ 10	$NOT OFFERED
IN STATE	$ 10	$NOT OFFERED
OUT-OF-STATE	$1490	$NOT OFFERED

REQUIREMENTS FOR ADMISSIONS:
  High school equivalency diploma
  High school diploma
  21 years of age or older, with or without a
    high school diploma or equivalency
  Admission requirements modified

ADDITIONAL SERVICES OFFERED:
  Learning Lab
  Learning Lab has a specialist with a masters degree
    or above in Learning Disabilities
  Diagnostic testing services on campus
  Diagnostic testing services off campus
  Remedial and/or tutorial help available
  Reader services for the blind available for LD
  Handicapped student services works with LD

MODIFICATIONS TO TRADITIONAL LEARNING ENVIRONMENT:
  Oral presentation in lieu of written exams
  Use of calculator for all math courses
  Tape recorders to record class lectures
  Someone else may take class notes
  Multiple choice exams only
  Essay exams only
  Student takes exams in separate rooms
  Students have exams read to them
  Students take typewritten exams
  Longer time allowed to complete exams
  Submit papers on cassette tape
  Extended time limits for graduation
  Physical education may be waived

MAJORS OFFERED:

  AREA STUDIES
  BIOLOGICAL SCIENCES
  BUSINESS AND MANAGEMENT
  COMMUNICATIONS
  COMPUTER SCIENCES
  EDUCATION
  ENGINEERING TECHNOLOGIES
  FINE AND APPLIED ARTS
  FOREIGN LANGUAGES
  HEALTH
  HOME ECONOMICS
  HUMANITIES
  MATHEMATICS
  PHYSICAL SCIENCES
  PSYCHOLOGY
  PUBLIC SERVICES
  SOCIAL SCIENCES
  GENERAL LIBERAL ARTS

==

SAN JOSE CITY COLLEGE
2100 MOORPARK AVENUE
SAN JOSE, CA 95128
408-298-2181

KEY CONTACT: Attn: MARTHA GLAZER

SIZE OF SCHOOL: LARGE

APPLICATION DEADLINE: NONE

```
        APPROXIMATE TUITION    ROOM AND BOARD

IN DISTRICT        $  10        $NOT OFFERED
IN STATE           $  10        $NOT OFFERED
OUT-OF-STATE       $1930        $NOT OFFERED
```

REQUIREMENTS FOR ADMISSIONS:
  High school equivalency diploma
  High school diploma
  21 years of age or older, with or without a
    high school diploma or equivalency
  Admission requirements modified
  Placement tests
  State/District residency

ADDITIONAL SERVICES OFFERED:
  Learning Lab
  Learning Lab has a specialist with a masters degree
    or above in Learning Disabilities
  Diagnostic testing services off campus
  Remedial and/or tutorial help available
  Reader services for the blind available for LD
  Special Education department
  Handicapped student services works with LD

MODIFICATIONS TO TRADITIONAL LEARNING ENVIRONMENT:
  Oral presentation in lieu of written exams
  Use of calculator for all math courses
  Has an adaptive physical education program
  Tape recorders to record class lectures
  Someone else may take class notes
  Multiple choice exams only
  Essay exams only
  Student takes exams in separate rooms
  Students have exams read to them
  Students take typewritten exams
  Longer time allowed to complete exams
  Submit papers on cassette tape
  Extended time limits for graduation
  Physical education may be waived

MAJORS OFFERED:

  AREA STUDIES
  BIOLOGICAL SCIENCES
  BUSINESS AND MANAGEMENT
  COMMUNICATIONS
  EDUCATION
  FINE AND APPLIED ARTS
  FOREIGN LANGUAGES
  HEALTH

```
HOME ECONOMICS
HUMANITIES
MATHEMATICS
PHYSICAL SCIENCES
PSYCHOLOGY
PUBLIC SERVICES
SOCIAL SCIENCES
GENERAL LIBERAL ARTS
```

==

```
SANTA ANA COLLEGE
17TH AT BRISTOL
SANTA ANA, CA 92706
714-667-3010
```

KEY CONTACT: Attn: CHERYL DUNN-HOANZL
                     LEARNING DISABILITIES PROGRAM

SIZE OF SCHOOL: LARGE

APPLICATION DEADLINE: NONE

	APPROXIMATE TUITION	ROOM AND BOARD
IN DISTRICT	$ 10	$NOT OFFERED
IN STATE	$ 10	$NOT OFFERED
OUT-OF-STATE	$2250	$NOT OFFERED

REQUIREMENTS FOR ADMISSIONS:
   High school equivalency diploma
   High school diploma
   21 years of age or older, with or without a
      high school diploma or equivalency

ADDITIONAL SERVICES OFFERED:
   Learning Lab
   Learning Lab has a specialist with a masters degree
      or above in Learning Disabilities
   Diagnostic testing services on campus
   Remedial and/or tutorial help available
   Reader services for the blind available for LD
   Special Education department

MODIFICATIONS TO TRADITIONAL LEARNING ENVIRONMENT:
   Oral presentation in lieu of written exams
   Use of calculator for all math courses
   Tape recorders to record class lectures
   Someone else may take class notes
   Multiple choice exams only
   Essay exams only

Student takes exams in seperate rooms
Students have exams read to them
Students take typewritten exams
Longer time allowed to complete exams
Submit papers on cassette tape
Extended time limits for graduation
Physical education may be waived

MAJORS OFFERED:

AGRICULTURE
ARCHITECTURE
AREA STUDIES
BIOLOGICAL SCIENCES
BUSINESS AND MANAGEMENT
COMMUNICATIONS
COMPUTER SCIENCES
EDUCATION
ENGINEERING TECHNOLOGIES
FINE AND APPLIED ARTS
FOREIGN LANGUAGES
HEALTH
HOME ECONOMICS
HUMANITIES
MATHEMATICS
PHYSICAL SCIENCES
PSYCHOLOGY
PUBLIC SERVICES
SOCIAL SCIENCES
GENERAL LIBERAL ARTS

===

SANTA BARBARA CITY COLLEGE
721 CLIFF DRIVE
SANTA BARBARA, CA 93109
805-963-4091

KEY CONTACT: Attn: Handicapped Student Services

SIZE OF SCHOOL: LARGE

APPLICATION DEADLINE: AUGUST 15

	APPROXIMATE TUITION	ROOM AND BOARD
IN DISTRICT	$ 0	$NOT OFFERED
IN STATE	$ 0	$NOT OFFERED
OUT-OF-STATE	$2600	$NOT OFFERED

REQUIREMENTS FOR ADMISSIONS:
  High school equivalency diploma
  High school diploma
  21 years of age or older, with or without a
    high school diploma or equivalency
  Admission requirements modified
  State/District residency

ADDITIONAL SERVICES OFFERED:
  Learning Lab
  Learning Lab has a specialist with a masters degree
    or above in Learning Disabilities
  Remedial and/or tutorial help available
  Reader services for the blind available for LD
  Handicapped student services works with LD

MODIFICATIONS TO TRADITIONAL LEARNING ENVIRONMENT:
  Use of calculator for all math courses
  Tape recorders to record class lectures
  Someone else may take class notes
  Multiple choice exams only
  Essay exams only
  Student takes exams in separate rooms
  Students have exams read to them
  Students take typewritten exams
  Longer time allowed to complete exams
  Submit papers on cassette tape
  Extended time limits for graduation
  Physical education may be waived

MAJORS OFFERED:

  AREA STUDIES
  BIOLOGICAL SCIENCES
  BUSINESS AND MANAGEMENT
  COMMUNICATIONS
  COMPUTER SCIENCES
  ENGINEERING TECHNOLOGIES
  FINE AND APPLIED ARTS
  FOREIGN LANGUAGES
  HEALTH
  HUMANITIES
  MATHEMATICS
  PHYSICAL SCIENCES
  PSYCHOLOGY
  SOCIAL SCIENCES
  GENERAL LIBERAL ARTS

===

SANTA MONICA COLLEGE
1900 PICO BLVD
SANTA MONICA, CA 90405
213-450-5150

KEY CONTACT: Attn: VICKIE PENNINGTON, COORDINATOR
                     DISABLED STUDENTS CENTER

SIZE OF SCHOOL: LARGE

APPLICATION DEADLINE: NONE

           APPROXIMATE TUITION   ROOM AND BOARD

IN DISTRICT $ 5 $NOT OFFERED
IN STATE $ 5 $NOT OFFERED
OUT-OF-STATE $2160 $NOT OFFERED

REQUIREMENTS FOR ADMISSIONS:
  High school equivalency diploma
  High school diploma
  Untimed or oral ACT Scores accepted
  Untimed or oral SAT Scores accepted
  University or College sponsored tests
  Placement tests

ADDITIONAL SERVICES OFFERED:
  Learning Lab
  Learning Lab has a specialist with a masters degree
    or above in Learning Disabilities
  Diagnostic testing services on campus
  Remedial and/or tutorial help available
  Reader services for the blind available for LD
  Special Education department
  Handicapped student services works with LD

MODIFICATIONS TO TRADITIONAL LEARNING ENVIRONMENT:
  Oral presentation in lieu of written exams
  Has an adaptive physical education program
  Tape recorders to record class lectures
  Someone else may take class notes
  Student takes exams in separate rooms
  Students have exams read to them
  Students take typewritten exams
  Longer time allowed to complete exams
  Submit papers on cassette tape
  Extended time limits for graduation
  Physical education may be waived

MAJORS OFFERED:

  AGRICULTURE
  ARCHITECTURE
  AREA STUDIES
  BIOLOGICAL SCIENCES
  BUSINESS AND MANAGEMENT
  COMMUNICATIONS
  COMPUTER SCIENCES
  EDUCATION
  ENGINEERING TECHNOLOGIES
  FINE AND APPLIED ARTS
  FOREIGN LANGUAGES
  HEALTH
  HOME ECONOMICS
  HUMANITIES
  MATHEMATICS
  PHYSICAL SCIENCES
  PSYCHOLOGY
  PUBLIC SERVICES
  SOCIAL SCIENCES
  GENERAL LIBERAL ARTS

===

SANTA ROSA JUNIOR COLLEGE
1501 MENDOCINO AVENUE
SANTA ROSA, CA 95401
707-527-4211

KEY CONTACT: Attn: ELIZABETH CARLSON, DEPT. CHAIR.
                    LEARNING SERVICES

SIZE OF SCHOOL: LARGE

APPLICATION DEADLINE: NONE

        APPROXIMATE TUITION   ROOM AND BOARD

IN DISTRICT $ 15 $1725
IN STATE $ 15 $1725
OUT-OF-STATE $2175 $1725

REQUIREMENTS FOR ADMISSIONS:
   18 years of age or older, with a
     high school diploma or equivalency
   Personal interview for LD program
   Placement tests - LD assesment given within program

ADDITIONAL SERVICES OFFERED:
  Learning Lab
  Learning Lab has a specialist with a masters degree
    or above in Learning Disabilities
  Diagnostic testing services on campus
  Remedial and/or tutorial help available
  Reader services for the blind available for LD
  Special Education department
  Handicapped student services works with LD

MODIFICATIONS TO TRADITIONAL LEARNING ENVIRONMENT:
  Oral presentation in lieu of written exams
  Has an adaptive physical education program
  Tape recorders to record class lectures
  Someone else may take class notes
  Students have exams read to them

MAJORS OFFERED:

  AGRICULTURE
  BUSINESS AND MANAGEMENT
  COMPUTER SCIENCES
  ENGINEERING TECHNOLOGIES
  HEALTH
  PUBLIC SERVICES
  GENERAL LIBERAL ARTS

==

SIERRA COLLEGE
5000 ROCKLIN ROAD
ROCKLIN, CA 95677
916-624-3333

KEY CONTACT: Attn: DENISE STONE, LD SPECIALIST

SIZE OF SCHOOL: LARGE

APPLICATION DEADLINE: NONE

        APPROXIMATE TUITION   ROOM AND BOARD

IN DISTRICT $ 30 $NOT OFFERED
IN STATE $ 30 $NOT OFFERED
OUT-OF-STATE $2390 $NOT OFFERED

REQUIREMENTS FOR ADMISSIONS:
  21 years of age or older, with or without a
    high school diploma or equivalency
  Untimed or oral ACT Scores accepted
  Untimed or oral SAT Scores accepted

University or College sponsored tests
Admission requirements modified
Personal interview
Placement tests
Recommendations

ADDITIONAL SERVICES OFFERED:
Learning Lab
Learning Lab has a specialist with a masters degree
    or above in Learning Disabilities
Diagnostic testing services on campus
Diagnostic testing services off campus
Reader services for the blind available for LD
Special Education department
Handicapped student services works with LD

MODIFICATIONS TO TRADITIONAL LEARNING ENVIRONMENT:
Oral presentation in lieu of written exams
Has an adaptive physical education program
Tape recorders to record class lectures
Someone else may take class notes
Student takes exams in separate rooms
Students have exams read to them
Students take typewritten exams
Longer time allowed to complete exams
Submit papers on cassette tape
Extended time limits for graduation
Physical education may be waived

MAJORS OFFERED:

AGRICULTURE
ARCHITECTURE
BIOLOGICAL SCIENCES
BUSINESS AND MANAGEMENT
COMPUTER SCIENCES
EDUCATION
ENGINEERING TECHNOLOGIES
FOREIGN LANGUAGES
HEALTH
HOME ECONOMICS
HUMANITIES
MATHEMATICS
PHYSICAL SCIENCES
PSYCHOLOGY
SOCIAL SCIENCES
GENERAL LIBERAL ARTS

===

SKYLINE COLLEGE
3300 COLLEGE DRIVE
SAN BRUNO, CA 94066
415-355-7000

KEY CONTACT: Attn: LINDA VAN SCIVER, COUNSELOR

SIZE OF SCHOOL: MEDIUM

APPLICATION DEADLINE: AUGUST 20

	APPROXIMATE TUITION	ROOM AND BOARD
IN DISTRICT	$ 20	$NOT OFFERED
IN STATE	$ 20	$NOT OFFERED
OUT-OF-STATE	$1850	$NOT OFFERED

REQUIREMENTS FOR ADMISSIONS:
  Personal interview
  Placement tests
  Recommendations
  State/District residency

ADDITIONAL SERVICES OFFERED:
  Learning Lab
  Learning Lab has a specialist with a masters degree
    or above in Learning Disabilities
  Diagnostic testing services off campus
  Remedial and/or tutorial help available
  Reader services for the blind available for LD
  Handicapped student services works with LD

MODIFICATIONS TO TRADITIONAL LEARNING ENVIRONMENT:
  Oral presentation in lieu of written exams (most)
  Has an adaptive physical education program
  Tape recorders to record class lectures (most)
  Someone else may take class notes
  Student takes exams in separate rooms (sometimes)
  Students have exams read to them
  Students take typewritten exams
  Longer time allowed to complete exams
  Extended time limits for graduation
  Physical education may be waived

MAJORS OFFERED:

  BIOLOGICAL SCIENCES
  BUSINESS AND MANAGEMENT
  COMPUTER SCIENCES
  EDUCATION
  FINE AND APPLIED ARTS

```
FOREIGN LANGUAGES
HEALTH
HOME ECONOMICS
HUMANITIES
MATHEMATICS
PHYSICAL SCIENCES
PSYCHOLOGY
SOCIAL SCIENCES
GENERAL LIBERAL ARTS
```

==

```
SOUTHWESTERN COLLEGE
900 OTAY LAKES ROAD
CHULA VISTA, CA 92010
714-421-1193
```

KEY CONTACT: Attn: Handicapped Student Services

SIZE OF SCHOOL: LARGE

APPLICATION DEADLINE: AUGUST 15

	APPROXIMATE TUITION	ROOM AND BOARD
IN DISTRICT	$ 0	$NOT OFFERED
IN STATE	$ 0	$NOT OFFERED
OUT-OF-STATE	$1600	$NOT OFFERED

REQUIREMENTS FOR ADMISSIONS:
  High school equivalency diploma
  High school diploma
  21 years of age or older, with or without a
    high school diploma or equivalency
  Admission requirements modified
  Placement tests
  State/District residency

ADDITIONAL SERVICES OFFERED:
  Learning Lab
  Learning Lab has a specialist with a masters degree
    or above in Learning Disabilities
  Diagnostic testing services on campus
  Remedial and/or tutorial help available
  Reader services for the blind available for LD
  Handicapped student services works with LD

MODIFICATIONS TO TRADITIONAL LEARNING ENVIRONMENT:
  Oral presentation in lieu of written exams
  Use of calculator for all math courses
  Has an adaptive physical education program

Tape recorders to record class lectures
Someone else may take class notes
Multiple choice exams only
Essay exams only
Student takes exams in separate rooms
Students have exams read to them
Students take typewritten exams
Longer time allowed to complete exams
Submit papers on cassette tape
Take limited course load and graduate within time
    required
Extended time limits for graduation
Physical education may be waived

MAJORS OFFERED:

AGRICULTURE
ARCHITECTURE
BIOLOGICAL SCIENCES
BUSINESS AND MANAGEMENT
COMPUTER SCIENCES
ENGINEERING TECHNOLOGIES
FINE AND APPLIED ARTS
FOREIGN LANGUAGES
HEALTH
HOME ECONOMICS
HUMANITIES
MATHEMATICS
PHYSICAL SCIENCES
PSYCHOLOGY
SOCIAL SCIENCES
GENERAL LIBERAL ARTS

==

TAFT COLLEGE
TAFT, CA 93268
805-763-4282

KEY CONTACT: Attn: KAREN KUCKREJA
                    COLLEGE SPECIALIST/ENABLER

SIZE OF SCHOOL: SMALL

APPLICATION DEADLINE: NONE

         APPROXIMATE TUITION   ROOM AND BOARD

IN DISTRICT $ 0 $1630
IN STATE $ 0 $1630
OUT-OF-STATE $2250 $1630

REQUIREMENTS FOR ADMISSIONS:
  High school equivalency diploma
  18 years of age or older, with or without a
    high school diploma or equivalency
  University or College sponsored tests
  Placement tests
  Recommendations
  State/District residency
  All disabled stucdents are mainstreamed

ADDITIONAL SERVICES OFFERED:
  Diagnostic testing services on campus
  Diagnostic testing services off campus
  Remedial and/or tutorial help available
  Reader services for the blind available for LD
    students
  Special Education department
  Handicapped student services works with LD
  Tutoral center for all students

MODIFICATIONS TO TRADITIONAL LEARNING ENVIRONMENT:
  No specific LD program, however will accomodate when
    and where deemed appropriate

MAJORS OFFERED:

  BIOLOGICAL SCIENCES
  BUSINESS AND MANAGEMENT
  COMMUNICATIONS
  COMPUTER SCIENCES
  ENGINEERING TECHNOLOGIES
  FINE AND APPLIED ARTS
  HUMANITIES
  MATHEMATICS
  PHYSICAL SCIENCES
  PSYCHOLOGY
  SOCIAL SCIENCES
  GENERAL LIBERAL ARTS

==

VENTURA COLLEGE
4667 TELEGRAPH ROAD
VENTURA, CA 93003
805-642-3211

KEY CONTACT: Attn: JEFFREY BARACH

SIZE OF SCHOOL: LARGE

APPLICATION DEADLINE: NONE

```
          APPROXIMATE TUITION   ROOM AND BOARD

IN DISTRICT        $  0         $NOT OFFERED
IN STATE           $  0         $NOT OFFERED
OUT-OF-STATE       $2160        $NOT OFFERED
```

REQUIREMENTS FOR ADMISSIONS:
  High school equivalency diploma
  High school diploma
  21 years of age or older, with or without a
    high school diploma or equivalency

ADDITIONAL SERVICES OFFERED:
  Learning Lab
  Learning Lab has a specialist with a masters degree
    or above in Learning Disabilities
  Diagnostic testing services on campus
  Diagnostic testing services off campus
  Remedial and/or tutorial help available
  Reader services for the blind available for LD
  Special Education department
  Handicapped student services works with LD

MODIFICATIONS TO TRADITIONAL LEARNING ENVIRONMENT:
  Oral presentation in lieu of written exams
  Has an adaptive physical education program
  Tape recorders to record class lectures
  Someone else may take class notes
  Multiple choice exams only
  Essay exams only
  Student takes exams in separate rooms
  Students have exams read to them
  Students take typewritten exams
  Longer time allowed to complete exams
  Submit papers on cassette tape
  Extended time limits for graduation
  Physical education may be waived

MAJORS OFFERED:

  AGRICULTURE
  ARCHITECTURE
  AREA STUDIES
  BIOLOGICAL SCIENCES
  BUSINESS AND MANAGEMENT
  COMMUNICATIONS
  COMPUTER SCIENCES
  EDUCATION
  ENGINEERING TECHNOLOGIES
  FINE AND APPLIED ARTS
  FOREIGN LANGUAGES

    HEALTH
    HOME ECONOMICS
    HUMANITIES
    MATHEMATICS
    PHYSICAL SCIENCES
    PSYCHOLOGY
    PUBLIC SERVICES
    SOCIAL SCIENCES
    GENERAL LIBERAL ARTS

==

WEST HILL COMMUNITY COLLEGE
300 CHERRY LANE
COALINGA, CA 93210
209-935-0801

KEY CONTACT: Attn: P.J. DEMARIS

SIZE OF SCHOOL: SMALL

APPLICATION DEADLINE: NONE

          APPROXIMATE TUITION   ROOM AND BOARD

IN DISTRICT $ 30 $2350
IN STATE $ 30 $2350
OUT-OF-STATE $2160 $2350

REQUIREMENTS FOR ADMISSIONS:
   18 years of age or older, with or without a
      high school diploma or equivalency
   Untimed or oral ACT Scores accepted
   Untimed or oral SAT Scores accepted
   University or College sponsored tests
   Placement tests

ADDITIONAL SERVICES OFFERED:
   Learning Lab
   Diagnostic testing services on campus
   Remedial and/or tutorial help available
   Reader services for the blind available for LD
   Handicapped student services works with LD

MODIFICATIONS TO TRADITIONAL LEARNING ENVIRONMENT:
   Oral presentation in lieu of written exams
   Use of calculator for all math courses
   Tape recorders to record class lectures
   Someone else may take class notes
   Students take typewritten exams
   Longer time allowed to complete exams

Submit papers on cassette tape
Extended time limits for graduation
Physical education may be waived

MAJORS OFFERED:

AGRICULTURE
BIOLOGICAL SCIENCES
BUSINESS AND MANAGEMENT
COMMUNICATIONS
COMPUTER SCIENCES
EDUCATION
ENGINEERING TECHNOLOGIES
FINE AND APPLIED ARTS
HEALTH
HUMANITIES
MATHEMATICS
PHYSICAL SCIENCES
PSYCHOLOGY
SOCIAL SCIENCES
GENERAL LIBERAL ARTS

===

YUBA COLLEGE
2088 NORTH BEALE ROAD
MARYSVILLE, CA 95901
916-742-7351

KEY CONTACT: Attn: HELEN DAVID SHAW, LD SPECIALIST

SIZE OF SCHOOL: MEDIUM

APPLICATION DEADLINE: SEPTEMBER 6

          APPROXIMATE TUITION   ROOM AND BOARD

IN DISTRICT $ 40 $2295
IN STATE $ 40 $2295
OUT-OF-STATE $1800 $2295

REQUIREMENTS FOR ADMISSIONS:
Untimed or oral ACT Scores accepted
Untimed or oral SAT Scores accepted
University or College sponsored tests
Personal interview
Placement tests
Recommendations

ADDITIONAL SERVICES OFFERED:
  Learning Lab
  Learning Lab has a specialist with a masters degree
    or above in Learning Disabilities
  Diagnostic testing services on campus
  Remedial and/or tutorial help available
  Reader services for the blind available for LD
    students (in some cases)
  Handicapped student services works with LD

MODIFICATIONS TO TRADITIONAL LEARNING ENVIRONMENT:
  Has an adaptive physical education program
  Tape recorders to record class lectures
  Student takes exams in separate rooms
  Students have exams read to them
  Longer time allowed to complete exams
  Extended time limits for graduation
  Modifications vary depending on individual students,
    courses, instructors

MAJORS OFFERED:

  AGRICULTURE
  AREA STUDIES
  BIOLOGICAL SCIENCES
  BUSINESS AND MANAGEMENT
  COMMUNICATIONS
  COMPUTER SCIENCES
  EDUCATION
  ENGINEERING TECHNOLOGIES
  FINE AND APPLIED ARTS
  HEALTH
  HOME ECONOMICS
  HUMANITIES
  PHYSICAL SCIENCES
  PUBLIC SERVICES
  SOCIAL SCIENCES
  GENERAL LIBERAL ARTS

===

DENVER AURARIA COMMUNITY COLLEGE
1111 WEST COLFAX
DENVER, CO 80204
303-629-3285

KEY CONTACT: Attn: WILLIAM R. RICHARDS, DIRECTOR
                    DEVELOPMENTAL STUDIES

SIZE OF SCHOOL: MEDIUM

APPLICATION DEADLINE: NONE

APPROXIMATE TUITION	ROOM AND BOARD
IN DISTRICT	$ 735	$NOT OFFERED
IN STATE	$ 735	$NOT OFFERED
OUT-OF-STATE	$2890	$NOT OFFERED

REQUIREMENTS FOR ADMISSIONS:
  University or College sponsored tests

ADDITIONAL SERVICES OFFERED:
  Learning Lab
  Learning Lab has a specialist with a masters degree
    or above in Learning Disabilities
  Diagnostic testing services on campus
  Remedial and/or tutorial help available
  Reader services for the blind available for LD
  Special Education department
  Handicapped student services works with LD

MODIFICATIONS TO TRADITIONAL LEARNING ENVIRONMENT:
  Oral presentation in lieu of written exams
  Has an adaptive physical education program
  Tape recorders to record class lectures
  Someone else may take class notes
  Student takes exams in separate rooms
  Students have exams read to them
  Students take typewritten exams
  Longer time allowed to complete exams
  Extended time limits for graduation
  Physical education may be waived

MAJORS OFFERED:

  BUSINESS AND MANAGEMENT
  COMPUTER SCIENCES
  ENGINEERING TECHNOLOGIES
  HEALTH
  PUBLIC SERVICES
  GENERAL LIBERAL ARTS

==

COMMUNITY COLLEGE OF DENVER - NORTH CAMPUS
3645 WEST 112TH AVENUE
WESTMINSTER, CO 80030
303-466-8811

KEY CONTACT: Attn: Handicapped Student Services

SIZE OF SCHOOL: MEDIUM

APPLICATION DEADLINE: NONE

```
      APPROXIMATE TUITION    ROOM AND BOARD

IN DISTRICT       $ 800        $NOT OFFERED
IN STATE          $ 800        $NOT OFFERED
OUT-OF-STATE      $2800        $NOT OFFERED
```

REQUIREMENTS FOR ADMISSIONS:
  University or College sponsored tests
  Placement tests

ADDITIONAL SERVICES OFFERED:
  Learning Lab
  Learning Lab has a specialist with a masters degree
    or above in Learning Disabilities
  Diagnostic testing services on campus
  Diagnostic testing services off campus
  Remedial and/or tutorial help available
  Reader services for the blind available for LD
  Handicapped student services works with LD

MODIFICATIONS TO TRADITIONAL LEARNING ENVIRONMENT:
  Oral presentation in lieu of written exams
  Tape recorders to record class lectures
  Someone else may take class notes
  Student takes exams in separate rooms
  Students have exams read to them
  Students take typewritten exams
  Longer time allowed to complete exams
  Extended time limits for graduation
  Physical education may be waived

MAJORS OFFERED:

  AGRICULTURE
  BUSINESS AND MANAGEMENT
  COMPUTER SCIENCES
  ENGINEERING TECHNOLOGIES
  HEALTH
  PUBLIC SERVICES
  GENERAL LIBERAL ARTS

===

HOUSATONIC COMMUNITY COLLEGE
510 BARNUM AVENUE
BRIDGEPORT, CT 06608
203-579-6475

KEY CONTACT: Attn: NATALIE BIEBER
                    LD RESCOURCE SPECIALIST

SIZE OF SCHOOL: SMALL

APPLICATION DEADLINE: NONE

         APPROXIMATE TUITION   ROOM AND BOARD

IN DISTRICT $ 500 $NOT OFFERED
IN STATE $ 500 $NOT OFFERED
OUT-OF-STATE $1600 $NOT OFFERED

REQUIREMENTS FOR ADMISSIONS:
  High school equivalency diploma
  High school diploma
  Admission requirements modified
  Personal interview
  Placement tests

ADDITIONAL SERVICES OFFERED:
  Learning Lab
  Learning Lab has a specialist with a masters degree
    or above in Learning Disabilities
  Diagnostic testing services on campus
  Remedial and/or tutorial help available
  Handicapped student services works with LD

MODIFICATIONS TO TRADITIONAL LEARNING ENVIRONMENT:
  Oral presentation in lieu of written exams
  Tape recorders to record class lectures
  Someone else may take class notes
  Student takes exams in separate rooms
  Students have exams read to them
  Students take typewritten exams
  Longer time allowed to complete exams
  Submit papers on cassette tape
  Extended time limits for graduation
  Modifications are flexible according to students
    unique needs

MAJORS OFFERED:

  BIOLOGICAL SCIENCES
  BUSINESS AND MANAGEMENT
  ENGINEERING TECHNOLOGIES
  FINE AND APPLIED ARTS
  HEALTH
  HUMANITIES
  MATHEMATICS
  PHYSICAL SCIENCES

PUBLIC SERVICES
SOCIAL SCIENCES
GENERAL LIBERAL ARTS

==

MOHEGAN COMMUNTIY COLLEGE
MAHAN DRIVE
NORWICH, CT 06360
203-886-1931

KEY CONTACT: Attn: LOUIDA JONES
                    DIRECTOR OF ADMISSIONS

SIZE OF SCHOOL: SMALL

APPLICATION DEADLINE: NONE

        APPROXIMATE TUITION   ROOM AND BOARD

IN DISTRICT $ 500 $NOT OFFERED
IN STATE $ 500 $NOT OFFERED
OUT-OF-STATE $1500 $NOT OFFERED

REQUIREMENTS FOR ADMISSIONS:
  High school equivalency diploma
  High school diploma
  21 years of age or older, with or without a
    high school diploma or equivalency
  Placement tests

ADDITIONAL SERVICES OFFERED:
  Remedial and/or tutorial help available
  Reader services for the blind available for LD
    students

MODIFICATIONS TO TRADITIONAL LEARNING ENVIRONMENT:
  All modifications left up to individual faculty

MAJORS OFFERED:

  BUSINESS AND MANAGEMENT
  COMPUTER SCIENCES
  HEALTH
  LIBRARY SCIENCE
  PUBLIC SERVICES
  GENERAL LIBERAL ARTS

==

```
ART INSTITUTE OF FORT LAUDERDALE
FORT LAUDERDALE, FL 33316
305-463-3000
```

KEY CONTACT: Attn: Handicapped Student Services

SIZE OF SCHOOL: SMALL

APPLICATION DEADLINE: NONE

```
        APPROXIMATE TUITION   ROOM AND BOARD

IN DISTRICT        $4170        $2235
IN STATE           $4170        $2235
OUT-OF-STATE       $4170        $2235
```

REQUIREMENTS FOR ADMISSIONS:
  High school equivalency diploma
  Personal interview

MODIFICATIONS TO TRADITIONAL LEARNING ENVIRONMENT:
  Use of calculator for all math courses
  Tape recorders to record class lectures
  Someone else may take class notes
  Students have exams read to them
  Students take typewritten exams
  Extended time limits for graduation
  Physical education may be waived

MAJORS OFFERED:

  FINE AND APPLIED ARTS

===

```
MANATEE JUNIOR COLLEGE
5840 26TH STREET WEST
BRADENTON, FL 33507
813-755-1511
```

KEY CONTACT: Attn: Handicapped Student Services

SIZE OF SCHOOL: MEDIUM

APPLICATION DEADLINE: NONE

```
        APPROXIMATE TUITION   ROOM AND BOARD

IN DISTRICT        $ 650        $NOT OFFERED
IN STATE           $ 650        $NOT OFFERED
OUT-OF-STATE       $1400        $NOT OFFERED
```

REQUIREMENTS FOR ADMISSIONS:
  High school equivalency diploma
  High school diploma
  21 years of age or older, with or without a
    high school diploma or equivalency
  Open admissions

ADDITIONAL SERVICES OFFERED:
  Learning Lab
  Learning Lab has a specialist with a masters degree
    or above in Learning Disabilities
  Diagnostic testing services off campus
  Remedial and/or tutorial help available
  Reader services for the blind available for LD

MODIFICATIONS TO TRADITIONAL LEARNING ENVIRONMENT:
  Has an adaptive physical education program
  Tape recorders to record class lectures
  Someone else may take class notes
  Student takes exams in separate rooms
  Students have exams read to them
  Students take typewritten exams
  Longer time allowed to complete exams
  Physical education may be waived

MAJORS OFFERED:

  AGRICULTURE
  ARCHITECTURE
  BIOLOGICAL SCIENCES
  BUSINESS AND MANAGEMENT
  COMMUNICATIONS
  COMPUTER SCIENCES
  EDUCATION
  ENGINEERING TECHNOLOGIES
  FINE AND APPLIED ARTS
  HEALTH
  HOME ECONOMICS
  HUMANITIES
  PUBLIC SERVICES
  SOCIAL SCIENCES
  GENERAL LIBERAL ARTS

==

MIAMI-DADE COMMUNITY COLLEGE
11011 SOUTHWEST 104TH STREET
MIAMI, FL 33176
305-596-1345

KEY CONTACT: Attn: DIANNE B. ROSSMAN
                    LEARNING DISABILITIES COORDINATOR

SIZE OF SCHOOL: LARGE

APPLICATION DEADLINE: NONE

	APPROXIMATE TUITION	ROOM AND BOARD
IN DISTRICT	$ 590	$NOT OFFERED
IN STATE	$ 590	$NOT OFFERED
OUT-OF-STATE	$1250	$NOT OFFERED

REQUIREMENTS FOR ADMISSIONS:
  High school equivalency diploma
  High school diploma
  21 years of age or older, with or without a
    high school diploma or equivalency
  Untimed or oral ACT Scores accepted
  Untimed or oral SAT Scores accepted
  University or College sponsored tests
  Personal interview
  Placement tests
  Recommendations

ADDITIONAL SERVICES OFFERED:
  Learning Lab
  Learning Lab has a specialist with a masters degree
    or above in Learning Disabilities
  Diagnostic testing services on campus
  Diagnostic testing services off campus
  Remedial and/or tutorial help available
  Reader services for the blind available for LD
  Handicapped student services works with LD

MODIFICATIONS TO TRADITIONAL LEARNING ENVIRONMENT:
  Oral presentation in lieu of written exams
  Use of calculator for all math courses
  Tape recorders to record class lectures
  Student takes exams in separate rooms
  Students have exams read to them
  Longer time allowed to complete exams
  Extended time limits for graduation
  Physical education may be waived

MAJORS OFFERED:

  AGRICULTURE
  ARCHITECTURE
  AREA STUDIES
  BIOLOGICAL SCIENCES

```
BUSINESS AND MANAGEMENT
COMMUNICATIONS
COMPUTER SCIENCES
EDUCATION
ENGINEERING TECHNOLOGIES
FINE AND APPLIED ARTS
HEALTH
HOME ECONOMICS
HUMANITIES
MATHEMATICS
PHYSICAL SCIENCES
PSYCHOLOGY
PUBLIC SERVICES
SOCIAL SCIENCES
GENERAL LIBERAL ARTS
```

==

```
PENSACOLA JUNIOR COLLEGE
1000 COLLEGE BLVD
PENSACOLA, FL 32504
904-476-5410

KEY CONTACT: Attn:  DR. ELIAS G. ASMAR
                    COORDINATOR, HANDICAPPED SERVICES

SIZE OF SCHOOL: LARGE

APPLICATION DEADLINE: NONE

        APPROXIMATE TUITION    ROOM AND BOARD

IN DISTRICT        $ 570         $NOT OFFERED
IN STATE           $ 570         $NOT OFFERED
OUT-OF-STATE       $1140         $NOT OFFERED

REQUIREMENTS FOR ADMISSIONS:
  High school equivalency diploma
  High school diploma
  ACT Scores required
  Untimed or oral ACT Scores accepted
  Placement tests

ADDITIONAL SERVICES OFFERED:
  Learning Lab
  Learning Lab has a specialist with a masters degree
    or above in Learning Disabilities
  Diagnostic testing services off campus
  Remedial and/or tutorial help available
  Handicapped student services works with LD
```

MODIFICATIONS TO TRADITIONAL LEARNING ENVIRONMENT:
  Oral presentation in lieu of written exams
  Use of calculator for all math courses
  Tape recorders to record class lectures
  Someone else may take class notes
  Students have exams read to them
  Students take typewritten exams
  Longer time allowed to complete exams
  Extended time limits for graduation
  Physical education may be waived

MAJORS OFFERED:

  AGRICULTURE
  BIOLOGICAL SCIENCES
  BUSINESS AND MANAGEMENT
  COMMUNICATIONS
  COMPUTER SCIENCES
  EDUCATION
  ENGINEERING TECHNOLOGIES
  FINE AND APPLIED ARTS
  FOREIGN LANGUAGES
  HEALTH
  HOME ECONOMICS
  HUMANITIES
  LIBRARY SCIENCE
  MATHEMATICS
  MILITARY SCIENCES
  PHYSICAL SCIENCES
  PSYCHOLOGY
  SOCIAL SCIENCES
  GENERAL LIBERAL ARTS

===

SEMINOLE COMMUNITY COLLEGE
SANFORD, FL 32771
305-323-1450

KEY CONTACT: Attn: MIDGE MYCOFF, COORDINATOR
                    VOC. ED. FOR HANDICAPPED

SIZE OF SCHOOL: MEDIUM

APPLICATION DEADLINE: NONE

           APPROXIMATE TUITION   ROOM AND BOARD

IN DISTRICT $ 575 $NOT OFFERED
IN STATE $ 575 $NOT OFFERED
OUT-OF-STATE $1280 $NOT OFFERED

REQUIREMENTS FOR ADMISSIONS:
  High school equivalency diploma
  High school diploma
  ACT Scores required
  Untimed or oral ACT Scores accepted
  Untimed or oral SAT Scores accepted
  State/District residency

ADDITIONAL SERVICES OFFERED:
  Learning Lab
  Learning Lab has a specialist with a masters degree
    or above in Learning Disabilities
  Diagnostic testing services off campus
  Remedial and/or tutorial help available
  Reader services for the blind available for LD
  Special Education department

MODIFICATIONS TO TRADITIONAL LEARNING ENVIRONMENT:
  Tape recorders to record class lectures
  Someone else may take class notes
  Extended time limits for graduation
  Physical education may be waived

MAJORS OFFERED:

    AGRICULTURE
    BUSINESS AND MANAGEMENT
    COMPUTER SCIENCES
    ENGINEERING TECHNOLOGIES
    HEALTH
    PUBLIC SERVICES
    GENERAL LIBERAL ARTS

==

REIHARDT COLLEGE
WALESKA, GA 30183
404-479-1454

KEY CONTACT: Attn: CONNIE COGDELL, DIRECTOR,
                    ACADEMIC SUPPORT OFFICE

SIZE OF SCHOOL: SMALL

APPLICATION DEADLINE: NONE

        APPROXIMATE TUITION   ROOM AND BOARD

IN DISTRICT $2700 $1800
IN STATE $2700 $1800
OUT-OF-STATE $2700 $1800

REQUIREMENTS FOR ADMISSIONS:
  High school equivalency diploma
  High school diploma
  Untimed or oral ACT Scores accepted
  Untimed or oral SAT Scores accepted
  WAIS scores required
  High school grade point average 2.0
  Admission requirements modified
  Personal interview
  Copies of the high school IEP for LD students
    applying for admission

ADDITIONAL SERVICES OFFERED:
  Remedial and/or tutorial help available
  Reader services for the blind available for LD
  Handicapped student services works with LD

MODIFICATIONS TO TRADITIONAL LEARNING ENVIRONMENT:
  Oral presentation in lieu of written exams
  Use of calculator for all math courses
  Tape recorders to record class lectures
  Someone else may take class notes
  Student takes exams in separate rooms
  Students have exams read to them
  Longer time allowed to complete exams
  Take limited course load and graduate within time
    required
  Extended time limits for graduation

MAJORS OFFERED:

  AGRICULTURE
  BUSINESS AND MANAGEMENT
  EDUCATION
  FINE AND APPLIED ARTS
  HEALTH
  HUMANITIES
  GENERAL LIBERAL ARTS

==

CHICAGO CITY COLLEGE - WILBUR WRIGHT
3400 NORTH AUSTIN AVENUE
CHICAGO, IL 60634
312-777-7900

KEY CONTACT: Attn: SERENE NATHAN, COORDINATOR
                    DISABLED STUDENT SERVICES

SIZE OF SCHOOL: MEDIUM

APPLICATION DEADLINE: AUGUST 20

         APPROXIMATE TUITION   ROOM AND BOARD

IN DISTRICT $ 690 $NOT OFFERED
IN STATE $1090 $NOT OFFERED
OUT-OF-STATE $1660 $NOT OFFERED

REQUIREMENTS FOR ADMISSIONS:
   High school diploma
   ACT Scores required
   Untimed or oral ACT Scores accepted
   University or College sponsored tests
   Particular rank in class (not specified)
   Admission requirements modified
   Personal interview
   Placement tests
   Recommendations
   State/District residency

ADDITIONAL SERVICES OFFERED:
   Learning Lab
   Diagnostic testing services off campus
   Reader services for the blind available for LD
   Handicapped student services works with LD

MODIFICATIONS TO TRADITIONAL LEARNING ENVIRONMENT:
   Oral presentation in lieu of written exams
   Use of calculator for all math courses
   Tape recorders to record class lectures
   Someone else may take class notes
   Student takes exams in separate rooms
   Students have exams read to them
   Longer time allowed to complete exams
   Submit papers on cassette tape
   Extended time limits for graduation
   Physical education may be waived

MAJORS OFFERED:

   AGRICULTURE
   ARCHITECTURE
   BIOLOGICAL SCIENCES
   BUSINESS AND MANAGEMENT
   COMMUNICATIONS
   COMPUTER SCIENCES
   EDUCATION
   ENGINEERING TECHNOLOGIES
   FINE AND APPLIED ARTS
   FOREIGN LANGUAGES
   HEALTH

```
HOME ECONOMICS
HUMANITIES
LIBRARY SCIENCE
MATHEMATICS
PHYSICAL SCIENCES
PSYCHOLOGY
PUBLIC SERVICES
SOCIAL SCIENCES
GENERAL LIBERAL ARTS
```

==

```
COLLEGE OF LAKE COUNTY
1931 WEST WASHINGTON STREET
GRAYSLAKE, IL 60030
312-223-6601
```

KEY CONTACT: Attn: JACQUELINE HASSETT

SIZE OF SCHOOL: LARGE

APPLICATION DEADLINE: NONE

	APPROXIMATE TUITION	ROOM AND BOARD
IN DISTRICT	$ 540	$NOT OFFERED
IN STATE	$1710	$NOT OFFERED
OUT-OF-STATE	$2520	$NOT OFFERED

REQUIREMENTS FOR ADMISSIONS:
  University or College sponsored tests
  Admission requirements modified
  Personal interview
  Placement tests
  Recommendations

ADDITIONAL SERVICES OFFERED:
  Learning Lab
  Diagnostic testing services off campus
  Remedial and/or tutorial help available
  Reader services for the blind available for LD
  Handicapped student services works with LD

MODIFICATIONS TO TRADITIONAL LEARNING ENVIRONMENT:
  Has an adaptive physical education program
  Tape recorders to record class lectures
  Someone else may take class notes
  Multiple choice exams only
  Student takes exams in separate rooms
  Students have exams read to them
  Students take typewritten exams

Longer time allowed to complete exams
Extended time limits for graduation
Physical education may be waived
Most modifications depend on instructor/student
   relationship and objectives of class

MAJORS OFFERED:

BIOLOGICAL SCIENCES
BUSINESS AND MANAGEMENT
COMMUNICATIONS
EDUCATION
ENGINEERING TECHNOLOGIES
FINE AND APPLIED ARTS
FOREIGN LANGUAGES
HEALTH
HUMANITIES
MATHEMATICS
PHYSICAL SCIENCES
PSYCHOLOGY
SOCIAL SCIENCES
GENERAL LIBERAL ARTS

===

JOHN WOOD COMMUNITY COLLEGE
1919 NORTH 18TH STREET
·QUINCY, IL 62301
217-224-6500

KEY CONTACT: Attn: RITA BUDDEMEYER

SIZE OF SCHOOL: MEDIUM

APPLICATION DEADLINE: NONE

APPROXIMATE TUITION   ROOM AND BOARD

	APPROXIMATE TUITION	ROOM AND BOARD
IN DISTRICT	$ 580	$2000
IN STATE	$1795	$2000
OUT-OF-STATE	$2700	$2000

REQUIREMENTS FOR ADMISSIONS:
   Placement tests
   Open admissions

ADDITIONAL SERVICES OFFERED:
   Learning Lab
   Diagnostic testing services on campus
   Remedial and/or tutorial help available
   Reader services for the blind available for LD

Handicapped student services works with LD

MODIFICATIONS TO TRADITIONAL LEARNING ENVIRONMENT:
   Oral presentation in lieu of written exams
   Has an adaptive physical education program
   Tape recorders to record class lectures
   Someone else may take class notes
   Student takes exams in separate rooms
   Students have exams read to them
   Students take typewritten exams
   Longer time allowed to complete exams
   Submit papers on cassette tape
   Take limited course load and graduate within time
      required
   Extended time limits for graduation
   Physical education may be waived
   Modifications made through agreement with instructor

MAJORS OFFERED:

   AGRICULTURE
   BIOLOGICAL SCIENCES
   BUSINESS AND MANAGEMENT
   COMMUNICATIONS
   COMPUTER SCIENCES
   EDUCATION
   ENGINEERING TECHNOLOGIES
   FINE AND APPLIED ARTS
   FOREIGN LANGUAGES
   HEALTH
   HUMANITIES
   MATHEMATICS
   PHYSICAL SCIENCES
   PSYCHOLOGY
   SOCIAL SCIENCES
   GENERAL LIBERAL ARTS

==

LAKE LAND COLLEGE
SOUTH ROUTE 45
MATTOON, IL 61938
217-235-3131

KEY CONTACT: Attn: JOYCE GUCKERT, DIRECTOR OF
                     TUTORIAL SERVICES

SIZE OF SCHOOL: MEDIUM

APPLICATION DEADLINE: NONE

```
              APPROXIMATE TUITION    ROOM AND BOARD

IN DISTRICT          $ 650         $NOT OFFERED
IN STATE             $1360         $NOT OFFERED
OUT-OF-STATE         $2260         $NOT OFFERED
```

REQUIREMENTS FOR ADMISSIONS:
  Recommendations
  State/District residency

ADDITIONAL SERVICES OFFERED:
  Learning Lab
  Diagnostic testing services on campus
  Remedial and/or tutorial help available

MODIFICATIONS TO TRADITIONAL LEARNING ENVIRONMENT:
  Oral presentation in lieu of written exams
  Tape recorders to record class lectures
  Someone else may take class notes
  Student takes exams in separate rooms
  Students have exams read to them
  Students take typewritten exams
  Longer time allowed to complete exams

MAJORS OFFERED:

    AGRICULTURE
    BIOLOGICAL SCIENCES
    BUSINESS AND MANAGEMENT
    COMMUNICATIONS
    COMPUTER SCIENCES
    EDUCATION
    ENGINEERING TECHNOLOGIES
    FINE AND APPLIED ARTS
    FOREIGN LANGUAGES
    HEALTH
    HOME ECONOMICS
    HUMANITIES
    MATHEMATICS
    MILITARY SCIENCES
    PHYSICAL SCIENCES
    PSYCHOLOGY
    PUBLIC SERVICES
    SOCIAL SCIENCES
    GENERAL LIBERAL ARTS

==
```
```

```
MALLINCKRODT COLLEGE
1041 RIDGE ROAD
WILMETTE, IL 60091
312-256-1094
```

KEY CONTACT: Attn: Handicapped Student Services

SIZE OF SCHOOL: SMALL

APPLICATION DEADLINE: NONE

	APPROXIMATE TUITION	ROOM AND BOARD
IN DISTRICT	$2400	$NOT OFFERED
IN STATE	$2400	$NOT OFFERED
OUT-OF-STATE	$2400	$NOT OFFERED

REQUIREMENTS FOR ADMISSIONS:
  High school equivalency diploma
  High school diploma
  ACT Scores required
  University or College sponsored tests
  Personal interview
  Placement tests
  Recommendations
  Essay

ADDITIONAL SERVICES OFFERED:
  Remedial and/or tutorial help available

MODIFICATIONS TO TRADITIONAL LEARNING ENVIRONMENT:
  Use of calculator for all math courses
  Tape recorders to record class lectures
  Someone else may take class notes
  Students take typewritten exams
  Longer time allowed to complete exams
  Take limited course load and graduate within time
    required
  Extended time limits for graduation
  Physical education may be waived

MAJORS OFFERED:

BUSINESS AND MANAGEMENT

===

```
MCHENRY COUNTY COLLEGE
ROUTE 14 AND LUCAS ROAD
CRYSTAL LAKE, IL 60014
815-455-3700
```

KEY CONTACT: Attn: ED ELSNER, DIRECTOR
                     SPECIAL PROGRAMS

SIZE OF SCHOOL: MEDIUM

APPLICATION DEADLINE: NONE

          APPROXIMATE TUITION   ROOM AND BOARD

IN DISTRICT $ 660 $NOT OFFERED
IN STATE $1488 $NOT OFFERED
OUT-OF-STATE $2289 $NOT OFFERED

REQUIREMENTS FOR ADMISSIONS:
  Untimed or oral ACT Scores accepted
  Untimed or oral SAT Scores accepted
  Open admissions

ADDITIONAL SERVICES OFFERED:
  Learning Lab
  Learning Lab has a specialist with a masters degree
    or above in Learning Disabilities
  Diagnostic testing services on campus
  Remedial and/or tutorial help available
  Reader services for the blind available for LD
  Special Education department
  Handicapped student services works with LD

MODIFICATIONS TO TRADITIONAL LEARNING ENVIRONMENT:
  Oral presentation in lieu of written exams
  Use of calculator for all math courses
  Tape recorders to record class lectures
  Someone else may take class notes
  Student takes exams in separate rooms
  Students have exams read to them
  Students take typewritten exams
  Longer time allowed to complete exams
  Submit papers on cassette tape
  Extended time limits for graduation
  Physical education may be waived

MAJORS OFFERED:

  AGRICULTURE
  BUSINESS AND MANAGEMENT
  COMPUTER SCIENCES
  ENGINEERING TECHNOLOGIES
  PUBLIC SERVICES
  GENERAL LIBERAL ARTS

===

PARKLAND COLLEGE
2400 WEST BRADLEY AVENUE
CHAMPAIGN, IL 61820
217-351-2246

KEY CONTACT: Attn: Handicapped Student Services

SIZE OF SCHOOL: MEDIUM

APPLICATION DEADLINE: NONE

	APPROXIMATE TUITION	ROOM AND BOARD
IN DISTRICT	$ 510	$NOT OFFERED
IN STATE	$2650	$NOT OFFERED
OUT-OF-STATE	$3170	$NOT OFFERED

REQUIREMENTS FOR ADMISSIONS:
  High school equivalency diploma
  High school diploma
  21 years of age or older, with or without a
    high school diploma or equivalency

ADDITIONAL SERVICES OFFERED:
  Learning Lab
  Learning Lab has a specialist with a masters degree
    or above in Learning Disabilities
  Diagnostic testing services off campus
  Remedial and/or tutorial help available
  Reader services for the blind available for LD
  Handicapped student services works with LD

MODIFICATIONS TO TRADITIONAL LEARNING ENVIRONMENT:
  Oral presentation in lieu of written exams
  Use of calculator for all math courses
  Tape recorders to record class lectures
  Someone else may take class notes
  Multiple choice exams only
  Essay exams only
  Student takes exams in separate rooms
  Students have exams read to them
  Students take typewritten exams
  Longer time allowed to complete exams
  Submit papers on cassette tape
  Take limited course load and graduate within time
    required
  Extended time limits for graduation
  Physical education may be waived

MAJORS OFFERED:

  AGRICULTURE
  BIOLOGICAL SCIENCES
  BUSINESS AND MANAGEMENT
  EDUCATION
  ENGINEERING TECHNOLOGIES
  FINE AND APPLIED ARTS
  HUMANITIES
  MATHEMATICS
  MILITARY SCIENCES
  PHYSICAL SCIENCES
  SOCIAL SCIENCES
  GENERAL LIBERAL ARTS

==

REND LAKE COLLEGE
RR 1
INA, IL 62846
618-437-5231

KEY CONTACT: Attn: THOMAS BURKE, COUNSELOR

SIZE OF SCHOOL: SMALL

APPLICATION DEADLINE: NONE

          APPROXIMATE TUITION   ROOM AND BOARD

IN DISTRICT $ 360 $NOT OFFERED
IN STATE $1420 $NOT OFFERED
OUT-OF-STATE $2530 $NOT OFFERED

REQUIREMENTS FOR ADMISSIONS:
  Untimed or oral ACT Scores accepted
  Untimed or oral SAT Scores accepted
  Placement tests

ADDITIONAL SERVICES OFFERED:
  Learning Lab
  Learning Lab has a specialist with a masters degree
    or above in Learning Disabilities
  Diagnostic testing services off campus
  Remedial and/or tutorial help available
  Reader services for the blind available for LD
    students
  Handicapped student services works with LD

MODIFICATIONS TO TRADITIONAL LEARNING ENVIRONMENT:
  Oral presentation in lieu of written exams
  Use of calculator for all math courses
  Tape recorders to record class lectures
  Someone else may take class notes
  Multiple choice exams only
  Essay exams only
  Student takes exams in separate rooms
  Students have exams read to them
  Students take typewritten exams
  Longer time allowed to complete exams
  Submit papers on cassette tape

MAJORS OFFERED:

  AGRICULTURE
  BUSINESS AND MANAGEMENT
  ENGINEERING TECHNOLOGIES
  HEALTH
  PUBLIC SERVICES
  GENERAL LIBERAL ARTS

===

TRITON COLLEGE
2000 FIFTH AVENUE
RIVER GROVE, IL 60171
312-456-5000

KEY CONTACT: Attn: Handicapped Student Services

SIZE OF SCHOOL: LARGE

APPLICATION DEADLINE: NONE

	APPROXIMATE TUITION	ROOM AND BOARD
IN DISTRICT	$ 675	$NOT OFFERED
IN STATE	$1750	$NOT OFFERED
OUT-OF-STATE	$2400	$NOT OFFERED

REQUIREMENTS FOR ADMISSIONS:
  High school equivalency diploma
  High school diploma
  21 years of age or older, with or without a
    high school diploma or equivalency
  Admission requirements modified
  Placement tests

ADDITIONAL SERVICES OFFERED:
  Learning Lab
  Learning Lab has a specialist with a masters degree
    or above in Learning Disabilities
  Remedial and/or tutorial help available
  Reader services for the blind available for LD
  Handicapped student services works with LD

MODIFICATIONS TO TRADITIONAL LEARNING ENVIRONMENT:
  Tape recorders to record class lectures
  Someone else may take class notes
  Student takes exams in separate rooms
  Students have exams read to them
  Students take typewritten exams
  Longer time allowed to complete exams
  Submit papers on cassette tape
  Extended time limits for graduation
  Physical education may be waived

MAJORS OFFERED:

  ARCHITECTURE
  BIOLOGICAL SCIENCES
  BUSINESS AND MANAGEMENT
  COMMUNICATIONS
  EDUCATION
  ENGINEERING TECHNOLOGIES
  FINE AND APPLIED ARTS
  HEALTH
  HOME ECONOMICS
  HUMANITIES
  PHYSICAL SCIENCES
  GENERAL LIBERAL ARTS

===

WILLIAM RAINEY HARPER COLLEGE
PALATINE, IL 60067
312-397-3000

KEY CONTACT: Attn: DR. GEORGE VOGEL, DEAN

SIZE OF SCHOOL: LARGE

APPLICATION DEADLINE: NONE

         APPROXIMATE TUITION   ROOM AND BOARD

IN DISTRICT $ 750 $NOT OFFERED
IN STATE $1700 $NOT OFFERED
OUT-OF-STATE $2500 $NOT OFFERED

REQUIREMENTS FOR ADMISSIONS:
  High school equivalency diploma
  High school diploma
  21 years of age or older, with or without a
    high school diploma or equivalency

ADDITIONAL SERVICES OFFERED:
  Learning Lab
  Learning Lab has a specialist with a masters degree
    or above in Learning Disabilities
  Diagnostic testing services on campus
  Remedial and/or tutorial help available

MODIFICATIONS TO TRADITIONAL LEARNING ENVIRONMENT:
  Oral presentation in lieu of written exams
  Use of calculator for all math courses
  Tape recorders to record class lectures
  Someone else may take class notes
  Multiple choice exams only
  Essay exams only
  Student takes exams in separate rooms
  Students have exams read to them
  Students take typewritten exams
  Longer time allowed to complete exams
  Submit papers on cassette tape
  Physical education may be waived

MAJORS OFFERED:

  BIOLOGICAL SCIENCES
  BUSINESS AND MANAGEMENT
  EDUCATION
  ENGINEERING TECHNOLOGIES
  FINE AND APPLIED ARTS
  HUMANITIES
  MATHEMATICS
  PHYSICAL SCIENCES
  SOCIAL SCIENCES
  GENERAL LIBERAL ARTS

==

INDIANA BUSINESS COLLEGE
802 NORTH MERIDIAN STREET
INDIANAPOLIS, IN 46204
317-634-8337

KEY CONTACT: Attn: MRS. JEANETTE LLYOD
                    REGISTRA & PLACEMENT DIRECTOR

SIZE OF SCHOOL: SMALL

APPLICATION DEADLINE: NONE

APPROXIMATE TUITION   ROOM AND BOARD

IN DISTRICT	$2100	$NOT OFFERED
IN STATE	$2100	$NOT OFFERED
OUT-OF-STATE	$2100	$NOT OFFERED

REQUIREMENTS FOR ADMISSIONS:
  High school equivalency diploma
  High school diploma
  Admission requirements modified
  Personal interview
  Recommendations

ADDITIONAL SERVICES OFFERED:
  Learning Lab
  Diagnostic testing services off campus
  Remedial and/or tutorial help available
  Reader services for the blind available for LD
  Handicapped student services works with LD

MODIFICATIONS TO TRADITIONAL LEARNING ENVIRONMENT:
  Longer time allowed to complete exams

MAJORS OFFERED:

  BUSINESS AND MANAGEMENT
  COMPUTER SCIENCES

==

INDIANA UNIVERSITY - EAST
2325 CHESTER BLVD
RICHMOND, IN 47374
317-966-8261

KEY CONTACT: Attn: Handicapped Student Services

SIZE OF SCHOOL: SMALL

APPLICATION DEADLINE: NONE

APPROXIMATE TUITION   ROOM AND BOARD

IN DISTRICT	$ 935	$NOT OFFERED
IN STATE	$ 935	$NOT OFFERED
OUT-OF-STATE	$2265	$NOT OFFERED

REQUIREMENTS FOR ADMISSIONS:
  High school equivalency diploma
  High school diploma
  21 years of age or older, with or without a
  Admission requirements modified

ADDITIONAL SERVICES OFFERED:
  Learning Lab
  Diagnostic testing services on campus
  Diagnostic testing services off campus
  Remedial and/or tutorial help available
  Reader services for the blind available for LD

MODIFICATIONS TO TRADITIONAL LEARNING ENVIRONMENT:
  Use of calculator for all math courses
  Tape recorders to record class lectures
  Someone else may take class notes
  Multiple choice exams only
  Essay exams only
  Student takes exams in separate rooms
  Students have exams read to them
  Students take typewritten exams
  Longer time allowed to complete exams
  Submit papers on cassette tape

MAJORS OFFERED:

  BUSINESS AND MANAGEMENT
  COMPUTER SCIENCES
  EDUCATION
  ENGINEERING TECHNOLOGIES
  PUBLIC SERVICES
  SOCIAL SCIENCES
  GENERAL LIBERAL ARTS

==

INDIANA VOCATIONAL TECHNICAL COLLEGE
1315 EAST WASHINGTON STREET
INDIANAPOLIS, IN 46202
317-635-6100

KEY CONTACT: Attn: NINNA SCHEIBER
                    MANAGER SPECIAL NEEDS

SIZE OF SCHOOL: MEDIUM

APPLICATION DEADLINE: NONE

```
       APPROXIMATE TUITION    ROOM AND BOARD

IN DISTRICT        $ 985      $NOT OFFERED
IN STATE           $ 985      $NOT OFFERED
OUT-OF-STATE       $1660      $NOT OFFERED
```

REQUIREMENTS FOR ADMISSIONS:
  Personal interview
  Placement tests
  Recommendations
  Essay

ADDITIONAL SERVICES OFFERED:
  Learning Lab
  Learning Lab has a specialist with a masters degree
    or above in Learning Disabilities
  Diagnostic testing services on campus
  Diagnostic testing services off campus
  Remedial and/or tutorial help available
  Reader services for the blind available for LD
  Special Education department
  Handicapped student services works with LD

MODIFICATIONS TO TRADITIONAL LEARNING ENVIRONMENT:
  Oral presentation in lieu of written exams
  Tape recorders to record class lectures
  Someone else may take class notes
  Student takes exams in seperate rooms
  Students have exams read to them
  Students take typewritten exams
  Longer time allowed to complete exams
  Submit papers on cassette tape
  Extended time limits for graduation
  Physical education may be waived

MAJORS OFFERED:

  BUSINESS AND MANAGEMENT
  COMPUTER SCIENCES
  ENGINEERING TECHNOLOGIES
  HEALTH
  PUBLIC SERVICES

==

VICENNES UNIVERSITY
1002 NORTH FIRST STREET
VINCENNES, IN 47591
812-885-4313

KEY CONTACT: Attn: GEORGE VARNS

SIZE OF SCHOOL: MEDIUM

APPLICATION DEADLINE: AUGUST 22

	APPROXIMATE TUITION	ROOM AND BOARD
IN DISTRICT	$ 980	$1800
IN STATE	$1010	$1800
OUT-OF-STATE	$2670	$1800

REQUIREMENTS FOR ADMISSIONS:
  High school equivalency diploma
  High school diploma
  SAT Scores required
  Untimed or oral SAT Scores accepted
  University or College sponsored tests
  Admission requirements modified
  Personal interview
  Placement tests

ADDITIONAL SERVICES OFFERED:
  Learning Lab
  Learning Lab has a specialist with a masters degree
    or above in Learning Disabilities
  Diagnostic testing services on campus
  Remedial and/or tutorial help available
  Reader services for the blind available for LD
  Special Education department
  Handicapped student services works with LD
  A developmental semester is available

MODIFICATIONS TO TRADITIONAL LEARNING ENVIRONMENT:
  Oral presentation in lieu of written exams
  Use of calculator for some math courses
  Has an adaptive physical education program
  Tape recorders to record class lectures
  Someone else may take class notes
  Student takes exams in separate rooms
  Students have exams read to them
  Students take typewritten exams
  Longer time allowed to complete exams
  Submit papers on cassette tape
  Extended time limits for graduation
  Physical education may be waived

MAJORS OFFERED:

  AGRICULTURE
  ARCHITECTURE
  BIOLOGICAL SCIENCES
  BUSINESS AND MANAGEMENT

```
COMMUNICATIONS
COMPUTER SCIENCES
EDUCATION
ENGINEERING TECHNOLOGIES
FINE AND APPLIED ARTS
FOREIGN LANGUAGES
HEALTH
HOME ECONOMICS
HUMANITIES
LIBRARY SCIENCE
MATHEMATICS
MILITARY SCIENCES
PHYSICAL SCIENCES
PSYCHOLOGY
PUBLIC SERVICES
SOCIAL SCIENCES
GENERAL LIBERAL ARTS
```

===

```
DES MOINES AREA COMMUNITY COLLEGE - ANKENY
2006 ANKENY BLVD
ANKENY, IA 50021
515-964-6215

KEY CONTACT: Attn:  DENNIS HINER
                    SPECIAL NEEDS COORDINATOR

SIZE OF SCHOOL: MEDIUM

APPLICATION DEADLINE: NONE

        APPROXIMATE TUITION    ROOM AND BOARD

IN DISTRICT       $1355        $NOT OFFERED
IN STATE          $1355        $NOT OFFERED
OUT-OF-STATE      $2710        $NOT OFFERED

REQUIREMENTS FOR ADMISSIONS:
  High school equivalency diploma
  High school diploma
  University or College sponsored tests

ADDITIONAL SERVICES OFFERED:
  Learning Lab
  Remedial and/or tutorial help available
  Reader services for the blind available for LD
  Handicapped student services works with LD
```

MODIFICATIONS TO TRADITIONAL LEARNING ENVIRONMENT:
  Oral presentation in lieu of written exams
  Tape recorders to record class lectures
  Someone else may take class notes
  Student takes exams in separate rooms
  Students have exams read to them
  Longer time allowed to complete exams
  Submit papers on cassette tape
  Extended time limits for graduation
  Physical education may be waived
  Modifications depend on faculty

MAJORS OFFERED:

  BIOLOGICAL SCIENCES
  BUSINESS AND MANAGEMENT
  COMMUNICATIONS
  COMPUTER SCIENCES
  EDUCATION
  ENGINEERING TECHNOLOGIES
  FINE AND APPLIED ARTS
  FOREIGN LANGUAGES
  HEALTH
  HUMANITIES
  MATHEMATICS
  PHYSICAL SCIENCES
  PSYCHOLOGY
  PUBLIC SERVICES
  SOCIAL SCIENCES
  GENERAL LIBERAL ARTS

===

IOWA CENTRAL COMMUNITY COLLEGE
330 AVENUE M
FORT DODGE, IA 50533
515-576-7201

KEY CONTACT: Attn: MARVIN LEWIS
                    I.C.E. PROGRAM DIRECTOR

SIZE OF SCHOOL: SMALL

APPLICATION DEADLINE: NONE

         APPROXIMATE TUITION   ROOM AND BOARD

IN DISTRICT $ 725 $1795
IN STATE $ 725 $1795
OUT-OF-STATE $1035 $1795

REQUIREMENTS FOR ADMISSIONS:
  Untimed or oral ACT Scores accepted
  Untimed or oral SAT Scores accepted
  Admission requirements modified
  Personal interview
  Placement tests

ADDITIONAL SERVICES OFFERED:
  Learning Lab
  Diagnostic testing services on campus
  Diagnostic testing services off campus
  Remedial and/or tutorial help available
  Special Education department

MODIFICATIONS TO TRADITIONAL LEARNING ENVIRONMENT:
  Oral presentation in lieu of written exams
  Use of calculator for all math courses
  Has an adaptive physical education program
  Tape recorders to record class lectures
  Someone else may take class notes
  Student takes exams in separate rooms
  Students have exams read to them
  Longer time allowed to complete exams
  Submit papers on cassette tape
  Extended time limits for graduation
  Physical education may be waived
  Modifications allowed on a case by case basis

MAJORS OFFERED:

  AGRICULTURE
  BUSINESS AND MANAGEMENT
  COMPUTER SCIENCES
  EDUCATION
  ENGINEERING TECHNOLOGIES
  FINE AND APPLIED ARTS
  HEALTH
  HOME ECONOMICS
  LIBRARY SCIENCE
  PUBLIC SERVICES
  GENERAL LIBERAL ARTS

===

IOWA WESTERN COMMUNITY COLLEGE
BOX 4C-2700 COLLEGE ROAD
COUNCIL BLUFFS, IA 51502
712-325-3288

KEY CONTACT: Attn: RAY OLSON
                    DIRECTOR OF SPECIAL NEEDS

SIZE OF SCHOOL: SMALL

APPLICATION DEADLINE: NONE

	APPROXIMATE TUITION	ROOM AND BOARD
IN DISTRICT	$ 870	$2175
IN STATE	$ 870	$2175
OUT-OF-STATE	$1300	$2175

REQUIREMENTS FOR ADMISSIONS:
  High school equivalency diploma
  High school diploma
  ACT Scores required
  Untimed or oral ACT Scores accepted
  Admission requirements modified
  Personal interview
  Placement tests
  Recommendations

ADDITIONAL SERVICES OFFERED:
  Learning Lab
  Learning Lab has a specialist with a masters degree
    or above in Learning Disabilities
  Diagnostic testing services on campus
  Remedial and/or tutorial help available
  Reader services for the blind available for LD
  Special Education department
  Handicapped student services works with LD

MODIFICATIONS TO TRADITIONAL LEARNING ENVIRONMENT:
  Oral presentation in lieu of written exams
  Use of calculator for all math courses
  Tape recorders to record class lectures
  Someone else may take class notes
  Student takes exams in separate rooms
  Students have exams read to them
  Students take typewritten exams
  Longer time allowed to complete exams
  Submit papers on cassette tape
  Extended time limits for graduation
  Physical education may be waived

MAJORS OFFERED:

  BUSINESS AND MANAGEMENT
  COMPUTER SCIENCES
  ENGINEERING TECHNOLOGIES
  HEALTH
  PUBLIC SERVICES
  GENERAL LIBERAL ARTS

KIRKWOOD COMMUNITY COLLEGE
6301 KIRKWOOD BLVD SW
CEDAR RAPIDS, IA 52406
319-398-5517

KEY CONTACT: Attn: J. GOODRON

SIZE OF SCHOOL: MEDIUM

APPLICATION DEADLINE: NONE

          APPROXIMATE TUITION   ROOM AND BOARD

IN DISTRICT $ 690 $NOT OFFERED
IN STATE $ 690 $NOT OFFERED
OUT-OF-STATE $1320 $NOT OFFERED

REQUIREMENTS FOR ADMISSIONS:
  High school equivalency diploma
  High school diploma
  21 years of age or older, with or without a
    high school diploma or equivalency
  Admission requirements modified

ADDITIONAL SERVICES OFFERED:
  Learning Lab
  Diagnostic testing services off campus
  Remedial and/or tutorial help available
  Handicapped student services works with LD

MODIFICATIONS TO TRADITIONAL LEARNING ENVIRONMENT:
  Oral presentation in lieu of written exams
  Tape recorders to record class lectures
  Someone else may take class notes
  Student takes exams in separate rooms
  Students have exams read to them
  Longer time allowed to complete exams
  Submit papers on cassette tape
  Physical education may be waived

MAJORS OFFERED:

  AGRICULTURE
  ARCHITECTURE
  AREA STUDIES
  BIOLOGICAL SCIENCES
  BUSINESS AND MANAGEMENT
  COMMUNICATIONS
  COMPUTER SCIENCES
  EDUCATION
  ENGINEERING TECHNOLOGIES

```
FINE AND APPLIED ARTS
FOREIGN LANGUAGES
HEALTH
HUMANITIES
LIBRARY SCIENCE
MATHEMATICS
MILITARY SCIENCES
PHYSICAL SCIENCES
PSYCHOLOGY
PUBLIC SERVICES
SOCIAL SCIENCES
GENERAL LIBERAL ARTS
```

==

NORTH IOWA AREA COMMUNITY COLLEGE
500 COLLEGE DRIVE
MASON CITY, IA 50401
515-421-4246

KEY CONTACT: Attn: Handicapped Student Services

SIZE OF SCHOOL: SMALL

APPLICATION DEADLINE: SEPTEMBER 9

	APPROXIMATE TUITION	ROOM AND BOARD
IN DISTRICT	$ 720	$1800
IN STATE	$ 720	$1800
OUT-OF-STATE	$1050	$1800

REQUIREMENTS FOR ADMISSIONS:
  High school equivalency diploma
  High school diploma
  21 years of age or older, with or without a
    high school diploma or equivalency
  Admission requirements modified

ADDITIONAL SERVICES OFFERED:
  Learning Lab
  Remedial and/or tutorial help available
  Reader services for the blind available for LD
  Handicapped student services works with LD

MODIFICATIONS TO TRADITIONAL LEARNING ENVIRONMENT:
  Oral presentation in lieu of written exams
  Use of calculator for all math courses
  Tape recorders to record class lectures
  Someone else may take class notes
  Multiple choice exams only

```
     Essay exams only
     Student takes exams in separate rooms
     Students have exams read to them
     Students take typewritten exams
     Longer time allowed to complete exams
     Submit papers on cassette tape
     Extended time limits for graduation
     Physical education may be waived
```

MAJORS OFFERED:

```
     AGRICULTURE
     ARCHITECTURE
     BIOLOGICAL SCIENCES
     BUSINESS AND MANAGEMENT
     COMMUNICATIONS
     COMPUTER SCIENCES
     EDUCATION
     ENGINEERING TECHNOLOGIES
     FINE AND APPLIED ARTS
     FOREIGN LANGUAGES
     HEALTH
     HOME ECONOMICS
     HUMANITIES
     MATHEMATICS
     PHYSICAL SCIENCES
     PSYCHOLOGY
     PUBLIC SERVICES
     SOCIAL SCIENCES
```

==

```
NORTHWEST IOWA TECHNICAL COLLEGE
HIGHWAAY 18 WEST
SHELDON, IA 51201
712-324-2587
```

KEY CONTACT: Attn: JOHN PELL
                    SPECIAL NEEDS COORDINATOR

SIZE OF SCHOOL: SMALL

APPLICATION DEADLINE: NONE

	APPROXIMATE TUITION	ROOM AND BOARD
IN DISTRICT	$ 865	$NOT OFFERED
IN STATE	$ 865	$NOT OFFERED
OUT-OF-STATE	$1265	$NOT OFFERED

REQUIREMENTS FOR ADMISSIONS:
  Personal interview

ADDITIONAL SERVICES OFFERED:
  Learning Lab
  Diagnostic testing services on campus
  Remedial and/or tutorial help available
  Reader services for the blind available for LD
  Handicapped student services works with LD

MODIFICATIONS TO TRADITIONAL LEARNING ENVIRONMENT:
  Oral presentation in lieu of written exams
  Use of calculator for all math courses
  Tape recorders to record class lectures
  Someone else may take class notes
  Multiple choice exams only
  Student takes exams in separate rooms
  Students have exams read to them
  Longer time allowed to complete exams
  Extended time limits for graduation

MAJORS OFFERED:

  AGRICULTURE
  BUSINESS AND MANAGEMENT
  COMPUTER SCIENCES
  ENGINEERING TECHNOLOGIES
  HEALTH

===

JOHNSON COUNTY COMMUNITY COLLEGE
COLLEGE BLVD AT QUIVIRA ROAD
OVERLAND PARK, KS 66210
913-677-8503

KEY CONTACT: Attn: JOANNE BODNER
                    PROGRAM SPECIALIST

SIZE OF SCHOOL: MEDIUM

APPLICATION DEADLINE: NONE

	APPROXIMATE TUITION	ROOM AND BOARD
IN DISTRICT	$ 525	$NOT OFFERED
IN STATE	$ 525	$NOT OFFERED
OUT-OF-STATE	$1575	$NOT OFFERED

REQUIREMENTS FOR ADMISSIONS:
  Placement tests
  Recommendations

ADDITIONAL SERVICES OFFERED:
  Diagnostic testing services off campus
  Remedial and/or tutorial help available
  Reader services for the blind available for LD
  Handicapped student services works with LD

MODIFICATIONS TO TRADITIONAL LEARNING ENVIRONMENT:
  Oral presentation in lieu of written exams
  Tape recorders to record class lectures
  Someone else may take class notes
  Student takes exams in separate rooms
  Students have exams read to them
  Students take typewritten exams
  Longer time allowed to complete exams
  Take limited course load and graduate within time
    required
  Extended time limits for graduation
  Most accomodations at the discretion of individual
    instructors

MAJORS OFFERED:

  AGRICULTURE
  BUSINESS AND MANAGEMENT
  COMPUTER SCIENCES
  ENGINEERING TECHNOLOGIES
  HEALTH
  PUBLIC SERVICES
  GENERAL LIBERAL ARTS

==

KANSAS CITY KANSAS COMMUNITY COLLEGE
7250 STATE AVENUE
KANSAS CITY, KS 66112
913-334-1100

KEY CONTACT: Attn: LINDA DEMARIAS, COORDINATOR
                    DISABLED STUDENT SERVICES

SIZE OF SCHOOL: MEDIUM

APPLICATION DEADLINE: NONE

```
        APPROXIMATE TUITION    ROOM AND BOARD

IN DISTRICT      $ 600        $NOT OFFERED
IN STATE         $ 600        $NOT OFFERED
OUT-OF-STATE     $1770        $NOT OFFERED
```

REQUIREMENTS FOR ADMISSIONS:
  High school equivalency diploma
  High school diploma
  Open door policy

ADDITIONAL SERVICES OFFERED:
  Learning Lab
  Remedial and/or tutorial help available
  Reader services for the blind available for LD
  Handicapped student services works with LD

MODIFICATIONS TO TRADITIONAL LEARNING ENVIRONMENT:
  Oral presentation in lieu of written exams
  Tape recorders to record class lectures
  Someone else may take class notes
  Student takes exams in separate rooms
  Students have exams read to them
  Students take typewritten exams
  Longer time allowed to complete exams
  Submit papers on cassette tape
  Take limited course load and graduate within time
    required
  Extended time limits for graduation

MAJORS OFFERED:

  AGRICULTURE
  BIOLOGICAL SCIENCES
  BUSINESS AND MANAGEMENT
  COMMUNICATIONS
  COMPUTER SCIENCES
  EDUCATION
  ENGINEERING TECHNOLOGIES
  FINE AND APPLIED ARTS
  FOREIGN LANGUAGES
  HEALTH
  HOME ECONOMICS
  HUMANITIES
  MATHEMATICS
  PHYSICAL SCIENCES
  PSYCHOLOGY
  PUBLIC SERVICES
  SOCIAL SCIENCES
  GENERAL LIBERAL ARTS

DELGADO COLLEGE - CITY PARK
615 CITY PARK AVENUE
NEW ORLEANS, LA 70119

KEY CONTACT: Attn: Handicapped Student Services

SIZE OF SCHOOL: LARGE

APPLICATION DEADLINE: NONE

         APPROXIMATE TUITION   ROOM AND BOARD

IN DISTRICT $ 460 $NOT OFFERED
IN STATE $ 460 $NOT OFFERED
OUT-OF-STATE $1090 $NOT OFFERED

REQUIREMENTS FOR ADMISSIONS:
  High school equivalency diploma
  High school diploma
  21 years of age or older, with or without a
    high school diploma or equivalency
  Admission requirements modified

ADDITIONAL SERVICES OFFERED:
  Learning Lab
  Learning Lab has a specialist with a masters degree
    or above in Learning Disabilities
  Diagnostic testing services on campus
  Remedial and/or tutorial help available
  Reader services for the blind available for LD
  Handicapped student services works with LD

MODIFICATIONS TO TRADITIONAL LEARNING ENVIRONMENT:
  Oral presentation in lieu of written exams
  Use of calculator for all math courses
  Tape recorders to record class lectures
  Someone else may take class notes
  Multiple choice exams only
  Essay exams only
  Student takes exams in separate rooms
  Students have exams read to them
  Students take typewritten exams
  Longer time allowed to complete exams
  Submit papers on cassette tape
  Extended time limits for graduation
  Physical education may be waived

MAJORS OFFERED:

  ARCHITECTURE
  BIOLOGICAL SCIENCES

```
BUSINESS AND MANAGEMENT
COMPUTER SCIENCES
ENGINEERING TECHNOLOGIES
FINE AND APPLIED ARTS
HEALTH
LIBRARY SCIENCE
PUBLIC SERVICES
GENERAL LIBERAL ARTS
```

===

HOWARD COMMUNITY COLLEGE
LITTLE PATUXENT PARKWAY
COLUMBIA, MD 21044
301-992-4822

KEY CONTACT: Attn: BARBARA GREENFELD
                     LEARNING DISABILITIES SPECIALIST

SIZE OF SCHOOL: MEDIUM

APPLICATION DEADLINE: NONE

	APPROXIMATE TUITION	ROOM AND BOARD
IN DISTRICT	$ 840	$NOT OFFERED
IN STATE	$1680	$NOT OFFERED
OUT-OF-STATE	$3360	$NOT OFFERED

REQUIREMENTS FOR ADMISSIONS:
  Untimed or oral ACT Scores accepted
  Untimed or oral SAT Scores accepted
  University or College sponsored tests
  Placement tests
  Essay
  Open admissions

ADDITIONAL SERVICES OFFERED:
  Remedial and/or tutorial help available
  Reader services for the blind available for LD
  Handicapped student services works with LD

MODIFICATIONS TO TRADITIONAL LEARNING ENVIRONMENT:
  Oral presentation in lieu of written exams
  Tape recorders to record class lectures
  Someone else may take class notes
  Student takes exams in separate rooms
  Students have exams read to them
  Students take typewritten exams
  Longer time allowed to complete exams
  Submit papers on cassette tape

Extended time limits for graduation
Physical education may be waived
All modifications are available and are arranged on a
    case by case basis by specialists, instructors and
    students

MAJORS OFFERED:

    BIOLOGICAL SCIENCES
    BUSINESS AND MANAGEMENT
    COMPUTER SCIENCES
    EDUCATION
    ENGINEERING TECHNOLOGIES
    FINE AND APPLIED ARTS
    HEALTH
    PHYSICAL SCIENCES
    PSYCHOLOGY
    SOCIAL SCIENCES
    GENERAL LIBERAL ARTS

==

MONTGOMERY COLLEGE - GERMANTOWN
20200 OBSERVATION ROAD
GERMANTOWN, MD 20874
301-972-2000

KEY CONTACT: Attn: Handicapped Student Services

SIZE OF SCHOOL: SMALL

APPLICATION DEADLINE: AUGUST 29

        APPROXIMATE TUITION   ROOM AND BOARD

IN DISTRICT $ 990 $NOT OFFERED
IN STATE $1950 $NOT OFFERED
OUT-OF-STATE $2675 $NOT OFFERED

REQUIREMENTS FOR ADMISSIONS:
  High school equivalency diploma
  High school diploma
  18 years of age or older, with or without a
    high school diploma or equivalency
  Untimed or oral ACT Scores accepted
  Untimed or oral SAT Scores accepted
  University or College sponsored tests
  Personal interview
  Placement tests
  Essay

ADDITIONAL SERVICES OFFERED:
  Learning Lab
  Learning Lab has a specialist with a masters degree
    or above in Learning Disabilities
  Diagnostic testing services on campus
  Remedial and/or tutorial help available
  Reader services for the blind available for LD
  Handicapped student services works with LD

MODIFICATIONS TO TRADITIONAL LEARNING ENVIRONMENT:
  Oral presentation in lieu of written exams
  Tape recorders to record class lectures
  Someone else may take class notes
  Student takes exams in separate rooms
  Students have exams read to them
  Students take typewritten exams
  Longer time allowed to complete exams
  Submit papers on cassette tape
  Physical education may be waived

MAJORS OFFERED:

  BUSINESS AND MANAGEMENT
  COMPUTER SCIENCES
  EDUCATION
  ENGINEERING TECHNOLOGIES
  GENERAL LIBERAL ARTS

===

MONTGOMERY COLLEGE - TAKOMA PARK
TAKOMA AVENUE AND FENTON STREET
TAKOMA PARK, MD 20912
301-587-4090

KEY CONTACT: Attn: MRS. LYNCH, COUNSELOR

SIZE OF SCHOOL: MEDIUM

APPLICATION DEADLINE: AUGUST 29

	APPROXIMATE TUITION	ROOM AND BOARD
IN DISTRICT	$ 990	$NOT OFFERED
IN STATE	$1950	$NOT OFFERED
OUT-OF-STATE	$2675	$NOT OFFERED

REQUIREMENTS FOR ADMISSIONS:
  High school equivalency diploma
  High school diploma

   21 years of age or older, with or without a
     high school diploma or equivalency
   Placement tests (recommended)

ADDITIONAL SERVICES OFFERED:
   Learning Lab
   Learning Lab has a specialist with a masters degree
     or above in Learning Disabilities
   Diagnostic testing services on campus
   Remedial and/or tutorial help available
   Reader services for the blind available for LD

MODIFICATIONS TO TRADITIONAL LEARNING ENVIRONMENT:
   Oral presentation in lieu of written exams
   Use of calculator for all math courses
   Tape recorders to record class lectures
   Someone else may take class notes
   Students have exams read to them
   Longer time allowed to complete exams
   Physical education may be waived
   Other modifications may be arranged

MAJORS OFFERED:

   BUSINESS AND MANAGEMENT
   COMPUTER SCIENCES
   EDUCATION
   ENGINEERING TECHNOLOGIES
   FINE AND APPLIED ARTS
   HEALTH
   HOME ECONOMICS
   GENERAL LIBERAL ARTS

==

PRINCE GEORGE'S COMMUNITY COLLEGE
301 LARGO ROAD
LARGO, MD 20772

KEY CONTACT: Attn: CARRIE JOHNSON, COUNSELOR

SIZE OF SCHOOL: LARGE

APPLICATION DEADLINE: NONE

	APPROXIMATE TUITION	ROOM AND BOARD
IN DISTRICT	$ 730	$NOT OFFERED
IN STATE	$1630	$NOT OFFERED
OUT-OF-STATE	$2780	$NOT OFFERED

REQUIREMENTS FOR ADMISSIONS:
  High school equivalency diploma
  High school diploma
  21 years of age or older, with or without a
    high school diploma or equivalency
  University or College sponsored tests
  Placement tests

ADDITIONAL SERVICES OFFERED:
  Learning Lab
  Diagnostic testing services on campus
  Remedial and/or tutorial help available
  Reader services for the blind available for LD
  Handicapped student services works with LD

MODIFICATIONS TO TRADITIONAL LEARNING ENVIRONMENT:
  Oral presentation in lieu of written exams
  Tape recorders to record class lectures
  Someone else may take class notes
  Longer time allowed to complete exams
  Extended time limits for graduation
  Physical education may be waived
  Other modifications may be arranged

MAJORS OFFERED:

  BUSINESS AND MANAGEMENT
  COMPUTER SCIENCES
  EDUCATION
  ENGINEERING TECHNOLOGIES
  FINE AND APPLIED ARTS
  HEALTH
  PUBLIC SERVICES
  GENERAL LIBERAL ARTS

==

UNIVERSITY OF MASSACHUSETTS
STOCKBRIDGE SCHOOL OF ARGRICULTURE
AMHERST, MA 01003
413-545-2222

KEY CONTACT: Attn: DR. JOHN W. DENISON

SIZE OF SCHOOL: SMALL

APPLICATION DEADLINE: MARCH 1

```
        APPROXIMATE TUITION    ROOM AND BOARD

IN DISTRICT      $1630          $2890
IN STATE         $1630          $2890
OUT-OF-STATE     $4185          $2890
```

REQUIREMENTS FOR ADMISSIONS:
  High school equivalency diploma
  High school diploma
  21 years of age or older, with or without a
    high school diploma or equivalency
  SAT Scores required
  Untimed or oral SAT Scores accepted
  Particular rank in class   50%
  Recommendations

ADDITIONAL SERVICES OFFERED:
  Diagnostic testing services on campus
  Remedial and/or tutorial help available
  Reader services for the blind available for LD
  Special Education department
  Handicapped student services works with LD

MODIFICATIONS TO TRADITIONAL LEARNING ENVIRONMENT:
  Oral presentation in lieu of written exams
  Tape recorders to record class lectures
  Someone else may take class notes
  Student takes exams in separate rooms
  Students have exams read to them
  Longer time allowed to complete exams
  Submit papers on cassette tape
  Extended time limits for graduation
  Modifications are made on an individual case basis at
    the discretion of the professor

MAJORS OFFERED:

  AGRICULTURE

==

NORTHERN ESSEX COMMUNITY COLLEGE
100 ELLIOTT STREET
HAVERHILL, MA 01830
617-374-0721

KEY CONTACT: Attn: JAN SCHEERER, COUNSELOR FOR
                    LEARNING DISABLED STUDENTS

SIZE OF SCHOOL: MEDIUM

APPLICATION DEADLINE: NONE

	APPROXIMATE TUITION	ROOM AND BOARD
IN DISTRICT	$ 725	$NOT OFFERED
IN STATE	$1035	$NOT OFFERED
OUT-OF-STATE	$2340	$NOT OFFERED

REQUIREMENTS FOR ADMISSIONS:
  Open admissions policy

ADDITIONAL SERVICES OFFERED:
  Learning Lab
  Learning Lab has a specialist with a masters degree
    or above in Learning Disabilities
  Diagnostic testing services on campus
  Diagnostic testing services off campus
  Remedial and/or tutorial help available
  Reader services for the blind available for LD
  Handicapped student services works with LD

MODIFICATIONS TO TRADITIONAL LEARNING ENVIRONMENT:
  Oral presentation in lieu of written exams
  Tape recorders to record class lectures
  Someone else may take class notes
  Student takes exams in separate rooms
  Students have exams read to them
  Students take typewritten exams
  Longer time allowed to complete exams
  Submit papers on cassette tape
  Extended time limits for graduation
  Physical education may be waived
  All of the above modifications have been acceptable
    depending on instructor

MAJORS OFFERED:

  BUSINESS AND MANAGEMENT
  COMPUTER SCIENCES
  ENGINEERING TECHNOLOGIES
  HEALTH
  GENERAL LIBERAL ARTS

===

GRAND RAPIDS JUNIOR COLLEGE
143 BOSTWICK, NE
GRAND RAPIDS, MI 49503
616-456-4884

KEY CONTACT: Attn: DORIS PARSONS

SIZE OF SCHOOL: LARGE

APPLICATION DEADLINE: SEPTEMBER 1

          APPROXIMATE TUITION   ROOM AND BOARD

IN DISTRICT $ 868 $NOT OFFERED
IN STATE $1457 $NOT OFFERED
OUT-OF-STATE $2170 $NOT OFFERED

REQUIREMENTS FOR ADMISSIONS:
  High school equivalency diploma
  High school diploma
  Untimed or oral ACT Scores accepted
  Untimed or oral SAT Scores accepted
  University or College sponsored tests
  Personal interview
  Placement tests
  Recommendations
  Open admissions

ADDITIONAL SERVICES OFFERED:
  Learning Lab
  Diagnostic testing services on campus
  Diagnostic testing services off campus
  Remedial and/or tutorial help available
  Reader services for the blind available for LD
  Handicapped student services works with LD

MODIFICATIONS TO TRADITIONAL LEARNING ENVIRONMENT:
  Oral presentation in lieu of written exams
  Has an adaptive physical education program
  Tape recorders to record class lectures
  Someone else may take class notes
  Student takes exams in separate rooms
  Students have exams read to them
  Longer time allowed to complete exams
  Extended time limits for graduation

MAJORS OFFERED:

  ARCHITECTURE
  BIOLOGICAL SCIENCES
  BUSINESS AND MANAGEMENT
  COMPUTER SCIENCES
  EDUCATION
  ENGINEERING TECHNOLOGIES
  HEALTH
  HOME ECONOMICS
  HUMANITIES
  LIBRARY SCIENCE

MATHEMATICS
PHYSICAL SCIENCES
PSYCHOLOGY
PUBLIC SERVICES
SOCIAL SCIENCES
GENERAL LIBERAL ARTS

===

SCHOOLCRAFT COLLEGE
18600 HAGGERTY ROAD
LIVONIA, MI 48152
313-591-6400

KEY CONTACT: Attn: Handicapped Student Services

SIZE OF SCHOOL: MEDIUM

APPLICATION DEADLINE: NONE

	APPROXIMATE TUITION	ROOM AND BOARD
IN DISTRICT	$ 810	$NOT OFFERED
IN STATE	$1020	$NOT OFFERED
OUT-OF-STATE	$1400	$NOT OFFERED

REQUIREMENTS FOR ADMISSIONS:
  High school equivalency diploma
  High school diploma
  21 years of age or older, with or without a
    high school diploma or equivalency

ADDITIONAL SERVICES OFFERED:
  Learning Lab
  Learning Lab has a specialist with a masters degree
    or above in Learning Disabilities
  Diagnostic testing services on campus
  Remedial and/or tutorial help available
  Reader services for the blind available for LD
  Handicapped student services works with LD

MODIFICATIONS TO TRADITIONAL LEARNING ENVIRONMENT:
  Tape recorders to record class lectures
  Someone else may take class notes
  Students have exams read to them
  Students take typewritten exams
  Longer time allowed to complete exams
  Take limited course load and graduate within time
    required
  Extended time limits for graduation
  Physical education may be waived

MAJORS OFFERED:

   BIOLOGICAL SCIENCES
   BUSINESS AND MANAGEMENT
   COMPUTER SCIENCES
   EDUCATION
   ENGINEERING TECHNOLOGIES
   FINE AND APPLIED ARTS
   MATHEMATICS
   PHYSICAL SCIENCES
   SOCIAL SCIENCES
   GENERAL LIBERAL ARTS

==

WASHTENAW COMMUNITY COLLEGE
4800 HURON RIVER DRIVE
ANN ARBOR, MI 48106
313-973-3544

KEY CONTACT: Attn: JOHN WEIR

SIZE OF SCHOOL: MEDIUM

APPLICATION DEADLINE: JULY 15

	APPROXIMATE TUITION	ROOM AND BOARD
IN DISTRICT	$ 590	$NOT OFFERED
IN STATE	$ 995	$NOT OFFERED
OUT-OF-STATE	$1330	$NOT OFFERED

REQUIREMENTS FOR ADMISSIONS:
  High school equivalency diploma
  High school diploma
  21 years of age or older, with or without a
    high school diploma or equivalency

ADDITIONAL SERVICES OFFERED:
  Learning Lab
  Learning Lab has a specialist with a masters degree
    or above in Learning Disabilities
  Remedial and/or tutorial help available
  Reader services for the blind available for LD
  Handicapped student services works with LD

MODIFICATIONS TO TRADITIONAL LEARNING ENVIRONMENT:
  Oral presentation in lieu of written exams
  Tape recorders to record class lectures
  Someone else may take class notes
  Multiple choice exams only

```
Essay exams only
Student takes exams in separate rooms
Students have exams read to them
Students take typewritten exams
Longer time allowed to complete exams
Submit papers on cassette tape
Physical education may be waived
```

MAJORS OFFERED:

```
BUSINESS AND MANAGEMENT
COMPUTER SCIENCES
ENGINEERING TECHNOLOGIES
HEALTH
PUBLIC SERVICES
GENERAL LIBERAL ARTS
```

==

```
WAYNE COUNTY COMMUNITY COLLEGE
801 WEST FORT STREET
DETROIT, MI 48226
313-496-2655
```

KEY CONTACT: Attn: Handicapped Student Services

SIZE OF SCHOOL: LARGE

APPLICATION DEADLINE: NONE

	APPROXIMATE TUITION	ROOM AND BOARD
IN DISTRICT	$ 625	$NOT OFFERED
IN STATE	$ 890	$NOT OFFERED
OUT-OF-STATE	$1155	$NOT OFFERED

REQUIREMENTS FOR ADMISSIONS:
```
  21 years of age or older, with or without a
     high school diploma or equivalency
  Admission requirements modified
  Placement tests
```

ADDITIONAL SERVICES OFFERED:
```
  Learning Lab
  Learning Lab has a specialist with a masters degree
     or above in Learning Disabilities
  Diagnostic testing services off campus
  Remedial and/or tutorial help available
  Reader services for the blind available for LD
  Handicapped student services works with LD
```

MODIFICATIONS TO TRADITIONAL LEARNING ENVIRONMENT:
  Oral presentation in lieu of written exams
  Use of calculator for all math courses
  Tape recorders to record class lectures
  Someone else may take class notes
  Multiple choice exams only
  Essay exams only
  Student takes exams in separate rooms
  Students have exams read to them
  Students take typewritten exams
  Longer time allowed to complete exams
  Submit papers on cassette tape
  Physical education may ·be waived

MAJORS OFFERED:

    BUSINESS AND MANAGEMENT
    COMPUTER SCIENCES
    ENGINEERING TECHNOLOGIES
    HEALTH
    PUBLIC SERVICES
    GENERAL LIBERAL ARTS

==

BRAINERD COMMUNITY COLLEGE
BOX 467
BRAINERD, MN 56401
218-828-2508

KEY CONTACT: Attn: Handicapped Student Services

SIZE OF SCHOOL: SMALL

APPLICATION DEADLINE: NONE

	APPROXIMATE TUITION	ROOM AND BOARD
IN DISTRICT	$1135	$NOT OFFERED
IN STATE	$1135	$NOT OFFERED
OUT-OF-STATE	$2270	$NOT OFFERED

REQUIREMENTS FOR ADMISSIONS:
  21 years of age or older, with or without a
    high school diploma or equivalency
  Admission requirements modified

ADDITIONAL SERVICES OFFERED:
  Remedial and/or tutorial help available
  Handicapped student services works with LD

MODIFICATIONS TO TRADITIONAL LEARNING ENVIRONMENT:
    Oral presentation in lieu of written exams
    Tape recorders to record class lectures
    Someone else may take class notes
    Multiple choice exams only
    Essay exams only
    Student takes exams in separate rooms
    Students have exams read to them
    Students take typewritten exams
    Longer time allowed to complete exams
    Submit papers on cassette tape
    Extended time limits for graduation
    Physical education may be waived

MAJORS OFFERED:

    BIOLOGICAL SCIENCES
    BUSINESS AND MANAGEMENT
    COMMUNICATIONS
    EDUCATION
    ENGINEERING TECHNOLOGIES
    FINE AND APPLIED ARTS
    HEALTH
    HUMANITIES
    MATHEMATICS
    PHYSICAL SCIENCES
    SOCIAL SCIENCES
    GENERAL LIBERAL ARTS

==

GOLDEN VALLEY LUTHERAN COLLEGE
6125 OLSON HIGHWAY
MINNEAPOLIS, MN 55422
612-542-1212

KEY CONTACT: Attn: MARY SICILIA

SIZE OF SCHOOL: SMALL

APPLICATION DEADLINE: SEPTEMBER 1

	APPROXIMATE TUITION	ROOM AND BOARD
IN DISTRICT	$4860	$2315
IN STATE	$4860	$2315
OUT-OF-STATE	$4860	$2315

REQUIREMENTS FOR ADMISSIONS:
    High school equivalency diploma
    High school diploma

ACT Scores required
SAT Scores required
Admission requirements modified
Personal interview
Recommendations

ADDITIONAL SERVICES OFFERED:
  Learning Lab
  Learning Lab has a specialist with a masters degree
    or above in Learning Disabilities
  Diagnostic testing services on campus
  Remedial and/or tutorial help available
  Reader services for the blind available for LD

MODIFICATIONS TO TRADITIONAL LEARNING ENVIRONMENT:
  Oral presentation in lieu of written exams
  Use of calculator for all math courses
  Tape recorders to record class lectures
  Someone else may take class notes
  Student takes exams in separate rooms
  Students have exams read to them
  Students take typewritten exams
  Longer time allowed to complete exams
  Submit papers on cassette tape
  Extended time limits for graduation
  Physical education may be waived

MAJORS OFFERED:

  BUSINESS AND MANAGEMENT
  COMPUTER SCIENCES
  EDUCATION
  FINE AND APPLIED ARTS
  HEALTH
  SOCIAL SCIENCES
  THEOLOGY
  GENERAL LIBERAL ARTS

===

INVER HILLS COMMUNITY COLLEGE
8445 COLLEGE TRAIL
INVER GROVE HEIGHTS, MN 55075
612-455-9621

KEY CONTACT: Attn: GINI SPURR, DIRECTOR
                    HANDICAPPED STUDENT SERVICES

SIZE OF SCHOOL: MEDIUM

APPLICATION DEADLINE: NONE

```
        APPROXIMATE TUITION    ROOM AND BOARD

IN DISTRICT      $  855       $NOT OFFERED
IN STATE         $  855       $NOT OFFERED
OUT-OF-STATE     $1710        $NOT OFFERED
```

REQUIREMENTS FOR ADMISSIONS:
  High school equivalency diploma
  High school diploma
  Placement tests

ADDITIONAL SERVICES OFFERED:
  Learning Lab
  Learning Lab has a specialist with a masters degree
    or above in Learning Disabilities
  Diagnostic testing services off campus
  Remedial and/or tutorial help available
  Reader services for the blind available for LD
  Handicapped student services works with LD
  Taping of textbooks, notetakers and typing services
    are also available

MODIFICATIONS TO TRADITIONAL LEARNING ENVIRONMENT:
  Tape recorders to record class lectures
  Someone else may take class notes
  Student takes exams in separate rooms
  Students have exams read to them
  Students take typewritten exams
  Longer time allowed to complete exams
  Extended time limits for graduation
  Physical education may be waived
  The type of exam given in class is the decision of
    the instructor
  All instructors will work with the handicapped
    student in meeting their individual needs
  Student is responsible for contacting the instructor
    before or during the first week of class
  An advocate is available to assist students.

MAJORS OFFERED:

  AGRICULTURE
  AREA STUDIES
  BIOLOGICAL SCIENCES
  BUSINESS AND MANAGEMENT
  COMPUTER SCIENCES
  EDUCATION
  ENGINEERING TECHNOLOGIES
  FINE AND APPLIED ARTS
  FOREIGN LANGUAGES
  HEALTH

```
HOME ECONOMICS
HUMANITIES
MATHEMATICS
PHYSICAL SCIENCES
PSYCHOLOGY
SOCIAL SCIENCES
GENERAL LIBERAL ARTS
```

==

NORMANDALE COMMUNITY COLLEGE
9700 FRANCE AVENUE SOUTH
BLOMMINGTON, MN 55431
612-830-9320

KEY CONTACT: Attn: Handicapped Student Services

SIZE OF SCHOOL: MEDIUM

APPLICATION DEADLINE: SEPTEMBER 1

	APPROXIMATE TUITION	ROOM AND BOARD
IN DISTRICT	$ 990	$NOT OFFERED
IN STATE	$ 990	$NOT OFFERED
OUT-OF-STATE	$1980	$NOT OFFERED

REQUIREMENTS FOR ADMISSIONS:
  High school equivalency diploma
  High school diploma

ADDITIONAL SERVICES OFFERED:
  Learning Lab
  Learning Lab has a specialist with a masters degree
    or above in Learning Disabilities
  Remedial and/or tutorial help available
  Reader services for the blind available for LD
  Special Education department
  Handicapped student services works with LD

MODIFICATIONS TO TRADITIONAL LEARNING ENVIRONMENT:
  Oral presentation in lieu of written exams
  Has an adaptive physical education program
  Tape recorders to record class lectures
  Someone else may take class notes
  Student takes exams in separate rooms
  Students take typewritten exams
  Longer time allowed to complete exams
  Submit papers on cassette tape
  Physical education may be waived

MAJORS OFFERED:

    AGRICULTURE
    ARCHITECTURE
    AREA STUDIES
    BIOLOGICAL SCIENCES
    BUSINESS AND MANAGEMENT
    COMMUNICATIONS
    COMPUTER SCIENCES
    EDUCATION
    ENGINEERING TECHNOLOGIES
    FINE AND APPLIED ARTS
    FOREIGN LANGUAGES
    HEALTH
    HOME ECONOMICS
    HUMANITIES
    LIBRARY SCIENCE
    MATHEMATICS
    MILITARY SCIENCES
    PHYSICAL SCIENCES
    PSYCHOLOGY
    PUBLIC SERVICES
    SOCIAL SCIENCES
    THEOLOGY
    GENERAL LIBERAL ARTS

===

NORTHEAST MISSISSIPPI JUNIOR COLLEGE
CUNNINGHAM BLVD
BOONEVILLE, MS 38829
601-728-7751

KEY CONTACT: Attn: JOE M. CHILDERS, DEAN

SIZE OF SCHOOL: MEDIUM

APPLICATION DEADLINE: NONE

         APPROXIMATE TUITION   ROOM AND BOARD

IN DISTRICT $ 500 $1360
IN STATE $ 500 $1360
OUT-OF-STATE $1080 $1360

REQUIREMENTS FOR ADMISSIONS:
   High school equivalency diploma
   High school diploma
   ACT Scores required

ADDITIONAL SERVICES OFFERED:
  Learning Lab
  Diagnostic testing services on campus
  Remedial and/or tutorial help available

MODIFICATIONS TO TRADITIONAL LEARNING ENVIRONMENT:
  Has an adaptive physical education program
  Someone else may take class notes
  Take limited course load and graduate within time
    required
  Extended time limits for graduation
  Physical education may be waived

MAJORS OFFERED:

  AGRICULTURE
  ARCHITECTURE
  AREA STUDIES
  BIOLOGICAL SCIENCES
  BUSINESS AND MANAGEMENT
  COMMUNICATIONS
  COMPUTER SCIENCES
  EDUCATION
  ENGINEERING TECHNOLOGIES
  FINE AND APPLIED ARTS
  FOREIGN LANGUAGES
  HEALTH
  HOME ECONOMICS
  HUMANITIES
  LIBRARY SCIENCE
  MATHEMATICS
  MILITARY SCIENCES
  PHYSICAL SCIENCES
  PSYCHOLOGY
  PUBLIC SERVICES
  SOCIAL SCIENCES
  THEOLOGY
  GENERAL LIBERAL ARTS

==

MINERAL AREA COLLEGE
FLAT RIVER, MO 63601
314-431-4593

KEY CONTACT: Attn: MARGARET SCOBEE
                    VOCATIONAL RESOURCE EDUCATOR

SIZE OF SCHOOL: SMALL

APPLICATION DEADLINE: AUGUST 15

```
        APPROXIMATE TUITION    ROOM AND BOARD

IN DISTRICT       $ 360       $NOT OFFERED
IN STATE          $ 660       $NOT OFFERED
OUT-OF-STATE      $ 830       $NOT OFFERED
```

REQUIREMENTS FOR ADMISSIONS:
  21 years of age or older, with or without a
    high school diploma or equivalency
  Untimed or oral ACT Scores accepted
  Untimed or oral SAT Scores accepted
  Open door policy
  GED or high school diploma must be earned before a
    degree may be granted from Mineral Area College

ADDITIONAL SERVICES OFFERED:
  Learning Lab
  Diagnostic testing services on campus
  Diagnostic testing services off campus
  Remedial and/or tutorial help available
  Reader services for the blind available for LD
  Special Education department
  Handicapped student services works with LD

MODIFICATIONS TO TRADITIONAL LEARNING ENVIRONMENT:
  Oral presentation in lieu of written reports
  Has an adaptive physical education program
  Tape recorders to record class lectures
  Someone else may take class notes
  Student takes exams in separate rooms
  Students have exams read to them
  Longer time allowed to complete exams
  Extended time limits for graduation
  Physical education may be waived

MAJORS OFFERED:

  BUSINESS AND MANAGEMENT
  ENGINEERING TECHNOLOGIES
  HEALTH
  PUBLIC SERVICES
  GENERAL LIBERAL ARTS

==

PENN VALLEY COMMUNITY COLLEGE
3201 SOUTHWEST TRAFFICWAY
KANSAS CITY, MO 64111
816-932-7610

KEY CONTACT: Attn: JUDITH FLYNN
                     MANAGER, LEARNING CENTER

SIZE OF SCHOOL: MEDIUM

APPLICATION DEADLINE: NONE

	APPROXIMATE TUITION	ROOM AND BOARD
IN DISTRICT	$ 600	$NOT OFFERED
IN STATE	$ 810	$NOT OFFERED
OUT-OF-STATE	$1410	$NOT OFFERED

REQUIREMENTS FOR ADMISSIONS:
   21 years of age or older, with or without a
      high school diploma or equivalency
   Students without a GED or High School diploma are
      admitted as "Special Students", required to take a
      battery of tests and are limited as to the number
      of hours they can take

ADDITIONAL SERVICES OFFERED:
   Learning Lab
   Remedial and/or tutorial help available
   PVCC has no program designed to assist LD students
      specifically but they may use the services of the
      Learning Center

MODIFICATIONS TO TRADITIONAL LEARNING ENVIRONMENT:
   Any modifications depend on the individual instructor

MAJORS OFFERED:

   BIOLOGICAL SCIENCES
   BUSINESS AND MANAGEMENT
   COMMUNICATIONS
   COMPUTER SCIENCES
   EDUCATION
   ENGINEERING TECHNOLOGIES
   FINE AND APPLIED ARTS
   FOREIGN LANGUAGES
   HEALTH
   HOME ECONOMICS
   HUMANITIES
   MATHEMATICS
   PHYSICAL SCIENCES
   PSYCHOLOGY
   PUBLIC SERVICES
   SOCIAL SCIENCES
   GENERAL LIBERAL ARTS

```
ST. LOUIS COMMUNITY COLLEGE - FLORISSANT VALLEY
3400 PERSHALL ROAD
ST. LOUIS, MO 63135
314-595-4244
```

KEY CONTACT: Attn: IVA PRESBERRY, COORDINATOR

SIZE OF SCHOOL: LARGE

APPLICATION DEADLINE: NONE

	APPROXIMATE TUITION	ROOM AND BOARD
IN DISTRICT	$ 675	$NOT OFFERED
IN STATE	$ 975	$NOT OFFERED
OUT-OF-STATE	$1300	$NOT OFFERED

REQUIREMENTS FOR ADMISSIONS:
  High school equivalency diploma
  18 years of age or older, with or without a
    high school diploma or equivalency
  Untimed or oral ACT Scores accepted
  Untimed or oral SAT Scores accepted
  University or College sponsored tests
  Personal interview
  Placement tests
  Recommendations
  Essay

ADDITIONAL SERVICES OFFERED:
  Learning Lab
  Remedial and/or tutorial help available
  Reader services for the blind available for LD
  Handicapped student services works with LD

MODIFICATIONS TO TRADITIONAL LEARNING ENVIRONMENT:
  Oral presentation in lieu of written exams
  Use of calculator for all math courses
  Someone else may take class notes
  Multiple choice exams only
  Student takes exams in separate rooms
  Students have exams read to them
  Students take typewritten exams
  Longer time allowed to complete exams
  Take limited course load and graduate within time
    required
  Extended time limits for graduation
  Physical education may be waived

MAJORS OFFERED:

  BIOLOGICAL SCIENCES
  BUSINESS AND MANAGEMENT
  COMMUNICATIONS
  COMPUTER SCIENCES
  ENGINEERING TECHNOLOGIES
  FINE AND APPLIED ARTS
  FOREIGN LANGUAGES
  HEALTH
  HOME ECONOMICS
  HUMANITIES
  MATHEMATICS
  PHYSICAL SCIENCES
  PSYCHOLOGY
  SOCIAL SCIENCES
  GENERAL LIBERAL ARTS

==

CENTRAL COMMUNITY COLLEGE
HASTINGS CAMPUS
P.O. BOX 1024
HASTINGS, NE 68901
402-463-9811

KEY CONTACT: Attn: PEG JOHNSON

SIZE OF SCHOOL: SMALL

APPLICATION DEADLINE: NONE

         APPROXIMATE TUITION   ROOM AND BOARD

IN DISTRICT $ 575 $1325
IN STATE $ 575 $1325
OUT-OF-STATE $ 865 $1325
REQUIREMENTS FOR ADMISSIONS:
  Admission requirements modified

MODIFICATIONS TO TRADITIONAL LEARNING ENVIRONMENT:
  Tape recorders to record class lectures

MAJORS OFFERED:

  AGRICULTURE
  BUSINESS AND MANAGEMENT
  COMPUTER SCIENCES
  ENGINEERING TECHNOLOGIES
  HEALTH
  PUBLIC SERVICES

NEBRASKA WESTERN COLLEGE
1602 EAST 27TH, NE
SCOTTSBLUFF, NE 69361
308-635-3606

KEY CONTACT: Attn: JEAN ROBERTS, COUNSELOR

SIZE OF SCHOOL: SMALL

APPLICATION DEADLINE: NONE

APPROXIMATE TUITION   ROOM AND BOARD

	TUITION	ROOM AND BOARD
IN DISTRICT	$ 620	$1700
IN STATE	$ 620	$1700
OUT-OF-STATE	$ 825	$1700

REQUIREMENTS FOR ADMISSIONS:
  21 years of age or older, with or without a
    high school diploma or equivalency
  Admission requirements modified
  Placement tests

ADDITIONAL SERVICES OFFERED:
  Learning Lab
  Learning Lab has a specialist with a masters degree
    or above in Learning Disabilities
  Diagnostic testing services on campus
  Remedial and/or tutorial help available
  Reader services for the blind available for LD

MODIFICATIONS TO TRADITIONAL LEARNING ENVIRONMENT:
  Oral presentation in lieu of written exams
  Use of calculator for all math courses
  Tape recorders to record class lectures
  Someone else may take class notes
  Longer time allowed to complete exams
  Submit papers on cassette tape
  Extended time limits for graduation
  Physical education may be waived

MAJORS OFFERED:

  AGRICULTURE
  BUSINESS AND MANAGEMENT
  COMPUTER SCIENCES
  HEALTH
  ENGINEERING TECHNOLOGIES
  PUBLIC SERVICES
  GENERAL LIBERAL ARTS

```
SOUTHEAST COMMUNITY COLLEGE - LINCOLN
8800 "O" STREET
LINCOLN, NE 68520
402-47-3333
```

KEY CONTACT: Attn: GERALD GRUBER
                    DEAN OF STUDENT SERVICES

SIZE OF SCHOOL: SMALL

APPLICATION DEADLINE: NONE

APPROXIMATE TUITION		ROOM AND BOARD
IN DISTRICT	$ 775	$NOT OFFERED
IN STATE	$ 775	$NOT OFFERED
OUT-OF-STATE	$1225	$NOT OFFERED

REQUIREMENTS FOR ADMISSIONS:
  High school equivalency diploma
  High school diploma
  University or College sponsored tests
  Placement tests

ADDITIONAL SERVICES OFFERED:
  Learning Lab
  Learning Lab has a specialist with a masters degree
    or above in Learning Disabilities
  Diagnostic testing services on campus
  Diagnostic testing services off campus
  Remedial and/or tutorial help available
  Reader services for the blind available for LD
  Handicapped student services works with LD

MODIFICATIONS TO TRADITIONAL LEARNING ENVIRONMENT:
  Tape recorders to record class lectures
  Someone else may take class notes
  Take limited course load and graduate within time
    required
  Extended time limits for graduation

MAJORS OFFERED:

  BUSINESS AND MANAGEMENT
  COMPUTER SCIENCES
  ENGINEERING TECHNOLOGIES
  HEALTH
  PUBLIC SERVICES

==

NEW HAMPSHIRE VOCATIONAL TECHNICAL COLLEGE
505 AMHERST STREET
NASHUA, NH 03063
603-882-6923

KEY CONTACT: Attn: J.T. FISCHER, ADMISSIONS

SIZE OF SCHOOL: SMALL

APPLICATION DEADLINE: NONE

	APPROXIMATE TUITION	ROOM AND BOARD
IN DISTRICT	$1200	$NOT OFFERED
IN STATE	$1200	$NOT OFFERED
OUT-OF-STATE	$3200	$NOT OFFERED

REQUIREMENTS FOR ADMISSIONS:
  High school equivalency diploma
  High school diploma
  University or College sponsored tests
  Personal interview
  Recommendations

ADDITIONAL SERVICES OFFERED:
  Remedial and/or tutorial help available

MODIFICATIONS TO TRADITIONAL LEARNING ENVIRONMENT:
  All modifications depend on consultation with faculty

MAJORS OFFERED:

  BUSINESS AND MANAGEMENT
  COMPUTER SCIENCES
  ENGINEERING TECHNOLOGIES

==

UNIVERSITY OF NEW HAMPSHIRE
THOMPSON SCHOOL OF APPLIED SCIENCE
DURHAM, NH 03824
603-862-1360

KEY CONTACT: Attn: ANN C. BERQUIST
                    LEARNING SKILLS COORDINATOR

SIZE OF SCHOOL: SMALL

APPLICATION DEADLINE: FEBRUARY 1

```
        APPROXIMATE TUITION    ROOM AND BOARD

IN DISTRICT        $1950        $2275
IN STATE           $1950        $2275
OUT-OF-STATE       $5050        $2275
```

REQUIREMENTS FOR ADMISSIONS:
  High school equivalency diploma
  High school diploma
  ACT Scores required
  Untimed or oral ACT Scores accepted
  SAT Scores required
  Untimed or oral SAT Scores accepted
  Recommendations
  Essay
  Admission requirements and modifications are under
    consideration at present and may be changed

ADDITIONAL SERVICES OFFERED:
  Diagnostic testing services on campus
  Diagnostic testing services off campus
  Remedial and/or tutorial help available
  Reader services for the blind available for LD
  Handicapped student services works with LD

MODIFICATIONS TO TRADITIONAL LEARNING ENVIRONMENT:
  Oral presentation in lieu of written exams
  Use of calculator for all math courses
  Tape recorders to record class lectures
  Someone else may take class notes
  Student takes exams in separate rooms
  Students have exams read to them
  Students take typewritten exams
  Longer time allowed to complete exams
  Extended time limits for graduation

MAJORS OFFERED:

  AGRICULTURE
  ARCHITECTURE
  BIOLOGICAL SCIENCES
  BUSINESS AND MANAGEMENT
  PHYSICAL SCIENCES

===

BROOKDALE COMMUNITY COLLEGE
NEWMAN SPRINGS ROAD
LINCROFT, NJ 07738
201-842-1900

KEY CONTACT: Attn: Handicapped Student Services

SIZE OF SCHOOL: LARGE

APPLICATION DEADLINE: NONE

	APPROXIMATE TUITION	ROOM AND BOARD
IN DISTRICT	$ 750	$NOT OFFERED
IN STATE	$1500	$NOT OFFERED
OUT-OF-STATE	$3000	$NOT OFFERED

REQUIREMENTS FOR ADMISSIONS:
  High school equivalency diploma
  High school diploma
  18 years of age or older, with or without a
    high school diploma or equivalency
  University or College sponsored tests
  Personal interview

ADDITIONAL SERVICES OFFERED:
  Learning Lab
  Learning Lab has a specialist with a masters degree
    or above in Learning Disabilities
  Diagnostic testing services on campus
  Remedial and/or tutorial help available
  Handicapped student services works with LD

MODIFICATIONS TO TRADITIONAL LEARNING ENVIRONMENT:
  Oral presentation in lieu of written exams
  Tape recorders to record class lectures
  Someone else may take class notes
  Student takes exams in separate rooms
  Students have exams read to them
  Longer time allowed to complete exams
  Submit papers on cassette tape
  Extended time limits for graduation

MAJORS OFFERED:

  BIOLOGICAL SCIENCES
  BUSINESS AND MANAGEMENT
  COMMUNICATIONS
  EDUCATION
  ENGINEERING TECHNOLOGIES
  FINE AND APPLIED ARTS
  FOREIGN LANGUAGES
  HUMANITIES
  MATHEMATICS
  PHYSICAL SCIENCES
  PSYCHOLOGY

PUBLIC SERVICES
SOCIAL SCIENCES
GENERAL LIBERAL ARTS

===

BURLINGTON COUNTY COLLEGE
PEMBERTON-BROWNS MILLS ROAD
PEMBERTON, NJ 08068
609-893-4005

KEY CONTACT: Attn: DR. DOUGLAS A. DEVOLL
                    ASSOC. DEAN OF STUDENT DEVELOPMENT

SIZE OF SCHOOL: MEDIUM

APPLICATION DEADLINE: NONE

         APPROXIMATE TUITION   ROOM AND BOARD

IN DISTRICT $ 840 $NOT OFFERED
IN STATE $ 930 $NOT OFFERED
OUT-OF-STATE $2310 $NOT OFFERED

REQUIREMENTS FOR ADMISSIONS:
  High school equivalency diploma
  High school diploma
  University or College sponsored tests
  Placement tests

ADDITIONAL SERVICES OFFERED:
  Remedial and/or tutorial help available
  Handicapped student services works with LD

MODIFICATIONS TO TRADITIONAL LEARNING ENVIRONMENT:
  Oral presentation in lieu of written exams
  Use of calculator for all math courses
  Has an adaptive physical education program
  Tape recorders to record class lectures
  Someone else may take class notes
  Students have exams read to them
  Longer time allowed to complete exams
  Extended time limits for graduation

MAJORS OFFERED:

  ARCHITECTURE
  BIOLOGICAL SCIENCES
  BUSINESS AND MANAGEMENT
  COMMUNICATIONS
  COMPUTER SCIENCES

```
EDUCATION
ENGINEERING TECHNOLOGIES
FINE AND APPLIED ARTS
FOREIGN LANGUAGES
HEALTH
HUMANITIES
MATHEMATICS
PHYSICAL SCIENCES
PSYCHOLOGY
SOCIAL SCIENCES
GENERAL LIBERAL ARTS
```

==

```
OCEAN COUNTY COLLEGE
ONE COLLEGE DRIVE
TOMS RIVER, NJ 08753
201-255-4000
```

KEY CONTACT: Attn: NANCY POLONITZA, COUNSELOR

SIZE OF SCHOOL: MEDIUM

APPLICATION DEADLINE: NONE

	APPROXIMATE TUITION	ROOM AND BOARD
IN DISTRICT	$ 805	$NOT OFFERED
IN STATE	$ 925	$NOT OFFERED
OUT-OF-STATE	$2800	$NOT OFFERED

REQUIREMENTS FOR ADMISSIONS:
  High school equivalency diploma
  High school diploma
  18 years of age or older, with or without a
    high school diploma or equivalency
  Untimed or oral ACT Scores accepted
  Untimed or oral SAT Scores accepted
  Placement tests
  Essay
  Open admissions

ADDITIONAL SERVICES OFFERED:
  Diagnostic testing services off campus
  Remedial and/or tutorial help available
  Handicapped student services works with LD

MODIFICATIONS TO TRADITIONAL LEARNING ENVIRONMENT:
  Use of calculator for all math courses
  Tape recorders to record class lectures
  Extended time limits for graduation

Other modifications can be arranged depending on
   faculty

MAJORS OFFERED:

   BUSINESS AND MANAGEMENT
   COMPUTER SCIENCES
   EDUCATION
   ENGINEERING TECHNOLOGIES
   FINE AND APPLIED ARTS
   FOREIGN LANGUAGES
   HUMANITIES
   MATHEMATICS
   PHYSICAL SCIENCES
   PSYCHOLOGY
   SOCIAL SCIENCES
   GENERAL LIBERAL ARTS

===

BROOME COMMUNITY COLLEGE
P.O. BOX 1017
BINGHAMTON, NY 13902
607-771-5001

KEY CONTACT: Attn: MARY SCHWIN
                    COORDINATOR FOR DISABLED

SIZE OF SCHOOL: MEDIUM

APPLICATION DEADLINE: NONE

        APPROXIMATE TUITION   ROOM AND BOARD

IN DISTRICT $ 865 $NOT OFFERED
IN STATE $ 865 $NOT OFFERED
OUT-OF-STATE $1665 $NOT OFFERED

REQUIREMENTS FOR ADMISSIONS:
   21 years of age or older, with or without a
      high school diploma or equivalency
   SAT Scores required
   Untimed or oral SAT Scores accepted
   No High School Diploma or equivalency required for
      entry but placement tests must be taken

ADDITIONAL SERVICES OFFERED:
   Learning Lab
   Diagnostic testing services on campus
   Diagnostic testing services off campus
   Remedial and/or tutorial help available

Reader services for the blind available for LD
Handicapped student services works with LD

MODIFICATIONS TO TRADITIONAL LEARNING ENVIRONMENT:
 Oral presentation in lieu of written exams
 Use of calculator for all math courses
 Has an adaptive physical education program
 Tape recorders to record class lectures
 Someone else may take class notes
 Student takes exams in separate rooms
 Students have exams read to them
 Longer time allowed to complete exams
 Submit papers on cassette tape
 Extended time limits for graduation
 Physical education may be waived

MAJORS OFFERED:

 BUSINESS AND MANAGEMENT
 COMPUTER SCIENCES
 ENGINEERING TECHNOLOGIES
 HEALTH
 GENERAL LIBERAL ARTS

==

ELIZABETH SETON COLLEGE
1061 NORTH BROADWAY
YONKERS, NY 10701
914-969-4000

KEY CONTACT: Attn: KATHRYN LANSON, COORDINATOR
                    COLLEGE ASSISTANCE PROGRAM

SIZE OF SCHOOL: SMALL

APPLICATION DEADLINE: NONE

         APPROXIMATE TUITION   ROOM AND BOARD

IN DISTRICT $3200 $2600
IN STATE $3200 $2600
OUT-OF-STATE $3200 $2600

REQUIREMENTS FOR ADMISSIONS:
 High school equivalency diploma
 High school diploma
 Untimed or oral ACT Scores accepted
 Untimed or oral SAT Scores accepted
 WAIS scores required
 High school grade point average 2.0

Personal interview
Placement tests
Recommendations
Essay

ADDITIONAL SERVICES OFFERED:
  Learning Lab
  Learning Lab has a specialist with a masters degree
    or above in Learning Disabilities
  Diagnostic testing services on campus
  Diagnostic testing services off campus
  Remedial and/or tutorial help available
  Reader services for the blind available for LD
  Handicapped student services works with LD

MODIFICATIONS TO TRADITIONAL LEARNING ENVIRONMENT:
  Oral presentation in lieu of written exams
  Use of calculator for all math courses
  Has an adaptive physical education program
  Tape recorders to record class lectures
  Someone else may take class notes
  Student takes exams in separate rooms
  Students have exams read to them
  Longer time allowed to complete exams
  Submit papers on cassette tape
  Take limited course load and graduate within time
    required
  Extended time limits for graduation
  Physical education may be waived

MAJORS OFFERED:

  BUSINESS AND MANAGEMENT
  COMMUNICATIONS
  EDUCATION
  FINE AND APPLIED ARTS
  HEALTH
  PHYSICAL SCIENCES
  GENERAL LIBERAL ARTS

==

HERKIMER COMMUNITY COLLEGE
RESERVOIR ROAD
HERKIMER, NY 13350
315-866-0300

KEY CONTACT: Attn: P.M. BAIN, PLACEMENT COUNSELOR

SIZE OF SCHOOL: SMALL

APPLICATION DEADLINE: NONE

	APPROXIMATE TUITION	ROOM AND BOARD
IN DISTRICT	$ 880	$NOT OFFERED
IN STATE	$ 880	$NOT OFFERED
OUT-OF-STATE	$1660	$NOT OFFERED

REQUIREMENTS FOR ADMISSIONS:
  Admission requirements modified
  Personal interview

ADDITIONAL SERVICES OFFERED:
  Remedial and/or tutorial help available

MODIFICATIONS TO TRADITIONAL LEARNING ENVIRONMENT:
  Oral presentation in lieu of written exams
  Use of calculator for all math courses
  Tape recorders to record class lectures
  Someone else may take class notes
  Student takes exams in separate rooms
  Longer time allowed to complete exams

MAJORS OFFERED:

  AGRICULTURE
  ARCHITECTURE
  AREA STUDIES
  BIOLOGICAL SCIENCES
  BUSINESS AND MANAGEMENT
  COMMUNICATIONS
  COMPUTER SCIENCES
  EDUCATION
  ENGINEERING TECHNOLOGIES
  FINE AND APPLIED ARTS
  HEALTH
  HUMANITIES
  MATHEMATICS
  PHYSICAL SCIENCES
  PSYCHOLOGY
  PUBLIC SERVICES
  SOCIAL SCIENCES
  GENERAL LIBERAL ARTS

===

HUDSON VALLEY COMMUNITY COLLEGE
80 VANDENBURGH AVENUE
TROY, NY 12180
518-283-1100

KEY CONTACT: Attn: PABLO E. NEGRON JR., COORDINATOR
                     DISABLED STUDENT SERVICES

SIZE OF SCHOOL: MEDIUM

APPLICATION DEADLINE: NONE

         APPROXIMATE TUITION   ROOM AND BOARD

IN DISTRICT $1200 $NOT OFFERED
IN STATE $1200 $NOT OFFERED
OUT-OF-STATE $2300 $NOT OFFERED

REQUIREMENTS FOR ADMISSIONS:
   High school equivalency diploma
   High school diploma
   21 years of age or older, with or without a
      high school diploma or equivalency

ADDITIONAL SERVICES OFFERED:
   Learning Lab
   Diagnostic testing services off campus
   Remedial and/or tutorial help available
   Reader services for the blind available for LD
   Handicapped student services works with LD

MODIFICATIONS TO TRADITIONAL LEARNING ENVIRONMENT:
   Tape recorders to record class lectures
   Someone else may take class notes
   Student takes exams in separate rooms
   Students have exams read to them
   Students take typewritten exams
   Longer time allowed to complete exams

MAJORS OFFERED:

   BIOLOGICAL SCIENCES
   BUSINESS AND MANAGEMENT
   ENGINEERING TECHNOLOGIES
   HEALTH
   HUMANITIES
   MATHEMATICS
   PHYSICAL SCIENCES
   SOCIAL SCIENCES
   GENERAL LIBERAL ARTS

==

NASSAU COMMUNITY COLLEGE
STEWART AVENUE
GARDEN CITY, NY 11530
516-222-7345

KEY CONTACT: Attn: DR. VICTOR MARGOLIS, COORDINATOR
                    DISABLED STUDENT SERVICES

SIZE OF SCHOOL: LARGE

APPLICATION DEADLINE: JULY 8

          APPROXIMATE TUITION   ROOM AND BOARD

IN DISTRICT $1160 $NOT OFFERED
IN STATE $1160 $NOT OFFERED
OUT-OF-STATE $2320 $NOT OFFERED

REQUIREMENTS FOR ADMISSIONS:
  High school equivalency diploma
  High school diploma
  21 years of age or older, with or without a
    high school diploma or equivalency
  University or College sponsored tests
  Personal interview
  Placement tests
  Recommendations

ADDITIONAL SERVICES OFFERED:
  Diagnostic testing services off campus
  Remedial and/or tutorial help available
  Reader services for the blind available for LD
  Handicapped student services works with LD

MODIFICATIONS TO TRADITIONAL LEARNING ENVIRONMENT:
  Oral presentation in lieu of written exams
  Use of calculator for all math courses
  Has an adaptive physical education program
  Tape recorders to record class lectures
  Someone else may take class notes
  Multiple choice exams only
  Essay exams only
  Student takes exams in separate rooms
  Students have exams read to them
  Students take typewritten exams
  Longer time allowed to complete exams
  Submit papers on cassette tape
  Extended time limits for graduation
  All modifications depend on individual teacher

MAJORS OFFERED:

    AGRICULTURE
    ARCHITECTURE
    BIOLOGICAL SCIENCES
    BUSINESS AND MANAGEMENT
    COMMUNICATIONS
    COMPUTER SCIENCES
    ENGINEERING TECHNOLOGIES
    FINE AND APPLIED ARTS
    FOREIGN LANGUAGES
    HEALTH
    HUMANITIES
    MATHEMATICS
    PHYSICAL SCIENCES
    PSYCHOLOGY
    PUBLIC SERVICES
    SOCIAL SCIENCES
    GENERAL LIBERAL ARTS

===

ROCKLAND COMMUNITY COLLEGE
145 COLLEGE ROAD
SUFFERN, NY 10901
914-356-4650

KEY CONTACT: Attn: ELLEN SPEGEL, COORDINATOR
                     DISABLED STUDENT SERVICES

SIZE OF SCHOOL: MEDIUM

APPLICATION DEADLINE: SEPTEMBER 1

        APPROXIMATE TUITION   ROOM AND BOARD

IN DISTRICT $1160 $NOT OFFERED
IN STATE $1160 $NOT OFFERED
OUT-OF-STATE $2250 $NOT OFFERED

REQUIREMENTS FOR ADMISSIONS:
    16 years of age or older, with or without a
       high school diploma or equivalency
    Placement tests

ADDITIONAL SERVICES OFFERED:
    Learning Lab
    Remedial and/or tutorial help available
    Reader services for the blind available for LD
    Handicapped student services works with LD

MODIFICATIONS TO TRADITIONAL LEARNING ENVIRONMENT:
   Oral presentation in lieu of written exams
   Use of calculator for all math courses
   Tape recorders to record class lectures
   Someone else may take class notes
   Student takes exams in separate rooms
   Students have exams read to them
   Students take typewritten exams
   Longer time allowed to complete exams
   Submit papers on cassette tape
   Extended time limits for graduation
   Physical education may be waived

MAJORS OFFERED:

   BIOLOGICAL SCIENCES
   BUSINESS AND MANAGEMENT
   COMMUNICATIONS
   COMPUTER SCIENCES
   ENGINEERING TECHNOLOGIES
   FINE AND APPLIED ARTS
   FOREIGN LANGUAGES
   HEALTH
   HUMANITIES
   MATHEMATICS
   PHYSICAL SCIENCES
   PSYCHOLOGY
   SOCIAL SCIENCES
   GENERAL LIBERAL ARTS

===

TOMPKINS CORTLAND COMMUNITY COLLEGE
170 NORTH STREET
DRYDEN, NY 13053
607-844-8211

KEY CONTACT: Attn: MARLENE BLUMIN, COORDINATOR
                     BASIC SKILLS DEVELOPMENT

SIZE OF SCHOOL: MEDIUM

APPLICATION DEADLINE: NONE

	APPROXIMATE TUITION	ROOM AND BOARD
IN DISTRICT	$1000	$NOT OFFERED
IN STATE	$1000	$NOT OFFERED
OUT-OF-STATE	$1000	$NOT OFFERED

REQUIREMENTS FOR ADMISSIONS:
  Untimed or oral ACT Scores accepted
  Untimed or oral SAT Scores accepted
  WAIS scores required (preferred)
  University or College sponsored tests
  Admission requirements modified
  Personal interview
  Placement tests

ADDITIONAL SERVICES OFFERED:
  Learning Lab
  Learning Lab has a specialist with a masters degree
    or above in Learning Disabilities
  Diagnostic testing services on campus
  Tutorial help available
  Reader services for the blind available for LD
  Handicapped student services works with LD

MODIFICATIONS TO TRADITIONAL LEARNING ENVIRONMENT:
  Oral presentation in lieu of written exams
  Has an adaptive physical education program
  Tape recorders to record class lectures
  Someone else may take class notes
  Student takes exams in separate rooms
  Students have exams read to them
  Students take typewritten exams
  Longer time allowed to complete exams
  Submit papers on cassette tape
  Take limited course load and graduate within time
    required
  Extended time limits for graduation
  Physical education may be waived

MAJORS OFFERED:

  BUSINESS AND MANAGEMENT
  COMMUNICATIONS
  COMPUTER SCIENCES
  ENGINEERING TECHNOLOGIES
  HEALTH
  PUBLIC SERVICES
  GENERAL LIBERAL ARTS

==

ANSON TECHNICAL COLLEGE
P.O. BOX 68
ANSONVILLE, NC 28007
704-826-8333

```
KEY CONTACT: Attn:   ALGIE C. GATEWOOD
                     DEAN OF STUDENTS

SIZE OF SCHOOL: SMALL

APPLICATION DEADLINE: NONE

        APPROXIMATE TUITION    ROOM AND BOARD

IN DISTRICT        $ 175        $NOT OFFERED
IN STATE           $ 175        $NOT OFFERED
OUT-OF-STATE       $ 815        $NOT OFFERED
```

REQUIREMENTS FOR ADMISSIONS:
   High school equivalency diploma
   High school diploma
   University or College sponsored tests
   Admission requirements modified
   Personal interview

ADDITIONAL SERVICES OFFERED:
   Learning Lab
   Diagnostic testing services on campus
   Remedial and/or tutorial help available
   Handicapped student services works with LD

MODIFICATIONS TO TRADITIONAL LEARNING ENVIRONMENT:
   Oral presentation in lieu of written exams
   Tape recorders to record class lectures
   Someone else may take class notes
   Students have exams read to them
   Students take typewritten exams
   Longer time allowed to complete exams
   Submit papers on cassette tape
   Extended time limits for graduation
   Physical education may be waived

MAJORS OFFERED:

   BUSINESS AND MANAGEMENT
   COMPUTER SCIENCES
   ENGINEERING TECHNOLOGIES
   HEALTH
   PUBLIC SERVICES
   GENERAL LIBERAL ARTS

==

CALDWELL COMMUNITY COLLEGE AND TECHNICAL INSTITUTE
1000 HICKORY BLVD
HUDSON, NC 28638
704-728-4323

KEY CONTACT: Attn: ELAINE SETZER, COUNSELOR

SIZE OF SCHOOL: SMALL

APPLICATION DEADLINE: NONE

	APPROXIMATE TUITION	ROOM AND BOARD
IN DISTRICT	$ 225	$NOT OFFERED
IN STATE	$ 225	$NOT OFFERED
OUT-OF-STATE	$1040	$NOT OFFERED

REQUIREMENTS FOR ADMISSIONS:
  High school equivalency diploma
  High school diploma
  21 years of age or older, with or without a
    high school diploma or equivalency
  University or College sponsored tests
  Admission requirements modified
  Placement tests

ADDITIONAL SERVICES OFFERED:
  Learning Lab
  Diagnostic testing services on campus
  Remedial and/or tutorial help available
  Reader services for the blind available for LD
  Handicapped student services works with LD

MODIFICATIONS TO TRADITIONAL LEARNING ENVIRONMENT:
  Oral presentation in lieu of written exams
  Use of calculator for all math courses
  Has an adaptive physical education program
  Tape recorders to record class lectures
  Someone else may take class notes
  Student takes exams in separate rooms
  Students have exams read to them
  Longer time allowed to complete exams
  Physical education may be waived

MAJORS OFFERED:

  BIOLOGICAL SCIENCES
  BUSINESS AND MANAGEMENT
  COMMUNICATIONS
  COMPUTER SCIENCES
  EDUCATION

```
ENGINEERING TECHNOLOGIES
HEALTH
MATHEMATICS
PHYSICAL SCIENCES
GENERAL LIBERAL ARTS
```

==

```
CENTRAL PIEDMONT COMMUNITY COLLEGE
P.O. BOX 35009
CHARLOTTE, NC 28235
704-373-6687
```

KEY CONTACT: Attn: Handicapped Student Services

SIZE OF SCHOOL: LARGE

APPLICATION DEADLINE: NONE

	APPROXIMATE TUITION	ROOM AND BOARD
IN DISTRICT	$ 160	$NOT OFFERED
IN STATE	$ 160	$NOT OFFERED
OUT-OF-STATE	$ 800	$NOT OFFERED

REQUIREMENTS FOR ADMISSIONS:
  High school equivalency diploma
  High school diploma
  18 years of age or older, with or without a
    high school diploma or equivalency
  University or College sponsored tests
  Admission requirements modified
  Personal interview
  Placement tests

ADDITIONAL SERVICES OFFERED:
  Learning Lab
  Learning Lab has a specialist with a masters degree
    or above in Learning Disabilities
  Diagnostic testing services on campus
  Remedial and/or tutorial help available
  Reader services for the blind available for LD
  Special Education department
  Handicapped student services works with LD

MODIFICATIONS TO TRADITIONAL LEARNING ENVIRONMENT:
  Oral presentation in lieu of written exams
  Use of calculator for all math courses
  Has an adaptive physical education program
  Tape recorders to record class lectures
  Someone else may take class notes

     Students have exams read to them
     Longer time allowed to complete exams
     Submit papers on cassette tape
     Extended time limits for graduation
     All services are specially designed for each student

MAJORS OFFERED:

     AGRICULTURE
     ARCHITECTURE
     BIOLOGICAL SCIENCES
     BUSINESS AND MANAGEMENT
     COMMUNICATIONS
     COMPUTER SCIENCES
     EDUCATION
     ENGINEERING TECHNOLOGIES
     FINE AND APPLIED ARTS
     FOREIGN LANGUAGES
     HEALTH
     HUMANITIES
     LIBRARY SCIENCE
     MATHEMATICS
     PHYSICAL SCIENCES
     PSYCHOLOGY
     PUBLIC SERVICES
     SOCIAL SCIENCES
     GENERAL LIBERAL ARTS

===

FORSYTH TECHNICAL INSTITUTE
2100 SILAS CREEK PARKWAY
WINSTON-SALEM, NC 27103
919-723-0371

KEY CONTACT: Attn: SUSAN Q. PHELPS, DEAN

SIZE OF SCHOOL: SMALL

APPLICATION DEADLINE: AUGUST 18

          APPROXIMATE TUITION   ROOM AND BOARD

IN DISTRICT $ 180 $NOT OFFERED
IN STATE $ 180 $NOT OFFERED
OUT-OF-STATE $ 815 $NOT OFFERED

REQUIREMENTS FOR ADMISSIONS:
  High school equivalency diploma
  High school diploma
  Untimed or oral ACT Scores accepted

Untimed or oral SAT Scores accepted
University or College sponsored tests
Personal interview
Placement tests

ADDITIONAL SERVICES OFFERED:
Learning Lab
Learning Lab has a specialist with a masters degree
  or above in Learning Disabilities
Diagnostic testing services on campus
Diagnostic testing services off campus
Remedial and/or tutorial help available
Reader services for the blind available for LD
Handicapped student services works with LD

MODIFICATIONS TO TRADITIONAL LEARNING ENVIRONMENT:
Oral presentation in lieu of written exams
Tape recorders to record class lectures
Someone else may take class notes
Students have exams read to them
Students take typewritten exams
Longer time allowed to complete exams
Submit papers on cassette tape
Extended time limits for graduation

MAJORS OFFERED:

AGRICULTURE
BUSINESS AND MANAGEMENT
COMPUTER SCIENCES
ENGINEERING TECHNOLOGIES
HEALTH
PUBLIC SERVICES

==

NORTH DAKOTA STATE SCHOOL OF SCIENCE
800 NORTH 6TH STREET
WAHPETON, ND 58075
701-671-2201

KEY CONTACT: Attn: PAULA AHLES
                    SPECIAL NEEDS COUNSELOR

SIZE OF SCHOOL: MEDIUM

APPLICATION DEADLINE: JULY 1

```
        APPROXIMATE TUITION   ROOM AND BOARD

IN DISTRICT        $ 630      $1600
IN STATE           $ 630      $1600
OUT-OF-STATE       $1195      $1600
```

REQUIREMENTS FOR ADMISSIONS:
  High school equivalency diploma
  ACT Scores required
  Untimed or oral ACT Scores accepted
  Untimed or oral SAT Scores accepted
  University or College sponsored tests
  Personal interview

ADDITIONAL SERVICES OFFERED:
  Learning Lab
  Remedial and/or tutorial help available
  Reader services for the blind available for LD
  Handicapped student services works with LD

MODIFICATIONS TO TRADITIONAL LEARNING ENVIRONMENT:
  Oral presentation in lieu of written exams
  Use of calculator for all math courses
  Tape recorders to record class lectures
  Someone else may take class notes
  Student takes exams in separate rooms
  Students have exams read to them
  Students take typewritten exams
  Longer time allowed to complete exams
  Submit papers on cassette tape
  Extended time limits for graduation
  Physical education may be waived

MAJORS OFFERED:

  BUSINESS AND MANAGEMENT
  COMPUTER SCIENCES
  EDUCATION
  ENGINEERING TECHNOLOGIES
  HEALTH
  GENERAL LIBERAL ARTS

==

CUYAHOGA COMMUNITY COLLEGE - METROPOLITAN
2900 COMMUNITY COLLEGE AVENUE
CLEVELAND, OH 44115
216-241-5365

KEY CONTACT: Attn: PENNY GOLDSTINE, COUNSELOR

SIZE OF SCHOOL: MEDIUM

APPLICATION DEADLINE: NONE

	APPROXIMATE TUITION	ROOM AND BOARD
IN DISTRICT	$ 445	$NOT OFFERED
IN STATE	$ 590	$NOT OFFERED
OUT-OF-STATE	$ 925	$NOT OFFERED

REQUIREMENTS FOR ADMISSIONS:
   Untimed or oral ACT Scores accepted
   Untimed or oral SAT Scores accepted
   University or College sponsored tests
   Personal interview
   Placement tests
   Recommendations

ADDITIONAL SERVICES OFFERED:
   Diagnostic testing services off campus
   Remedial and/or tutorial help available
   Reader services for the blind available for LD
   Handicapped student services works with LD

MODIFICATIONS TO TRADITIONAL LEARNING ENVIRONMENT:
   Oral presentation in lieu of written exams
   Use of calculator for all math courses
   Has an adaptive physical education program
   Tape recorders to record class lectures
   Someone else may take class notes
   Multiple choice exams only
   Essay exams only
   Student takes exams in separate rooms
   Students have exams read to them
   Students take typewritten exams
   Longer time allowed to complete exams
   Submit papers on cassette tape
   Extended time limits for graduation
   Physical education may be waived

MAJORS OFFERED:

   AGRICULTURE
   ARCHITECTURE
   BIOLOGICAL SCIENCES
   COMMUNICATIONS
   COMPUTER SCIENCES
   FINE AND APPLIED ARTS
   FOREIGN LANGUAGES
   HOME ECONOMICS
   LIBRARY SCIENCE

MATHEMATICS
PHYSICAL SCIENCES
PSYCHOLOGY
PUBLIC SERVICES
SOCIAL SCIENCES
THEOLOGY
GENERAL LIBERAL ARTS

==

CUYAHOGA COMMUNITY COLLEGE - WESTERN
11000 WEST PLEASANT VALLEY ROAD
PARMA, OH 44130
216-842-7773

KEY CONTACT: Attn: LOUIS NIRO

SIZE OF SCHOOL: LARGE

APPLICATION DEADLINE: NONE

	APPROXIMATE TUITION	ROOM AND BOARD
IN DISTRICT	$ 720	$NOT OFFERED
IN STATE	$ 945	$NOT OFFERED
OUT-OF-STATE	$1485	$NOT OFFERED

REQUIREMENTS FOR ADMISSIONS:
   University or College sponsored tests
   Admission requirements modified
   Personal interview
   Placement tests
   Recommendations

ADDITIONAL SERVICES OFFERED:
   Learning Lab
   Diagnostic testing services on campus
   Remedial and/or tutorial help available
   Reader services for the blind available for LD
   Handicapped student services works with LD

MODIFICATIONS TO TRADITIONAL LEARNING ENVIRONMENT:
   Oral presentation in lieu of written exams
   Has an adaptive physical education program
   Tape recorders to record class lectures
   Someone else may take class notes
   Student takes exams in separate rooms
   Students have exams read to them
   Students take typewritten exams
   Longer time allowed to complete exams
   Submit papers on cassette tape

```
    Extended time limits for graduation
    Physical education may be waived
```

MAJORS OFFERED:

```
    BUSINESS AND MANAGEMENT
    COMPUTER SCIENCES
    ENGINEERING TECHNOLOGIES
    HEALTH
    PUBLIC SERVICES
    GENERAL LIBERAL ARTS
```

==

```
NORTHEASTERN OKLAHOMA AGRGICULTURE & MECHANICAL COLLEGE
3RD AND I, NE
MIAMI, OK 74354
918-542-8441
```

KEY CONTACT: Attn: DR. J.D. WILHOIT, ASSOC. DEAN

SIZE OF SCHOOL: SMALL

APPLICATION DEADLINE: NONE

	APPROXIMATE TUITION	ROOM AND BOARD
IN DISTRICT	$ 340	$1275
IN STATE	$ 340	$1275
OUT-OF-STATE	$ 880	$1275

REQUIREMENTS FOR ADMISSIONS:
```
    High school equivalency diploma
    High school diploma
    21 years of age or older, with or without a
      high school diploma or equivalency
    ACT Scores required
    Untimed or oral ACT Scores accepted
    Admission requirements modified
```

ADDITIONAL SERVICES OFFERED:
```
    Learning Lab
    Learning Lab has a specialist with a masters degree
      or above in Learning Disabilities
    Diagnostic testing services on campus
    Diagnostic testing services off campus
    Remedial and/or tutorial help available
    Special Education department
```

MODIFICATIONS TO TRADITIONAL LEARNING ENVIRONMENT:
  Oral presentation in lieu of written exams
  Tape recorders to record class lectures
  Someone else may take class notes
  Students have exams read to them
  Students take typewritten exams
  Longer time allowed to complete exams
  Submit papers on cassette tape
  Take limited course load and graduate within time
    required
  Extended time limits for graduation
  Physical education may be waived

MAJORS OFFERED:

  AGRICULTURE
  BIOLOGICAL SCIENCES
  BUSINESS AND MANAGEMENT
  COMMUNICATIONS
  EDUCATION
  ENGINEERING TECHNOLOGIES
  FINE AND APPLIED ARTS
  HEALTH
  HOME ECONOMICS
  MATHEMATICS
  PHYSICAL SCIENCES
  PUBLIC SERVICES
  SOCIAL SCIENCES
  GENERAL LIBERAL ARTS

===

TULSA JUNIOR COLLEGE
6111 EAST SKELLY DRIVE
TULSA, OK 74135
918-622-5100

KEY CONTACT: Attn: BOBBIE WOODWARD
                    DIRECTOR OF HANDICAPPED

SIZE OF SCHOOL: LARGE

APPLICATION DEADLINE: NONE

          APPROXIMATE TUITION   ROOM AND BOARD

IN DISTRICT $ 345 $NOT OFFERED
IN STATE $ 345 $NOT OFFERED
OUT-OF-STATE $ 905 $NOT OFFERED

REQUIREMENTS FOR ADMISSIONS:
  High school equivalency diploma
  ACT Scores required

ADDITIONAL SERVICES OFFERED:
  Diagnostic testing services on campus
  Remedial and/or tutorial help available
  Reader services for the blind available for LD
  Handicapped student services works with LD

MODIFICATIONS TO TRADITIONAL LEARNING ENVIRONMENT:
  Oral presentation in lieu of written exams
  Use of calculator for all math courses
  Tape recorders to record class lectures
  Someone else may take class notes
  Students have exams read to them

MAJORS OFFERED:

  AGRICULTURE
  ARCHITECTURE
  BIOLOGICAL SCIENCES
  BUSINESS AND MANAGEMENT
  COMMUNICATIONS
  COMPUTER SCIENCES
  EDUCATION
  ENGINEERING TECHNOLOGIES
  FINE AND APPLIED ARTS
  FOREIGN LANGUAGES
  HEALTH
  HUMANITIES
  LIBRARY SCIENCE
  MATHEMATICS
  PHYSICAL SCIENCES
  PSYCHOLOGY
  PUBLIC SERVICES
  SOCIAL SCIENCES
  GENERAL LIBERAL ARTS

===

BLUE MOUNTAIN COMMUNITY COLLEGE
P.O. BOX 100
PENDLETON, OR 97801
503-276-1260

KEY CONTACT: Attn: CYNTHIA HILDEN
                  DEVELOPMENTAL ED COORDINATOR

SIZE OF SCHOOL: SMALL

APPLICATION DEADLINE: NONE

APPROXIMATE TUITION   ROOM AND BOARD

IN DISTRICT	$ 540	$NOT OFFERED
IN STATE	$ 800	$NOT OFFERED
OUT-OF-STATE	$2160	$NOT OFFERED

REQUIREMENTS FOR ADMISSIONS:
  19 years of age or older, with or without a
    high school diploma or equivalency
  University or College sponsored tests
  Admission requirements modified
  Placement tests
  Essay

ADDITIONAL SERVICES OFFERED:
  Learning Lab
  Learning Lab has a specialist with a masters degree
    or above in Learning Disabilities
  Remedial and/or tutorial help available
  Reader services for the blind available for LD
  Handicapped student services works with LD

MODIFICATIONS TO TRADITIONAL LEARNING ENVIRONMENT:
  Oral presentation in lieu of written exams
  Use of calculator for all math courses
  Tape recorders to record class lectures
  Someone else may take class notes
  Student takes exams in separate rooms
  Students have exams read to them
  Students take typewritten exams
  Longer time allowed to complete exams
  Extended time limits for graduation
  Physical education may be waived

MAJORS OFFERED:

  AGRICULTURE
  BUSINESS AND MANAGEMENT
  COMPUTER SCIENCES
  ENGINEERING TECHNOLOGIES
  HEALTH
  PUBLIC SERVICES
  GENERAL LIBERAL ARTS

===

CLACKAMAS COMMUNITY COLLEGE
OREGON CITY, OR 97045
503-657-8400

KEY CONTACT: Attn: DEBBIE DERR
                     HANDICAP SPECIALIST

SIZE OF SCHOOL: MEDIUM

APPLICATION DEADLINE: NONE

          APPROXIMATE TUITION   ROOM AND BOARD

IN DISTRICT $ 600 $NOT OFFERED
IN STATE $ 600 $NOT OFFERED
OUT-OF-STATE $2190 $NOT OFFERED

REQUIREMENTS FOR ADMISSIONS:
  Untimed or oral SAT Scores accepted
  University or College sponsored tests
  Admission requirements modified
  Personal interview
  Placement tests

ADDITIONAL SERVICES OFFERED:
  Learning Lab
  Diagnostic testing services off campus
  Remedial and/or tutorial help available
  Reader services for the blind available for LD
  Handicapped student services works with LD
  In the process of expanding program

MODIFICATIONS TO TRADITIONAL LEARNING ENVIRONMENT:
  Oral presentation in lieu of written exams
  Use of calculator for all math courses
  Has an adaptive physical education program
  Tape recorders to record class lectures
  Someone else may take class notes
  Student takes exams in separate rooms
  Students have exams read to them
  Students take typewritten exams
  Longer time allowed to complete exams
  Submit papers on cassette tape
  Take limited course load and graduate within time
    required
  Extended time limits for graduation
  Physical education may be waived

MAJORS OFFERED:

  AGRICULTURE
  AREA STUDIES
  BIOLOGICAL SCIENCES
  BUSINESS AND MANAGEMENT
  COMMUNICATIONS

```
COMPUTER SCIENCES
EDUCATION
ENGINEERING TECHNOLOGIES
FINE AND APPLIED ARTS
FOREIGN LANGUAGES
HEALTH
HOME ECONOMICS
HUMANITIES
MATHEMATICS
PHYSICAL SCIENCES
PSYCHOLOGY
PUBLIC SERVICES
SOCIAL SCIENCES
THEOLOGY
GENERAL LIBERAL ARTS
```

===

```
PORTLAND COMMUNITY COLLEGE
12000 SW 49TH AVENUE
PORTLAND, OR 97219
503-244-6111
```

KEY CONTACT: Attn: CAROLEE SCHMEER, LD SPECIALIST

SIZE OF SCHOOL: LARGE

APPLICATION DEADLINE: NONE

	APPROXIMATE TUITION	ROOM AND BOARD
IN DISTRICT	$ 540	$NOT OFFERED
IN STATE	$1140	$NOT OFFERED
OUT-OF-STATE	$2925	$NOT OFFERED

REQUIREMENTS FOR ADMISSIONS:
  Untimed or oral ACT Scores accepted
  Untimed or oral SAT Scores accepted
  University or College sponsored tests
  Personal interview
  Placement tests
  Open door policy

ADDITIONAL SERVICES OFFERED:
  Learning Lab
  Learning Lab has a specialist with a masters degree
    or above in Learning Disabilities
  Diagnostic testing services on campus
  Remedial and/or tutorial help available
  Reader services for the blind available for LD
  Handicapped student services works with LD

MODIFICATIONS TO TRADITIONAL LEARNING ENVIRONMENT:
  Oral presentation in lieu of written exams
  Use of calculator for all math courses
  Has an adaptive physical education program
  Tape recorders to record class lectures
  Someone else may take class notes
  Longer time allowed to complete exams
  Submit papers on cassette tape
  Take limited course load and graduate within time
    required
  Extended time limits for graduation
  Physical education may be waived

MAJORS OFFERED:

  COMMUNICATIONS
  EDUCATION
  ENGINEERING TECHNOLOGIES
  HOME ECONOMICS
  GENERAL LIBERAL ARTS

==

COMMUNITY COLLEGE OF ALLEGHENY COUNTY
808 RIDGE AVENUE
PITTSBURGH, PA 15212
412-237-2511

KEY CONTACT: Attn: MARY BETH DOYLE

SIZE OF SCHOOL: MEDIUM

APPLICATION DEADLINE: NONE

	APPROXIMATE TUITION	ROOM AND BOARD
IN DISTRICT	$ 790	$NOT OFFERED
IN STATE	$1585	$NOT OFFERED
OUT-OF-STATE	$2375	$NOT OFFERED

REQUIREMENTS FOR ADMISSIONS:
  High school equivalency diploma
  High school diploma
  University or College sponsored tests
  Placement tests

ADDITIONAL SERVICES OFFERED:
  Learning Lab
  Learning Lab has a specialist with a masters degree
    or above in Learning Disabilities
  Diagnostic testing services on campus

Diagnostic testing services off campus
Remedial and/or tutorial help available
Handicapped student services works with LD

MODIFICATIONS TO TRADITIONAL LEARNING ENVIRONMENT:
Oral presentation in lieu of written exams
Has an adaptive physical education program
Tape recorders to record class lectures
Someone else may take class notes
Student takes exams in separate rooms
Students have exams read to them
Students take typewritten exams
Longer time allowed to complete exams

MAJORS OFFERED:

BIOLOGICAL SCIENCES
BUSINESS AND MANAGEMENT
COMMUNICATIONS
COMPUTER SCIENCES
EDUCATION
ENGINEERING TECHNOLOGIES
FINE AND APPLIED ARTS
FOREIGN LANGUAGES
HEALTH
HUMANITIES
MATHEMATICS
PHYSICAL SCIENCES
PUBLIC SERVICES
SOCIAL SCIENCES
GENERAL LIBERAL ARTS

===

DELAWARE COUNTY COMMUNITY COLLEGE
MEDIA, PA 19063
215-353-5400

KEY CONTACT: Attn: STUART J. DIX, COUNSELOR

SIZE OF SCHOOL: MEDIUM

APPLICATION DEADLINE: SEPTEMBER 4

	APPROXIMATE TUITION	ROOM AND BOARD
IN DISTRICT	$ 365	$NOT OFFERED
IN STATE	$ 810	$NOT OFFERED
OUT-OF-STATE	$1175	$NOT OFFERED

REQUIREMENTS FOR ADMISSIONS:
   21 years of age or older, with or without a
     high school diploma or equivalency
   ACT Scores required
   Untimed or oral ACT Scores accepted
   Untimed or oral SAT Scores accepted
   University or College sponsored tests
   Placement tests
   Essay
   State/District residency

ADDITIONAL SERVICES OFFERED:
   Learning Lab
   Remedial and/or tutorial help available
   Reader services for the blind available for LD
   Handicapped student services works with LD

MODIFICATIONS TO TRADITIONAL LEARNING ENVIRONMENT:
   Oral presentation in lieu of written exams
   Use of calculator for all math courses
   Tape recorders to record class lectures
   Someone else may take class notes
   Student takes exams in separate rooms
   Students have exams read to them
   Students take typewritten exams
   Longer time allowed to complete exams
   Submit papers on cassette tape
   Extended time limits for graduation
   Physical education may be waived

MAJORS OFFERED:

   BUSINESS AND MANAGEMENT
   ENGINEERING TECHNOLOGIES
   PHYSICAL SCIENCES
   GENERAL LIBERAL ARTS

===

NORTHHAMPTON COUNTY AREA COMMUNITY COLLEGE
3835 GREEN POND ROAD
BETHLEHEM, PA 18017
215-861-5500

KEY CONTACT: Attn: WENDY P. COLE, LD SPECIALIST

SIZE OF SCHOOL: MEDIUM

APPLICATION DEADLINE: NONE

```
      APPROXIMATE TUITION    ROOM AND BOARD

IN DISTRICT       $ 960      $NOT OFFERED
IN STATE          $1990      $NOT OFFERED
OUT-OF-STATE      $3025      $NOT OFFERED
```

REQUIREMENTS FOR ADMISSIONS:
  Untimed or oral ACT Scores accepted
  Untimed or oral SAT Scores accepted
  University or College sponsored tests
  Personal interview
  Placement tests

ADDITIONAL SERVICES OFFERED:
  Learning Lab
  Learning Lab has a specialist with a masters degree
    or above in Learning Disabilities
  Diagnostic testing services on campus
  Diagnostic testing services off campus
  Remedial and/or tutorial help available
  Handicapped student services works with LD

MODIFICATIONS TO TRADITIONAL LEARNING ENVIRONMENT:
  Oral presentation in lieu of written exams
  Use of calculator for all math courses
  Tape recorders to record class lectures
  Someone else may take class notes
  Student takes exams in separate rooms
  Students have exams read to them
  Students take typewritten exams
  Longer time allowed to complete exams
  Submit papers on cassette tape
  Take limited course load and graduate within time
    required
  Extended time limits for graduation
  Physical education may be waived

MAJORS OFFERED:

  ARCHITECTURE
  BIOLOGICAL SCIENCES
  BUSINESS AND MANAGEMENT
  EDUCATION
  ENGINEERING TECHNOLOGIES
  FINE AND APPLIED ARTS
  MATHEMATICS
  PHYSICAL SCIENCES
  GENERAL LIBERAL ARTS

==

```
PENNSYLVANIA INSTITUTE OF TECHNOLOGY
800 MANCHESTER AVENUE
MEDIA, PA 19063
215-565-7900

KEY CONTACT: Attn:  MARTHA FITZGERALD
                    DIRECTOR OF SPECIAL PROGAMS

SIZE OF SCHOOL: SMALL

APPLICATION DEADLINE: NONE

        APPROXIMATE TUITION   ROOM AND BOARD

IN DISTRICT       $1225         $NOT OFFERED
IN STATE          $1225         $NOT OFFERED
OUT-OF-STATE      $1225         $NOT OFFERED

REQUIREMENTS FOR ADMISSIONS:
  High school equivalency diploma
  High school diploma
  Admission requirements modified
  Personal interview
  Placement tests

ADDITIONAL SERVICES OFFERED:
  Learning Lab
  Diagnostic testing services on campus
  Remedial and/or tutorial help available

MODIFICATIONS TO TRADITIONAL LEARNING ENVIRONMENT:
  Oral presentation in lieu of written exams
  Use of calculator for all math courses
  Tape recorders to record class lectures
  Someone else may take class notes
  Students have exams read to them
  Longer time allowed to complete exams
  Extended time limits for graduation
  Physical education may be waived

MAJORS OFFERED:

ENGINEERING TECHNOLOGIES

===========================================================

DRAUGHON'S JUNIOR COLLEGE OF BUSINESS
NASHVILLE, TN 37217
615-361-7555

KEY CONTACT: Attn:  BILL GREENE, DEAN OF ADMISSIONS
```

SIZE OF SCHOOL: SMALL

APPLICATION DEADLINE: NONE

	APPROXIMATE TUITION	ROOM AND BOARD
IN DISTRICT	$2160	$NOT OFFERED
IN STATE	$2160	$NOT OFFERED
OUT-OF-STATE	$2160	$NOT OFFERED

REQUIREMENTS FOR ADMISSIONS:
  High school equivalency diploma
  High school diploma

ADDITIONAL SERVICES OFFERED:
  Remedial and/or tutorial help available

MODIFICATIONS TO TRADITIONAL LEARNING ENVIRONMENT:
  Oral presentation in lieu of written exams
  Use of calculator for all math courses
  Tape recorders to record class lectures
  Someone else may take class notes
  Student takes exams in separate rooms
  Students take typewritten exams
  Longer time allowed to complete exams
  Extended time limits for graduation
  Physical education may be waived

MAJORS OFFERED:

  BUSINESS AND MANAGEMENT
  COMPUTER SCIENCES
  HEALTH

==

WALTERS STATE COMMUNITY COLLEGE
DAVY CROCKET PARKWAY
MORRISTOWN, TN 37814
615-581-2121

KEY CONTACT: Attn: ANN BOWEN, COORDINATOR OF
                     HANDICAPPED SERVICES

SIZE OF SCHOOL: MEDIUM

APPLICATION DEADLINE: NONE

```
            APPROXIMATE TUITION    ROOM AND BOARD

IN DISTRICT        $ 470        $NOT OFFERED
IN STATE           $ 470        $NOT OFFERED
OUT-OF-STATE       $2230        $NOT OFFERED
```

REQUIREMENTS FOR ADMISSIONS:
  High school equivalency diploma
  High school diploma

ADDITIONAL SERVICES OFFERED:
  Diagnostic testing services on campus
  Diagnostic testing services off campus
  Remedial and/or tutorial help available
  Reader services for the blind available for LD
  Handicapped student services works with LD

MODIFICATIONS TO TRADITIONAL LEARNING ENVIRONMENT:
  Oral presentation in lieu of written exams
  Use of calculator for all math courses
  Has an adaptive physical education program
  Tape recorders to record class lectures
  Someone else may take class notes
  Student takes exams in separate rooms
  Students have exams read to them
  Students take typewritten exams
  Longer time allowed to complete exams
  Submit papers on cassette tape
  Take limited course load and graduate within time
    required
  Extended time limits for graduation
  Physical education may be waived

MAJORS OFFERED:

  AGRICULTURE
  BUSINESS AND MANAGEMENT
  COMPUTER SCIENCES
  EDUCATION
  ENGINEERING TECHNOLOGIES
  FINE AND APPLIED ARTS
  HEALTH
  GENERAL LIBERAL ARTS

==

AMARILLO COLLEGE
AMARILLO, TX 79178
806-376-9341

KEY CONTACT: Attn: KAY HENARD, PHD, DIVISION
                     CHAIRMAN ACCESS CENTER

SIZE OF SCHOOL: MEDIUM

APPLICATION DEADLINE: NONE

          APPROXIMATE TUITION   ROOM AND BOARD

IN DISTRICT $ 240 $NOT OFFERED
IN STATE $ 380 $NOT OFFERED
OUT-OF-STATE $ 655 $NOT OFFERED

REQUIREMENTS FOR ADMISSIONS:
    18 years of age or older, with or without a
      high school diploma or equivalency
    Placement tests

ADDITIONAL SERVICES OFFERED:
    Learning Lab
    Learning Lab has a specialist with a masters degree
      or above in Learning Disabilities
    Diagnostic testing services on campus
    Remedial and/or tutorial help available
    Reader services for the blind available for LD
    Handicapped student services works with LD

MODIFICATIONS TO TRADITIONAL LEARNING ENVIRONMENT:
    Oral presentation in lieu of written exams
    Use of calculator for all math courses
    Has an adaptive physical education program
    Someone else may take class notes
    Tape recorders to record class lectures
    Student takes exams in separate rooms
    Students have exams read to them
    Students take typewritten exams
    Longer time allowed to complete exams

MAJORS OFFERED:

    ARCHITECTURE
    BIOLOGICAL SCIENCES
    BUSINESS AND MANAGEMENT
    COMMUNICATIONS
    COMPUTER SCIENCES
    EDUCATION
    ENGINEERING TECHNOLOGIES
    FINE AND APPLIED ARTS
    FOREIGN LANGUAGES
    HEALTH
    HOME ECONOMICS

```
HUMANITIES
LIBRARY SCIENCE
MATHEMATICS
PHYSICAL SCIENCES
PSYCHOLOGY
PUBLIC SERVICES
SOCIAL SCIENCES
THEOLOGY
GENERAL LIBERAL ARTS
```

==

```
ANGELINA COLLEGE
LUFKIN, TX 75902
713-639-1301
```

KEY CONTACT: Attn: FREDERICK W. KANKE
DEAN OF ADMISSIONS

SIZE OF SCHOOL: SMALL

APPLICATION DEADLINE: NONE

	APPROXIMATE TUITION	ROOM AND BOARD
IN DISTRICT	$ 250	$1600
IN STATE	$ 250	$1600
OUT-OF-STATE	$ 650	$1600

REQUIREMENTS FOR ADMISSIONS:
  High school equivalency diploma
  High school diploma
  21 years of age or older, with or without a
    high school diploma or equivalency
  Untimed or oral ACT Scores accepted
  Untimed or oral SAT Scores accepted
  University or College sponsored tests
  Personal interview
  Recommendations
ADDITIONAL SERVICES OFFERED:
  Learning Lab
  Learning Lab has a specialist with a masters degree
    or above in Learning Disabilities
  Diagnostic testing services on campus
  Remedial and/or tutorial help available

MODIFICATIONS TO TRADITIONAL LEARNING ENVIRONMENT:
  Oral presentation in lieu of written exams
  Use of calculator for all math courses
  Has an adaptive physical education program
  Tape recorders to record class lectures

    Someone else may take class notes
    Longer time allowed to complete exams
    Submit papers on cassette tape
    Extended time limits for graduation
    Physical education may be waived

MAJORS OFFERED:

    AGRICULTURE
    BIOLOGICAL SCIENCES
    BUSINESS AND MANAGEMENT
    COMMUNICATIONS
    COMPUTER SCIENCES
    EDUCATION
    ENGINEERING TECHNOLOGIES
    FINE AND APPLIED ARTS
    HEALTH
    HUMANITIES
    MATHEMATICS
    PHYSICAL SCIENCES
    GENERAL LIBERAL ARTS

===

BEE COUNTY COLLEGE
BEEVILLE, TX 78102
512-358-3130

KEY CONTACT: Attn: PATRICIA MEYERS
                    SPECIAL NEEDS COUNSELOR

SIZE OF SCHOOL: SMALL

APPLICATION DEADLINE: NONE

        APPROXIMATE TUITION   ROOM AND BOARD

IN DISTRICT $ 230 $1930
IN STATE $ 350 $1930
OUT-OF-STATE $1280 $1930

REQUIREMENTS FOR ADMISSIONS:
    University or College sponsored tests
    Admission requirements modified
    Placement tests
    Recommendations

ADDITIONAL SERVICES OFFERED:
    Learning Lab
    Learning Lab has a specialist with a masters degree
      or above in Learning Disabilities

Reader services for the blind available for LD
Handicapped student services works with LD

MODIFICATIONS TO TRADITIONAL LEARNING ENVIRONMENT:
Oral presentation in lieu of written exams
Use of calculator for all math courses
Has an adaptive physical education program
Tape recorders to record class lectures
Someone else may take class notes
Multiple choice exams only
Students have exams read to them
Students take typewritten exams
Longer time allowed to complete exams
Submit papers on cassette tape
Extended time limits for graduation
Physical education may be waived

MAJORS OFFERED:

AGRICULTURE
BUSINESS AND MANAGEMENT
COMPUTER SCIENCES
ENGINEERING TECHNOLOGIES
HEALTH
PUBLIC SERVICES
GENERAL LIBERAL ARTS

==

CEDAR VALLEY COLLEGE
3030 NORTH DALLAS AVENUE
LANCASTER, TX 75134
214-372-8200

KEY CONTACT: Attn: GALE FRAZIER
                    SPECIAL SERVICES DIRECTOR

SIZE OF SCHOOL: SMALL

APPLICATION DEADLINE: NONE

	APPROXIMATE TUITION	ROOM AND BOARD
IN DISTRICT	$ 260	$NOT OFFERED
IN STATE	$ 610	$NOT OFFERED
OUT-OF-STATE	$6030	$NOT OFFERED

REQUIREMENTS FOR ADMISSIONS:
Untimed or oral ACT Scores accepted
Untimed or oral SAT Scores accepted
WAIS scores required

University or College sponsored tests
Personal interview
Placement tests
Recommendations

ADDITIONAL SERVICES OFFERED:
  Learning Lab
  Learning Lab has a specialist with a masters degree
    or above in Learning Disabilities
  Diagnostic testing services on campus
  Diagnostic testing services off campus
  Remedial and/or tutorial help available
  Reader services for the blind available for LD
  Handicapped student services works with LD

MODIFICATIONS TO TRADITIONAL LEARNING ENVIRONMENT:
  Tape recorders to record class lectures
  Someone else may take class notes
  Student takes exams in separate rooms
  Students have exams read to them
  Students take typewritten exams
  Longer time allowed to complete exams
  Submit papers on cassette tape
  Extended time limits for graduation

MAJORS OFFERED:

  BUSINESS AND MANAGEMENT
  PSYCHOLOGY
  SOCIAL SCIENCES
  THEOLOGY
  GENERAL LIBERAL ARTS

===

COLLEGE OF THE MAINLAND
8001 PALMER HIGHWAY
TEXAS CITY, TX 77590
713-480-6416

KEY CONTACT: Attn: MARCELLA DERRICK

SIZE OF SCHOOL: MEDIUM

APPLICATION DEADLINE: AUGUST 17

        APPROXIMATE TUITION   ROOM AND BOARD

IN DISTRICT $ 150 $NOT OFFERED
IN STATE $ 170 $NOT OFFERED
OUT-OF-STATE $ 420 $NOT OFFERED

REQUIREMENTS FOR ADMISSIONS:
  High school equivalency diploma
  High school diploma
  Untimed or oral ACT Scores accepted
  Untimed or oral SAT Scores accepted
  University or College sponsored tests
  Admission requirements modified
  Placement tests
  State/District residency

MODIFICATIONS TO TRADITIONAL LEARNING ENVIRONMENT:
  Use of calculator for all math courses
  Tape recorders to record class lectures
  Someone else may take class notes
  Multiple choice exams only
  Essay exams only
  Student takes exams in separate rooms
  Students have exams read to them
  Take limited course load and graduate within time
    required
  Extended time limits for graduation
  Physical education may be waived

MAJORS OFFERED:

  AGRICULTURE
  ARCHITECTURE
  BIOLOGICAL SCIENCES
  BUSINESS AND MANAGEMENT
  COMPUTER SCIENCES
  EDUCATION
  ENGINEERING TECHNOLOGIES
  FINE AND APPLIED ARTS
  FOREIGN LANGUAGES
  HEALTH
  HOME ECONOMICS
  HUMANITIES
  LIBRARY SCIENCE
  MATHEMATICS
  MILITARY SCIENCES
  PHYSICAL SCIENCES
  PSYCHOLOGY
  SOCIAL SCIENCES
  GENERAL LIBERAL ARTS

===

EASTFIELD COLLEGE
3737 MOTLEY DRIVE
MESQUITE, TX 75150
214-746-3100

KEY CONTACT: Attn: REVA O. RATTAN, SPECIALIST

SIZE OF SCHOOL: MEDIUM

APPLICATION DEADLINE: NONE

	APPROXIMATE TUITION	ROOM AND BOARD
IN DISTRICT	$ 275	$NOT OFFERED
IN STATE	$ 535	$NOT OFFERED
OUT-OF-STATE	$1495	$NOT OFFERED

REQUIREMENTS FOR ADMISSIONS:
  Untimed or oral ACT Scores accepted
  Untimed or oral SAT Scores accepted
  Admission requirements modified
  Personal interview
  Placement tests
  Recommendations

ADDITIONAL SERVICES OFFERED:
  Diagnostic testing services off campus
  Remedial and/or tutorial help available
  Reader services for the blind available for LD
  Handicapped student services works with LD

MODIFICATIONS TO TRADITIONAL LEARNING ENVIRONMENT:
  Oral presentation in lieu of written exams
  Has an adaptive physical education program
  Someone else may take class notes
  Student takes exams in separate rooms
  Students have exams read to them
  Students take typewritten exams
  Longer time allowed to complete exams
  Submit papers on cassette tape
  Extended time limits for graduation
  Physical education may be waived

MAJORS OFFERED:

  BUSINESS AND MANAGEMENT
  COMPUTER SCIENCES
  ENGINEERING TECHNOLOGIES
  HEALTH
  PUBLIC SERVICES
  GENERAL LIBERAL ARTS

==

EL CENTRO COLLEGE OF THE DALLAS COUNTY COMMUNITY
COLLEGE DISTRICT
MAIN AND LAMAR
DALLAS, TX 75202
214-746-2311

KEY CONTACT: Attn: JIM HANDY, COUNSELOR

SIZE OF SCHOOL: MEDIUM

APPLICATION DEADLINE: NONE

	APPROXIMATE TUITION	ROOM AND BOARD
IN DISTRICT	$ 205	$NOT OFFERED
IN STATE	$ 465	$NOT OFFERED
OUT-OF-STATE	$1005	$NOT OFFERED

REQUIREMENTS FOR ADMISSIONS:
  18 years of age or older, with or without a
    high school diploma or equivalency
  Untimed or oral ACT Scores accepted
  Untimed or oral SAT Scores accepted
  University or College sponsored tests
  Admission requirements modified
  Personal interview

ADDITIONAL SERVICES OFFERED:
  Learning Lab
  Diagnostic testing services off campus
  Remedial and/or tutorial help available
  Reader services for the blind available for LD
  Handicapped student services works with LD

MODIFICATIONS TO TRADITIONAL LEARNING ENVIRONMENT:
  Oral presentation in lieu of written exams
  Use of calculator for all math courses
  Has an adaptive physical education program
  Tape recorders to record class lectures
  Someone else may take class notes
  Student takes exams in separate rooms
  Students have exams read to them
  Students take typewritten exams
  Longer time allowed to complete exams
  Submit papers on cassette tape
  Take limited course load and graduate within time
    required
  Extended time limits for graduation
  Physical education may be waived
  Modifications depend on instructor

MAJORS OFFERED:

  BUSINESS AND MANAGEMENT
  COMPUTER SCIENCES
  ENGINEERING TECHNOLOGIES
  HEALTH
  PUBLIC SERVICES
  GENERAL LIBERAL ARTS

==

EL PASO COMMUNITY COLLEGE
EL PASO, TX 79998
915-594-2300

KEY CONTACT: Attn: ANN LEMKE, COUNSELOR

SIZE OF SCHOOL: LARGE

APPLICATION DEADLINE: NONE

        APPROXIMATE TUITION   ROOM AND BOARD

IN DISTRICT $ 440 $NOT OFFERED
IN STATE $ 440 $NOT OFFERED
OUT-OF-STATE $1680 $NOT OFFERED

REQUIREMENTS FOR ADMISSIONS:
  High school equivalency diploma
  High school diploma
  21 years of age or older, with or without a
    high school diploma or equivalency
  Untimed or oral ACT Scores accepted
  Untimed or oral SAT Scores accepted
  University or College sponsored tests
  Personal interview
  Recommendations

ADDITIONAL SERVICES OFFERED:
  Diagnostic testing services on campus
  Remedial and/or tutorial help available
  Reader services for the blind available for LD
  Handicapped student services works with LD

MODIFICATIONS TO TRADITIONAL LEARNING ENVIRONMENT:
  Oral presentation in lieu of written exams
  Has an adaptive physical education program
  Tape recorders to record class lectures
  Someone else may take class notes
  Student takes exams in separate rooms
  Students have exams read to them

Longer time allowed to complete exams
Physical education may be waived

MAJORS OFFERED:

BIOLOGICAL SCIENCES
BUSINESS AND MANAGEMENT
COMMUNICATIONS
COMPUTER SCIENCES
EDUCATION
FINE AND APPLIED ARTS
FOREIGN LANGUAGES
HEALTH
HUMANITIES
MATHEMATICS
MILITARY SCIENCES
PHYSICAL SCIENCES
PSYCHOLOGY
SOCIAL SCIENCES
GENERAL LIBERAL ARTS

===

GRAYSON COUNTY COLLEGE
6101 HIGHWAY 691
DENISON, TX 75020
214-465-6030

KEY CONTACT: Attn: CHARLOTTE BULLARD, COUNSELOR

SIZE OF SCHOOL: MEDIUM

APPLICATION DEADLINE: NONE

	APPROXIMATE TUITION	ROOM AND BOARD
IN DISTRICT	$ 240	$2875
IN STATE	$ 270	$2875
OUT-OF-STATE	$ 500	$2875

REQUIREMENTS FOR ADMISSIONS:
  High school equivalency diploma
  High school diploma
  21 years of age or older, with or without a
    high school diploma or equivalency
  Untimed or oral ACT Scores accepted
  Untimed or oral SAT Scores accepted
  Placement tests

ADDITIONAL SERVICES OFFERED:
  Learning Lab
  Learning Lab has a specialist with a masters degree
    or above in Learning Disabilities
  Diagnostic testing services on campus
  Diagnostic testing services off campus
  Remedial and/or tutorial help available
  Reader services for the blind available for LD
  Handicapped student services works with LD

MODIFICATIONS TO TRADITIONAL LEARNING ENVIRONMENT:
  Tape recorders to record class lectures
  Someone else may take class notes
  Student takes exams in separate rooms
  Students have exams read to them
  Students take typewritten exams
  Longer time allowed to complete exams
  Submit papers on cassette tape
  Extended time limits for graduation
  Physical education may be waived

MAJORS OFFERED:

  AGRICULTURE
  BIOLOGICAL SCIENCES
  BUSINESS AND MANAGEMENT
  COMMUNICATIONS
  EDUCATION
  ENGINEERING TECHNOLOGIES
  FINE AND APPLIED ARTS
  HEALTH
  HOME ECONOMICS
  HUMANITIES
  MATHEMATICS
  PHYSICAL SCIENCES
  GENERAL LIBERAL ARTS

===

MCLENNAN COMMUNITY COLLEGE
1400 COLLEGE DRIVE
WACO, TX 76708
817-756-6551

KEY CONTACT: Attn: JOHN PATTERSON

SIZE OF SCHOOL: MEDIUM

APPLICATION DEADLINE: NONE

```
              APPROXIMATE TUITION    ROOM AND BOARD

IN DISTRICT        $ 240         $NOT OFFERED
IN STATE           $ 265         $NOT OFFERED
OUT-OF-STATE       $ 600         $NOT OFFERED
```

REQUIREMENTS FOR ADMISSIONS:
  High school equivalency diploma
  High school diploma
  ACT Scores required
  Untimed or oral ACT Scores accepted
  University or College sponsored tests
  Admission requirements modified
  Personal interview
  Placement tests
  Recommendations

ADDITIONAL SERVICES OFFERED:
  Learning Lab
  Diagnostic testing services off campus
  Remedial and/or tutorial help available
  Reader services for the blind available for LD
  Handicapped student services works with LD

MODIFICATIONS TO TRADITIONAL LEARNING ENVIRONMENT:
  Oral presentation in lieu of written exams
  Has an adaptive physical education program
  Tape recorders to record class lectures
  Someone else may take class notes
  Student takes exams in separate rooms
  Students have exams read to them
  Students take typewritten exams
  Longer time allowed to complete exams
  Submit papers on cassette tape
  Take limited course load and graduate within time
     required
  Extended time limits for graduation
  Physical education may be waived

MAJORS OFFERED:

  AGRICULTURE
  ARCHITECTURE
  BIOLOGICAL SCIENCES
  BUSINESS AND MANAGEMENT
  COMMUNICATIONS
  COMPUTER SCIENCES
  EDUCATION
  FINE AND APPLIED ARTS
  HEALTH
  HUMANITIES

```
MATHEMATICS
PHYSICAL SCIENCES
PSYCHOLOGY
SOCIAL SCIENCES
THEOLOGY
GENERAL LIBERAL ARTS
```

==

```
SAN ANTONIO COLLEGE
1300 SAN PEDRO AVENUE
SAN ANTONIO, TX 78284
512-733-2309
```

KEY CONTACT: Attn: THOMAS HOY, COUNSELOR

SIZE OF SCHOOL: LARGE

APPLICATION DEADLINE: NONE

	APPROXIMATE TUITION	ROOM AND BOARD
IN DISTRICT	$ 110	$NOT OFFERED
IN STATE	$ 160	$NOT OFFERED
OUT-OF-STATE	$ 270	$NOT OFFERED

REQUIREMENTS FOR ADMISSIONS:
  High school equivalency diploma
  High school diploma
  Untimed or oral ACT Scores accepted
  Untimed or oral SAT Scores accepted
  University or College sponsored tests
  Admission requirements modified
  Placement tests
  Recommendations

ADDITIONAL SERVICES OFFERED:
  Remedial and/or tutorial help available
  Reader services for the blind available for LD
  Handicapped student services works with LD

MODIFICATIONS TO TRADITIONAL LEARNING ENVIRONMENT:
  Oral presentation in lieu of written exams
  Has an adaptive physical education program
  Tape recorders to record class lectures
  Someone else may take class notes
  Student takes exams in separate rooms
  Students have exams read to them
  Students take typewritten exams
  Longer time allowed to complete exams
  Submit papers on cassette tape

Extended time limits for graduation
Physical education may be waived

MAJORS OFFERED:

BUSINESS AND MANAGEMENT
COMPUTER SCIENCES
ENGINEERING TECHNOLOGIES
HEALTH
PUBLIC SERVICES
GENERAL LIBERAL ARTS

==

TARRANT COUNTY JUNIOR COLLEGE
1500 HOUSTON
FORT WORTH, TX 76102
817-336-7851

KEY CONTACT: Attn: ELIZABETH DAVIS

SIZE OF SCHOOL: LARGE

APPLICATION DEADLINE: NONE

	APPROXIMATE TUITION	ROOM AND BOARD
IN DISTRICT	$ 140	$NOT OFFERED
IN STATE	$ 230	$NOT OFFERED
OUT-OF-STATE	$1300	$NOT OFFERED

REQUIREMENTS FOR ADMISSIONS:
  High school equivalency diploma
  High school diploma
  21 years of age or older, with or without a
    high school diploma or equivalency
  University or College sponsored tests
  Personal interview
  Placement tests
  Recommendations
  Essay
  State/District residency

ADDITIONAL SERVICES OFFERED:
  Diagnostic testing services off campus
  Remedial and/or tutorial help available
  Reader services for the blind available for LD
  Handicapped student services works with LD

MODIFICATIONS TO TRADITIONAL LEARNING ENVIRONMENT:
  Oral presentation in lieu of written exams

```
     Tape recorders to record class lectures
     Someone else may take class notes
     Student takes exams in separate rooms
     Students have exams read to them
     Students take typewritten exams
     Longer time allowed to complete exams
     Physical education may be waived
```

MAJORS OFFERED:

```
     AGRICULTURE
     BUSINESS AND MANAGEMENT
     COMPUTER SCIENCES
     ENGINEERING TECHNOLOGIES
     HEALTH
     PUBLIC SERVICES
     GENERAL LIBERAL ARTS
```

===

```
WHARTON COUNTY JUNIOR COLLEGE
911 BOLING HIGHWAY
WHARTON, TX 77488
409-532-4560
```

KEY CONTACT: Attn: Handicapped Student Services

SIZE OF SCHOOL: SMALL

APPLICATION DEADLINE: AUGUST 25

	APPROXIMATE TUITION	ROOM AND BOARD
IN DISTRICT	$ 330	$1380
IN STATE	$ 430	$1380
OUT-OF-STATE	$1515	$1380

REQUIREMENTS FOR ADMISSIONS:
  High school equivalency diploma
  High school diploma
  ACT Scores required
  Untimed or oral ACT Scores accepted
  Untimed or oral SAT Scores accepted
  University or College sponsored tests
  Placement tests

ADDITIONAL SERVICES OFFERED:
  Learning Lab
  Diagnostic testing services on campus
  Remedial and/or tutorial help available
  Reader services for the blind available for LD

Handicapped student services works with LD

MODIFICATIONS TO TRADITIONAL LEARNING ENVIRONMENT:
  Oral presentation in lieu of written exams
  Use of calculator for all math courses
  Tape recorders to record class lectures
  Someone else may take class notes
  Multiple choice exams only
  Essay exams only
  Student takes exams in separate rooms
  Students have exams read to them
  Longer time allowed to complete exams
  Submit papers on cassette tape
  Take limited course load and graduate within time
    required
  Extended time limits for graduation

MAJORS OFFERED:

  AGRICULTURE
  BIOLOGICAL SCIENCES
  BUSINESS AND MANAGEMENT
  COMMUNICATIONS
  COMPUTER SCIENCES
  ENGINEERING TECHNOLOGIES
  FINE AND APPLIED ARTS
  FOREIGN LANGUAGES
  HEALTH
  HOME ECONOMICS
  HUMANITIES
  MATHEMATICS
  PHYSICAL SCIENCES
  PUBLIC SERVICES
  SOCIAL SCIENCES
  GENERAL LIBERAL ARTS

==

J. SARGEANT REYNOLDS COMMUNITY COLLEGE
RICHMOND, VA 23241
804-257-0204

KEY CONTACT: Attn: WENDELL A. HOWLETT
                     DIRECTOR, SPECIAL PROGRAMS

SIZE OF SCHOOL: MEDIUM

APPLICATION DEADLINE: NONE

```
       APPROXIMATE TUITION    ROOM AND BOARD

IN DISTRICT        $ 560        $NOT OFFERED
IN STATE           $ 560        $NOT OFFERED
OUT-OF-STATE       $2245        $NOT OFFERED
```

REQUIREMENTS FOR ADMISSIONS:
  High school equivalency diploma
  High school diploma
  University or College sponsored tests
  Placement tests

ADDITIONAL SERVICES OFFERED:
  Learning Lab
  Diagnostic testing services on campus
  Remedial and/or tutorial help available
  Reader services for the blind available for LD

MODIFICATIONS TO TRADITIONAL LEARNING ENVIRONMENT:
  Oral presentation in lieu of written exams
  Tape recorders to record class lectures
  Someone else may take class notes
  Students have exams read to them
  Students take typewritten exams
  Longer time allowed to complete exams

MAJORS OFFERED:

  BIOLOGICAL SCIENCES
  BUSINESS AND MANAGEMENT
  EDUCATION
  ENGINEERING TECHNOLOGIES
  MATHEMATICS
  PHYSICAL SCIENCES
  GENERAL LIBERAL ARTS

===

THOMAS NELSON COMMUNITY COLLEGE
HAMPTON, VA 23670
804-825-2800

KEY CONTACT: Attn: TOM KELLEN, COUNSELOR

SIZE OF SCHOOL: MEDIUM

APPLICATION DEADLINE: NONE

```
         APPROXIMATE TUITION   ROOM AND BOARD

IN DISTRICT      $ 610        $NOT OFFERED
IN STATE         $ 610        $NOT OFFERED
OUT-OF-STATE     $2610        $NOT OFFERED
```

REQUIREMENTS FOR ADMISSIONS:
   High school equivalency diploma
   High school diploma
   21 years of age or older, with or without a
      high school diploma or equivalency
   Placement tests
   WAIS scores are required as part of a total
      diagnostic package
   Personal interview encouraged

ADDITIONAL SERVICES OFFERED:
   Learning Lab
   Diagnostic testing services off campus
   Remedial and/or tutorial help available
   Reader services for the blind available for LD
   Handicapped student services works with LD

MODIFICATIONS TO TRADITIONAL LEARNING ENVIRONMENT:
   Use of calculator for all math courses
   Tape recorders to record class lectures
   Someone else may take class notes
   Student takes exams in separate rooms
   Students have exams read to them
   Students take typewritten exams
   Longer time allowed to complete exams
   Submit papers on cassette tape
   Physical education may be waived

MAJORS OFFERED:

   BUSINESS AND MANAGEMENT
   EDUCATION
   ENGINEERING TECHNOLOGIES
   FINE AND APPLIED ARTS
   PHYSICAL SCIENCES
   GENERAL LIBERAL ARTS

==

CLARK COLLEGE
1800 EAST MCLOUGHLIN BLVD
VANCOUVER, WA 98663
206-699-0262

KEY CONTACT: Attn: DUANE HENRY, COORDINATOR
                     DISABLED SERVICES

SIZE OF SCHOOL: MEDIUM

APPLICATION DEADLINE: NONE

         APPROXIMATE TUITION   ROOM AND BOARD

IN DISTRICT $ 305 $NOT OFFERED
IN STATE $ 305 $NOT OFFERED
OUT-OF-STATE $1190 $NOT OFFERED

REQUIREMENTS FOR ADMISSIONS:
  Admission requirements modified
  Placement tests
  If it is determined through diagnostic testing that a
   student can be successful they can enter the program

ADDITIONAL SERVICES OFFERED:
  Learning Lab
  Diagnostic testing services on campus
  Diagnostic testing services off campus
  Remedial and/or tutorial help available
  Reader services for the blind available for LD
  Handicapped student services works with LD

MODIFICATIONS TO TRADITIONAL LEARNING ENVIRONMENT:
  Oral presentation in lieu of written exams
  Use of calculator for all math courses
  Has an adaptive physical education program
  Tape recorders to record class lectures
  Someone else may take class notes
  Student takes exams in separate rooms
  Students have exams read to them
  Students take typewritten exams
  Longer time allowed to complete exams
  Extended time limits for graduation
  Physical education may be waived

MAJORS OFFERED:

  AGRICULTURE
  ARCHITECTURE
  AREA STUDIES
  BIOLOGICAL SCIENCES
  BUSINESS AND MANAGEMENT
  COMMUNICATIONS
  COMPUTER SCIENCES
  EDUCATION
  ENGINEERING TECHNOLOGIES

```
FINE AND APPLIED ARTS
FOREIGN LANGUAGES
HEALTH
HOME ECONOMICS
HUMANITIES
LIBRARY SCIENCE
MATHEMATICS
PHYSICAL SCIENCES
PSYCHOLOGY
PUBLIC SERVICES
SOCIAL SCIENCES
THEOLOGY
GENERAL LIBERAL ARTS
```

===

```
EVERETT COMMUNITY COLLEGE
801 WETMORE AVENUE
EVERETT, WA 98201
206-259-7151

KEY CONTACT: Attn:  DIANE CANTOS, DIRECTOR
                    DISABLED STUDENT SERVICES

SIZE OF SCHOOL: MEDIUM

APPLICATION DEADLINE: NONE

       APPROXIMATE TUITION    ROOM AND BOARD

IN DISTRICT      $ 520        $NOT OFFERED
IN STATE         $ 520        $NOT OFFERED
OUT-OF-STATE     $2040        $NOT OFFERED

ADDITIONAL SERVICES OFFERED:
  Learning Lab
  Remedial and/or tutorial help available
  Reader services for the blind available for LD
  Handicapped student services works with LD

MODIFICATIONS TO TRADITIONAL LEARNING ENVIRONMENT:
  Oral presentation in lieu of written exams
  Use of calculator for all math courses
  Has an adaptive physical education program
  Tape recorders to record class lectures
  Someone else may take class notes
  Student takes exams in separate rooms
  Students have exams read to them
  Students take typewritten exams
  Longer time allowed to complete exams
  Submit papers on cassette tape
```

Extended time limits for graduation
Physical education may be waived

MAJORS OFFERED:

BIOLOGICAL SCIENCES
BUSINESS AND MANAGEMENT
COMMUNICATIONS
COMPUTER SCIENCES
ENGINEERING TECHNOLOGIES
FINE AND APPLIED ARTS
FOREIGN LANGUAGES
HEALTH
HUMANITIES
MATHEMATICS
PHYSICAL SCIENCES
PSYCHOLOGY
SOCIAL SCIENCES
GENERAL LIBERAL ARTS

==

FORT STEILACOOM COMMUNITY COLLEGE
9401 FARWEST DRIVE SW
TACOMA, WA 98498
206-964-6501

KEY CONTACT: Attn: BARRY BRODNIAK, SPECIAL PROGRAMS
                    COORDINATOR

SIZE OF SCHOOL: MEDIUM

APPLICATION DEADLINE: NONE

           APPROXIMATE TUITION   ROOM AND BOARD

IN DISTRICT $ 575 $NOT OFFERED
IN STATE $ 575 $NOT OFFERED
OUT-OF-STATE $2260 $NOT OFFERED

REQUIREMENTS FOR ADMISSIONS:
  18 years of age or older, with or without a
     high school diploma or equivalency
  Placement tests

ADDITIONAL SERVICES OFFERED:
  Learning Lab
  Diagnostic testing services on campus
  Diagnostic testing services off campus
  Remedial and/or tutorial help available
  Reader services for the blind available for LD

Special Education department
Handicapped student services works with LD

MODIFICATIONS TO TRADITIONAL LEARNING ENVIRONMENT:
    Oral presentation in lieu of written exams
    Has an adaptive physical education program
    Tape recorders to record class lectures
    Someone else may take class notes
    Student takes exams in separate rooms
    Students have exams read to them
    Students take typewritten exams
    Longer time allowed to complete exams
    Submit papers on cassette tape
    Extended time limits for graduation
    Physical education may be waived

MAJORS OFFERED:

    BUSINESS AND MANAGEMENT
    COMPUTER SCIENCES
    ENGINEERING TECHNOLOGIES
    HEALTH
    PUBLIC SERVICES
    GENERAL LIBERAL ARTS

==

LOWER COLUMBIA COLLEGE
LONGVIEW, WA 98632
206-577-2300

KEY CONTACT: Attn: CAROL MCNAIR, COORDINATOR
                    DISABLED STUDENT SERVICES

SIZE OF SCHOOL: MEDIUM

APPLICATION DEADLINE: NONE

        APPROXIMATE TUITION   ROOM AND BOARD

IN DISTRICT $ 520 $NOT OFFERED
IN STATE $ 520 $NOT OFFERED
OUT-OF-STATE $2040 $NOT OFFERED

REQUIREMENTS FOR ADMISSIONS:
    University or College sponsored tests
    Placement tests
    Recommendations
    Open admissions

ADDITIONAL SERVICES OFFERED:
  Learning Lab
  Diagnostic testing services on campus
  Remedial and/or tutorial help available
  Reader services for the blind available for LD
  Handicapped student services works with LD

MODIFICATIONS TO TRADITIONAL LEARNING ENVIRONMENT:
  Tape recorders to record class lectures
  Someone else may take class notes
  Extended time limits for graduation
  All other modifications with the approval of
    instructor

MAJORS OFFERED:

  AGRICULTURE
  BIOLOGICAL SCIENCES
  BUSINESS AND MANAGEMENT
  ENGINEERING TECHNOLOGIES
  FINE AND APPLIED ARTS
  HEALTH
  HUMANITIES
  MATHEMATICS
  PHYSICAL SCIENCES
  PSYCHOLOGY
  SOCIAL SCIENCES
  GENERAL LIBERAL ARTS

==

OLYMPIC COLEGE
16TH AND CHESTER
BREMERTON, WA 98310
206-478-4541

KEY CONTACT: Attn: Handicapped Student Services

SIZE OF SCHOOL: MEDIUM

APPLICATION DEADLINE: NONE

         APPROXIMATE TUITION   ROOM AND BOARD

IN DISTRICT $ 580 $NOT OFFERED
IN STATE $ 580 $NOT OFFERED
OUT-OF-STATE $2285 $NOT OFFERED

REQUIREMENTS FOR ADMISSIONS:
  High school equivalency diploma
  Personal interview

ADDITIONAL SERVICES OFFERED:
  Diagnostic testing services off campus
  Remedial and/or tutorial help available
  Reader services for the blind available for LD
  Handicapped student services works with LD

MODIFICATIONS TO TRADITIONAL LEARNING ENVIRONMENT:
  Oral presentation in lieu of written exams
  Use of calculator for all math courses
  Has an adaptive physical education program
  Tape recorders to record class lectures
  Someone else may take class notes
  Take limited course load and graduate within time
    required
  Extended time limits for graduation
  All other modifications depend on instructor

MAJORS OFFERED:

  AGRICULTURE
  BIOLOGICAL SCIENCES
  BUSINESS AND MANAGEMENT
  COMMUNICATIONS
  COMPUTER SCIENCES
  EDUCATION
  ENGINEERING TECHNOLOGIES
  FINE AND APPLIED ARTS
  FOREIGN LANGUAGES
  HEALTH
  HOME ECONOMICS
  HUMANITIES
  MATHEMATICS
  PHYSICAL SCIENCES
  PSYCHOLOGY
  PUBLIC SERVICES
  SOCIAL SCIENCES
  GENERAL LIBERAL ARTS

===

SEATTLE CENTRAL COMMUNITY COLLEGE
1801 BROADWAY
SEATTLE, WA 98122
206-587-6918

KEY CONTACT: Attn: KATHERN J. CARLSTROM

SIZE OF SCHOOL: MEDIUM

APPLICATION DEADLINE: NONE

```
      APPROXIMATE TUITION   ROOM AND BOARD

IN DISTRICT        $ 580      $NOT OFFERED
IN STATE           $ 580      $NOT OFFERED
OUT-OF-STATE       $2285      $NOT OFFERED
```

REQUIREMENTS FOR ADMISSIONS:
  Placement tests

ADDITIONAL SERVICES OFFERED:
  Learning Lab
  Diagnostic testing services on campus
  Reader services for the blind available for LD
  Handicapped student services works with LD

MODIFICATIONS TO TRADITIONAL LEARNING ENVIRONMENT:
  Oral presentation in lieu of written exams
  Use of calculator for all math courses
  Tape recorders to record class lectures
  Someone else may take class notes
  Students have exams read to them
  Longer time allowed to complete exams
  Extended time limits for graduation
  Physical education may be waived

MAJORS OFFERED:

  BUSINESS AND MANAGEMENT
  COMPUTER SCIENCES .
  ENGINEERING TECHNOLOGIES
  HEALTH
  PUBLIC SERVICES
  GENERAL LIBERAL ARTS

===

SKAGIT VALLEY COLLEGE
2405 COLLEGE WAY
MT. VERNON, WA 98273
206-428-1155

KEY CONTACT: Attn: STAN POPE, COUNSELOR

SIZE OF SCHOOL: MEDIUM

APPLICATION DEADLINE: NONE

```
          APPROXIMATE TUITION    ROOM AND BOARD

IN DISTRICT        $ 580         $NOT OFFERED
IN STATE           $ 580         $NOT OFFERED
OUT-OF-STATE       $2285         $NOT OFFERED
```

REQUIREMENTS FOR ADMISSIONS:
  High school equivalency diploma
  High school diploma
  University or College sponsored tests
  Placement tests

ADDITIONAL SERVICES OFFERED:
  Learning Lab
  Learning Lab has a specialist with a masters degree
    or above in Learning Disabilities
  Diagnostic testing services on campus
  Remedial and/or tutorial help available

MODIFICATIONS TO TRADITIONAL LEARNING ENVIRONMENT:
  Oral presentation in lieu of written exams
  Tape recorders to record class lectures
  Someone else may take class notes
  Student takes exams in separate rooms
  Students have exams read to them
  Students take typewritten exams
  Longer time allowed to complete exams
  Take limited course load and graduate within time
    required
  Extended time limits for graduation
  Physical education may be waived

MAJORS OFFERED:

  AGRICULTURE
  BIOLOGICAL SCIENCES
  BUSINESS AND MANAGEMENT
  COMMUNICATIONS
  COMPUTER SCIENCES
  EDUCATION
  ENGINEERING TECHNOLOGIES
  FINE AND APPLIED ARTS
  FOREIGN LANGUAGES
  HEALTH
  HUMANITIES
  MATHEMATICS
  PHYSICAL SCIENCES
  PSYCHOLOGY
  PUBLIC SERVICES
  SOCIAL SCIENCES
  GENERAL LIBERAL ARTS

SOUTH SEATTLE COMMUNITY COLLEGE
6000 16TH AVENUE, SW
SEATTLE, WA 98106
206-764-5378

KEY CONTACT: Attn: Handicapped Student Services

SIZE OF SCHOOL: MEDIUM

APPLICATION DEADLINE: NONE

	APPROXIMATE TUITION	ROOM AND BOARD
IN DISTRICT	$ 505	$NOT OFFERED
IN STATE	$ 505	$NOT OFFERED
OUT-OF-STATE	$2025	$NOT OFFERED

REQUIREMENTS FOR ADMISSIONS:
  High school equivalency diploma
  Untimed or oral ACT Scores accepted
  SAT Scores required
  Untimed or oral SAT Scores accepted
  Admission requirements modified
  Personal interview
  Placement tests
  Recommendations

ADDITIONAL SERVICES OFFERED:
  Learning Lab
  Diagnostic testing services on campus
  Remedial and/or tutorial help available
  Reader services for the blind available for LD
  Handicapped student services works with LD

MODIFICATIONS TO TRADITIONAL LEARNING ENVIRONMENT:
  Oral presentation in lieu of written exams
  Tape recorders to record class lectures
  Someone else may take class notes
  Students have exams read to them
  Students take typewritten exams
  Longer time allowed to complete exams
  Submit papers on cassette tape
  Take limited course load and graduate within time
    required
  Extended time limits for graduation
  Physical education may be waived

MAJORS OFFERED:

  AGRICULTURE
  BUSINESS AND MANAGEMENT

ENGINEERING TECHNOLOGIES
PUBLIC SERVICES
GENERAL LIBERAL ARTS

==

SPOKANE FALLS COMMUNITY COLLEGE
WEST 3410 FORT GEORGE WRIGHT DRIVE
SPOKANE, WA 99204
509-456-2815

KEY CONTACT: Attn: Handicapped Student Services

SIZE OF SCHOOL: MEDIUM

APPLICATION DEADLINE: NONE

	APPROXIMATE TUITION	ROOM AND BOARD
IN DISTRICT	$ 595	$NOT OFFERED
IN STATE	$ 595	$NOT OFFERED
OUT-OF-STATE	$2300	$NOT OFFERED

REQUIREMENTS FOR ADMISSIONS:
  High school equivalency diploma
  High school diploma
  Placement tests

ADDITIONAL SERVICES OFFERED:
  Learning Lab
  Remedial and/or tutorial help available
  Reader services for the blind available for LD
  Handicapped student services works with LD

MODIFICATIONS TO TRADITIONAL LEARNING ENVIRONMENT:
  Oral presentation in lieu of written exams
  Tape recorders to record class lectures
  Someone else may take class notes
  Students have exams read to them
  Students take typewritten exams
  Longer time allowed to complete exams
  Submit papers on cassette tape
  Extended time limits for graduation
  Physical education may be waived

MAJORS OFFERED:

  BUSINESS AND MANAGEMENT
  COMPUTER SCIENCES
  ENGINEERING TECHNOLOGIES
  HEALTH

HOME ECONOMICS
PUBLIC SERVICES
GENERAL LIBERAL ARTS

==

YAKIMA VALLEY COMMUNITY COLLEGE
16TH AVENUE AND NOB HILL BLVD
YAKIMA, WA 98907
509-575-2373

KEY CONTACT: Attn: MARK CORNETT

SIZE OF SCHOOL: MEDIUM

APPLICATION DEADLINE: NONE

     APPROXIMATE TUITION   ROOM AND BOARD

IN DISTRICT $ 585 $2340
IN STATE $ 585 $2340
OUT-OF-STATE $2290 $2340

REQUIREMENTS FOR ADMISSIONS:
  High school equivalency diploma
  High school diploma
  Placement tests

ADDITIONAL SERVICES OFFERED:
  Learning Lab
  Remedial and/or tutorial help available
  Reader services for the blind available for LD
  Handicapped student services works with LD

MODIFICATIONS TO TRADITIONAL LEARNING ENVIRONMENT:
  Oral presentation in lieu of written exams
  Use of calculator for all math courses
  Tape recorders to record class lectures
  Student takes exams in separate rooms
  Students have exams read to them
  Longer time allowed to complete exams
  Submit papers on cassette tape
  Extended time limits for graduation
  Physical education may be waived
  All modifications made with the approval of faculty

MAJORS OFFERED:

  BUSINESS AND MANAGEMENT
  ENGINEERING TECHNOLOGIES
  FINE AND APPLIED ARTS

```
HEALTH
HOME ECONOMICS
GENERAL LIBERAL ARTS
```

==

```
GATEWAY TECHNICAL INSTITUTE-RACINE
1001 SOUTH MAIN STREET
RACINE, WI 53403
414-631-7300
```

KEY CONTACT: Attn: JO KRON-BAILEY
                    LEARNING SKILLS SPECIALIST

SIZE OF SCHOOL: MEDIUM

APPLICATION DEADLINE: NONE

	APPROXIMATE TUITION	ROOM AND BOARD
IN DISTRICT	$1350	$NOT OFFERED
IN STATE	$1350	$NOT OFFERED
OUT-OF-STATE	$2800	$NOT OFFERED

REQUIREMENTS FOR ADMISSIONS:
   Untimed or oral ACT Scores accepted
   Untimed or oral SAT Scores accepted
   Admission requirements modified
   Personal interview
   Placement tests
   Recommendations

ADDITIONAL SERVICES OFFERED:
   Learning Lab
   Diagnostic testing services on campus
   Diagnostic testing services off campus
   Remedial and/or tutorial help available
   Reader services for the blind available for LD
   Special Education department
   Handicapped student services works with LD

MODIFICATIONS TO TRADITIONAL LEARNING ENVIRONMENT:
   Oral presentation in lieu of written exams
   Use of calculator for all math courses
   Tape recorders to record class lectures
   Someone else may take class notes
   Student takes exams in separate rooms
   Students have exams read to them
   Students take typewritten exams
   Longer time allowed to complete exams
   Submit papers on cassette tape

```
    Extended time limits for graduation
    Physical education may be waived
```

MAJORS OFFERED:

```
    AGRICULTURE
    BUSINESS AND MANAGEMENT
    COMMUNICATIONS
    COMPUTER SCIENCES
    ENGINEERING TECHNOLOGIES
    HEALTH
    HOME ECONOMICS
```

===

```
MID-STATE TECHNICAL INSTITUTE
110 WEST THIRD STREET
MARCHFIELD, WI 54449
715-387-3538
```

KEY CONTACT: Attn: SALLEY CUTLER

SIZE OF SCHOOL: SMALL

APPLICATION DEADLINE: NONE

	APPROXIMATE TUITION	ROOM AND BOARD
IN DISTRICT	$ 660	$NOT OFFERED
IN STATE	$ 660	$NOT OFFERED
OUT-OF-STATE	$1960	$NOT OFFERED

REQUIREMENTS FOR ADMISSIONS:
```
    21 years of age or older, with or without a
       high school diploma or equivalency
    Untimed or oral ACT Scores accepted
    Untimed or oral SAT Scores accepted
    Admission requirements modified
    Personal interview
    Placement tests
    Recommendations
    Essay
```

ADDITIONAL SERVICES OFFERED:
```
    Learning Lab
    Diagnostic testing services on campus
    Diagnostic testing services off campus
    Remedial and/or tutorial help available
    Reader services for the blind available for LD
    Special Education department
    Handicapped student services works with LD
```

MODIFICATIONS TO TRADITIONAL LEARNING ENVIRONMENT:
   Oral presentation in lieu of written exams
   Use of calculator for all math courses
   Tape recorders to record class lectures
   Someone else may take class notes
   Student takes exams in separate rooms
   Students have exams read to them
   Students take typewritten exams
   Longer time allowed to complete exams
   Extended time limits for graduation
   Modifications depend on class

MAJORS OFFERED:

   AGRICULTURE
   HEALTH SERVICES

==

MORAINE PARK TECHNICAL INSTITUTE
2151 NORTH MAIN STREET
WEST BEND, WI 53095
414-334-3413

KEY CONTACT: Attn: PETER VAN GROLL
                    SPECIAL NEEDS COORDINATOR

SIZE OF SCHOOL: MEDIUM
APPLICATION DEADLINE: NONE

          APPROXIMATE TUITION   ROOM AND BOARD

IN DISTRICT $ 900 $NOT OFFERED
IN STATE $2000 $NOT OFFERED
OUT-OF-STATE $3500 $NOT OFFERED

REQUIREMENTS FOR ADMISSIONS:
   Admission requirements modified
   Personal interview
   Placement tests
   Recommendations

ADDITIONAL SERVICES OFFERED:
   Learning Lab
   Diagnostic testing services on campus
   Remedial and/or tutorial help available
   Reader services for the blind available for LD
   Handicapped student services works with LD

MODIFICATIONS TO TRADITIONAL LEARNING ENVIRONMENT:
  Use of calculator for all math courses
  Tape recorders to record class lectures
  Someone else may take class notes
  Students have exams read to them
  Students take typewritten exams
  Longer time allowed to complete exams
  Submit papers on cassette tape
  Extended time limits for graduation
  Modifications depend on course and instructor

MAJORS OFFERED:

  BUSINESS AND MANAGEMENT
  COMPUTER SCIENCES
  HEALTH

==

SOUTHWEST WISCONSIN VOCATIONAL TECHNICAL INSTITUTE
BRONSON BLVD
FENNIMORE, WI 53809
608-822-3262

KEY CONTACT: Attn: JOANN PERTZ, ADMINISTRATOR
                    STUDENT SERVICES

SIZE OF SCHOOL: SMALL

APPLICATION DEADLINE: NONE

         APPROXIMATE TUITION   ROOM AND BOARD

IN DISTRICT $ 660 $NOT OFFERED
IN STATE $ 660 $NOT OFFERED
OUT-OF-STATE $1955 $NOT OFFERED

REQUIREMENTS FOR ADMISSIONS:
  Personal interview
  A high school diploma is a requirement for any
    student pursing an associate degree program or the
    Practical Nursing program
  In some cases students with learning disabilities
    work with special needs instructors along with the
    regular curriculum
  Placement test are reguired for some programs

ADDITIONAL SERVICES OFFERED:
  Learning Lab
  Diagnostic testing services on campus
  Diagnostic testing services off campus

Remedial and/or tutorial help available
Reader services for the blind available for LD
Special Education department

MODIFICATIONS TO TRADITIONAL LEARNING ENVIRONMENT:
  Oral presentation in lieu of written exams
  Use of calculator for all math courses
  Tape recorders to record class lectures
  Someone else may take class notes
  Students have exams read to them
  Longer time allowed to complete exams
  Extended time limits for graduation
  Physical education may be waived

MAJORS OFFERED:

  AGRICULTURE
  BUSINESS AND MANAGEMENT
  COMPUTER SCIENCES
  ENGINEERING TECHNOLOGIES
  HEALTH
  PUBLIC SERVICES

===

WISCONSIN INDIANHEAD TECHNICAL INSTITUTE
1900 COLLEGE DRIVE
RICE LAKE, WI 54868
715-234-7082

KEY CONTACT: Attn: DR. GEORGE THEIR
                    STUDENT SERVICES ADMINISTRATOR

SIZE OF SCHOOL: SMALL

APPLICATION DEADLINE: AUGUST 1

        APPROXIMATE TUITION   ROOM AND BOARD

IN DISTRICT $ 365 $NOT OFFERED
IN STATE $1055 $NOT OFFERED
OUT-OF-STATE $2205 $NOT OFFERED

REQUIREMENTS FOR ADMISSIONS:
  University or College sponsored tests
  Personal interview
  Placement tests

ADDITIONAL SERVICES OFFERED:
  Learning Lab
  Learning Lab has a specialist with a masters degree
    or above in Learning Disabilities
  Diagnostic testing services on campus
  Diagnostic testing services off campus
  Remedial and/or tutorial help available
  Reader services for the blind available for LD
  Handicapped student services works with LD

MODIFICATIONS TO TRADITIONAL LEARNING ENVIRONMENT:
  Oral presentation in lieu of written exams
  Use of calculator for all math courses
  Tape recorders to record class lectures
  Student takes exams in separate rooms
  Students have exams read to them
  Longer time allowed to complete exams

MAJORS OFFERED:

  AGRICULTURE
  BUSINESS AND MANAGEMENT
  ENGINEERING TECHNOLOGIES
  HEALTH

==

FOUR-YEAR COLLEGES

ALABAMA A&M UNIVERSITY
BOX 284
NORMAL, AL 35762
205-859-7468

KEY CONTACT: Attn: Handicapped Student Services

SIZE OF SCHOOL: MEDIUM

APPLICATION DEADLINE: NONE

         APPROXIMATE TUITION   ROOM AND BOARD

IN STATE $ 680 $1500
OUT-OF-STATE $1300 $1500

REQUIREMENTS FOR ADMISSIONS:
  High school equivalency diploma
  High school diploma
  ACT Scores required
  SAT Scores required
  High school grade point average   'C'
  Admission requirements modified

ADDITIONAL SERVICES OFFERED:
  Learning Lab
  Learning Lab has a specialist with a masters degree
    or above in Learning Disabilities
  Diagnostic testing services on campus
  Diagnostic testing services off campus
  Remedial and/or tutorial help available
  Special Education department
  Handicapped student services works with LD

MODIFICATIONS TO TRADITIONAL LEARNING ENVIRONMENT:
  Use of calculator for all math courses
  Has an adaptive physical education program
  Tape recorders to record class lectures
  Someone else may take class notes
  Longer time allowed to complete exams (depends on
    instructer)
  Submit papers on cassette tape (depends on
    instructer)
  Extended time limits for graduation
  Physical education may be waived (depends on physical
    condition)

MAJORS OFFERED:

  AGRICULTURE
  ARCHITECTURE

```
AREA STUDIES
BIOLOGICAL SCIENCES
BUSINESS AND MANAGEMENT
COMMUNICATIONS
COMPUTER SCIENCES
EDUCATION
ENGINEERING TECHNOLOGIES
FINE AND APPLIED ARTS
FOREIGN LANGUAGES
HEALTH
HOME ECONOMICS
HUMANITIES
LAW
LIBRARY SCIENCE
MATHEMATICS
MILITARY SCIENCES
PHYSICAL SCIENCES
PSYCHOLOGY
PUBLIC SERVICES
SOCIAL SCIENCES
```

===

```
UNIVERSITY OF MONTEVALLO
OAK STREET
MONTEVALLO, AL 35115
205-665-2521
```

KEY CONTACT: Attn: ELAINE ELLEDGE,
                    SPECIAL SERVICES DIRECTOR

SIZE OF SCHOOL: SMALL

APPLICATION DEADLINE: NONE

	APPROXIMATE TUITION	ROOM AND BOARD
IN STATE	$1030	$1750
OUT-OF-STATE	$1630	$1750

REQUIREMENTS FOR ADMISSIONS:
  The same as for any student

ADDITIONAL SERVICES OFFERED:
  Learning Lab
  Diagnostic testing services on campus
  Remedial and/or tutorial help available

MODIFICATIONS TO TRADITIONAL LEARNING ENVIRONMENT:
  Tape recorders to record class lectures

MAJORS OFFERED:

BIOLOGICAL SCIENCES
BUSINESS AND MANAGEMENT
COMMUNICATIONS
EDUCATION
ENGINEERING TECHNOLOGIES
FINE AND APPLIED ARTS
FOREIGN LANGUAGES
HEALTH
HOME ECONOMICS
LAW
HUMANITIES
MATHEMATICS
PHYSICAL SCIENCES
PSYCHOLOGY
PUBLIC SERVICES
SOCIAL SCIENCES

===

ARIZONA STATE UNIVERSITY
TEMPE, ARIZONA 85287
602-965-3255

KEY CONTACT: Attn: ANN RISPOLI - LEARNING SPECIALIST

SIZE OF SCHOOL: LARGE

APPLICATION DEADLINE: JULY 29

	APPROXIMATE TUITION	ROOM AND BOARD
IN STATE	$ 850	$2400
OUT-OF-STATE	$3500	$2400

REQUIREMENTS FOR ADMISSIONS:
  High school equivalency diploma
  High school diploma
  ACT Scores required
  SAT Scores required
  Particular rank in class 50%
  High school grade point average 2.5
  Admission requirements modified
  Recommendations
  Upward trend in high school
  Prior academic work will be considered

ADDITIONAL SERVICES OFFERED:
  Learning Lab

Learning Lab has a specialist with a masters degree
  or above in Learning Disabilities
Diagnostic testing services on campus
Diagnostic testing services off campus
Remedial and/or tutorial help available
Handicapped student services works with LD

MODIFICATIONS TO TRADITIONAL LEARNING ENVIRONMENT:
  Tape recorders to record class lectures
  Someone else may take class notes
  Multiple choice exams only
  Essay exams only
  Student takes exams in separate rooms
  Students have exams read to them
  Students take typewritten exams
  Longer time allowed to complete exams
  Submit papers on cassette tape
  Take limited course load and graduate within time
    required
  Extended time limits for graduation
  Physical education may be waived

MAJORS OFFERED:

  AGRICULTURE
  ARCHITECTURE DESIGN
  BIOLOGICAL SCIENCES
  BUSINESS AND MANAGEMENT
  COMMUNICATIONS
  COMPUTER SCIENCES
  EDUCATION
  ENGINEERING TECHNOLOGIES
  FOREIGN LANGUAGES
  HEALTH
  HOME ECONOMICS
  HUMANITIES
  MATHEMATICS
  PHYSICAL SCIENCES
  PSYCHOLOGY
  PUBLIC SERVICES
  SOCIAL SCIENCES
  THEOLOGY

==

NORTHERN ARIZONA UNIVERSITY
BOX 4084
FLAGSTAFF, AZ 86011
602-523-2108

```
KEY CONTACT: Attn:   LINDA PRICE, COORDINATOR
                     DISABLED STUDENT SERVICES

SIZE OF SCHOOL: MEDIUM

APPLICATION DEADLINE: JULY 15

         APPROXIMATE TUITION    ROOM AND BOARD

IN STATE          $ 755         $1830
OUT-OF-STATE      $ 755         $1830
```

REQUIREMENTS FOR ADMISSIONS:
  High school equivalency diploma
  High school diploma
  ACT Scores required (recommended)
  Untimed or oral ACT Scores accepted
  Particular rank in class 50%
  High school grade point average 2.5

ADDITIONAL SERVICES OFFERED:
  Diagnostic testing services on campus
  Remedial and/or tutorial help available
  Reader services for the blind available for LD
  Handicapped student services works with LD

MODIFICATIONS TO TRADITIONAL LEARNING ENVIRONMENT:
  Oral presentation in lieu of written exams
  Use of calculator for all math courses
  Has an adaptive physical education program
  Tape recorders to record class lectures
  Someone else may take class notes
  Student takes exams in separate rooms
  Students have exams read to them
  Longer time allowed to complete exams
  Physical education not required

MAJORS OFFERED:

  AGRICULTURE
  ARCHITECTURE
  AREA STUDIES
  BIOLOGICAL SCIENCES
  BUSINESS AND MANAGEMENT
  COMMUNICATIONS
  COMPUTER SCIENCES
  EDUCATION
  ENGINEERING TECHNOLOGIES
  FINE AND APPLIED ARTS
  FOREIGN LANGUAGES
  HEALTH

HOME ECONOMICS
HUMANITIES
LAW
MATHEMATICS
PHYSICAL SCIENCES
PSYCHOLOGY
PUBLIC SERVICES
SOCIAL SCIENCES

===

COLLEGE OF THE OZARKS
CLARKSVILLE, AR 72830
501-754-8715

KEY CONTACT: Attn: C. DOUGLAS SADDLER
                     DIRECTOR SPECIAL LEARNING CENTER

SIZE OF SCHOOL: SMALL

APPLICATION DEADLINE: JUNE 1

        APPROXIMATE TUITION   ROOM AND BOARD

IN STATE $1425 $1350
OUT-OF-STATE $1425 $1350

REQUIREMENTS FOR ADMISSIONS:
  WAIS scores required
  Admission requirements modified
  Personal interview

ADDITIONAL SERVICES OFFERED:
  Learning Lab
  Learning Lab has a specialist with a masters degree
    or above in Learning Disabilities
  Diagnostic testing services on campus
  Diagnostic testing services off campus
  Remedial and/or tutorial help available
  Reader services for the blind available for LD
  Handicapped student services works with LD

MODIFICATIONS TO TRADITIONAL LEARNING ENVIRONMENT:
  Use of calculator for all math courses
  Tape recorders to record class lectures
  Someone else may take class notes
  Student takes exams in separate rooms
  Students have exams read to them
  Students take typewritten exams
  Longer time allowed to complete exams
  Submit papers on cassette tape

Extended time limits for graduation
Physical education may be waived

MAJORS OFFERED:

AREA STUDIES
BIOLOGICAL SCIENCES
BUSINESS AND MANAGEMENT
COMMUNICATIONS
EDUCATION
FINE AND APPLIED ARTS
FOREIGN LANGUAGES
HEALTH
HUMANITIES
MATHEMATICS
PHYSICAL SCIENCES
PSYCHOLOGY
PUBLIC SERVICES
SOCIAL SCIENCES
THEOLOGY

===

SOUTHERN ARKANSAS UNIVERSITY
MAGNOLIA, AR 71753
501-234-5120

KEY CONTACT: Attn: DONALD HAEFNER
                    V.P. FOR STUDENT AFFAIRS

SIZE OF SCHOOL: SMALL

APPLICATION DEADLINE: NONE

	APPROXIMATE TUITION	ROOM AND BOARD
IN STATE	$ 720	$1430
OUT-OF-STATE	$1150	$1430

REQUIREMENTS FOR ADMISSIONS:
  High school equivalency diploma
  High school diploma
  21 years of age or older, with or without a
    high school diploma or equivalency
  ACT Scores required
  Untimed or oral ACT Scores accepted
  SAT Scores required
  Untimed or oral SAT Scores accepted
  University or College sponsored tests
  Particular rank in class 75%
  Admission requirements modified

State/District residency
In State residents admitted regardless of high school
   average
Out of State residents must be in the upper 50% to
   75% of high school graduating class

ADDITIONAL SERVICES OFFERED:
   Learning Lab
   Diagnostic testing services on campus
   Diagnostic testing services off campus
   Remedial and/or tutorial help available
   Reader services for the blind available for LD
      students through Arkansas State Rehab services

MODIFICATIONS TO TRADITIONAL LEARNING ENVIRONMENT:
   Oral presentation in lieu of written exams
   Has an adaptive physical education program
   Tape recorders to record class lectures
   Someone else may take class notes
   Student takes exams in separate rooms
   Students have exams read to them
   Students take typewritten exams
   Longer time allowed to complete exams
   Submit papers on cassette tape
   Extended time limits for graduation
   Physical education may be waived

MAJORS OFFERED:

   AGRICULTURE
   AREA STUDIES
   BIOLOGICAL SCIENCES
   BUSINESS AND MANAGEMENT
   COMMUNICATIONS
   COMPUTER SCIENCES
   EDUCATION
   FINE AND APPLIED ARTS
   FOREIGN LANGUAGES
   HEALTH
   HUMANITIES
   LAW
   LIBRARY SCIENCE
   MATHEMATICS
   PHYSICAL SCIENCES
   PSYCHOLOGY
   PUBLIC SERVICES
   SOCIAL SCIENCES

===

UNIVERSITY OF ARKANSAS
FAYETTEVILLE, AR 72701
501-575-5346

KEY CONTACT: Attn: JIM HEMAUER, COORDINATOR
DISABLED STUDENT SERVICES

SIZE OF SCHOOL: LARGE

APPLICATION DEADLINE: NONE

	APPROXIMATE TUITION	ROOM AND BOARD
IN STATE	$ 900	$2650
OUT-OF-STATE	$2160	$2650

REQUIREMENTS FOR ADMISSIONS:
High school equivalency diploma
High school diploma
Effective Fall 1985, admission requirements will be
raised from open admission policy. At this time
ACT/SAT scores will be used for placement but are
not required. No modifications of admission
requirements are made for disabled students.

ADDITIONAL SERVICES OFFERED:
Learning Lab
Learning Lab has a specialist with a masters degree
or above in Learning Disabilities
Diagnostic testing services on campus
Diagnostic testing services off campus
Remedial and/or tutorial help available
Reader services for the blind available for LD
Special education department
Handicapped student services works with LD

MODIFICATIONS TO TRADITIONAL LEARNING ENVIRONMENT:
Oral presentation in lieu of written exams
Use of calculator for all math courses
Has an adaptive physical education program
Tape recorders to record class lectures
Someone else may take class notes
Student takes exams in separate rooms
Students have exams read to them
Students take typewritten exams
Longer time allowed to complete exams
Submit papers on cassette tape
Take limited course load and graduate within time
required
Extended time limits for graduation

MAJORS OFFERED:

  AGRICULTURE
  ARCHITECTURE
  BIOLOGICAL SCIENCES
  BUSINESS AND MANAGEMENT
  COMMUNICATIONS
  COMPUTER SCIENCES
  EDUCATION
  ENGINEERING TECHNOLOGIES
  FINE AND APPLIED ARTS
  FOREIGN LANGUAGES
  HEALTH
  HOME ECONOMICS
  HUMANITIES
  LAW
  LIBRARY SCIENCE
  MATHEMATICS
  PHYSICAL SCIENCES
  PSYCHOLOGY
  PUBLIC SERVICES
  SOCIAL SCIENCES

===

UNIVERSITY OF ARKANSAS - LITTLE ROCK
33RD AND UNIVERSITY AVENUES
LITTLE ROCK, AR 72204

KEY CONTACT: Attn: NEYLAND HESTER
                    DIRECTOR ADMINISTRATIVE SERVICES

SIZE OF SCHOOL: MEDIUM

APPLICATION DEADLINE: NONE

     APPROXIMATE TUITION   ROOM AND BOARD

IN STATE $ 800 $ NOT OFFERED
OUT-OF-STATE $1940 $ NOT OFFERED

REQUIREMENTS FOR ADMISSIONS:
  21 years of age or older, with or without a
    high school diploma or equivalency
  ACT Scores required
  Untimed or oral ACT Scores accepted
  SAT Scores required
  Untimed or oral SAT Scores accepted
  High school grade point average 'C'
  Placement tests for English and Math

ADDITIONAL SERVICES OFFERED:
Learning Lab
Learning Lab has a specialist with a masters degree
  or above in Learning Disabilities
Diagnostic testing services on campus
Diagnostic testing services off campus
Remedial and/or tutorial help available
Reader services for the blind available for LD
Special education department
Handicapped student services works with LD

MODIFICATIONS TO TRADITIONAL LEARNING ENVIRONMENT:
Oral presentation in lieu of written exams
Use of calculator for all math courses
Has an adaptive physical education program
Tape recorders to record class lectures
Someone else may take class notes
Students have exams read to them
Students take typewritten exams
Extended time limits for graduation
Physical education may be waived

MAJORS OFFERED:

BIOLOGICAL SCIENCES
BUSINESS AND MANAGEMENT
COMMUNICATIONS
COMPUTER SCIENCES
EDUCATION
ENGINEERING TECHNOLOGIES
FINE AND APPLIED ARTS
FOREIGN LANGUAGES
HEALTH
HUMANITIES
LIBRARY SCIENCE
MATHEMATICS
MILITARY SCIENCES
PHYSICAL SCIENCES
PSYCHOLOGY
PUBLIC SERVICES
SOCIAL SCIENCES

===

BIOLA UNIVERSITY
13800 BIOLA AVENUE
LA MIRADA, CA 90639

KEY CONTACT: Attn: JANE HIGA
                    DEAN FOR STUDENT AFFAIRS

SIZE OF SCHOOL: SMALL

APPLICATION DEADLINE: JULY 31

	APPROXIMATE TUITION	ROOM AND BOARD
IN STATE	$4470	$2500
OUT-OF-STATE	$4470	$2500

REQUIREMENTS FOR ADMISSIONS:
  High school equivalency diploma
  High school diploma
  SAT Scores required
  Untimed or oral SAT Scores accepted
  University or College sponsored tests
  Admission requirements modified
  Personal interview
  Placement tests
  Recommendations
  Essay

ADDITIONAL SERVICES OFFERED:
  Learning Lab
  Diagnostic testing services on campus
  Diagnostic testing services off campus
  Remedial and/or tutorial help available
  Reader services for the blind available for LD
  Handicapped student services works with LD

MODIFICATIONS TO TRADITIONAL LEARNING ENVIRONMENT:
  Oral presentation in lieu of written exams
  Use of calculator for all math courses
  Has an adaptive physical education program
  Tape recorders to record class lectures
  Someone else may take class notes
  Multiple choice exams only
  Essay exams only
  Student takes exams in separate rooms
  Students have exams read to them
  Students take typewritten exams
  Longer time allowed to complete exams
  Submit papers on cassette tape
  Extended time limits for graduation
  Physical education may be waived

MAJORS OFFERED:

  AREA STUDIES
  BIOLOGICAL SCIENCES
  BUSINESS AND MANAGEMENT
  COMMUNICATIONS

```
COMPUTER SCIENCES
EDUCATION
FINE AND APPLIED ARTS
FOREIGN LANGUAGES
HEALTH
HUMANITIES
MATHEMATICS
PHYSICAL SCIENCES
PSYCHOLOGY
PUBLIC SERVICES
SOCIAL SCIENCES
THEOLOGY
```

==

```
CALIFORNIA POLYTECHNIC STATE UNIVERSITY
SAN LUIS OBISPO, CA 93407
805-546-2311

KEY CONTACT: Attn:  ANN FRYER
                    LEARNING DISABILITIES SPECIALIST

SIZE OF SCHOOL: LARGE

APPLICATION DEADLINE: NOVEMBER 30
```

	APPROXIMATE TUITION	ROOM AND BOARD
IN STATE	$ 650	$2895
OUT-OF-STATE	$3150	$2895

```
REQUIREMENTS FOR ADMISSIONS:
  High school equivalency diploma
  High school diploma
  SAT Scores required (used as indicator)
  Untimed or oral SAT Scores accepted
  Admission requirements modified
  Personal interview
  Recommendations (two required)

ADDITIONAL SERVICES OFFERED:
  Learning Lab
  Diagnostic testing services on campus
  Diagnostic testing services off campus
  Remedial and/or tutorial help available
  Reader services for the blind available for LD
  Special Education department
  Handicapped student services works with LD
  Handicapped student services has LD specialist
```

MODIFICATIONS TO TRADITIONAL LEARNING ENVIRONMENT:
  Oral presentation in lieu of written exams
  Use of calculator for all math courses
  Has an adaptive physical education program
  Tape recorders to record class lectures
  Someone else may take class notes
  Student takes exams in separate rooms
  Students have exams read to them
  Longer time allowed to complete exams
  Submit papers on cassette tape
  Extended time limits for graduation

MAJORS OFFERED:

  AGRICULTURE
  ARCHITECTURE
  BIOLOGICAL SCIENCES
  BUSINESS AND MANAGEMENT
  COMMUNICATIONS
  COMPUTER SCIENCES
  EDUCATION
  ENGINEERING TECHNOLOGIES
  FINE AND APPLIED ARTS
  HOME ECONOMICS
  HUMANITIES
  MATHEMATICS
  PHYSICAL SCIENCES
  PUBLIC SERVICES
  SOCIAL SCIENCES

===

CALIFORNIA STATE UNIVERSITY - CHICO
CHICO, CA 95929
916-895-6321

KEY CONTACT: Attn: PATRICIA STEWART, LD SPECIALIST

SIZE OF SCHOOL: LARGE

APPLICATION DEADLINE: AUGUST

         APPROXIMATE TUITION   ROOM AND BOARD

IN STATE $ 600 $2700
OUT-OF-STATE $4350 $2700

REQUIREMENTS FOR ADMISSIONS:
  High school diploma
  ACT Scores required
  Untimed or oral ACT Scores accepted

```
SAT Scores required
Untimed or oral SAT Scores accepted
University or College sponsored tests
Particular rank in class (upper 1/3 in-state)
                         (upper 1/6 out of state)
High school grade point average (combination of
  g.p.a. and SAT or ACT, tables available)
Admission requirements modified if borderline grades
Personal interview
Placement tests
Recommendations
English and Math placement
Writing proficiency in Jr. year
```

ADDITIONAL SERVICES OFFERED:
```
Diagnostic testing services on campus
Diagnostic testing services off campus
Remedial and/or tutorial help available
Reader services for the blind available for LD
Special Education department
Handicapped student services works with LD
Limited tutoring
```

MODIFICATIONS TO TRADITIONAL LEARNING ENVIRONMENT:
```
Oral presentation in lieu of written exams
Use of calculator for all math courses
Has an adaptive physical education program
Tape recorders to record class lectures
Someone else may take class notes
Student takes exams in separate rooms
Students have exams read to them
Students take typewritten exams
Longer time allowed to complete exams
Take limited course load and graduate within time
  required
Extended time limits for graduation
Physical education may be waived
```

MAJORS OFFERED:

```
AGRICULTURE
AREA STUDIES
BIOLOGICAL SCIENCES
BUSINESS AND MANAGEMENT
COMMUNICATIONS
COMPUTER SCIENCES
EDUCATION
ENGINEERING TECHNOLOGIES
FINE AND APPLIED ARTS
FOREIGN LANGUAGES
HEALTH
```

    HOME ECONOMICS
    HUMANITIES
    MATHEMATICS
    PHYSICAL SCIENCES
    PSYCHOLOGY
    PUBLIC SERVICES
    SOCIAL SCIENCES

==

CALIFORNIA STATE UNIVERSITY - DOMINQUEZ HILLS
CARSON, CA 90747
213-516-3600

KEY CONTACT: Attn: MARK MATSUI, COORDINATOR
                     HANDICAPPED STUDENT SERVICES

SIZE OF SCHOOL: MEDIUM

APPLICATION DEADLINE: AUGUST 15

        APPROXIMATE TUITION   ROOM AND BOARD

IN STATE $ 625 $2410
OUT-OF-STATE $1995 $2410

REQUIREMENTS FOR ADMISSIONS:
  High school equivalency diploma
  High school diploma
  ACT Scores required
  Untimed or oral ACT Scores accepted
  SAT Scores required
  Untimed or oral SAT Scores accepted
  Particular rank in class (eligibility index for
    freshman)
  High school grade point average (eligibility index
    for freshman)

ADDITIONAL SERVICES OFFERED:
  Learning Lab
  Diagnostic testing services on campus
  Diagnostic testing services off campus
  Remedial and/or tutorial help available
  Reader services for the blind available for LD
  Handicapped student services works with LD
  All support services through Disabled Student
    Services Office

MODIFICATIONS TO TRADITIONAL LEARNING ENVIRONMENT:
  Oral presentation in lieu of written exams
  Use of calculator for all math courses

```
Has an adaptive physical education program
Tape recorders to record class lectures
Someone else may take class notes
Student takes exams in separate rooms
Students have exams read to them
Students take typewritten exams
Longer time allowed to complete exams
Submit papers on cassette tape
Extended time limits for graduation
Physical education may be waived
All class accomodations are worked out individually,
    there are very few general rules
```

MAJORS OFFERED:

```
BIOLOGICAL SCIENCES
BUSINESS AND MANAGEMENT
COMMUNICATIONS
COMPUTER SCIENCES
EDUCATION
FINE AND APPLIED ARTS
FOREIGN LANGUAGES
HEALTH
HUMANITIES
MATHEMATICS
PHYSICAL SCIENCES
PSYCHOLOGY
PUBLIC SERVICES
SOCIAL SCIENCES
```

==

```
CALIFORNIA STATE UNIVERSITY - FRESNO
SHAW ANDCEDAR AVENUES
FRESNO, CA 93740
209-294-2192
```

KEY CONTACT: Attn: Handicapped Student Services

SIZE OF SCHOOL: LARGE

APPLICATION DEADLINE: JUNE 3

	APPROXIMATE TUITION	ROOM AND BOARD
IN STATE	$ 600	$2940
OUT OF-STATE	$3700	$2940

REQUIREMENTS FOR ADMISSIONS:
  High school equivalency diploma
  High school diploma

```
ACT Scores required
Untimed or oral ACT Scores accepted
SAT Scores required
Untimed or oral SAT Scores accepted
University or College sponsored tests
Placement tests
```

ADDITIONAL SERVICES OFFERED:
```
  Learning Lab
  Learning Lab has a specialist with a masters degree
   or above in Learning Disabilities
  Diagnostic testing services on campus
  Remedial and/or tutorial help available
  Reader services for the blind available for LD
  Handicapped student services works with LD
```

MODIFICATIONS TO TRADITIONAL LEARNING ENVIRONMENT:
```
  Oral presentation in lieu of written exams
  Use of calculator for all math courses
  Has an adaptive physical education program
  Tape recorders to record class lectures
  Someone else may take class notes
  Student takes exams in separate rooms
  Students have exams read to them
  Students take typewritten exams
  Longer time allowed to complete exams
  Extended time limits for graduation
  Physical education may be waived
```

MAJORS OFFERED:

```
  AGRICULTURE
  BIOLOGICAL SCIENCES
  BUSINESS AND MANAGEMENT
  COMMUNICATIONS
  EDUCATION
  ENGINEERING TECHNOLOGIES
  FINE AND APPLIED ARTS
  FOREIGN LANGUAGES
  HEALTH
  HOME ECONOMICS
  HUMANITIES
  MATHEMATICS
  PHYSICAL SCIENCES
  PSYCHOLOGY
  PUBLIC SERVICES
  SOCIAL SCIENCES
```

==

CALIFORNIA STATE UNIVERSITY - LONG BEACH
1250 BELLFLOWER BOULEVARD
LONG BEACH, CA 90840
213-498-4141

KEY CONTACT: Attn: HELEN IRLEN OR DAVID SANFILIPPO
                    HANDICAPPED STUDENT SERVICES

SIZE OF SCHOOL: LARGE

APPLICATION DEADLINE: NONE

	APPROXIMATE TUITION	ROOM AND BOARD
IN STATE	$ 450	$2700
OUT-OF-STATE	$2745	$2700

REQUIREMENTS FOR ADMISSIONS:
  High school equivalency diploma
  High school diploma
  ACT Scores (recommended)
  Untimed or oral ACT Scores accepted
  SAT Scores (recommended)
  Untimed or oral SAT Scores accepted
  High school grade point average 2.0 preferred
  Admission requirements modified
  Personal interview
  Recommendations
  Essay

ADDITIONAL SERVICES OFFERED:
  Learning Lab
  Learning Lab has a specialist with a masters degree
    or above in Learning Disabilities
  Diagnostic testing services on campus
  Diagnostic testing services off campus
  Remedial and/or tutorial help available
  Reader services for the blind available for LD
  Special Education department
  Handicapped student services works with LD
  Has extensive research component

MODIFICATIONS TO TRADITIONAL LEARNING ENVIRONMENT:
  Oral presentation in lieu of written exams
  Use of calculator for all math courses
  Has an adaptive physical education program
  Tape recorders to record class lectures
  Someone else may take class notes
  Multiple choice exams only (if necessary)
  Essay exams only (if necessary)
  Student takes exams in separate rooms

```
    Students have exams read to them
    Students take typewritten exams
    Longer time allowed to complete exams
    Submit papers on cassette tape
    Extended time limits for graduation
    Physical education may be waived
    In the process of developing a word processing center
        for students
    Standardized exams for graduation may be waived
```

MAJORS OFFERED:

```
    ARCHITECTURE
    AREA STUDIES
    BIOLOGICAL SCIENCES
    BUSINESS AND MANAGEMENT
    COMMUNICATIONS
    COMPUTER SCIENCES
    EDUCATION
    ENGINEERING TECHNOLOGIES
    FINE AND APPLIED ARTS
    FOREIGN LANGUAGES
    HEALTH
    HOME ECONOMICS
    HUMANITIES
    MATHEMATICS
    MILITARY SCIENCES
    PHYSICAL SCIENCES
    PSYCHOLOGY
    PUBLIC SERVICES
    SOCIAL SCIENCES
```

===

```
CALIFORNIA STATE UNIVERSITY - SACRAMENTO
6000 J STREET
SACRAMENTO, CA 95819
916-454-6111

KEY CONTACT: Attn:  SUSAN EILAND-RICKMAN
                    L.D. SPECIALIST

SIZE OF SCHOOL: LARGE

APPLICATION DEADLINE: NONE
```

	APPROXIMATE TUITION	ROOM AND BOARD
IN STATE	$ 600	$2400
OUT-OF-STATE	$3150	$2400

REQUIREMENTS FOR ADMISSIONS:
  High school equivalency diploma
  High school diploma
  ACT Scores required
  Untimed or oral ACT Scores accepted
  SAT Scores required
  Untimed or oral SAT Scores accepted
  High school grade point average (minimum 3.21)
  Admission requirements modified
  Personal interview
  Placement tests
  Recommendations

ADDITIONAL SERVICES OFFERED:
  Learning Lab
  Learning Lab has a specialist with a masters degree
    or above in Learning Disabilities
  Diagnostic testing services on campus
  Remedial and/or tutorial help available
  Reader services for the blind available for LD
  Special Education department
  Handicapped student services works with LD

MODIFICATIONS TO TRADITIONAL LEARNING ENVIRONMENT:
  Oral presentation in lieu of written exams
  Tape recorders to record class lectures
  Someone else may take class notes
  Multiple choice exams only
  Essay exams only
  Student takes exams in separate rooms
  Students have exams read to them
  Students take typewritten exams
  Longer time allowed to complete exams
  Submit papers on cassette tape
  Extended time limits for graduation

MAJORS OFFERED:

  BIOLOGICAL SCIENCES
  BUSINESS AND MANAGEMENT
  COMMUNICATIONS
  COMPUTER SCIENCES
  EDUCATION
  ENGINEERING TECHNOLOGIES
  FINE AND APPLIED ARTS
  FOREIGN LANGUAGES
  HEALTH
  HOME ECONOMICS
  HUMANITIES
  MATHEMATICS
  PHYSICAL SCIENCES

PSYCHOLOGY
PUBLIC SERVICES
SOCIAL SCIENCES

==

SAN DIEGO STATE UNIVERSITY
5300 CAMPANILE DRIVE
SAN DIEGO, CA 92182
619-265-6871

KEY CONTACT: Attn: DEIDRE SEMOFF JORDON
                     LEARNING DISABILITIES SPECIALIST

SIZE OF SCHOOL: LARGE

APPLICATION DEADLINE: NOVEMBER 30

        APPROXIMATE TUITION   ROOM AND BOARD

IN STATE $ 500 $2300
OUT-OF-STATE $3650 $2300

REQUIREMENTS FOR ADMISSIONS:
  High school equivalency diploma
  High school diploma
  21 years of age or older, with or without a
    high school diploma or equivalency
  ACT Scores required
  Untimed or oral ACT Scores accepted
  SAT Scores required
  Untimed or oral SAT Scores accepted
  University or College sponsored tests
  Admission requirements modified
  Personal interview
  Placement tests
  Recommendations
  Essay
  State/District residency (for tuition)

ADDITIONAL SERVICES OFFERED:
  Diagnostic testing services on campus
  Remedial and/or tutorial help available
  Reader services for the blind available for LD
  Handicapped student services works with LD
  L.D. specialist has masters in Special Ed

MODIFICATIONS TO TRADITIONAL LEARNING ENVIRONMENT:
  Oral presentation in lieu of written exams
  Use of calculator for all math courses
  Has an adaptive physical education program

```
Tape recorders to record class lectures
Someone else may take class notes
Student takes exams in separate rooms
Students have exams read to them
Students take typewritten exams
Longer time allowed to complete exams
Submit papers on cassette tape
Extended time limits for graduation
Physical education may be waived
```

MAJORS OFFERED:

```
AREA STUDIES .
BIOLOGICAL SCIENCES
BUSINESS AND MANAGEMENT
COMMUNICATIONS
COMPUTER SCIENCES
EDUCATION
ENGINEERING TECHNOLOGIES
FINE AND APPLIED ARTS
FOREIGN LANGUAGES
HEALTH
HOME ECONOMICS
HUMANITIES
MATHEMATICS
PHYSICAL SCIENCES
PSYCHOLOGY
PUBLIC SERVICES
SOCIAL SCIENCES
```

==

```
SAN DIEGO STATE UNIVERSITY
IMPERIAL VALLEY CAMPUS
720 HEBER AVENUE
CALEXICO, CA 92231
619-357-3721
```

KEY CONTACT: Attn: MS. CYNTHIA FLORES
                     ASSISTANT DEAN OF STUDENT AFFAIRES

SIZE OF SCHOOL: SMALL

APPLICATION DEADLINE: NONE

	APPROXIMATE TUITION	ROOM AND BOARD
IN STATE	$ 255	$ NOT OFFERED
OUT-OF-STATE	$2747	$ NOT OFFERED

REQUIREMENTS FOR ADMISSIONS:
  University or College sponsored tests
  Particular rank in class (56 transferrable units or
    more
  Admission requirements modified

ADDITIONAL SERVICES OFFERED:
  Remedial and/or tutorial help available
  Reader services for the blind available for LD

MODIFICATIONS TO TRADITIONAL LEARNING ENVIRONMENT:
  Oral presentation in lieu of written exams
  Tape recorders to record class lectures
  Someone else may take class notes
  Student takes exams in separate rooms
  Students have exams read to them
  Students take typewritten exams
  Longer time allowed to complete exams
  Submit papers on cassette tape
  Extended time limits for graduation
  Physical education may be waived

MAJORS OFFERED:

  AREA STUDIES
  BUSINESS AND MANAGEMENT
  EDUCATION
  FOREIGN LANGUAGES
  HUMANITIES
  PSYCHOLOGY
  PUBLIC SERVICES
  SOCIAL SCIENCES

==

UNIVERSITY OF CALIFORNIA - BERKELEY
120 SPROUL HALL
BERKELEY, CA 94720
415-642-0200

KEY CONTACT: Attn: DOROTHY STUMP, LD SPECIALIST

SIZE OF SCHOOL: LARGE

APPLICATION DEADLINE: NOVEMBER 30

        APPROXIMATE TUITION   ROOM AND BOARD

IN STATE $1360 $3500
OUT-OF-STATE $4720 $3500

REQUIREMENTS FOR ADMISSIONS:
   ACT Scores required
   SAT Scores required
   Admission requirements modified

ADDITIONAL SERVICES OFFERED:
   Learning Lab
   Learning Lab has a specialist with a masters degree
      or above in Learning Disabilities
   Reader services for the blind available for LD
   Handicapped student services works with LD

MODIFICATIONS TO TRADITIONAL LEARNING ENVIRONMENT:
   Tape recorders to record class lectures
   Someone else may take class notes
   Student takes exams in separate rooms
   Students have exams read to them
   Students take typewritten exams
   Longer time allowed to complete exams
   Physical education may be waived

MAJORS OFFERED:

   AGRICULTURE
   ARCHITECTURE
   AREA STUDIES
   BIOLOGICAL SCIENCES
   BUSINESS AND MANAGEMENT
   COMMUNICATIONS
   COMPUTER SCIENCES
   EDUCATION
   ENGINEERING TECHNOLOGIES
   FINE AND APPLIED ARTS
   FOREIGN LANGUAGES
   HEALTH
   HOME ECONOMICS
   HUMANITIES
   LIBRARY SCIENCE
   MATHEMATICS
   PHYSICAL SCIENCES
   PSYCHOLOGY
   PUBLIC SERVICES
   SOCIAL SCIENCES
   THEOLOGY

===

UNIVERSITY OF CALIFORNIA - IRVINE
IRVINE, CA 92717
714-833-5011

KEY CONTACT: Attn: PATRICIA L. ROMERO, COORDINATOR
                     DISABLED STUDENT SERVICES

SIZE OF SCHOOL: MEDIUM

APPLICATION DEADLINE: NONE

           APPROXIMATE TUITION   ROOM AND BOARD

IN STATE $1400 $3480
OUT-OF-STATE $4760 $3480

REQUIREMENTS FOR ADMISSIONS:
  High school equivalency diploma
  High school diploma
  ACT Scores required
  Untimed or oral ACT Scores accepted
  SAT Scores required
  Untimed or oral SAT Scores accepted
  University or College sponsored tests
  Admission requirements modified
  Placement tests
  Essay

ADDITIONAL SERVICES OFFERED:
  Learning Lab
  Diagnostic testing services off campus
  Remedial and/or tutorial help available
  Reader services for the blind available for LD
  Handicapped student services works with LD

MODIFICATIONS TO TRADITIONAL LEARNING ENVIRONMENT:
  Oral presentation in lieu of written exams
  Use of calculator for all math courses
  Tape recorders to record class lectures
  Someone else may take class notes
  Multiple choice exams only
  Essay exams only
  Student takes exams in separate rooms
  Students have exams read to them
  Students take typewritten exams
  Longer time allowed to complete exams
  Submit papers on cassette tape
  Extended time limits for graduation

MAJORS OFFERED:

  AREA STUDIES
  BIOLOGICAL SCIENCES
  BUSINESS AND MANAGEMENT
  COMPUTER SCIENCES

```
EDUCATION
ENGINEERING TECHNOLOGIES
FINE AND APPLIED ARTS
FOREIGN LANGUAGES
HUMANITIES
MATHEMATICS
PHYSICAL SCIENCES
PSYCHOLOGY
SOCIAL SCIENCES
```

==

UNIVERSITY OF CALIFORNIA - RIVERSIDE
RIVERSIDE, CA 92521
714-787-3411

KEY CONTACT: Attn: GAY C. GLASGOW
                     HANDICAPPED STUDENT SERVICES

SIZE OF SCHOOL: MEDIUM

APPLICATION DEADLINE: NONE

	APPROXIMATE TUITION	ROOM AND BOARD
IN STATE	$1370	$2640
OUT-OF-STATE	$3360	$2640

REQUIREMENTS FOR ADMISSIONS:
  High school diploma
  ACT Scores required
  SAT Scores required
  Admission requirements modified

ADDITIONAL SERVICES OFFERED:
  Learning Lab
  Learning Lab has a specialist with a masters degree
    or above in Learning Disabilities
  Remedial and/or tutorial help available
  Reader services for the blind available for LD
  Handicapped student services works with LD

MODIFICATIONS TO TRADITIONAL LEARNING ENVIRONMENT:
  Use of calculator for all math courses
  Tape recorders to record class lectures
  Someone else may take class notes
  Student takes exams in separate rooms
  Students have exams read to them
  Students take typewritten exams
  Longer time allowed to complete exams
  Submit papers on cassette tape

Extended time limits for graduation
Physical education may be waived

MAJORS OFFERED:

AGRICULTURE
AREA STUDIES
BIOLOGICAL SCIENCES
BUSINESS AND MANAGEMENT
COMPUTER SCIENCES
EDUCATION
FINE AND APPLIED ARTS
FOREIGN LANGUAGES
HEALTH
HUMANITIES
LAW
MATHEMATICS
PHYSICAL SCIENCES
PSYCHOLOGY
PUBLIC SERVICES
SOCIAL SCIENCES

==

COLORADO STATE UNIVERSITY
FORT COLLINS, CO 80523
303-491-7201

KEY CONTACT: Attn: MIKE RYAN, OFFICE OF RESOURCES
                    FOR DISABLED STUDENTS

SIZE OF SCHOOL: LARGE

APPLICATION DEADLINE: NONE

           APPROXIMATE TUITION   ROOM AND BOARD

IN STATE $1100 $2365
OUT-OF-STATE $4120 $2365

REQUIREMENTS FOR ADMISSIONS:
  High school diploma
  ACT Scores required
  Untimed or oral ACT Scores accepted
  SAT Scores required
  Untimed or oral SAT Scores accepted
  Particular rank in class 50%

ADDITIONAL SERVICES OFFERED:
  Learning Lab
  Diagnostic testing services on campus

Remedial and/or tutorial help available
Reader services for the blind available for LD
Handicapped student services works with LD

MODIFICATIONS TO TRADITIONAL LEARNING ENVIRONMENT:
Oral presentation in lieu of written exams
Use of calculator for all math courses
Has an adaptive physical education program
Tape recorders to record class lectures
Someone else may take class notes
Student takes exams in separate rooms
Students have exams read to them
Students take typewritten exams
Longer time allowed to complete exams
Submit papers on cassette tape
Take limited course load and graduate within time
    required
Extended time limits for graduation
Physical education may be waived

MAJORS OFFERED:

AGRICULTURE
ARCHITECTURE
AREA STUDIES
BIOLOGICAL SCIENCES
BUSINESS AND MANAGEMENT
COMMUNICATIONS
COMPUTER SCIENCES
EDUCATION
ENGINEERING TECHNOLOGIES
FINE AND APPLIED ARTS
FOREIGN LANGUAGES
HEALTH
HOME ECONOMICS
HUMANITIES
MATHEMATICS
PHYSICAL SCIENCES
PSYCHOLOGY
PUBLIC SERVICES
SOCIAL SCIENCES

==

FORT LEWIS COLLEGE
DURANGO, CO 81301
303-247-7184

KEY CONTACT: Attn: BOB LUNDQUIST, DIRECTOR
                    LEARNING ASSISTANCE CENTER
SIZE OF SCHOOL: MEDIUM

APPLICATION DEADLINE: NONE

APPROXIMATE TUITION   ROOM AND BOARD

	APPROXIMATE TUITION	ROOM AND BOARD
IN STATE	$ 850	$1815
OUT-OF-STATE	$3160	$1815

REQUIREMENTS FOR ADMISSIONS:
  High school diploma
  ACT Scores required
  Placement tests

ADDITIONAL SERVICES OFFERED:
  Learning Lab
  Diagnostic testing services on campus
  Remedial and/or tutorial help available

MODIFICATIONS TO TRADITIONAL LEARNING ENVIRONMENT:
  Oral presentation in lieu of written exams
  Use of calculator for all math courses
  Tape recorders to record class lectures
  Someone else may take class notes
  Multiple choice exams only
  Essay exams only
  Student takes exams in separate rooms
  Students have exams read to them
  Students take typewritten exams
  Longer time allowed to complete exams
  Submit papers on cassette tape
  Extended time limits for graduation
  Physical education may be waived

MAJORS OFFERED:

  AREA STUDIES
  BIOLOGICAL SCIENCES
  BUSINESS AND MANAGEMENT
  COMMUNICATIONS
  COMPUTER SCIENCES
  EDUCATION
  ENGINEERING TECHNOLOGIES
  FINE AND APPLIED ARTS
  FOREIGN LANGUAGES
  HEALTH
  HUMANITIES
  LAW
  MATHEMATICS
  PHYSICAL SCIENCES
  PSYCHOLOGY
  SOCIAL SCIENCES

METROPOLITAN STATE COLLEGE
1006 11TH STREET
DENVER, CO 80204
303-629-3058

KEY CONTACT: Attn: EVA DYER, LEARNING DISABILITIES
                    PROGRAM DIRECTOR

SIZE OF SCHOOL: LARGE

APPLICATION DEADLINE: AUGUST 15

     APPROXIMATE TUITION   ROOM AND BOARD

IN STATE $ 900 $ NOT OFFERED
OUT-OF-STATE $3270 $ NOT OFFERED

REQUIREMENTS FOR ADMISSIONS:
  High school equivalency diploma
  High school diploma

ADDITIONAL SERVICES OFFERED:
  Learning Lab
  Learning Lab has a specialist with a masters degree
    or above in Learning Disabilities
  Diagnostic testing services on campus
  Reader services for the blind available for LD
  Special Education department
  Handicapped student services works with LD
  Courses designed for LD students
  Special Learning Disabilities Program

MODIFICATIONS TO TRADITIONAL LEARNING ENVIRONMENT:
  Oral presentation in lieu of written exams
  Use of calculator for all math courses
  Has an adaptive physical education program
  Tape recorders to record class lectures
  Someone else may take class notes
  Multiple choice exams only
  Essay exams only
  Student takes exams in separate rooms
  Students have exams read to them
  Students take typewritten exams
  Longer time allowed to complete exams
  Submit papers on cassette tape
  Take limited course load and graduate within time
    required
  Extended time limits for graduation
  Physical education may be waived

MAJORS OFFERED:

    ARCHITECTURE
    BIOLOGICAL SCIENCES
    BUSINESS AND MANAGEMENT
    COMMUNICATIONS
    COMPUTER SCIENCES
    EDUCATION
    ENGINEERING TECHNOLOGIES
    FINE AND APPLIED ARTS
    FOREIGN LANGUAGES
    HEALTH
    HUMANITIES
    LAW
    MATHEMATICS
    PHYSICAL SCIENCES
    PSYCHOLOGY
    PUBLIC SERVICES
    SOCIAL SCIENCES

===

UNIVERSITY OF COLORADO
BOULDER, CO 80309
303-492-6694

KEY CONTACT: Attn: OFFICE OF DISABLED STUDENT SERVICES

SIZE OF SCHOOL: LARGE

APPLICATION DEADLINE: JULY 1

              APPROXIMATE TUITION   ROOM AND BOARD

IN STATE $1010 $2250
OUT-OF-STATE $4715 $2250

REQUIREMENTS FOR ADMISSIONS:
    High school equivalency diploma
    High school diploma
    ACT Scores required
    Untimed or oral ACT Scores accepted
    SAT Scores required
    Untimed or oral SAT Scores accepted
    Particular rank in class (50%)
    Admission requirements modified

ADDITIONAL SERVICES OFFERED:
    Learning Lab
    Learning Lab has a specialist with a masters degree
      or above in Learning Disabilities

```
Diagnostic testing services on campus
Diagnostic testing services off campus
Remedial and/or tutorial help available
Special Education department
Handicapped student services works with LD
```

MODIFICATIONS TO TRADITIONAL LEARNING ENVIRONMENT:
```
Use of calculator for all math courses
Tape recorders to record class lectures
Someone else may take class notes
Student takes exams in separate rooms
Students have exams read to them
Students take typewritten exams
Longer time allowed to complete exams
Take limited course load and graduate within time
   required
Physical education may be waived
```

MAJORS OFFERED:

```
ARCHITECTURE
AREA STUDIES
BIOLOGICAL SCIENCES
BUSINESS AND MANAGEMENT
COMMUNICATIONS
COMPUTER SCIENCES
EDUCATION
ENGINEERING TECHNOLOGIES
FINE AND APPLIED ARTS
FOREIGN LANGUAGES
HEALTH
HUMANITIES
MATHEMATICS
PHYSICAL SCIENCES
PSYCHOLOGY
PUBLIC SERVICES
SOCIAL SCIENCES
THEOLOGY
```

==

```
UNIVERSITY OF NORTHERN COLORADO
GREELEY, CO 80639
303-351-2881
```

KEY CONTACT: Attn: RESOURCES FOR THE DISABLED

SIZE OF SCHOOL: MEDIUM

APPLICATION DEADLINE: AUGUST 15

```
        APPROXIMATE TUITION    ROOM AND BOARD

IN STATE            $1340        $2475
OUT-OF-STATE        $4470        $2475
```

REQUIREMENTS FOR ADMISSIONS:
  ACT Scores required
  Particular rank in class 50%

ADDITIONAL SERVICES OFFERED:
  Learning Lab
  Diagnostic testing services off campus
  Reader services for the blind available for LD
  Special Education department
  Handicapped student services works with LD

MODIFICATIONS TO TRADITIONAL LEARNING ENVIRONMENT:
  Oral presentation in lieu of written exams
  Use of calculator for all math courses
  Tape recorders to record class lectures
  Someone else may take class notes
  Multiple choice exams only
  Essay exams only
  Student takes exams in separate rooms
  Students have exams read to them
  Students take typewritten exams
  Longer time allowed to complete exams
  Submit papers on cassette tape
  Extended time limits for graduation
  Physical education may be waived

MAJORS OFFERED:

  AREA STUDIES
  BIOLOGICAL SCIENCES
  BUSINESS AND MANAGEMENT
  COMMUNICATIONS
  COMPUTER SCIENCES
  EDUCATION
  FINE AND APPLIED ARTS
  FOREIGN LANGUAGES
  HEALTH
  HOME ECONOMICS
  HUMANITIES
  LAW
  MATHEMATICS
  MILITARY SCIENCES
  PHYSICAL SCIENCES
  PSYCHOLOGY
  SOCIAL SCIENCES

UNIVERSITY OF SOUTHERN COLORADO
2200 NORTH BONFORTE BOULEVARD
PUEBLO, CO 81001
303-549-2461

KEY CONTACT: Attn: DAVID GRISHAM, DIRECTOR
                     HANDICAPPED STUDENT SERVICES

SIZE OF SCHOOL: MEDIUM

APPLICATION DEADLINE: JULY 21

         APPROXIMATE TUITION   ROOM AND BOARD

IN STATE $1070 $2560
OUT-OF-STATE $3960 $2560

REQUIREMENTS FOR ADMISSIONS:
   High school equivalency diploma
   High school diploma
   ACT Scores required
   Open admissions policy

ADDITIONAL SERVICES OFFERED:
   Learning Lab
   Learning Lab has a specialist with a masters degree
      or above in Learning Disabilities
   Diagnostic testing services on campus
   Diagnostic testing services off campus
   Remedial and/or tutorial help available
   Reader services for the blind available for LD
   Handicapped student services works with LD

MODIFICATIONS TO TRADITIONAL LEARNING ENVIRONMENT:
   Oral presentation in lieu of written exams
   Use of calculator for all math courses
   Has an adaptive physical education program
   Tape recorders to record class lectures
   Someone else may take class notes
   Multiple choice exams only
   Essay exams only
   Student takes exams in separate rooms
   Students have exams read to them
   Students take typewritten exams
   Longer time allowed to complete exams
   Submit papers on cassette tape
   Take limited course load and graduate within time
      required
   Extended time limits for graduation
   Physical education may be waived

MAJORS OFFERED:

   AGRICULTURE
   AREA STUDIES
   BIOLOGICAL SCIENCES
   BUSINESS AND MANAGEMENT
   COMMUNICATIONS
   COMPUTER SCIENCES
   EDUCATION
   ENGINEERING TECHNOLOGIES
   FINE AND APPLIED ARTS
   FOREIGN LANGUAGES
   HEALTH
   HUMANITIES
   MATHEMATICS
   MILITARY SCIENCES
   PHYSICAL SCIENCES
   PSYCHOLOGY
   PUBLIC SERVICES
   SOCIAL SCIENCES

==

EASTERN CONNECTICUT STATE UNIVERSITY
WILLIMANTIC, CT 06226
203-456-2231

KEY CONTACT: Attn: SHIRLEY A. DOIRON, COORDINATOR
                    DISABLED STUDENT SERVICES

SIZE OF SCHOOL: MEDIUM

APPLICATION DEADLINE: JULY 15

        APPROXIMATE TUITION   ROOM AND BOARD

IN STATE $1090 $2250
OUT-OF-STATE $2220 $2250

REQUIREMENTS FOR ADMISSIONS:
  High school equivalency diploma
  ACT Scores required
  Untimed or oral ACT Scores accepted
  SAT Scores required
  Untimed or oral SAT Scores accepted
  Particular rank in class 50%
  Admission requirements modified
  Personal interview (sometimes)
  Recommendations

ADDITIONAL SERVICES OFFERED:

Learning Lab
Remedial and/or tutorial help available
Reader services for the blind available for LD
Handicapped student services works with LD

MODIFICATIONS TO TRADITIONAL LEARNING ENVIRONMENT:
Oral presentation in lieu of written exams
Use of calculator for all math courses
Has an adaptive physical education program
Tape recorders to record class lectures
Someone else may take class notes
Multiple choice exams only
Essay exams only
Student takes exams in separate rooms
Students have exams read to them
Students take typewritten exams
Longer time allowed to complete exams
Submit papers on cassette tape
Extended time limits for graduation
Physical education may be waived

No formal program for Learning Disabled students.
They work with each L.D. student on an individual
basis and make whatever modification they can with
the resources available.

MAJORS OFFERED:

AREA STUDIES
BIOLOGICAL SCIENCES
BUSINESS AND MANAGEMENT
COMPUTER SCIENCES
EDUCATION
FINE AND APPLIED ARTS
FOREIGN LANGUAGES
HEALTH
HUMANITIES
MATHEMATICS
MILITARY SCIENCES
PHYSICAL SCIENCES
PSYCHOLOGY
SOCIAL SCIENCES

==

UNIVERSITY OF HARTFORD
200 BLOOMFIELD AVENUE
WEST HARTFORD, CT 06117
203-243-4296

KEY CONTACT: Attn: Handicapped Student Services

SIZE OF SCHOOL: MEDIUM

APPLICATION DEADLINE: FEBRUARY 1

APPROXIMATE TUITION   ROOM AND BOARD

IN STATE $7150 $3190
OUT-OF-STATE $7150 $3190

REQUIREMENTS FOR ADMISSIONS:
  High school equivalency diploma
  High school diploma
  ACT Scores required
  SAT Scores required

ADDITIONAL SERVICES OFFERED:
  Learning Lab
  Remedial and/or tutorial help available
  Reader services for the blind available for LD
  Handicapped student services works with LD

MODIFICATIONS TO TRADITIONAL LEARNING ENVIRONMENT:
  Oral presentation in lieu of written exams
  Use of calculator for all math courses
  Tape recorders to record class lectures
  Someone else may take class notes
  Student takes exams in separate rooms
  Students have exams read to them
  Students take typewritten exams
  Longer time allowed to complete exams
  Submit papers on cassette tape
  Take limited course load and graduate within time
    required
  Extended time limits for graduation
  Physical education may be waived

MAJORS OFFERED:

  BIOLOGICAL SCIENCES
  BUSINESS AND MANAGEMENT
  COMMUNICATIONS
  COMPUTER SCIENCES
  EDUCATION
  ENGINEERING TECHNOLOGIES
  FINE AND APPLIED ARTS
  FOREIGN LANGUAGES
  HEALTH
  HUMANITIES
  MATHEMATICS
  PHYSICAL SCIENCES
  PSYCHOLOGY

```
PUBLIC SERVICES
SOCIAL SCIENCES
```

==

```
UNIVERSITY OF NEW HAVEN
300 ORANGE AVENUE
WEST HAVEN, CT 06516
203-934-6321
```

KEY CONTACT: Attn: GEORGE A. SCHAEFER, OFFICE OF
                     HANDICAPPED STUDENT SERVICES

SIZE OF SCHOOL: SMALL

APPLICATION DEADLINE: NONE

	APPROXIMATE TUITION	ROOM AND BOARD
IN STATE	$5150	$2850
OUT-OF-STATE	$5150	$2850

REQUIREMENTS FOR ADMISSIONS:
  High school equivalency diploma
  High school diploma
  ACT Scores required
  Untimed or oral ACT Scores accepted
  SAT Scores required
  Untimed or oral SAT Scores accepted
  Admission requirements modified

ADDITIONAL SERVICES OFFERED:
  Learning Lab
  Remedial and/or tutorial help available
  Reader services for the blind available for LD

MODIFICATIONS TO TRADITIONAL LEARNING ENVIRONMENT:
  Oral presentation in lieu of written exams
  Use of calculator for all math courses
  Tape recorders to record class lectures
  Someone else may take class notes
  Student takes exams in separate rooms
  Students have exams read to them
  Students take typewritten exams
  Longer time allowed to complete exams
  Physical education may be waived

MAJORS OFFERED:

  ARCHITECTURE
  BIOLOGICAL SCIENCES

```
BUSINESS AND MANAGEMENT
COMMUNICATIONS
COMPUTER SCIENCES
ENGINEERING TECHNOLOGIES
FINE AND APPLIED ARTS
HEALTH
HOME ECONOMICS
HUMANITIES
MATHEMATICS
PHYSICAL SCIENCES
PSYCHOLOGY
PUBLIC SERVICES
SOCIAL SCIENCES
```

===

AMERICAN UNIVERSITY
WASHINGTON, DC 20016
202-686-2211

KEY CONTACT: Attn: FAITH LEONARD, DIRECTOR
                    LEARNING SERVICES

SIZE OF SCHOOL: MEDIUM

APPLICATION DEADLINE: FEBRUARY 1

	APPROXIMATE TUITION	ROOM AND BOARD
IN STATE	$7070	$3400
OUT-OF-STATE	$7070	$3400

REQUIREMENTS FOR ADMISSIONS:
  High school equivalency diploma
  High school diploma
  ACT Scores required
  Untimed or oral ACT Scores accepted
  SAT Scores required
  Untimed or oral SAT Scores accepted
  WAIS scores required
  High school grade point average (minimum 2.0)
  Admission requirements modified
  Personal interview
  Placement tests
  Recommendations
  Essay

ADDITIONAL SERVICES OFFERED:
  Learning Lab
  Learning Lab has a specialist with a masters degree
    or above in Learning Disabilities

Diagnostic testing services on campus
Diagnostic testing services off campus
Remedial and/or tutorial help available
Reader services for the blind available for LD
Special Education department
Handicapped student services works with LD

MODIFICATIONS TO TRADITIONAL LEARNING ENVIRONMENT:
Oral presentation in lieu of written exams
Use of calculator for all math courses
Has an adaptive physical education program
Tape recorders to record class lectures
Someone else may take class notes
Student takes exams in separate rooms
Students have exams read to them
Students take typewritten exams
Longer time allowed to complete exams
Submit papers on cassette tape
Extended time limits for graduation

Individual arrangements made upon request by Ms.
Leonard, LD student and professors

MAJORS OFFERED:

AREA STUDIES
BIOLOGICAL SCIENCES
BUSINESS AND MANAGEMENT
COMMUNICATIONS
COMPUTER SCIENCES
EDUCATION
ENGINEERING TECHNOLOGIES
FINE AND APPLIED ARTS
FOREIGN LANGUAGES
HEALTH
HUMANITIES
LAW
MATHEMATICS
PHYSICAL SCIENCES
PSYCHOLOGY
PUBLIC SERVICES
SOCIAL SCIENCES

==

GEORGE WASHINGTON UNIVERSITY
WASHINGTON, DC 20052
202-676-6040

KEY CONTACT: Attn: LINDA DONNELS, DIRECTOR
                    DISABLED STUDENT SERVICES

SIZE OF SCHOOL: MEDIUM

APPLICATION DEADLINE: MARCH 1

APPROXIMATE TUITION   ROOM AND BOARD

IN STATE	$6300	$3750
OUT-OF-STATE	$6300	$3750

REQUIREMENTS FOR ADMISSIONS:
  High school diploma
  ACT Scores required
  Untimed or oral ACT Scores accepted
  SAT Scores required
  Untimed or oral SAT Scores accepted
  Particular rank in class
  High school grade point average
  Placement tests
  Recommendations

ADDITIONAL SERVICES OFFERED:
  Diagnostic testing services on campus
  Diagnostic testing services off campus
  Remedial and/or tutorial help available
  Reader services for the blind available for LD
  Special Education department
  Handicapped student services works with LD

MODIFICATIONS TO TRADITIONAL LEARNING ENVIRONMENT:
  Oral presentation in lieu of written exams
  Use of calculator for all math courses
  Has an adaptive physical education program
  Tape recorders to record class lectures
  Someone else may take class notes
  Multiple choice exams only
  Essay exams only
  Student takes exams in separate rooms
  Students have exams read to them
  Students take typewritten exams
  Longer time allowed to complete exams
  Submit papers on cassette tape
  Extended time limits for graduation
  Physical education may be waived

  All of the above modifications are negotiable and
  possible. There is not one policy. Student and
  professor work out modification for each course
  separately.

MAJORS OFFERED:

    AREA STUDIES
    BIOLOGICAL SCIENCES
    BUSINESS AND MANAGEMENT
    COMMUNICATIONS
    COMPUTER SCIENCES
    EDUCATION
    ENGINEERING TECHNOLOGIES
    FINE AND APPLIED ARTS
    FOREIGN LANGUAGES
    HEALTH
    HUMANITIES
    MATHEMATICS
    PHYSICAL SCIENCES
    PSYCHOLOGY
    PUBLIC SERVICES
    SOCIAL SCIENCES

==

TRINITY COLLEGE
MICHIGAN AVENUE AND FRANKLIN AVENUE, NE
WASHINGTON, DC 20017
202-269-2201

KEY CONTACT: Attn: EVELYN A. MCDONALD
                    DEAN OF STUDENTS

SIZE OF SCHOOL: SMALL

APPLICATION DEADLINE: NONE

        APPROXIMATE TUITION   ROOM AND BOARD

IN STATE $5900 $3800
OUT-OF-STATE $5900 $3800

REQUIREMENTS FOR ADMISSIONS:
  High school equivalency diploma
  High school diploma
  ACT Scores required
  Untimed or oral ACT Scores accepted
  Particular rank in class 50%
  High school grade point average 2.5 and above
  Admission requirements modified
  Personal interview
  Recommendations
  Essay

ADDITIONAL SERVICES OFFERED:
  Learning Lab
  Diagnostic testing services on campus
  Diagnostic testing services off campus
  Remedial and/or tutorial help available
  Reader services for the blind available for LD
  Handicapped student services works with LD

MODIFICATIONS TO TRADITIONAL LEARNING ENVIRONMENT:
  Oral presentation in lieu of written exams
  Use of calculator for all math courses
  Has an adaptive physical education program
  Tape recorders to record class lectures
  Someone else may take class notes
  Student takes exams in separate rooms
  Students have exams read to them
  Longer time allowed to complete exams
  Submit papers on cassette tape
  Extended time limits for graduation
  Physical education may be waived

MAJORS OFFERED:

  AREA STUDIES
  BIOLOGICAL SCIENCES
  BUSINESS AND MANAGEMENT
  COMMUNICATIONS
  EDUCATION
  ENGINEERING TECHNOLOGIES
  FINE AND APPLIED ARTS
  FOREIGN LANGUAGES
  HEALTH
  HUMANITIES
  LAW
  MATHEMATICS
  PHYSICAL SCIENCES
  PSYCHOLOGY
  SOCIAL SCIENCES
  THEOLOGY

==

FLAGLER COLLEGE
P.O. BOX 1027
ST. AUGUSTINE, FL 32084
904-829-6481

KEY CONTACT: Attn: Handicapped Student Services

SIZE OF SCHOOL: SMALL

APPLICATION DEADLINE: MAY 1

	APPROXIMATE TUITION	ROOM AND BOARD
IN STATE	$2830	$1800
OUT-OF-STATE	$2830	$1800

REQUIREMENTS FOR ADMISSIONS:
  SAT Scores required
  WAIS scores required
  Recommendations

ADDITIONAL SERVICES OFFERED:
  Learning Lab
  Learning Lab has a specialist with a masters degree
    or above in Learning Disabilities
  Diagnostic testing services off campus
  Reader services for the blind available for LD

MODIFICATIONS TO TRADITIONAL LEARNING ENVIRONMENT:
  Tape recorders to record class lectures
  Someone else may take class notes
  Students have exams read to them
  Students take typewritten exams
  Longer time allowed to complete exams
  Extended time limits for graduation
  Physical education may be waived

MAJORS OFFERED:

  AREA STUDIES
  BUSINESS AND MANAGEMENT
  COMPUTER SCIENCES
  EDUCATION
  FINE AND APPLIED ARTS
  FOREIGN LANGUAGES
  HUMANITIES
  LAW
  PSYCHOLOGY
  PUBLIC SERVICES
  SOCIAL SCIENCES
  THEOLOGY

===

FLORIDA A&M UNIVERSITY
TALLAHASSEE, FL 32307
904-599-3796

KEY CONTACT: Attn: TALMADGE FRAZIER, ASSISTANT
                    COORD. DISABLED STUDENT SERVICES

SIZE OF SCHOOL: MEDIUM

APPLICATION DEADLINE: JULY 23

    APPROXIMATE TUITION   ROOM AND BOARD

	APPROXIMATE TUITION	ROOM AND BOARD
IN STATE	$ 750	$1780
OUT-OF-STATE	$1980	$1790

REQUIREMENTS FOR ADMISSIONS:
  High school equivalency diploma
  High school diploma
  ACT Scores required
  Untimed or oral ACT Scores accepted
  SAT Scores required
  Untimed or oral SAT Scores accepted
  University or College sponsored tests
  High school grade point average 2.0
  Admission requirements modified
  Personal interview
  Placement tests
  Recommendations
  Essay

ADDITIONAL SERVICES OFFERED:
  Learning Lab
  Learning Lab has a specialist with a masters degree
    or above in Learning Disabilities
  Diagnostic testing services on campus
  Diagnostic testing services off campus
  Remedial and/or tutorial help available
  Reader services for the blind available for LD
  Special Education department
  Handicapped student services works with LD

MODIFICATIONS TO TRADITIONAL LEARNING ENVIRONMENT:
  Oral presentation in lieu of written exams
  Use of calculator for all math courses
  Has an adaptive physical education program
  Tape recorders to record class lectures
  Someone else may take class notes
  Student takes exams in separate rooms
  Students have exams read to them
  Students take typewritten exams
  Longer time allowed to complete exams
  Submit papers on cassette tape
  Extended time limits for graduation
  Physical education may be waived

MAJORS OFFERED:

    AGRICULTURE
    ARCHITECTURE
    BIOLOGICAL SCIENCES
    BUSINESS AND MANAGEMENT
    COMMUNICATIONS
    COMPUTER SCIENCES
    EDUCATION
    ENGINEERING TECHNOLOGIES
    FINE AND APPLIED ARTS
    HEALTH
    HUMANITIES
    MATHEMATICS
    PHYSICAL SCIENCES
    SOCIAL SCIENCES
    THEOLOGY

==

FLORIDA STATE UNIVERSITY
TALLAHASSEE, FL 32306
904-644-6200

KEY CONTACT: Attn: Handicapped Student Services

SIZE OF SCHOOL: LARGE

APPLICATION DEADLINE: JUNE 30

         APPROXIMATE TUITION   ROOM AND BOARD

IN STATE $ 840 $2300
OUT-OF-STATE $2030 $2300

REQUIREMENTS FOR ADMISSIONS:
  High school equivalency diploma
  High school diploma
  ACT Scores required
  SAT Scores required
  High school grade point average
  Admission requirements modified

ADDITIONAL SERVICES OFFERED:
  Learning Lab
  Learning Lab has a specialist with a masters degree
    or above in Learning Disabilities
  Diagnostic testing services on campus
  Reader services for the blind available for LD
  Special Education department
  Handicapped student services works with LD

MODIFICATIONS TO TRADITIONAL LEARNING ENVIRONMENT:
  Oral presentation in lieu of written exams
  Use of calculator for all math courses
  Tape recorders to record class lectures
  Someone else may take class notes
  Student takes exams in separate rooms
  Students have exams read to them
  Students take typewritten exams
  Longer time allowed to complete exams
  Submit papers on cassette tape
  Take limited course load and graduate within time
    required
  Physical education may be waived

MAJORS OFFERED:

  AGRICULTURE
  AREA STUDIES
  BIOLOGICAL SCIENCES
  BUSINESS AND MANAGEMENT
  COMMUNICATIONS
  COMPUTER SCIENCES
  EDUCATION
  ENGINEERING TECHNOLOGIES
  FINE AND APPLIED ARTS
  FOREIGN LANGUAGES
  HEALTH
  HOME ECONOMICS
  HUMANITIES
  MATHEMATICS
  MILITARY SCIENCES
  PHYSICAL SCIENCES
  PSYCHOLOGY
  PUBLIC SERVICES
  SOCIAL SCIENCES
  THEOLOGY

===

GEORGIA STATE UNIVERSITY
UNIVERSITY PLAZA
ATLANTA, GA 30303
404-658-2365

KEY CONTACT: Attn: Handicapped Student Services

SIZE OF SCHOOL: LARGE

APPLICATION DEADLINE: AUGUST 12

```
        APPROXIMATE TUITION    ROOM AND BOARD

IN STATE          $1050        $NOT OFFERED
OUT-OF-STATE      $3390        $NOT OFFERED
```

REQUIREMENTS FOR ADMISSIONS:
    High school equivalency diploma
    High school diploma
    SAT Scores required
    Untimed or oral SAT Scores accepted
    University or College sponsored tests
    Placement tests
    Essay

ADDITIONAL SERVICES OFFERED:
    Learning Lab
    Diagnostic testing services on campus
    Diagnostic testing services off campus
    Remedial and/or tutorial help available
    Reader services for the blind available for LD
    Handicapped student services works with LD

MODIFICATIONS TO TRADITIONAL LEARNING ENVIRONMENT:
    Oral presentation in lieu of written exams
    Has an adaptive physical education program
    Tape recorders to record class lectures
    Someone else may take class notes
    Multiple choice exams only
    Essay exams only
    Student takes exams in separate rooms
    Students have exams read to them
    Students take typewritten exams
    Longer time allowed to complete exams
    Submit papers on cassette tape
    Physical education may be waived
    These strategies are used based on individual needs

MAJORS OFFERED:

    BIOLOGICAL SCIENCES
    BUSINESS AND MANAGEMENT
    COMMUNICATIONS
    COMPUTER SCIENCES
    EDUCATION
    FINE AND APPLIED ARTS
    FOREIGN LANGUAGES
    HEALTH
    HOME ECONOMICS
    HUMANITIES
    MATHEMATICS
    PHYSICAL SCIENCES

```
PSYCHOLOGY
PUBLIC SERVICES
SOCIAL SCIENCES
```

===

```
UNIVERSITY OF GEORGIA
114 ACADEMIC BUILDING
ATHENS, GA 30602
404-542-2112
```

KEY CONTACT: Attn: Handicapped Student Services

SIZE OF SCHOOL: LARGE

APPLICATION DEADLINE: SEPTEMBER 1

	APPROXIMATE TUITION	ROOM AND BOARD
IN STATE	$1245	$2025
OUT-OF-STATE	$3210	$2025

REQUIREMENTS FOR ADMISSIONS:
  SAT Scores required
  High school grade point average B

ADDITIONAL SERVICES OFFERED:
  Learning Lab
  Learning Lab has a specialist with a masters degree
    or above in Learning Disabilities
  Diagnostic testing services on campus
  Reader services for the blind available for LD
  Special Education department

MODIFICATIONS TO TRADITIONAL LEARNING ENVIRONMENT:
  Use of calculator for all math courses
  Has an adaptive physical education program
  Tape recorders to record class lectures
  Someone else may take class notes
  Students have exams read to them
  Students take typewritten exams
  Longer time allowed to complete exams
  Submit papers on cassette tape
  Extended time limits for graduation
  Physical education may be waived

MAJORS OFFERED:

  AGRICULTURE
  ARCHITECTURE
  AREA STUDIES

```
BIOLOGICAL SCIENCES
BUSINESS AND MANAGEMENT
COMMUNICATIONS
COMPUTER SCIENCES
EDUCATION
ENGINEERING TECHNOLOGIES
FINE AND APPLIED ARTS
FOREIGN LANGUAGES
HEALTH
HOME ECONOMICS
HUMANITIES
MATHEMATICS
PHYSICAL SCIENCES
PSYCHOLOGY
PUBLIC SERVICES
SOCIAL SCIENCES
THEOLOGY
```

==

```
UNIVERSITY OF HAWAII
COLLEGE OF ARTS & SCIENCES
P.O. BOX 1357-1400 KAPIOLANI STREET
HILO, HI 96720
```

KEY CONTACT: Attn: Handicapped Student Services

SIZE OF SCHOOL: SMALL

APPLICATION DEADLINE: JULY 1

	APPROXIMATE TUITION	ROOM AND BOARD
IN STATE	$ 330	$2040
OUT-OF-STATE	$ 930	$2040

REQUIREMENTS FOR ADMISSIONS:
  High school equivalency diploma
  High school diploma
  SAT Scores required

ADDITIONAL SERVICES OFFERED:
  Learning Lab
  Learning Lab has a specialist with a masters degree
    or above in Learning Disabilities
  Diagnostic testing services off campus
  Remedial and/or tutorial help available
  Handicapped student services works with LD

MODIFICATIONS TO TRADITIONAL LEARNING ENVIRONMENT:
  Oral presentation in lieu of written exams
  Use of calculator for all math courses
  Tape recorders to record class lectures
  Someone else may take class notes
  Student takes exams in separate rooms
  Students have exams read to them
  Students take typewritten exams
  Longer time allowed to complete exams
  Submit papers on cassette tape
  Take limited course load and graduate within time
    required
  Extended time limits for graduation
  Physical education may be waived

MAJORS OFFERED:

  AGRICULTURE
  AREA STUDIES
  BIOLOGICAL SCIENCES
  BUSINESS AND MANAGEMENT
  EDUCATION
  FINE AND APPLIED ARTS
  HUMANITIES
  MATHEMATICS
  PHYSICAL SCIENCES
  PSYCHOLOGY
  SOCIAL SCIENCES

==

BOISE STATE UNIVERSITY
1910 UNIVERSITY DRIVE
BOISE, ID 83725
208-385-1177

KEY CONTACT: Attn: JANET CENTANNI
                    SPECIAL SERVICES COORDINATOR

SIZE OF SCHOOL: MEDIUM

APPLICATION DEADLINE: AUGUST 12

        APPROXIMATE TUITION   ROOM AND BOARD

IN STATE $ 800 $2095
OUT-OF-STATE $2700 $2095

REQUIREMENTS FOR ADMISSIONS:
  High school equivalency diploma
  High school diploma

```
ACT Scores required
Untimed or oral ACT Scores accepted
SAT Scores required
Untimed or oral SAT Scores accepted
Placement tests
SAT or ACT or WPC scores are required
Placement tests in English and Math are required for
   entry level courses in these subjects.
```

ADDITIONAL SERVICES OFFERED:
```
   Diagnostic testing services on campus
   Diagnostic testing services off campus
   Remedial and/or tutorial help available
   Handicapped student services works with LD
```

MODIFICATIONS TO TRADITIONAL LEARNING ENVIRONMENT:
```
   Oral presentation in lieu of written exams
   Has an adaptive physical education program
   Tape recorders to record class lectures
   Someone else may take class notes
   Student takes exams in separate rooms
   Students have exams read to them
   Students take typewritten exams
   Longer time allowed to complete exams
   Take limited course load and graduate within time
      required
   Extended time limits for graduation
   Physical education may be waived
   Modifications are possible, dependent on permission
      of the instructor
```

MAJORS OFFERED:

```
   ARCHITECTURE
   AREA STUDIES
   BIOLOGICAL SCIENCES
   BUSINESS AND MANAGEMENT
   COMMUNICATIONS
   COMPUTER SCIENCES
   EDUCATION
   FINE AND APPLIED ARTS
   HEALTH
   HUMANITIES
   MATHEMATICS
   PHYSICAL SCIENCES
   PSYCHOLOGY
   PUBLIC SERVICES
   SOCIAL SCIENCES
```

===

```
LEWIS-CLARK STATE COLLEGE
8TH AVENUE AND 6TH STREET
LEWISTON, ID 83501
208-746-2341
```

KEY CONTACT: Attn: DR. DACHLING
                     ACADEMIC VICE PRESIDENT

SIZE OF SCHOOL: SMALL

APPLICATION DEADLINE: NONE

	APPROXIMATE TUITION	ROOM AND BOARD
IN STATE	$ 740	$2170
OUT-OF-STATE	$2640	$2170

REQUIREMENTS FOR ADMISSIONS:
  High school equivalency diploma
  High school diploma
  21 years of age or older, with or without a
    high school diploma or equivalency
  ACT Scores required
  Untimed or oral ACT Scores accepted
  University or College sponsored tests
  Placement tests

ADDITIONAL SERVICES OFFERED:
  Learning Lab
  Learning Lab has a specialist with a masters degree
    or above in Learning Disabilities
  Diagnostic testing services on campus
  Diagnostic testing services off campus
  Remedial and/or tutorial help available
  Special Education department
  Handicapped student services works with LD

MODIFICATIONS TO TRADITIONAL LEARNING ENVIRONMENT:
  Oral presentation in lieu of written exams (some)
  Use of calculator for all math courses (some)
  Has an adaptive physical education program
  Tape recorders to record class lectures
  Longer time allowed to complete exams
  Extended time limits for graduation
  Physical education may be waived

MAJORS OFFERED:

  BIOLOGICAL SCIENCES
  BUSINESS AND MANAGEMENT
  EDUCATION

```
FINE AND APPLIED ARTS
HEALTH
HUMANITIES
MATHEMATICS
PHYSICAL SCIENCES
PUBLIC SERVICES
SOCIAL SCIENCES
```

===

UNIVERSITY OF IDAHO
MOSCOW, ID 83843
208-885-6326

KEY CONTACT: Attn: DIANNE S. MILHOLLIS
                     COORDINATOR HANDICAPPED SERVICES

SIZE OF SCHOOL: MEDIUM

APPLICATION DEADLINE: AUGUST 1

```
       APPROXIMATE TUITION    ROOM AND BOARD

IN STATE          $ 820        $1955
OUT-OF-STATE      $2820        $1955
```

REQUIREMENTS FOR ADMISSIONS:
  High school equivalency diploma
  High school diploma
  21 years of age or older, with or without a
    high school diploma or equivalency
  ACT Scores required
  SAT Scores required
  Admission requirements modified

ADDITIONAL SERVICES OFFERED:
  Learning Lab
  Diagnostic testing services on campus
  Remedial and/or tutorial help available
  Reader services for the blind available for LD
  Special Education department
  Handicapped student services works with LD

MODIFICATIONS TO TRADITIONAL LEARNING ENVIRONMENT:
  Oral presentation in lieu of written exams
  Use of calculator for all math courses
  Has an adaptive physical education program
  Tape recorders to record class lectures
  Someone else may take class notes
  Student takes exams in separate rooms
  Students have exams read to them

Students take typewritten exams
Longer time allowed to complete exams
Submit papers on cassette tape
Extended time limits for graduation
Physical education may be waived

MAJORS OFFERED:

AGRICULTURE
ARCHITECTURE
AREA STUDIES
BIOLOGICAL SCIENCES
BUSINESS AND MANAGEMENT
COMMUNICATIONS
COMPUTER SCIENCES
EDUCATION
ENGINEERING TECHNOLOGIES
FINE AND APPLIED ARTS
FOREIGN LANGUAGES
HEALTH
HOME ECONOMICS
HUMANITIES
MATHEMATICS
MILITARY SCIENCES
PHYSICAL SCIENCES
PSYCHOLOGY
PUBLIC SERVICES
SOCIAL SCIENCES

===

BARAT COLLEGE
700 EAST WESTLEIGH ROAD
LAKE FOREST, IL 60045
312-234-3000

KEY CONTACT: Attn: Handicapped Student Services

SIZE OF SCHOOL: SMALL

APPLICATION DEADLINE: NONE

	APPROXIMATE TUITION	ROOM AND BOARD
IN STATE	$4900	$2500
OUT-OF-STATE	$4900	$2500

REQUIREMENTS FOR ADMISSIONS:
  ACT Scores required
  Untimed or oral ACT Scores accepted
  SAT Scores required

Untimed or oral SAT Scores accepted
Admission requirements modified
Recommendations

ADDITIONAL SERVICES OFFERED:
  Learning Lab
  Learning Lab has a specialist with a masters degree
    or above in Learning Disabilities
  Diagnostic testing services on campus
  Remedial and/or tutorial help available
  Reader services for the blind available for LD
  Special Education department
  Handicapped student services works with LD

MODIFICATIONS TO TRADITIONAL LEARNING ENVIRONMENT:
  Oral presentation in lieu of written exams
  Tape recorders to record class lectures
  Multiple choice exams only
  Essay exams only
  Student takes exams in separate rooms
  Students have exams read to them
  Students take typewritten exams
  Longer time allowed to complete exams
  Submit papers on cassette tape
  Take limited course load and graduate within time
    required
  Extended time limits for graduation
  Physical education may be waived

MAJORS OFFERED:

  BUSINESS AND MANAGEMENT
  COMPUTER SCIENCES
  EDUCATION
  FINE AND APPLIED ARTS
  HEALTH
  HUMANITIES
  MATHEMATICS
  PHYSICAL SCIENCES
  PSYCHOLOGY
  PUBLIC SERVICES
  SOCIAL SCIENCES

===

MCKENDREE COLLEGE
LEBANON, IL 62258
618-537-4481

KEY CONTACT: Attn: GABRIELLE ROWE
                    LEARNING & COMMUNICATIONS CENTER

SIZE OF SCHOOL: SMALL

APPLICATION DEADLINE: NONE

	APPROXIMATE TUITION	ROOM AND BOARD
IN STATE	$3700	$2000
OUT-OF-STATE	$3700	$2000

REQUIREMENTS FOR ADMISSIONS:
  High school equivalency diploma
  High school diploma
  ACT Scores required
  Personal interview
  Placement tests

ADDITIONAL SERVICES OFFERED:
  Learning Lab
  Remedial and/or tutorial help available

MODIFICATIONS TO TRADITIONAL LEARNING ENVIRONMENT:
  Oral presentation in lieu of written exams
  Use of calculator for all math courses
  Has an adaptive physical education program
  Tape recorders to record class lectures
  Someone else may take class notes
  Multiple choice exams only
  Essay exams only
  Student takes exams in separate rooms
  Students have exams read to them
  Students take typewritten exams
  Longer time allowed to complete exams
  Submit papers on cassette tape
  Take limited course load and graduate within time
    required
  Extended time limits for graduation
  Physical education may be waived
  All modifications at the discretion of individual
    faculty

MAJORS OFFERED:

  BIOLOGICAL SCIENCES
  BUSINESS AND MANAGEMENT
  COMPUTER SCIENCES
  EDUCATION
  FINE AND APPLIED ARTS
  HEALTH
  HUMANITIES
  MATHEMATICS
  PHYSICAL SCIENCES

```
PSYCHOLOGY
PUBLIC SERVICES
SOCIAL SCIENCES
THEOLOGY
```

===

```
SOUTHERN ILLINOIS UNIVERSITY - CARBONDALE
CARBONDALE, IL 62901
618-453-4381
```

KEY CONTACT: Attn: BARBARA CORDONI, PROJECT ACHIEVE

SIZE OF SCHOOL: LARGE

APPLICATION DEADLINE: NONE

	APPROXIMATE TUITION	ROOM AND BOARD
IN STATE	$1310	$2240
OUT-OF-STATE	$3095	$2240

REQUIREMENTS FOR ADMISSIONS:
  High school diploma
  ACT Scores required
  Admission requirements modified

ADDITIONAL SERVICES OFFERED:
  Learning Lab
  Learning Lab has a specialist with a masters degree
    or above in Learning Disabilities
  Diagnostic testing services on campus
  Diagnostic testing services off campus
  Remedial and/or tutorial help available
  Reader services for the blind available for LD
  Special Education department
  Handicapped student services works with LD

MODIFICATIONS TO TRADITIONAL LEARNING ENVIRONMENT:
  Oral presentation in lieu of written exams
  Tape recorders to record class lectures
  Someone else may take class notes
  Multiple choice exams only
  Essay exams only
  Students have exams read to them
  Students take typewritten exams
  Longer time allowed to complete exams
  Submit papers on cassette tape
  Extended time limits for graduation
  Physical education may be waived

MAJORS OFFERED:

   AGRICULTURE
   ARCHITECTURE
   AREA STUDIES
   BIOLOGICAL SCIENCES
   BUSINESS AND MANAGEMENT
   COMMUNICATIONS
   COMPUTER SCIENCES
   EDUCATION
   ENGINEERING TECHNOLOGIES
   FINE AND APPLIED ARTS
   FOREIGN LANGUAGES
   HEALTH
   HOME ECONOMICS
   HUMANITIES
   LAW
   MATHEMATICS
   MILITARY SCIENCES
   PHYSICAL SCIENCES
   PSYCHOLOGY
   PUBLIC SERVICES
   SOCIAL SCIENCES
   THEOLOGY

===

SOUTHERN ILLINOIS UNIVERSITY - CARBONDALE
CARBONDALE, IL 62901
618-453-4381

KEY CONTACT: Attn: BARBARA CORDONI, PROJECT ACHIEVE

SIZE OF SCHOOL: LARGE

APPLICATION DEADLINE: NONE

     APPROXIMATE TUITION   ROOM AND BOARD

	APPROXIMATE TUITION	ROOM AND BOARD
IN STATE	$1310	$2240
OUT-OF-STATE	$3095	$2240

REQUIREMENTS FOR ADMISSIONS:
  High school diploma
  ACT Scores required
  Admission requirements modified

ADDITIONAL SERVICES OFFERED:
  Learning Lab
  Learning Lab has a specialist with a masters degree
    or above in Learning Disabilities

Diagnostic testing services on campus
Diagnostic testing services off campus
Remedial and/or tutorial help available
Reader services for the blind available for LD
Special Education department
Handicapped student services works with LD

MODIFICATIONS TO TRADITIONAL LEARNING ENVIRONMENT:
Oral presentation in lieu of written exams
Tape recorders to record class lectures
Someone else may take class notes
Multiple choice exams only
Essay exams only
Students have exams read to them
Students take typewritten exams
Longer time allowed to complete exams
Submit papers on cassette tape
Extended time limits for graduation
Physical education may be waived

MAJORS OFFERED:

AGRICULTURE
ARCHITECTURE
AREA STUDIES
BIOLOGICAL SCIENCES
BUSINESS AND MANAGEMENT
COMMUNICATIONS
COMPUTER SCIENCES
EDUCATION
ENGINEERING TECHNOLOGIES
FINE AND APPLIED ARTS
FOREIGN LANGUAGES
HEALTH
HOME ECONOMICS
HUMANITIES
LAW
MATHEMATICS
MILITARY SCIENCES
PHYSICAL SCIENCES
PSYCHOLOGY
PUBLIC SERVICES
SOCIAL SCIENCES
THEOLOGY

==

ST. XAVIER COLLEGE
3700 WEST 103RD STREET
CHICAGO, IL 60655
312-779-3300

KEY CONTACT: Attn: Handicapped Student Services

SIZE OF SCHOOL: SMALL

APPLICATION DEADLINE: AUGUST 15

         APPROXIMATE TUITION   ROOM AND BOARD

IN STATE $4050 $2250
OUT-OF-STATE $4050 $2250

REQUIREMENTS FOR ADMISSIONS:
  High school equivalency diploma
  High school diploma
  ACT Scores required
  SAT Scores required

ADDITIONAL SERVICES OFFERED:
  Learning Lab
  Learning Lab has a specialist with a masters degree
    or above in Learning Disabilities
  Diagnostic testing services on campus
  Remedial and/or tutorial help available
  Special Education department

MAJORS OFFERED:

  BIOLOGICAL SCIENCES
  BUSINESS AND MANAGEMENT
  COMMUNICATIONS
  EDUCATION
  FINE AND APPLIED ARTS
  FOREIGN LANGUAGES
  HEALTH
  HUMANITIES
  MATHEMATICS
  PHYSICAL SCIENCES
  PSYCHOLOGY
  PUBLIC SERVICES
  SOCIAL SCIENCES
  THEOLOGY

==

WESTERN ILLINOIS UNIVERSITY
900 WEST ADAMS STREET
MACOMB, IL 61455
309-298-1891

KEY CONTACT: Attn: MS. CANDICE MCLAUGHLIN
                    ADVISOR TO THE HANDICAPPED

SIZE OF SCHOOL: MEDIUM

APPLICATION DEADLINE: NONE

          APPROXIMATE TUITION   ROOM AND BOARD

IN STATE $1080 $1990
OUT-OF-STATE $2630 $1990

REQUIREMENTS FOR ADMISSIONS:
  High school equivalency diploma (if have comparable
    ACT of 19)
  High school diploma
  ACT Scores required
  Untimed or oral ACT Scores accepted
  Untimed or oral SAT Scores accepted
  WAIS scores required
  University or College sponsored tests
  Personal interview
  Placement tests

  Western will accept students who graduate in the
  upper 1/2 of their graduating class, regardless of
  the ACT score. We will accept students who graduate
  in the in the upper 2/3 of their class if they have
  an ACT composite of 15 or better.

  Students must meet regular admission requirements

ADDITIONAL SERVICES OFFERED:
  Learning Lab
  Remedial and/or tutorial help available
  Reader services for the blind available for LD
  Handicapped student services works with LD

MODIFICATIONS TO TRADITIONAL LEARNING ENVIRONMENT:
  Tape recorders to record class lectures
  Someone else may take class notes
  Student takes exams in separate rooms
  Students have exams read to them
  Students take typewritten exams
  Longer time allowed to complete exams
  Submit papers on cassette tape
  Extended time limits for graduation
  Physical education may be waived

  Students should have documentation of disability when
  applying to Western

MAJORS OFFERED:

    AGRICULTURE
    BIOLOGICAL SCIENCES
    BUSINESS AND MANAGEMENT
    COMMUNICATIONS
    COMPUTER SCIENCES
    EDUCATION
    ENGINEERING TECHNOLOGIES
    FINE AND APPLIED ARTS
    FOREIGN LANGUAGES
    HEALTH
    HOME ECONOMICS
    HUMANITIES
    LIBRARY SCIENCE
    MATHEMATICS
    PHYSICAL SCIENCES
    PSYCHOLOGY
    PUBLIC SERVICES
    SOCIAL SCIENCES

==

INDIANA UNIVERSITY - BLOOMINGTON
BLOOMINGTON, IN 47405
812-335-0661

KEY CONTACT: Attn: FRANCES DODSON RHOME

SIZE OF SCHOOL: LARGE

APPLICATION DEADLINE: JULY 15 .

        APPROXIMATE TUITION   ROOM AND BOARD

IN STATE $1300 $1980
OUT OF STATE $3640 $1980

REQUIREMENTS FOR ADMISSIONS:
    Particular rank in class   50%
    Admission requirements modified
    State on application Learning Disabled

ADDITIONAL SERVICES OFFERED:
    Learning Lab
    Remedial and/or tutorial help available
    Reader services for the blind available for LD
    Special Education department
    Handicapped student services works with LD

MODIFICATIONS TO TRADITIONAL LEARNING ENVIRONMENT:
  Oral presentation in lieu of written exams
  Has an adaptive physical education program
  Tape recorders to record class lectures
  Someone else may take class notes
  Multiple choice exams only
  Essay exams only
  Student takes exams in separate rooms
  Students have exams read to them
  Students take typewritten exams
  Longer time allowed to complete exams
  Submit papers on cassette tape
  Extended time limits for graduation
  Physical education may be waived

MAJORS OFFERED:

  AGRICULTURE
  AREA STUDIES
  BIOLOGICAL SCIENCES
  BUSINESS AND MANAGEMENT
  COMMUNICATIONS
  COMPUTER SCIENCES
  EDUCATION
  FINE AND APPLIED ARTS
  FOREIGN LANGUAGES
  HEALTH
  HOME ECONOMICS
  HUMANITIES
  MATHEMATICS
  PHYSICAL SCIENCES
  PSYCHOLOGY
  PUBLIC SERVICES
  SOCIAL SCIENCES

===

INDIANA UNIVERSITY - NORTHWEST
GARY, IN 46408
219-980-6821

KEY CONTACT: Attn: ROY MILLER, COUNSELOR TO DISABLED

SIZE OF SCHOOL: MEDIUM

APPLICATION DEADLINE: JULY 15

          APPROXIMATE TUITION   ROOM AND BOARD

IN STATE $1130 $NOT OFFERED
OUT-OF-STATE $2740 $NOT OFFERED

REQUIREMENTS FOR ADMISSIONS:
  High school equivalency diploma
  High school diploma
  SAT Scores required
  Untimed or oral SAT Scores accepted
  University or College sponsored tests
  Particular rank in class   50%
  Admission requirements modified
  Personal interview
  Placement tests
  Recommendations

ADDITIONAL SERVICES OFFERED:
  Learning Lab
  Diagnostic testing services off campus
  Remedial and/or tutorial help available
  Reader services for the blind available for LD
  Handicapped student services works with LD

MODIFICATIONS TO TRADITIONAL LEARNING ENVIRONMENT:
  Oral presentation in lieu of written exams
  Use of calculator for all math courses
  Tape recorders to record class lectures
  Someone else may take class notes
  Student takes exams in separate rooms
  Students have exams read to them
  Students take typewritten exams
  Longer time allowed to complete exams
  Take limited course load and graduate within time
    required
  Extended time limits for graduation
  Physical education may be waived

MAJORS OFFERED:

  BIOLOGICAL SCIENCES
  BUSINESS AND MANAGEMENT
  COMMUNICATIONS
  COMPUTER SCIENCES
  EDUCATION
  FINE AND APPLIED ARTS
  FOREIGN LANGUAGES
  HEALTH
  HUMANITIES
  LAW
  MATHEMATICS
  PHYSICAL SCIENCES
  PSYCHOLOGY
  PUBLIC SERVICES
  SOCIAL SCIENCES

INDIANA UNIVERSITY - PURDUE UNIVERSITY AT FORT WAYNE
2101 COLISEUM BOULEVARD EAST
FORT WAYNE, IN 46805
219-482-5626

KEY CONTACT: Attn: DEBRA FREIMUTH
                     DISABLED STUDENT COUNSELOR

SIZE OF SCHOOL: MEDIUM

APPLICATION DEADLINE: AUGUST 1

        APPROXIMATE TUITION   ROOM AND BOARD

IN STATE $1165 $NOT OFFERED
OUT-OF-STATE $2790 $NOT OFFERED

REQUIREMENTS FOR ADMISSIONS:
  High school equivalency diploma
  High school diploma
  ACT Scores required
  Untimed or oral ACT Scores accepted
  SAT Scores required
  Untimed or oral SAT Scores accepted
  University or College sponsored tests
  Admission requirements modified
  Placement tests
  Depending on the individual situation, ACT and SAT
    scores may be waived

ADDITIONAL SERVICES OFFERED:
  Remedial and/or tutorial help available
  Special Education department
  Handicapped student services works with LD

MODIFICATIONS TO TRADITIONAL LEARNING ENVIRONMENT:
  Oral presentation in lieu of written exams
  Use of calculator for all math courses
  Has an adaptive physical education program
  Tape recorders to record class lectures
  Someone else may take class notes
  Students have exams read to them
  Longer time allowed to complete exams
  Extended time limits for graduation
  Physical education may be waived
  Many modifications depend on individual professor

MAJORS OFFERED:

  ARCHITECTURE
  BIOLOGICAL SCIENCES

BUSINESS AND MANAGEMENT
COMMUNICATIONS
COMPUTER SCIENCES
EDUCATION
ENGINEERING TECHNOLOGIES
FINE AND APPLIED ARTS
FOREIGN LANGUAGES
HEALTH
HUMANITIES
LAW
MATHEMATICS
PHYSICAL SCIENCES
PSYCHOLOGY
PUBLIC SERVICES
SOCIAL SCIENCES

==

INDIANA UNIVERSITY - SOUTH BEND
1700 MISHAWAKA AVENUE
SOUTH BEND, IN 46634
219-237-4455

KEY CONTACT: Attn: JAMES BAUMGARTNER, COORDINATOR
                    SERVICES FOR THE HANDICAPPED

SIZE OF SCHOOL: MEDIUM

APPLICATION DEADLINE: JULY 15

        APPROXIMATE TUITION   ROOM AND BOARD

IN STATE $1195 $NOT OFFERED
OUT-OF-STATE $2925 $NOT OFFERED

REQUIREMENTS FOR ADMISSIONS:
  High school equivalency diploma
  High school diploma
  SAT Scores required
  Admission requirements modified

ADDITIONAL SERVICES OFFERED:
  Diagnostic testing services on campus
  Diagnostic testing services off campus
  Reader services for the blind available for LD
  Special Education department
  Handicapped student services works with LD

MODIFICATIONS TO TRADITIONAL LEARNING ENVIRONMENT:
  Oral presentation in lieu of written exams
  Use of calculator for all math courses

```
Tape recorders to record class lectures
Someone else may take class notes
Students have exams read to them
Students take typewritten exams
Longer time allowed to complete exams
Submit papers on cassette tape
Extended time limits for graduation
```

MAJORS OFFERED:

```
BIOLOGICAL SCIENCES
BUSINESS AND MANAGEMENT
COMMUNICATIONS
COMPUTER SCIENCES
EDUCATION
FINE AND APPLIED ARTS
FOREIGN LANGUAGES
HEALTH
HUMANITIES
MATHEMATICS
PHYSICAL SCIENCES
PSYCHOLOGY
PUBLIC SERVICES
SOCIAL SCIENCES
```

===

```
INDIANA UNIVERSITY - SOUTHEAST
4201 GRANT LINE ROAD
NEW ALBANY, IN 47150
812-945-2731
```

KEY CONTACT: Attn: LEE ANN S. WALLS, COORDINATOR
                    SERVICES FOR HANDICAPPED PERSONS

SIZE OF SCHOOL: MEDIUM

APPLICATION DEADLINE: JULY 15

         APPROXIMATE TUITION   ROOM AND BOARD

	APPROXIMATE TUITION	ROOM AND BOARD
IN STATE	$1130	$NOT OFFERED
OUT-OF-STATE	$2730	$NOT OFFERED

REQUIREMENTS FOR ADMISSIONS:
  High school equivalency diploma
  High school diploma
  21 years of age or older, with a high
    school diploma or equivalency
  ACT Scores required
  Untimed or oral ACT Scores accepted

```
    SAT Scores required
    Untimed or oral SAT Scores accepted
    University or College sponsored tests
    Particular rank in class   50%
    Admission requirements modified
    Placement tests
    State/District residency
```

ADDITIONAL SERVICES OFFERED:
```
    Diagnostic testing services off campus
    Remedial and/or tutorial help available
    Reader services for the blind available for LD
    Special Education department
    Handicapped student services works with LD
```

MODIFICATIONS TO TRADITIONAL LEARNING ENVIRONMENT:
```
    Has an adaptive physical education program
    Tape recorders to record class lectures
    Someone else may take class notes
    Take limited course load and graduate within time
      required
    Extended time limits for graduation
    Other modifications at discretion of individual
      faculty members
```

MAJORS OFFERED:
```
    BIOLOGICAL SCIENCES
    BUSINESS AND MANAGEMENT
    COMMUNICATIONS
    COMPUTER SCIENCES
    EDUCATION
    ENGINEERING TECHNOLOGIES
    FINE AND APPLIED ARTS
    FOREIGN LANGUAGES
    HEALTH
    HUMANITIES
    MATHEMATICS
    PHYSICAL SCIENCES
    PSYCHOLOGY
    SOCIAL SCIENCES
```

==

ST. JOSEPH'S COLLEGE
RENSSELAER, IN 47978
219-866-7111

KEY CONTACT: Attn: Handicapped Student Services

SIZE OF SCHOOL: SMALL

APPLICATION DEADLINE: AUGUST 1

APPROXIMATE TUITION   ROOM AND BOARD

	APPROXIMATE TUITION	ROOM AND BOARD
IN STATE	$4480	$2290
OUT-OF-STATE	$4480	$2290

REQUIREMENTS FOR ADMISSIONS:
  ACT Scores required
  SAT Scores required
  High school grade point average   2.0
  Admission requirements modified

ADDITIONAL SERVICES OFFERED:
  Learning Lab
  Learning Lab has a specialist with a masters degree
    or above in Learning Disabilities
  Diagnostic testing services off campus
  Reader services for the blind available for LD
  Handicapped student services works with LD

MODIFICATIONS TO TRADITIONAL LEARNING ENVIRONMENT:
  Oral presentation in lieu of written exams
  Tape recorders to record class lectures
  Someone else may take class notes
  Multiple choice exams only
  Essay exams only
  Student takes exams in separate rooms
  Students have exams read to them
  Students take typewritten exams
  Longer time allowed to complete exams
  Submit papers on cassette tape
  Take limited course load and graduate within time
    required
  Extended time limits for graduation
  Physical education may be waived

MAJORS OFFERED:

  BIOLOGICAL SCIENCES
  BUSINESS AND MANAGEMENT
  COMMUNICATIONS
  COMPUTER SCIENCES
  EDUCATION
  ENGINEERING TECHNOLOGIES
  FINE AND APPLIED ARTS
  HEALTH
  HUMANITIES
  MATHEMATICS
  PHYSICAL SCIENCES
  PSYCHOLOGY

```
SOCIAL SCIENCES
THEOLOGY
```

===

```
ST. MARY-OF-THE-WOODS COLLEGE
ST. MARY-OF-THE-WOODS, IN 47876
812-535-4141
```

KEY CONTACT: Attn: S. JEAN HAGELSKAMP

SIZE OF SCHOOL: SMALL

APPLICATION DEADLINE: NONE

           APPROXIMATE TUITION   ROOM AND BOARD

```
IN STATE             $4380         $2080
OUT-OF-STATE         $4380         $2080
```

REQUIREMENTS FOR ADMISSIONS:
  ACT Scores required
  SAT Scores required

MODIFICATIONS TO TRADITIONAL LEARNING ENVIRONMENT:
  Has an adaptive physical education program
  Tape recorders to record class lectures
  Someone else may take class notes
  Student takes exams in separate rooms
  Physical education may be waived

MAJORS OFFERED:

  BIOLOGICAL SCIENCES
  BUSINESS AND MANAGEMENT
  COMMUNICATIONS
  EDUCATION
  FINE AND APPLIED ARTS
  FOREIGN LANGUAGES
  HEALTH
  HOME ECONOMICS
  HUMANITIES
  LAW
  MATHEMATICS
  PHYSICAL SCIENCES
  PSYCHOLOGY
  PUBLIC SERVICES
  SOCIAL SCIENCES
  THEOLOGY

===

```
TAYLOR UNIVERSITY
READE AVENUE
UPLAND, IN 46989
317-998-2751
```

KEY CONTACT: Attn: Handicapped Student Services

SIZE OF SCHOOL: SMALL

APPLICATION DEADLINE: NONE

	APPROXIMATE TUITION	ROOM AND BOARD
IN STATE	$4780	$2215
OUT-OF-STATE	$4780	$2215

REQUIREMENTS FOR ADMISSIONS:
  ACT Scores required
  SAT Scores required
  Particular rank in class 50%

ADDITIONAL SERVICES OFFERED:
  Learning Lab
  Learning Lab has a specialist with a masters degree
    or above in Learning Disabilities
  Diagnostic testing services on campus
  Remedial and/or tutorial help available

MODIFICATIONS TO TRADITIONAL LEARNING ENVIRONMENT:
  Oral presentation in lieu of written exams
  Tape recorders to record class lectures
  Someone else may take class notes
  Multiple choice exams only
  Essay exams only
  Student takes exams in separate rooms
  Students have exams read to them
  Students take typewritten exams
  Longer time allowed to complete exams
  Submit papers on cassette tape
  Extended time limits for graduation
  Physical education may be waived

MAJORS OFFERED:

  BIOLOGICAL SCIENCES
  BUSINESS AND MANAGEMENT
  COMMUNICATIONS
  COMPUTER SCIENCES
  EDUCATION
  FINE AND APPLIED ARTS
  FOREIGN LANGUAGES

HEALTH
HUMANITIES
LAW
MATHEMATICS
PHYSICAL SCIENCES
PSYCHOLOGY
PUBLIC SERVICES
SOCIAL SCIENCES
THEOLOGY

==

MARYCREST COLLEGE
1607 WEST 12TH STREET
DAVENPORT, IA 52804
319-326-9226

KEY CONTACT: Attn: Handicapped Student Services

SIZE OF SCHOOL: SMALL

APPLICATION DEADLINE: NONE

        APPROXIMATE TUITION   ROOM AND BOARD

IN STATE $4250 $1990
OUT-OF-STATE $4250 $1990

REQUIREMENTS FOR ADMISSIONS:
  Admission requirements modified

ADDITIONAL SERVICES OFFERED:
  Has a specialist with a masters degree or above
    in Learning Disabilities
  Diagnostic testing services off campus
  Remedial and/or tutorial help available
  Reader services available for LD students

MODIFICATIONS TO TRADITIONAL LEARNING ENVIRONMENT:
  Oral presentation in lieu of written exams
  Use of calculator for all math courses
  Tape recorders to record class lectures
  Someone else may take class notes
  Student takes exams in separate rooms
  Students have exams read to them
  Students take typewritten exams
  Longer time allowed to complete exams
  Take limited course load and graduate within time
    required
  Extended time limits for graduation
  Physical education may be waived

MAJORS OFFERED:

    BIOLOGICAL SCIENCES
    BUSINESS AND MANAGEMENT
    COMMUNICATIONS
    COMPUTER SCIENCES
    EDUCATION
    FINE AND APPLIED ARTS
    FOREIGN LANGUAGES
    HEALTH
    HOME ECONOMICS
    HUMANITIES
    LAW
    LIBRARY SCIENCE
    PHYSICAL SCIENCES
    PUBLIC SERVICES
    SOCIAL SCIENCES

===

KANSAS STATE UNIVERSITY
MANHATTAN, KS 66506
913-532-6250

KEY CONTACT: Attn: GRETCHEN HOLDEN, COORDINATOR
                    FOR PHYSICALLY LIMITED STUDENTS

SIZE OF SCHOOL: LARGE

APPLICATION DEADLINE: NONE

         APPROXIMATE TUITION   ROOM AND BOARD

IN STATE $1075 $2000
OUT-OF-STATE $2655 $2000

REQUIREMENTS FOR ADMISSIONS:
  High school equivalency diploma
  High school diploma
  ACT Scores required
  Untimed or oral ACT Scores accepted
  SAT Scores required
  Untimed or oral SAT Scores accepted
  SAT scores can be used in lieu of ACT scores
  If out of state applicant, must rank 50% or above and
    have 2.5 grade point average

ADDITIONAL SERVICES OFFERED:
  Learning Lab
  Diagnostic testing services off campus
  Remedial and/or tutorial help available

Reader services for the blind available for LD
Handicapped student services works with LD

MODIFICATIONS TO TRADITIONAL LEARNING ENVIRONMENT:
Oral presentation in lieu of written exams
Has an adaptive physical education program
Tape recorders to record class lectures
Someone else may take class notes
Student takes exams in separate rooms
Students have exams read to them
Students take typewritten exams
Longer time allowed to complete exams
Extended time limits for graduation

MAJORS OFFERED:

AGRICULTURE
ARCHITECTURE
AREA STUDIES
BIOLOGICAL SCIENCES
BUSINESS AND MANAGEMENT
COMMUNICATIONS
COMPUTER SCIENCES
EDUCATION
ENGINEERING TECHNOLOGIES
FINE AND APPLIED ARTS
FOREIGN LANGUAGES
HEALTH
HOME ECONOMICS
HUMANITIES
LAW
MATHEMATICS
PHYSICAL SCIENCES
PSYCHOLOGY
PUBLIC SERVICES
SOCIAL SCIENCES

===

OTTAWA UNIVERSITY
TENTH AND CEDAR STREETS
OTTAWA, KS 66067
913-242-5200

KEY CONTACT: Attn: Handicapped Student Services

SIZE OF SCHOOL: SMALL

APPLICATION DEADLINE: AUGUST 1

```
        APPROXIMATE TUITION    ROOM AND BOARD

IN STATE          $3690          $2120
OUT-OF-STATE      $3690          $2120
```

REQUIREMENTS FOR ADMISSIONS:
  ACT Scores required
  SAT Scores required
  Admission requirements modified
  Recommendations

ADDITIONAL SERVICES OFFERED:
  Diagnostic testing services off campus

MODIFICATIONS TO TRADITIONAL LEARNING ENVIRONMENT:
  Oral presentation in lieu of written exams
  Has an adaptive physical education program
  Tape recorders to record class lectures
  Someone else may take class notes
  Multiple choice exams only
  Essay exams only
  Student takes exams in separate rooms
  Students have exams read to them
  Students take typewritten exams
  Longer time allowed to complete exams
  Submit papers on cassette tape
  Extended time limits for graduation
  Physical education may be waived

MAJORS OFFERED:

  AGRICULTURE
  AREA STUDIES
  BIOLOGICAL SCIENCES
  BUSINESS AND MANAGEMENT
  COMMUNICATIONS
  COMPUTER SCIENCES
  EDUCATION
  ENGINEERING TECHNOLOGIES
  FINE AND APPLIED ARTS
  FOREIGN LANGUAGES
  HEALTH
  HOME ECONOMICS
  HUMANITIES
  LAW
  MATHEMATICS
  PHYSICAL SCIENCES
  PSYCHOLOGY
  PUBLIC SERVICES
  SOCIAL SCIENCES
  THEOLOGY

PITTSBURG STATE UNIVERSITY
1701 SOUTH BROADWAY
PITTSBURG, KS 66762
316-231-7000

KEY CONTACT: Attn: Handicapped Student Services

SIZE OF SCHOOL: MEDIUM

APPLICATION DEADLINE: NONE

	APPROXIMATE TUITION	ROOM AND BOARD
IN STATE	$ 840	$2040
OUT-OF-STATE	$1795	$2040

REQUIREMENTS FOR ADMISSIONS:
  High school equivalency diploma
  High school diploma
  ACT Scores required
  Particular rank in class 50%

ADDITIONAL SERVICES OFFERED:
  Diagnostic testing services on campus
  Remedial and/or tutorial help available
  Special Education department
  Handicapped student services works with LD

MODIFICATIONS TO TRADITIONAL LEARNING ENVIRONMENT:
  Oral presentation in lieu of written exams
  Use of calculator for all math courses
  Tape recorders to record class lectures
  Someone else may take class notes
  Multiple choice exams only
  Essay exams only
  Student takes exams in separate rooms
  Students have exams read to them
  Students take typewritten exams
  Longer time allowed to complete exams
  Submit papers on cassette tape
  Extended time limits for graduation
  Physical education may be waived

MAJORS OFFERED:

  AGRICULTURE
  ARCHITECTURE
  BIOLOGICAL SCIENCES
  BUSINESS AND MANAGEMENT
  COMMUNICATIONS
  COMPUTER SCIENCES

```
EDUCATION
ENGINEERING TECHNOLOGIES
FINE AND APPLIED ARTS
FOREIGN LANGUAGES
HEALTH
HOME ECONOMICS
HUMANITIES
LIBRARY SCIENCE
MATHEMATICS
PHYSICAL SCIENCES
PSYCHOLOGY
PUBLIC SERVICES
SOCIAL SCIENCES
```

==

```
STERLING COLLEGE
NORTH BROADWAY
STERLING, KS 67579
316-278-2173
```

KEY CONTACT: Attn: Handicapped Student Services

SIZE OF SCHOOL: SMALL

APPLICATION DEADLINE: NONE

	APPROXIMATE TUITION	ROOM AND BOARD
IN STATE	$3600	$2100
OUT-OF-STATE	$3600	$2100

REQUIREMENTS FOR ADMISSIONS:
  High school equivalency diploma
  High school diploma
  High school grade point average 2.0

ADDITIONAL SERVICES OFFERED:
  Learning Lab
  Learning Lab has a specialist with a masters degree
     or above in Learning Disabilities
  Diagnostic testing services on campus

MODIFICATIONS TO TRADITIONAL LEARNING ENVIRONMENT:
  Oral presentation in lieu of written exams
  Use of calculator for all math courses
  Tape recorders to record class lectures
  Someone else may take class notes
  Multiple choice exams only
  Essay exams only
  Student takes exams in separate rooms

Students have exams read to them
Students take typewritten exams
Longer time allowed to complete exams
Submit papers on cassette tape
Take limited course load and graduate within time
    required
Extended time limits for graduation
Physical education may be waived

MAJORS OFFERED:

AGRICULTURE
BIOLOGICAL SCIENCES
BUSINESS AND MANAGEMENT
COMPUTER SCIENCES
EDUCATION
FINE AND APPLIED ARTS
HEALTH
HOME ECONOMICS
HUMANITIES
MATHEMATICS
PHYSICAL SCIENCES
PSYCHOLOGY
PUBLIC SERVICES
SOCIAL SCIENCES
THEOLOGY

==

UNIVERSITY OF KANSAS
COLLEGE OF HEALTH SCIENCES AND HOSPITAL
KANSAS CITY, KS 66103
913-588-7055

KEY CONTACT: Attn: Handicapped Student Services

SIZE OF SCHOOL: SMALL

APPLICATION DEADLINE: NONE

        APPROXIMATE TUITION   ROOM AND BOARD

IN STATE $ 860 $NOT OFFERED
OUT-OF-STATE $2440 $NOT OFFERED

REQUIREMENTS FOR ADMISSIONS:
  High school equivalency diploma
  High school diploma
  ACT Scores required
  Admission requirements modified

ADDITIONAL SERVICES OFFERED:
  Diagnostic testing services on campus
  Reader services for the blind available for LD
  Handicapped student services works with LD

MODIFICATIONS TO TRADITIONAL LEARNING ENVIRONMENT:
  Oral presentation in lieu of written exams
  Use of calculator for all math courses
  Tape recorders to record class lectures
  Someone else may take class notes
  Student takes exams in separate rooms
  Students have exams read to them
  Students take typewritten exams
  Longer time allowed to complete exams
  Submit papers on cassette tape
  Extended time limits for graduation
  Physical education may be waived

MAJORS OFFERED:

  HEALTH

==

WASHBURN UNIVERSITY OF TOPEKA
1700 COLLEGE STREET
TOPEKA, KS 66621
913-295-6574

KEY CONTACT: Attn: GREGG MOORE, ASSISTANT
                     DEAN OF STUDENTS

SIZE OF SCHOOL: MEDIUM

APPLICATION DEADLINE: NONE

            APPROXIMATE TUITION   ROOM AND BOARD

IN STATE $1470 $2200
OUT-OF-STATE $1995 $2200

REQUIREMENTS FOR ADMISSIONS:
  High school equivalency diploma
  High school diploma
  Untimed or oral ACT Scores accepted
  Untimed or oral SAT Scores accepted
  High school grade point average 2.0
  Placement tests

ADDITIONAL SERVICES OFFERED:
  Learning Lab
  Remedial and/or tutorial help available
  Reader services for the blind available for LD
  Special Education department
  Handicapped student services works with LD

MODIFICATIONS TO TRADITIONAL LEARNING ENVIRONMENT:
  Oral presentation in lieu of written exams
  Use of calculator for all math courses
  Tape recorders to record class lectures
  Someone else may take class notes
  Student takes exams in separate rooms
  Students have exams read to them
  Students take typewritten exams
  Longer time allowed to complete exams
  Submit papers on cassette tape
  Take limited course load and graduate within time
    required
  Extended time limits for graduation
  Physical education may be waived
  Specific modification depends on disability

MAJORS OFFERED:

  BIOLOGICAL SCIENCES
  BUSINESS AND MANAGEMENT
  COMMUNICATIONS
  COMPUTER SCIENCES
  EDUCATION
  FINE AND APPLIED ARTS
  FOREIGN LANGUAGES
  HEALTH
  HOME ECONOMICS
  HUMANITIES
  LAW
  MATHEMATICS
  MILITARY SCIENCES
  PHYSICAL SCIENCES
  PSYCHOLOGY
  PUBLIC SERVICES
  SOCIAL SCIENCES

==

BRESCIA COLLEGE
120 WEST 7TH STREET
OWENSBORO, KY 42301
502-685-3131

KEY CONTACT: Attn: MICHELE MOREK, ACADEMIC DEAN

SIZE OF SCHOOL: SMALL

APPLICATION DEADLINE: NONE

	APPROXIMATE TUITION	ROOM AND BOARD
IN STATE	$2895	$1840
OUT-OF-STATE	$2895	$1840

REQUIREMENTS FOR ADMISSIONS:
  High school equivalency diploma
  High school diploma
  ACT Scores required
  Untimed or oral ACT Scores accepted
  SAT Scores required
  Untimed or oral SAT Scores accepted
  Particular rank in class - upper 50%
  High school grade point average C or better
  Admission requirements modified
  Personal interview
  Placement tests
  Recommendations

ADDITIONAL SERVICES OFFERED:
  Learning Lab
  Diagnostic testing services on campus
  Diagnostic testing services off campus
  Remedial and/or tutorial help available
  Reader services for the blind available for LD
  Special Education department

MODIFICATIONS TO TRADITIONAL LEARNING ENVIRONMENT:
  Oral presentation in lieu of written exams
  Use of calculator for all math courses
  Tape recorders to record class lectures
  Someone else may take class notes
  Multiple choice exams only
  Essay exams only
  Student takes exams in separate rooms
  Students have exams read to them
  Students take typewritten exams
  Longer time allowed to complete exams
  Submit papers on cassette tape
  Extended time limits for graduation
  Modifications decided on individual basis

MAJORS OFFERED:

  BIOLOGICAL SCIENCES
  BUSINESS AND MANAGEMENT
  COMPUTER SCIENCES

EDUCATION
ENGINEERING TECHNOLOGIES
FINE AND APPLIED ARTS
FOREIGN LANGUAGES
HEALTH
HUMANITIES
MATHEMATICS
PHYSICAL SCIENCES
PSYCHOLOGY
SOCIAL SCIENCES

===

MURRAY STATE UNIVERSITY
MURRAY, KY 42071
502-762-3741

KEY CONTACT: Attn: DR. JODY ANDERSON, DIRECTOR
                     LEARNING CENTER

SIZE OF SCHOOL: MEDIUM

APPLICATION DEADLINE: AUGUST 1

        APPROXIMATE TUITION   ROOM AND BOARD

IN STATE $ 815 $1570
OUT-OF-STATE $2305 $1570

ADDITIONAL SERVICES OFFERED:
  Learning Lab has a specialist with a masters degree
    or above in Learning Disabilities
  Diagnostic testing services off campus
  Remedial and/or tutorial help available
  Reader services for the blind available for LD

MODIFICATIONS TO TRADITIONAL LEARNING ENVIRONMENT:
  Oral presentation in lieu of written exams
  Use of calculator for all math courses
  Tape recorders to record class lectures
  Someone else may take class notes
  Multiple choice exams only
  Essay exams only
  Student takes exams in separate rooms
  Students have exams read to them
  Students take typewritten exams
  Longer time allowed to complete exams
  Submit papers on cassette tape
  Extended time limits for graduation
  Physical education may be waived

MAJORS OFFERED:

```
AGRICULTURE
ARCHITECTURE
AREA STUDIES
BIOLOGICAL SCIENCES
BUSINESS AND MANAGEMENT
COMMUNICATIONS
COMPUTER SCIENCES
EDUCATION
ENGINEERING TECHNOLOGIES
FINE AND APPLIED ARTS
FOREIGN LANGUAGES
HEALTH
HOME ECONOMICS
HUMANITIES
LAW
LIBRARY SCIENCE
MATHEMATICS
MILITARY SCIENCES
PHYSICAL SCIENCES
PSYCHOLOGY
PUBLIC SERVICES
SOCIAL SCIENCES
```

===

UNIVERSITY OF KENTUCKY
LEXINGTON, KY 40506
606-257-1606

KEY CONTACT: Attn: JACOB KARNES, DIRECTOR
                     HANDICAPPED STUDENT SERVICES

SIZE OF SCHOOL: LARGE

APPLICATION DEADLINE: FEBRUARY 15

	APPROXIMATE TUITION	ROOM AND BOARD
IN STATE	$1020	$2320
OUT-OF-STATE	$2890	$2320

REQUIREMENTS FOR ADMISSIONS:
  High school equivalency diploma
  High school diploma
  ACT Scores required
  High school grade point average 2.0

ADDITIONAL SERVICES OFFERED:
  Diagnostic testing services on campus
  Remedial and/or tutorial help available
  Reader services for the blind available for LD
  Handicapped student services works with LD

MODIFICATIONS TO TRADITIONAL LEARNING ENVIRONMENT:
  Oral presentation in lieu of written exams
  Use of calculator for all math courses
  Tape recorders to record class lectures
  Someone else may take class notes
  Student takes exams in separate rooms
  Students have exams read to them
  Students take typewritten exams
  Longer time allowed to complete exams
  Submit papers on cassette tape
  Extended time limits for graduation
  Physical education may be waived

MAJORS OFFERED:

  AGRICULTURE
  ARCHITECTURE
  AREA STUDIES
  BIOLOGICAL SCIENCES
  BUSINESS AND MANAGEMENT
  COMMUNICATIONS
  COMPUTER SCIENCES
  EDUCATION
  ENGINEERING TECHNOLOGIES
  FINE AND APPLIED ARTS
  FOREIGN LANGUAGES
  HEALTH
  HOME ECONOMICS
  HUMANITIES
  LAW
  LIBRARY SCIENCE
  MATHEMATICS
  PHYSICAL SCIENCES
  PSYCHOLOGY
  PUBLIC SERVICES
  SOCIAL SCIENCES

===

UNIVERSITY OF LOUISVILLE
2211 SOUTH BROOK STREET
LOUISVILLE, KY 40292
502-588-6531

KEY CONTACT: Attn: Handicapped Student Services

SIZE OF SCHOOL: LARGE

APPLICATION DEADLINE: AUGUST 1

           APPROXIMATE TUITION   ROOM AND BOARD

IN STATE $1080 $1935
OUT-OF-STATE $2900 $1935

REQUIREMENTS FOR ADMISSIONS:
   High school equivalency diploma
   High school diploma
   ACT Scores required

ADDITIONAL SERVICES OFFERED:
   Learning Lab
   Learning Lab has a specialist with a masters degree
      or above in Learning Disabilities
   Diagnostic testing services off campus
   Remedial and/or tutorial help available
   Reader services for the blind available for LD
   Handicapped student services works with LD

MODIFICATIONS TO TRADITIONAL LEARNING ENVIRONMENT:
   Oral presentation in lieu of written exams
   Tape recorders to record class lectures
   Someone else may take class notes
   Students have exams read to them
   Students take typewritten exams
   Longer time allowed to complete exams
   Physical education may be waived

MAJORS OFFERED:

   ARCHITECTURE
   AREA STUDIES
   BIOLOGICAL SCIENCES
   BUSINESS AND MANAGEMENT
   COMMUNICATIONS
   COMPUTER SCIENCES
   EDUCATION
   ENGINEERING TECHNOLOGIES
   FINE AND APPLIED ARTS
   FOREIGN LANGUAGES
   HEALTH
   HOME ECONOMICS
   HUMANITIES
   LAW
   MATHEMATICS
   PHYSICAL SCIENCES
   PSYCHOLOGY

PUBLIC SERVICES
SOCIAL SCIENCES

===

NORTHWESTERN STATE UNIVERSITY
COLLEGE AVENUE
NATCHITOCHES, LA 71457
318-357-4503

KEY CONTACT: Attn: Handicapped Student Services

SIZE OF SCHOOL: MEDIUM

APPLICATION DEADLINE: NONE

         APPROXIMATE TUITION   ROOM AND BOARD

IN STATE $ 670 $1160
OUT-OF-STATE $1300 $1160

REQUIREMENTS FOR ADMISSIONS:
  High school equivalency diploma
  21 years of age or older, with or without a
    high school diploma or equivalency
  ACT Scores required
  University or College sponsored tests

ADDITIONAL SERVICES OFFERED:
  Learning Lab
  Diagnostic testing services on campus
  Diagnostic testing services off campus
  Remedial and/or tutorial help available
  Reader services for the blind available for LD
  Special Education department
  Handicapped student services works with LD

MODIFICATIONS TO TRADITIONAL LEARNING ENVIRONMENT:
  Has an adaptive physical education program
  Tape recorders to record class lectures
  Take limited course load and graduate within time
    required
  Extended time limits for graduation
  Physical education may be waived

MAJORS OFFERED:

  AGRICULTURE
  ARCHITECTURE
  AREA STUDIES
  BIOLOGICAL SCIENCES

```
BUSINESS AND MANAGEMENT
COMMUNICATIONS
COMPUTER SCIENCES
EDUCATION
ENGINEERING TECHNOLOGIES
FINE AND APPLIED ARTS
FOREIGN LANGUAGES
HEALTH
HOME ECONOMICS
HUMANITIES
LAW
LIBRARY SCIENCE
MATHEMATICS
MILITARY SCIENCES
PHYSICAL SCIENCES
PSYCHOLOGY
PUBLIC SERVICES
SOCIAL SCIENCES
THEOLOGY
```

==

```
XAVIER UNIVERSITY OF LOUISIANA
7325 PALMETTO STREET
NEW ORLEANS, LA 70125
504-486-7411
```

KEY CONTACT: Attn: Handicapped Student Services

SIZE OF SCHOOL: SMALL

APPLICATION DEADLINE: JULY 15

	APPROXIMATE TUITION	ROOM AND BOARD
IN STATE	$3400	$2250
OUT-OF-STATE	$3400	$2250

ADDITIONAL SERVICES OFFERED:
  Learning Lab
  Learning Lab has a specialist with a masters degree
    or above in Learning Disabilities
  Diagnostic testing services on campus
  Remedial and/or tutorial help available
  Reader services for the blind available for LD
  Special Education department

MODIFICATIONS TO TRADITIONAL LEARNING ENVIRONMENT:
  Oral presentation in lieu of written exams
  Use of calculator for all math courses
  Tape recorders to record class lectures

Someone else may take class notes
Multiple choice exams only
Essay exams only
Student takes exams in separate rooms
Students have exams read to them
Students take typewritten exams
Longer time allowed to complete exams
Submit papers on cassette tape
Physical education may be waived

MAJORS OFFERED:

BIOLOGICAL SCIENCES
BUSINESS AND MANAGEMENT
COMMUNICATIONS
COMPUTER SCIENCES
EDUCATION
ENGINEERING TECHNOLOGIES
FINE AND APPLIED ARTS
FOREIGN LANGUAGES
HEALTH
HUMANITIES
LAW
MATHEMATICS
PHYSICAL SCIENCES
PSYCHOLOGY
PUBLIC SERVICES
SOCIAL SCIENCES

===

BATES COLLEGE
LEWISTON, ME 04240
207-786-6000

KEY CONTACT: Attn: WILLIAM C. HISS
                     DEAN OF ADMISSIONS

SIZE OF SCHOOL: SMALL

APPLICATION DEADLINE: FEBRUARY 1

      APPROXIMATE TUITION   ROOM AND BOARD

IN STATE $8890 $2610
OUT-OF-STATE $8890 $2610

REQUIREMENTS FOR ADMISSIONS:
  High school equivalency diploma
  High school diploma
  SAT Scores required

Untimed or oral SAT Scores accepted
Personal interview (recommended)
Recommendations
Essay

ADDITIONAL SERVICES OFFERED:
Diagnostic testing services off campus
Remedial and/or tutorial help available
Reader services for the blind available for LD

MODIFICATIONS TO TRADITIONAL LEARNING ENVIRONMENT:
Use of calculator for all math courses
Has an adaptive physical education program
Tape recorders to record class lectures
Someone else may take class notes
Student takes exams in separate rooms,
Students have exams read to them
Students take typewritten exams
Longer time allowed to complete exams
Extended time limits for graduation
Physical education may be waived

MAJORS OFFERED:

BIOLOGICAL SCIENCES
FINE AND APPLIED ARTS
FOREIGN LANGUAGES
HUMANITIES
MATHEMATICS
PHYSICAL SCIENCES
PSYCHOLOGY
SOCIAL SCIENCES

===

UNITY COLLEGE
QUAKER HILL ROAD
UNITY, ME 04988

KEY CONTACT: Attn: Handicapped Student Services

SIZE OF SCHOOL: SMALL

APPLICATION DEADLINE: NONE

	APPROXIMATE TUITION	ROOM AND BOARD
IN STATE	$4630	$2860
OUT-OF-STATE	$4630	$2860

REQUIREMENTS FOR ADMISSIONS:
  High school equivalency diploma
  High school diploma
  ACT Scores recommended
  Untimed or oral ACT Scores accepted
  SAT Scores recommended
  Untimed or oral SAT Scores accepted
  University or College sponsored tests
  Admission requirements modified with WAIS protocol
  Personal interview
  Placement tests
  Recommendations
  Essay

ADDITIONAL SERVICES OFFERED:
  Learning Lab
  Learning Lab has a specialist with a masters degree
    or above in Learning Disabilities
  Diagnostic testing services on campus
  Remedial and/or tutorial help available

MODIFICATIONS TO TRADITIONAL LEARNING ENVIRONMENT:
  Use of calculator for most math courses
  Tape recorders to record class lectures
  Multiple choice exams only
  Essay exams only
  Student takes exams in separate rooms
  Students have exams read to them
  Students take typewritten exams
  Longer time allowed to complete exams
  Submit papers on cassette tape
  Take limited course load and graduate within time
    required
  Extended time limits for graduation
  All modifications depend on individual, course and
    instructor

MAJORS OFFERED:

  AGRICULTURE
  BIOLOGICAL SCIENCES
  PUBLIC SERVICES

===

UNIVERSITY OF NEW ENGLAND
ST. FRANCIS COLLEGE
11 HILL BEACH ROAD
BIDDEFORD, ME 04005
207-283-0171

KEY CONTACT: Attn: BARBARA BERKOVICH, DIRECTOR
                     LEARNING DISABILITIES PROGRAM

SIZE OF SCHOOL: SMALL

APPLICATION DEADLINE: NONE

         APPROXIMATE TUITION   ROOM AND BOARD

IN STATE $4950 $2780
OUT-OF-STATE $4950 $2780

REQUIREMENTS FOR ADMISSIONS:
  High school equivalency diploma
  High school diploma
  Untimed or oral ACT Scores accepted
  Untimed or oral SAT Scores accepted
  WAIS scores required
  University or College sponsored tests
  Admission requirements modified
  Personal interview
  Placement tests
  Recommendations
  Essay

ADDITIONAL SERVICES OFFERED:
  Learning Lab
  Learning Lab has a specialist with a masters degree
     or above in Learning Disabilities
  Diagnostic testing services off campus
  Remedial and/or tutorial help available
  Reader services for the blind available for LD
  Special Education department
  Handicapped student services works with LD

MODIFICATIONS TO TRADITIONAL LEARNING ENVIRONMENT:
  Oral presentation in lieu of written exams
  Use of calculator for all math courses
  Has an adaptive physical education program
  Tape recorders to record class lectures
  Student takes exams in separate rooms
  Students have exams read to them
  Students take typewritten exams
  Longer time allowed to complete exams
  Submit papers on cassette tape
  Extended time limits for graduation
  All modifications left up to individual instructor

MAJORS OFFERED:

  BIOLOGICAL SCIENCES

BUSINESS AND MANAGEMENT
EDUCATION
HEALTH
PHYSICAL SCIENCES
PSYCHOLOGY
PUBLIC SERVICES

==

TOWSON STATE UNIVERSITY
TOWSON, MD 21204
301-321-2112

KEY CONTACT: Attn: LYNNE DOWELL, AIDS COORDINATOR

SIZE OF SCHOOL: LARGE

APPLICATION DEADLINE: MARCH 1

         APPROXIMATE TUITION   ROOM AND BOARD

IN STATE $1350 $3380
OUT-OF-STATE $2450 $3380

REQUIREMENTS FOR ADMISSIONS:
  High school equivalency diploma
  High school diploma
  SAT Scores required
  Untimed or oral SAT Scores accepted

ADDITIONAL SERVICES OFFERED:
  Learning Lab
  Learning Lab has a specialist with a masters degree
    or above in Learning Disabilities
  Diagnostic testing services on campus
  Remedial and/or tutorial help available
  Reader services for the blind available for LD
  Handicapped student services works with LD

MODIFICATIONS TO TRADITIONAL LEARNING ENVIRONMENT:
  Oral presentation in lieu of written exams
  Use of calculator for all math courses
  Tape recorders to record class lectures
  Someone else may take class notes
  Student takes exams in separate rooms
  Students have exams read to them
  Students take typewritten exams
  Longer time allowed to complete exams
  Submit papers on cassette tape
  Extended time limits for graduation

MAJORS OFFERED:

   AREA STUDIES
   BIOLOGICAL SCIENCES
   BUSINESS AND MANAGEMENT
   COMMUNICATIONS
   COMPUTER SCIENCES
   EDUCATION
   FINE AND APPLIED ARTS
   FOREIGN LANGUAGES
   HEALTH
   HUMANITIES
   LIBRARY SCIENCE
   MILITARY SCIENCES
   PHYSICAL SCIENCES
   PSYCHOLOGY
   PUBLIC SERVICES
   SOCIAL SCIENCES

==

AMERICAN INTERNATIONAL COLLEGE
170 WILBRAHM ROAD
SPRINGFIELD, MA 01109
413-737-7000

KEY CONTACT: Attn: DR. CYNTHIA HALL

SIZE OF SCHOOL: SMALL

APPLICATION DEADLINE: NONE

	APPROXIMATE TUITION	ROOM AND BOARD
IN STATE	$4475	$2375
OUT-OF-STATE	$4475	$2375

REQUIREMENTS FOR ADMISSIONS:
  High school diploma
  SAT Scores required
  Untimed or oral SAT Scores accepted
  WAIS scores required
  Admission requirements modified
  Personal interview
  Recommendations

ADDITIONAL SERVICES OFFERED:
  Learning Lab has a specialist with a masters degree
    or above in Learning Disabilities
  Diagnostic testing services on campus
  Remedial and/or tutorial help available

Special Education department

MODIFICATIONS TO TRADITIONAL LEARNING ENVIRONMENT:
  Oral presentation in lieu of written exams
  Use of calculator for all math courses
  Tape recorders to record class lectures
  Someone else may take class notes
  Student takes exams in separate rooms
  Students have exams read to them
  Students take typewritten exams
  Longer time allowed to complete exams
  Submit papers on cassette tape
  Take limited course load and graduate within time
    required
  Extended time limits for graduation
  Physical education may be waived

MAJORS OFFERED:

  AREA STUDIES
  BIOLOGICAL SCIENCES
  BUSINESS AND MANAGEMENT
  COMPUTER SCIENCES
  EDUCATION
  FOREIGN LANGUAGES
  HEALTH
  HUMANITIES
  MATHEMATICS
  PHYSICAL SCIENCES
  PSYCHOLOGY
  PUBLIC SERVICES
  SOCIAL SCIENCES

===

BOSTON UNIVERSITY
BOSTON, MA 02215
617-353-2300

KEY CONTACT: Attn: ALFRED H. DEGRAFF, DIRECTOR
                     DISABLED STUDENT SERVICES

SIZE OF SCHOOL: LARGE

APPLICATION DEADLINE: FEBRUARY 1

        APPROXIMATE TUITION   ROOM AND BOARD

IN STATE $8420 $3780
OUT-OF-STATE $8420 $3780

REQUIREMENTS FOR ADMISSIONS:
  High school equivalency diploma
  High school diploma
  21 years of age or older, with or without a
    high school diploma or equivalency
  Untimed or oral ACT Scores accepted
  SAT Scores required
  Untimed or oral SAT Scores accepted
  High school grade point average (not specified)
  Admission requirements modified
  Recommendations
  Essay

ADDITIONAL SERVICES OFFERED:
  Diagnostic testing services off campus
  Remedial and/or tutorial help available
  Reader services for the blind available for LD
  Handicapped student services works with LD

MODIFICATIONS TO TRADITIONAL LEARNING ENVIRONMENT:
  Oral presentation in lieu of written exams
  Use of calculator for all math courses
  Tape recorders to record class lectures
  Someone else may take class notes
  Students have exams read to them
  Students take typewritten exams
  Longer time allowed to complete exams
  Submit papers on cassette tape
  Extended time limits for graduation
  Physical education may be waived

MAJORS OFFERED:

  ARCHITECTURE
  AREA STUDIES
  BIOLOGICAL SCIENCES
  BUSINESS AND MANAGEMENT
  COMMUNICATIONS
  COMPUTER SCIENCES
  EDUCATION
  ENGINEERING TECHNOLOGIES
  FINE AND APPLIED ARTS
  FOREIGN LANGUAGES
  HEALTH
  HUMANITIES
  LAW
  MATHEMATICS
  MILITARY SCIENCES
  PHYSICAL SCIENCES
  PSYCHOLOGY
  PUBLIC SERVICES

SOCIAL SCIENCES
THEOLOGY

==

BRADFORD COLLEGE
320 SOUTH MAIN STREET
BRADFORD, MA 01830
617-372-7161

KEY CONTACT: Attn: DIANE WALDRON, DIRECTOR
                     HANDICAPED STUDENT SERVICES

SIZE OF SCHOOL: SMALL

APPLICATION DEADLINE: NONE

      APPROXIMATE TUITION   ROOM AND BOARD

IN STATE $6235 $3390
OUT-OF-STATE $6235 $3390

REQUIREMENTS FOR ADMISSIONS:
  High school equivalency diploma
  High school diploma
  WAIS scores required
  Admission requirements modified
  Personal interview
  Recommendations
  Essay

ADDITIONAL SERVICES OFFERED:
  Learning Lab
  Learning Lab has a specialist with a masters degree
    or above in Learning Disabilities
  Remedial and/or tutorial help available
  Reader services for the blind available for LD

MODIFICATIONS TO TRADITIONAL LEARNING ENVIRONMENT:
  Oral presentation in lieu of written exams
  Use of calculator for all math courses
  Tape recorders to record class lectures
  Someone else may take class notes
  Student takes exams in separate rooms
  Students have exams read to them
  Longer time allowed to complete exams
  Submit papers on cassette tape

MAJORS OFFERED:

  BUSINESS AND MANAGEMENT

```
FINE AND APPLIED ARTS
FOREIGN LANGUAGES
HUMANITIES
PSYCHOLOGY
SOCIAL SCIENCES
```

===

```
CURRY COLLEGE
1071 BLUE HILL AVENUE
MILTON, MA 02186
617-333-0441
```

KEY CONTACT: Attn: DR. GERTRUDE M. WEBB, DIRECTOR
                    THE LEARNING CENTER

SIZE OF SCHOOL: SMALL

APPLICATION DEADLINE: NONE

	APPROXIMATE TUITION	ROOM AND BOARD
IN STATE	$6535	$3500
OUT-OF-STATE	$6535	$3500

REQUIREMENTS FOR ADMISSIONS:
  High school equivalency diploma
  High school diploma
  Untimed or oral SAT Scores accepted
  WAIS scores required
  Particular rank in class (not specified)
  High school grade point average (not specified)
  Personal interview
  Essay

ADDITIONAL SERVICES OFFERED:
  Learning Lab
  Learning Lab has many specialists with masters degree
    or above in Learning Disabilities
  Diagnostic testing services on campus
  Remedial and/or tutorial help available
  Reader services for the blind available for LD
  Special Education department

MODIFICATIONS TO TRADITIONAL LEARNING ENVIRONMENT:
  Student takes exams in separate rooms
  Longer time allowed to complete exams
  Extended time limits for graduation
  All other modifications are individualized by
    professors as warranted

MAJORS OFFERED:

  BIOLOGICAL SCIENCES
  BUSINESS AND MANAGEMENT
  COMMUNICATIONS
  EDUCATION
  FINE AND APPLIED ARTS
  HEALTH
  HUMANITIES
  LAW
  PHYSICAL SCIENCES
  PSYCHOLOGY
  PUBLIC SERVICES
  SOCIAL SCIENCES

===

EMMANUEL COLLEGE
400 THE FENWAY
BOSTON, MA 02115
617-277-9340

KEY CONTACT: Attn: Handicapped Student Services

SIZE OF SCHOOL: SMALL

APPLICATION DEADLINE: NONE

     APPROXIMATE TUITION   ROOM AND BOARD

IN STATE	$5300	$2900
OUT-OF-STATE	$5300	$2900

REQUIREMENTS FOR ADMISSIONS:
  High school equivalency diploma
  High school diploma
  SAT Scores required
  Admission requirements modified
  Recommendations

ADDITIONAL SERVICES OFFERED:
  Learning Lab
  Learning Lab has a specialist with a masters degree
    or above in Learning Disabilities
  Diagnostic testing services on campus
  Remedial and/or tutorial help available
  Reader services for the blind available for LD

MODIFICATIONS TO TRADITIONAL LEARNING ENVIRONMENT:
  Oral presentation in lieu of written exams
  Use of calculator for all math courses

```
Tape recorders to record class lectures
Someone else may take class notes
Multiple choice exams only
Essay exams only
Student takes exams in separate rooms
Students have exams read to them
Students take typewritten exams
Longer time allowed to complete exams
Submit papers on cassette tape
Extended time limits for graduation
Physical education may be waived
```

MAJORS OFFERED:

```
BIOLOGICAL SCIENCES
BUSINESS AND MANAGEMENT
COMMUNICATIONS
EDUCATION
ENGINEERING TECHNOLOGIES
FINE AND APPLIED ARTS
FOREIGN LANGUAGES
HEALTH
HUMANITIES
MATHEMATICS
PHYSICAL SCIENCES
PSYCHOLOGY
SOCIAL SCIENCES
THEOLOGY
```

==

HAMPSHIRE COLLEGE
AMHERST, MA 01002
413-549-4600

KEY CONTACT: Attn: Handicapped Student Services

SIZE OF SCHOOL: SMALL

APPLICATION DEADLINE: FEBRUARY 15

	APPROXIMATE TUITION	ROOM AND BOARD
IN STATE	$9260	$2890
OUT-OF-STATE	$9260	$2890

REQUIREMENTS FOR ADMISSIONS:
  High school equivalency diploma
  High school diploma
  21 years of age or older, with or without a
    high school diploma or equivalency

ADDITIONAL SERVICES OFFERED:
  Learning Lab
  Learning Lab has a specialist with a masters degree
    or above in Learning Disabilities
  Diagnostic testing services on campus
  Remedial and/or tutorial help available
  Reader services for the blind available for LD
  Handicapped student services works with LD

MODIFICATIONS TO TRADITIONAL LEARNING ENVIRONMENT:
  Oral presentation in lieu of written exams
  Use of calculator for all math courses
  Tape recorders to record class lectures
  Someone else may take class notes
  Essay exams only
  Student takes exams in separate rooms
  Students have exams read to them
  Students take typewritten exams
  Longer time allowed to complete exams
  Submit papers on cassette tape
  Extended time limits for graduation
  Physical education may be waived

MAJORS OFFERED:

  AGRICULTURE
  ARCHITECTURE
  AREA STUDIES
  BIOLOGICAL SCIENCES
  BUSINESS AND MANAGEMENT
  COMMUNICATIONS
  COMPUTER SCIENCES
  EDUCATION
  FINE AND APPLIED ARTS
  FOREIGN LANGUAGES
  HEALTH
  HUMANITIES
  LAW
  MATHEMATICS
  PHYSICAL SCIENCES
  PSYCHOLOGY
  PUBLIC SERVICES
  SOCIAL SCIENCES
  THEOLOGY

==

```
LESLEY COLLEGE
29 EVERETT STREET
CAMBRIDGE, MA 02238
617-868-9600
```

KEY CONTACT: Attn: KATHERINE MORGANTHAU, ADVISOR
                     TO HANDICAPPED STUDENTS

SIZE OF SCHOOL: SMALL

APPLICATION DEADLINE: MARCH 15

	APPROXIMATE TUITION	ROOM AND BOARD
IN STATE	$6050	$3750
OUT-OF-STATE	$6050	$3750

REQUIREMENTS FOR ADMISSIONS:
  High school equivalency diploma
  High school diploma
  ACT Scores required
  Untimed or oral ACT Scores accepted
  SAT Scores required
  Untimed or oral SAT Scores accepted
  Personal interview
  Recommendations
  Essay

ADDITIONAL SERVICES OFFERED:
  Remedial and/or tutorial help available

MODIFICATIONS TO TRADITIONAL LEARNING ENVIRONMENT:
  Oral presentation in lieu of written exams
  Tape recorders to record class lectures
  Someone else may take class notes
  Student takes exams in separate rooms
  Students have exams read to them
  Students take typewritten exams
  Longer time allowed to complete exams
  Extended time limits for graduation
  Physical education may be waived

MAJORS OFFERED:

  EDUCATION

==

```
SOUTHEASTERN MASSACHUSETTS UNIVERSITY
NORTH DARTMOUTH, MA 02747
617-999-8605
```

KEY CONTACT: Attn: CAROLE JOHNSON, ACTING DIRECTOR
                     HANDICAPPED STUDENT SERVICES

SIZE OF SCHOOL: MEDIUM

APPLICATION DEADLINE: NONE

         APPROXIMATE TUITION   ROOM AND BOARD

IN STATE $1405 $3200
OUT-OF-STATE $3550 $3200

REQUIREMENTS FOR ADMISSIONS:
  High school diploma
  SAT Scores required
  Admission requirements modified
  Personal interview
  Recommendations

ADDITIONAL SERVICES OFFERED:
  Diagnostic testing services on campus
  Diagnostic testing services off campus
  Remedial and/or tutorial help available
  Reader services for the blind available for LD
  Special Education department
  Handicapped student services works with LD

MODIFICATIONS TO TRADITIONAL LEARNING ENVIRONMENT:
  Oral presentation in lieu of written exams
  Tape recorders to record class lectures
  Someone else may take class notes
  Student takes exams in separate rooms
  Students have exams read to them
  Students take typewritten exams
  Longer time allowed to complete exams
  Extended time limits for graduation
  Physical education may be waived

MAJORS OFFERED:

  BIOLOGICAL SCIENCES
  BUSINESS AND MANAGEMENT
  COMPUTER SCIENCES
  EDUCATION
  FINE AND APPLIED ARTS
  FOREIGN LANGUAGES
  HEALTH
  HOME ECONOMICS
  HUMANITIES
  MATHEMATICS
  PHYSICAL SCIENCES

```
PSYCHOLOGY
SOCIAL SCIENCES
```

==

```
TUFTS UNIVERSITY
MEDFORD, MA 02155
617-381-3170
```

KEY CONTACT: Attn: Handicapped Student Services

SIZE OF SCHOOL: MEDIUM

APPLICATION DEADLINE: JANUARY 15

	APPROXIMATE TUITION	ROOM AND BOARD
IN STATE	$8800	$4050
OUT-OF-STATE	$8800	$4050

REQUIREMENTS FOR ADMISSIONS:
  High school equivalency diploma
  High school diploma
  ACT Scores required
  SAT Scores required
  Untimed or oral SAT Scores accepted

ADDITIONAL SERVICES OFFERED:
  Diagnostic testing services off campus
  Reader services for the blind available for LD

MODIFICATIONS TO TRADITIONAL LEARNING ENVIRONMENT:
  Oral presentation in lieu of written exams
  Use of calculator for all math courses
  Tape recorders to record class lectures
  Someone else may take class notes
  Multiple choice exams only
  Essay exams only
  Student takes exams in separate rooms
  Students have exams read to them
  Students take typewritten exams
  Longer time allowed to complete exams
  Submit papers on cassette tape
  Physical education may be waived

MAJORS OFFERED:

  AREA STUDIES
  BIOLOGICAL SCIENCES
  COMPUTER SCIENCES
  EDUCATION

```
ENGINEERING TECHNOLOGIES
FINE AND APPLIED ARTS
FOREIGN LANGUAGES
HEALTH
HUMANITIES
MATHEMATICS
PHYSICAL SCIENCES
PSYCHOLOGY
SOCIAL SCIENCES
```

==

```
UNIVERSITY OF LOWELL
ROLFE STREET
LOWELL, MA 01854
617-452-5000
```

KEY CONTACT: Attn: Handicapped Student Services

SIZE OF SCHOOL: MEDIUM

APPLICATION DEADLINE: APRIL 1

	APPROXIMATE TUITION	ROOM AND BOARD
IN STATE	$1340	$2470
OUT-OF-STATE	$3595	$2470

REQUIREMENTS FOR ADMISSIONS:
  High school diploma
  SAT Scores required

ADDITIONAL SERVICES OFFERED:
  Has a specialist with a masters degree or above
    in Learning Disabilities
  Diagnostic testing services on campus
  Remedial and/or tutorial help available
  Reader services for the blind available for LD
  Handicapped student services works with LD

MODIFICATIONS TO TRADITIONAL LEARNING ENVIRONMENT:
  Use of calculator for all math courses
  Has an adaptive physical education program
  Tape recorders to record class lectures
  Someone else may take class notes
  Multiple choice exams only
  Essay exams only
  Students have exams read to them
  Students take typewritten exams
  Longer time allowed to complete exams
  Submit papers on cassette tape

Take limited course load and graduate within time
   required
Physical education may be waived
Modifications at the discretion of professors

MAJORS OFFERED:

  AREA STUDIES
  BIOLOGICAL SCIENCES
  BUSINESS AND MANAGEMENT
  COMPUTER SCIENCES
  EDUCATION
  ENGINEERING TECHNOLOGIES
  FINE AND APPLIED ARTS
  FOREIGN LANGUAGES
  HEALTH
  HUMANITIES
  MATHEMATICS
  MILITARY SCIENCES
  PHYSICAL SCIENCES
  PSYCHOLOGY
  PUBLIC SERVICES
  SOCIAL SCIENCES

==

MARYGROVE COLLEGE
DETROIT, MI 48221
313-862-8000

KEY CONTACT: Attn: DARLENE VAN TIEM, DIRECTOR
                    LEARNING SKILLS CENTER

SIZE OF SCHOOL: SMALL

APPLICATION DEADLINE: AUGUST 15

        APPROXIMATE TUITION   ROOM AND BOARD

IN STATE $4045 $2430
OUT-OF-STATE $4045 $2430

REQUIREMENTS FOR ADMISSIONS:
  High school equivalency diploma
  High school diploma
  University or College sponsored tests
  Personal interview
  Placement tests
  Recommendations
  Essay

ADDITIONAL SERVICES OFFERED:
  Learning Lab
  Learning Lab has a specialist with a masters degree
    or above in Learning Disabilities
  Diagnostic testing services on campus
  Remedial and/or tutorial help available
  Special Education department

MODIFICATIONS TO TRADITIONAL LEARNING ENVIRONMENT:
  Tape recorders to record class lectures
  All modifications handled individually

MAJORS OFFERED:

  ARCHITECTURE
  BIOLOGICAL SCIENCES
  BUSINESS AND MANAGEMENT
  COMMUNICATIONS
  COMPUTER SCIENCES
  EDUCATION
  FINE AND APPLIED ARTS
  FOREIGN LANGUAGES
  HOME ECONOMICS
  HUMANITIES
  MATHEMATICS
  PHYSICAL SCIENCES
  PSYCHOLOGY
  PUBLIC SERVICES
  SOCIAL SCIENCES
  THEOLOGY

===

UNIVERSITY OF MICHIGAN - ANN ARBOR
ANN ARBOR, MI 48109
313-764-7433

KEY CONTACT: Attn: Handicapped Student Services

SIZE OF SCHOOL: LARGE

APPLICATION DEADLINE: MARCH 1

        APPROXIMATE TUITION   ROOM AND BOARD

IN STATE $2030 $2500
OUT-OF-STATE $5800 $2500

REQUIREMENTS FOR ADMISSIONS:
  High school equivalency diploma
  High school diploma

```
     ACT Scores required
     Untimed or oral ACT Scores accepted
     SAT Scores required
     Untimed or oral SAT Scores accepted
     University or College sponsored tests
     Personal interview
     Recommendations
```

ADDITIONAL SERVICES OFFERED:
```
     Remedial and/or tutorial help available
     Reader services for the blind available for LD
     Handicapped student services works with LD
```

MODIFICATIONS TO TRADITIONAL LEARNING ENVIRONMENT:
```
     Has an adaptive physical education program
     Tape recorders to record class lectures
     Someone else may take class notes
     Student takes exams in separate rooms
     Students have exams read to them
     Students take typewritten exams
     Longer time allowed to complete exams
     Submit papers on cassette tape
     Take limited course load and graduate within time
        required
     Extended time limits for graduation
```

MAJORS OFFERED:

```
     AGRICULTURE
     ARCHITECTURE
     AREA STUDIES
     BIOLOGICAL SCIENCES
     BUSINESS AND MANAGEMENT
     COMMUNICATIONS
     COMPUTER SCIENCES
     EDUCATION
     ENGINEERING TECHNOLOGIES
     FINE AND APPLIED ARTS
     FOREIGN LANGUAGES
     HEALTH
     HUMANITIES
     LIBRARY SCIENCE
     MATHEMATICS
     MILITARY SCIENCES
     PHYSICAL SCIENCES
     PSYCHOLOGY
     PUBLIC SERVICES
     SOCIAL SCIENCES
```

===

UNIVERSITY OF MICHIGAN - DEARBORN
4901 EVERGREEN ROAD
DEARBORN, MI 48128
313-593-5170

KEY CONTACT: Attn: Handicapped Student Services

SIZE OF SCHOOL: MEDIUM

APPLICATION DEADLINE: NONE

        APPROXIMATE TUITION   ROOM AND BOARD

IN STATE $1670 $NOT OFFERED
OUT-OF-STATE $5120 $NOT OFFERED

REQUIREMENTS FOR ADMISSIONS:
  ACT Scores required
  SAT Scores required

ADDITIONAL SERVICES OFFERED:
  Learning Lab
  Learning Lab has a specialist with a masters degree
    or above in Learning Disabilities
  Diagnostic testing services on campus
  Remedial and/or tutorial help available
  Reader services for the blind available for LD
  Handicapped student services works with LD

MODIFICATIONS TO TRADITIONAL LEARNING ENVIRONMENT:
  Tape recorders to record class lectures
  Someone else may take class notes
  Students have exams read to them
  Students take typewritten exams
  Longer time allowed to complete exams
  Extended time limits for graduation
  Physical education may be waived

MAJORS OFFERED:

  AREA STUDIES
  BIOLOGICAL SCIENCES
  BUSINESS AND MANAGEMENT
  COMMUNICATIONS
  COMPUTER SCIENCES
  EDUCATION
  ENGINEERING TECHNOLOGIES
  FINE AND APPLIED ARTS
  HEALTH
  HUMANITIES
  MATHEMATICS

```
PHYSICAL SCIENCES
PSYCHOLOGY
PUBLIC SERVICES
SOCIAL SCIENCES
```

===

```
WAYNE STATE UNIVERSITY
DETROIT, MI 48202
313-577-3577
```

KEY CONTACT: Attn: BETSY F. SCHRAUDER, DIRECTOR ERS

SIZE OF SCHOOL: LARGE

APPLICATION DEADLINE: NONE

	APPROXIMATE TUITION	ROOM AND BOARD
IN STATE	$1760	$1700
OUT-OF-STATE	$3860	$1700

REQUIREMENTS FOR ADMISSIONS:
  High school equivalency diploma
  High school diploma
  ACT Scores required (depends on average)
  Untimed or oral ACT Scores accepted
  SAT Scores required (depends on average)
  Untimed or oral SAT Scores accepted
  High school grade point average 2.75 or
    SAT of 850 or above, ACT of 20 or above
  Admission requirements modified
  Personal interview
  Placement tests
  Recommendations
  Essay

ADDITIONAL SERVICES OFFERED:
  Learning Lab
  Diagnostic testing services on campus
  Remedial and/or tutorial help available
  Reader services for the blind available for LD
  Special Education department
  Handicapped student services works with LD

MODIFICATIONS TO TRADITIONAL LEARNING ENVIRONMENT:
  Oral presentation in lieu of written exams
  Use of calculator for all math courses
  Has an adaptive physical education program
  Tape recorders to record class lectures
  Someone else may take class notes

```
Student takes exams in separate rooms
Students have exams read to them
Longer time allowed to complete exams
Extended time limits for graduation
Physical education may be waived
```

MAJORS OFFERED:

```
ARCHITECTURE
AREA STUDIES
BIOLOGICAL SCIENCES
BUSINESS AND MANAGEMENT
COMMUNICATIONS
COMPUTER SCIENCES
EDUCATION
ENGINEERING TECHNOLOGIES
FINE AND APPLIED ARTS
FOREIGN LANGUAGES
HEALTH
HOME ECONOMICS
HUMANITIES
LAW
LIBRARY SCIENCE
MATHEMATICS
MILITARY SCIENCES
PHYSICAL SCIENCES
PSYCHOLOGY
PUBLIC SERVICES
SOCIAL SCIENCES
THEOLOGY
```

===

```
AUGSBURG COLLEGE
731 21ST AVENUE SOUTH
MINNEAPOLIS, MN 55454
612-330-1001
```

KEY CONTACT: Attn: DONALD WARREN, DIRECTOR
                    ACADEMIC ENRICHMENT

SIZE OF SCHOOL: SMALL

APPLICATION DEADLINE: AUGUST 1

	APPROXIMATE TUITION	ROOM AND BOARD
IN STATE	$5160	$2335
OUT-OF-STATE	$5160	$2335

REQUIREMENTS FOR ADMISSIONS:
  High school equivalency diploma
  High school diploma
  ACT Scores required OR SAT scores OR PSAT scores
  Untimed or oral ACT Scores accepted
  Untimed or oral SAT Scores accepted
  Particular rank in class 33%
  High school grade point average 2.0
  Admission requirements modified
  Personal interview
  Placement tests
  Recommendations
  Essay

ADDITIONAL SERVICES OFFERED:
  Learning Lab
  Diagnostic testing services on campus
  Remedial and/or tutorial help available
  Reader services for the blind available for LD
  Special Education department

MODIFICATIONS TO TRADITIONAL LEARNING ENVIRONMENT:
  Oral presentation in lieu of written exams
  Use of calculator for all math courses
  Has an adaptive physical education program
  Tape recorders to record class lectures
  Someone else may take class notes
  Multiple choice exams only
  Student takes exams in separate rooms
  Students have exams read to them
  Students take typewritten exams
  Longer time allowed to complete exams
  Submit papers on cassette tape
  Extended time limits for graduation
  Physical education may be waived
  Currently working on waiver of foreign language
    requirement when appropriate

MAJORS OFFERED:

  AREA STUDIES
  BIOLOGICAL SCIENCES
  BUSINESS AND MANAGEMENT
  COMMUNICATIONS
  EDUCATION
  FINE AND APPLIED ARTS
  FOREIGN LANGUAGES
  HEALTH
  HUMANITIES
  LAW
  MATHEMATICS

```
PHYSICAL SCIENCES
PSYCHOLOGY
PUBLIC SERVICES
SOCIAL SCIENCES
```

==

```
CONCORDIA COLLEGE
MOORHEAD, MN 56560
218-299-3004
```

KEY CONTACT: Attn: DON DALE

SIZE OF SCHOOL: SMALL

APPLICATION DEADLINE: JUNE 1

	APPROXIMATE TUITION	ROOM AND BOARD
IN STATE	$5305	$1795
OUT-OF-STATE	$5305	$1795

REQUIREMENTS FOR ADMISSIONS:
  High school diploma
  ACT Scores required
  SAT Scores required
  Particular rank in class 50%
  Admission requirements modified

ADDITIONAL SERVICES OFFERED:
  Learning Lab has a specialist with a masters degree
    or above in Learning Disabilities
  Diagnostic testing services off campus
  Remedial and/or tutorial help available
  Reader services for the blind available for LD
  Handicapped student services works with LD

MODIFICATIONS TO TRADITIONAL LEARNING ENVIRONMENT:
  Use of calculator for all math courses
  Tape recorders to record class lectures
  Someone else may take class notes
  Student takes exams in separate rooms
  Students have exams read to them
  Longer time allowed to complete exams
  Physical education may be waived

MAJORS OFFERED:

  BIOLOGICAL SCIENCES
  BUSINESS AND MANAGEMENT
  COMMUNICATIONS

```
COMPUTER SCIENCES
EDUCATION
FINE AND APPLIED ARTS
FOREIGN LANGUAGES
HEALTH
HOME ECONOMICS
HUMANITIES
MATHEMATICS
PHYSICAL SCIENCES
PSYCHOLOGY
PUBLIC SERVICES
SOCIAL SCIENCES
```

===

```
MOORHEAD STATE UNIVERSITY
MOORHEAD, MN 56560
218-236-2161
```

KEY CONTACT: Attn: ROBERT PRATT PHD, COORDINATOR
                     SERVICES FOR HANDICAPPED STUDENTS

SIZE OF SCHOOL: MEDIUM

APPLICATION DEADLINE: AUGUST 15

	APPROXIMATE TUITION	ROOM AND BOARD
IN STATE	$1000	$1490
OUT-OF-STATE	$1690	$1490

ADDITIONAL SERVICES OFFERED:
  Diagnostic testing services off campus
  Remedial and/or tutorial help available
  Reader services for the blind available for LD
  Special Education department
  Handicapped student services works with LD

MODIFICATIONS TO TRADITIONAL LEARNING ENVIRONMENT:
  Oral presentation in lieu of written exams
  Use of calculator for all math courses
  Has an adaptive physical education program
  Tape recorders to record class lectures
  Someone else may take class notes
  Multiple choice exams only
  Essay exams only
  Student takes exams in separate rooms
  Students have exams read to them
  Students take typewritten exams
  Longer time allowed to complete exams
  Submit papers on cassette tape

Take limited course load and graduate within time
   required
Extended time limits for graduation
Physical education may be waived
Modifications made only if necessary

MAJORS OFFERED:

AREA STUDIES
BIOLOGICAL SCIENCES
BUSINESS AND MANAGEMENT
COMMUNICATIONS
COMPUTER SCIENCES
EDUCATION
FINE AND APPLIED ARTS
FOREIGN LANGUAGES
HEALTH
HUMANITIES
LAW
MATHEMATICS
PHYSICAL SCIENCES
PSYCHOLOGY
PUBLIC SERVICES
SOCIAL SCIENCES

===

ST. OLAF COLLEGE
NORTHFIELD, MN 55057
507-663-3025

KEY CONTACT: Attn: KATE CAMPBELL

SIZE OF SCHOOL: SMALL

APPLICATION DEADLINE: FEBRUARY 15

        APPROXIMATE TUITION   ROOM AND BOARD

IN STATE $6075 $2075
OUT-OF-STATE $6075 $2075

REQUIREMENTS FOR ADMISSIONS:
   ACT Scores required
   SAT Scores required
   Admission requirements modified

ADDITIONAL SERVICES OFFERED:
   Learning Lab
   Learning Lab has a specialist with a masters degree
      or above in Learning Disabilities

```
Diagnostic testing services on campus
Diagnostic testing services off campus
Remedial and/or tutorial help available
Handicapped student services works with LD
```

MODIFICATIONS TO TRADITIONAL LEARNING ENVIRONMENT:
```
Oral presentation in lieu of written exams
Use of calculator for all math courses
Has an adaptive physical education program
Tape recorders to record class lectures
Someone else may take class notes
Multiple choice exams only
Essay exams only
Student takes exams in separate rooms
Students have exams read to them
Students take typewritten exams
Longer time allowed to complete exams
Submit papers on cassette tape
Extended time limits for graduation
Physical education may be waived
```

MAJORS OFFERED:

```
AREA STUDIES
BIOLOGICAL SCIENCES
EDUCATION
ENGINEERING TECHNOLOGIES
FINE AND APPLIED ARTS
FOREIGN LANGUAGES
HEALTH
HOME ECONOMICS
HUMANITIES
MATHEMATICS
PHYSICAL SCIENCES
PSYCHOLOGY
PUBLIC SERVICES
SOCIAL SCIENCES
THEOLOGY
```

==

MISSISSIPPI VALLEY STATE UNIVERSITY
ITTA BENA, MS 38941
601-254-9041

KEY CONTACT: Attn: MARY CROWDER, COUNSELOR
                     SPECIAL SERVICES

SIZE OF SCHOOL: SMALL

APPLICATION DEADLINE: NONE

```
         APPROXIMATE TUITION    ROOM AND BOARD

IN STATE               $ 850        $1350
OUT-OF-STATE           $ 850        $1350
```

REQUIREMENTS FOR ADMISSIONS:
  High school equivalency diploma
  High school diploma
  ACT Scores required
  WAIS scores required
  All students must meet University admissions
    requirements

ADDITIONAL SERVICES OFFERED:
  Remedial and/or tutorial help available
  Reader services for the blind available for LD

MODIFICATIONS TO TRADITIONAL LEARNING ENVIRONMENT:
  Oral presentation in lieu of written exams
  Use of calculator for all math courses
  Has an adaptive physical education program
  Tape recorders to record class lectures
  Someone else may take class notes
  Students have exams read to them
  Students take typewritten exams
  Longer time allowed to complete exams
  Submit papers on cassette tape
  Take limited course load and graduate within time
    required
  Extended time limits for graduation
  Physical education may be waived

MAJORS OFFERED:

  BIOLOGICAL SCIENCES
  BUSINESS AND MANAGEMENT
  COMMUNICATIONS
  EDUCATION
  ENGINEERING TECHNOLOGIES
  FINE AND APPLIED ARTS
  HEALTH
  HUMANITIES
  MATHEMATICS
  PHYSICAL SCIENCES
  PUBLIC SERVICES
  SOCIAL SCIENCES

===

TOUGALOO COLLEGE
TOUGALOO, MS 39174
601-956-4941

KEY CONTACT: Attn: Handicapped Student Services

SIZE OF SCHOOL: SMALL

APPLICATION DEADLINE: NONE

	APPROXIMATE TUITION	ROOM AND BOARD
IN STATE	$2800	$1440
OUT-OF-STATE	$2800	$1440

REQUIREMENTS FOR ADMISSIONS:
  High school diploma
  ACT Scores required
  SAT Scores required
  High school grade point average 2.0
  Placement tests

ADDITIONAL SERVICES OFFERED:
  Learning Lab
  Learning Lab has a specialist with a masters degree
    or above in Learning Disabilities
  Remedial and/or tutorial help available

MODIFICATIONS TO TRADITIONAL LEARNING ENVIRONMENT:
  Has an adaptive physical education program
  Physical education may be waived

MAJORS OFFERED:

  AREA STUDIES
  BIOLOGICAL SCIENCES
  BUSINESS AND MANAGEMENT
  COMMUNICATIONS
  COMPUTER SCIENCES
  EDUCATION
  ENGINEERING TECHNOLOGIES
  FINE AND APPLIED ARTS
  HEALTH
  HUMANITIES
  MATHEMATICS
  PHYSICAL SCIENCES
  PSYCHOLOGY
  PUBLIC SERVICES
  SOCIAL SCIENCES

==

```
AVILA COLLEGE
11901 WORNALL ROAD
KANSAS CITY, MO 64145
816-942-8400
```

KEY CONTACT: Attn: Handicapped Student Services

SIZE OF SCHOOL: SMALL

APPLICATION DEADLINE: NONE

	APPROXIMATE TUITION	ROOM AND BOARD
IN STATE	$3600	$1900
OUT-OF-STATE	$3600	$1900

REQUIREMENTS FOR ADMISSIONS:
  High school equivalency diploma
  High school diploma
  ACT Scores required
  SAT Scores required
  High school grade point average C
  Admission requirements modified

ADDITIONAL SERVICES OFFERED:
  Learning Lab
  Learning Lab has a specialist with a masters degree
    or above in Learning Disabilities
  Diagnostic testing services on campus
  Remedial and/or tutorial help available
  Special Education department

MODIFICATIONS TO TRADITIONAL LEARNING ENVIRONMENT:
  Oral presentation in lieu of written exams
  Tape recorders to record class lectures
  Someone else may take class notes
  Multiple choice exams only
  Student takes exams in separate rooms
  Students have exams read to them
  Students take typewritten exams
  Longer time allowed to complete exams
  Physical education may be waived

MAJORS OFFERED:

  BIOLOGICAL SCIENCES
  BUSINESS AND MANAGEMENT
  COMMUNICATIONS
  COMPUTER SCIENCES
  EDUCATION
  FINE AND APPLIED ARTS

```
HEALTH
HUMANITIES
LAW
MATHEMATICS
PHYSICAL SCIENCES
PUBLIC SERVICES
SOCIAL SCIENCES
THEOLOGY
```

===

KANSAS CITY ART INSTITUTE
4415 WARWICK BOULEVARD
KANSAS CITY, MO 64111
816-561-4852

KEY CONTACT: Attn: Handicapped Student Services

SIZE OF SCHOOL: SMALL

APPLICATION DEADLINE: NONE

APPROXIMATE TUITION   ROOM AND BOARD

IN STATE $6150 $2455
OUT-OF-STATE $6150 $2455

REQUIREMENTS FOR ADMISSIONS:
  High school equivalency diploma
  High school diploma
  Admission requirements modified

ADDITIONAL SERVICES OFFERED:
  Diagnostic testing services off campus
  Remedial and/or tutorial help available

MODIFICATIONS TO TRADITIONAL LEARNING ENVIRONMENT:
  Oral presentation in lieu of written exams
  Use of calculator for all math courses
  Tape recorders to record class lectures
  Someone else may take class notes
  Multiple choice exams only
  Essay exams only
  Student takes exams in separate rooms
  Students have exams read to them
  Students take typewritten exams
  Longer time allowed to complete exams
  Submit papers on cassette tape
  Extended time limits for graduation
  Physical education may be waived

MAJORS OFFERED:

ARCHITECTURE
FINE AND APPLIED ARTS

==

LINDENWOOD COLLEGE
ST. CHARLES, MO 63301
314-723-7152

KEY CONTACT: Attn: AARON MILLER, PROVOST

SIZE OF SCHOOL: SMALL

APPLICATION DEADLINE: NONE

	APPROXIMATE TUITION	ROOM AND BOARD
IN STATE	$4800	$3200
OUT-OF-STATE	$4800	$3200

REQUIREMENTS FOR ADMISSIONS:
    High school diploma
    ACT Scores required
    Untimed or oral ACT Scores accepted
    SAT Scores required
    Untimed or oral SAT Scores accepted
    University or College sponsored tests
    High school grade point average 2.0
    Admission requirements modified
    Personal interview

ADDITIONAL SERVICES OFFERED:
    Remedial and/or tutorial help available
    Reader services for the blind available for LD
    Special Education department
    Handicapped student services works with LD

MODIFICATIONS TO TRADITIONAL LEARNING ENVIRONMENT:
    Oral presentation in lieu of written exams
    Use of calculator for all math courses
    Tape recorders to record class lectures
    Someone else may take class notes
    Students have exams read to them
    Longer time allowed to complete exams
    Submit papers on cassette tape
    Take limited course load and graduate within time
        required
    Extended time limits for graduation
    Physical education may be waived

MAJORS OFFERED:

  BIOLOGICAL SCIENCES
  BUSINESS AND MANAGEMENT
  COMMUNICATIONS
  COMPUTER SCIENCES
  EDUCATION
  ENGINEERING TECHNOLOGIES
  FINE AND APPLIED ARTS
  FOREIGN LANGUAGES
  HEALTH
  HUMANITIES
  MATHEMATICS
  PHYSICAL SCIENCES
  PSYCHOLOGY
  SOCIAL SCIENCES

===

MISSOURI VALLEY COLLEGE
MARSHALL, MO 65340
816-886-6924

KEY CONTACT: Attn: Handicapped Student Services

SIZE OF SCHOOL: SMALL

APPLICATION DEADLINE: NONE

	APPROXIMATE TUITION	ROOM AND BOARD
IN STATE	$3400	$1880
OUT-OF-STATE	$3400	$1880

REQUIREMENTS FOR ADMISSIONS:
  High school equivalency diploma
  High school diploma
  ACT Scores required
  SAT Scores required
  Recommendations

ADDITIONAL SERVICES OFFERED:
  Learning Lab
  Learning Lab has a specialist with a masters degree
    or above in Learning Disabilities
  Diagnostic testing services on campus
  Remedial and/or tutorial help available
  Special Education department

MODIFICATIONS TO TRADITIONAL LEARNING ENVIRONMENT:
    Oral presentation in lieu of written exams
    Use of calculator for all math courses
    Tape recorders to record class lectures
    Someone else may take class notes
    Multiple choice exams only
    Essay exams only
    Student takes exams in separate rooms
    Students have exams read to them
    Students take typewritten exams
    Longer time allowed to complete exams
    Submit papers on cassette tape
    Extended time limits for graduation
    Physical education may be waived

MAJORS OFFERED:

    AGRICULTURE
    BIOLOGICAL SCIENCES
    BUSINESS AND MANAGEMENT
    COMMUNICATIONS
    COMPUTER SCIENCES
    EDUCATION
    FINE AND APPLIED ARTS
    FOREIGN LANGUAGES
    HUMANITIES
    MATHEMATICS
    PHYSICAL SCIENCES
    PSYCHOLOGY
    SOCIAL SCIENCES
    THEOLOGY

===

MISSOURI WESTERN STATE COLLEGE
4525 DOWNS DRIVE
ST. JOSEPH, MO 64507
233-271-4211

KEY CONTACT: Attn: Handicapped Student Services

SIZE OF SCHOOL: MEDIUM

APPLICATION DEADLINE: NONE

	APPROXIMATE TUITION	ROOM AND BOARD
IN STATE	$ 780	$1460
OUT-OF-STATE	$1460	$1460

REQUIREMENTS FOR ADMISSIONS:
  High school equivalency diploma
  High school diploma

ADDITIONAL SERVICES OFFERED:
  Learning Lab
  Learning Lab has a specialist with a masters degree
    or above in Learning Disabilities
  Diagnostic testing services on campus
  Diagnostic testing services off campus
  Remedial and/or tutorial help available
  Reader services for the blind available for LD
  Handicapped student services works with LD

MODIFICATIONS TO TRADITIONAL LEARNING ENVIRONMENT:
  Oral presentation in lieu of written exams
  Use of calculator for all math courses
  Has an adaptive physical education program
  Tape recorders to record class lectures
  Someone else may take class notes
  Student takes exams in separate rooms
  Students have exams read to them
  Students take typewritten exams
  Longer time allowed to complete exams
  Submit papers on cassette tape
  Take limited course load and graduate within time
    required
  Extended time limits for graduation
  Physical education may be waived

MAJORS OFFERED:

  AGRICULTURE
  ARCHITECTURE
  BIOLOGICAL SCIENCES
  BUSINESS AND MANAGEMENT
  COMPUTER SCIENCES
  EDUCATION
  ENGINEERING TECHNOLOGIES
  FINE AND APPLIED ARTS
  HEALTH
  HUMANITIES
  LAW
  MATHEMATICS
  PHYSICAL SCIENCES
  PSYCHOLOGY
  PUBLIC SERVICES
  SOCIAL SCIENCES

==

NORTHEAST MISSOURI STATE UNIVERSITY
KIRKSVILLE, MO 63501
816-785-4114

KEY CONTACT: Attn: Handicapped Student Services

SIZE OF SCHOOL: MEDIUM

APPLICATION DEADLINE: NONE

        APPROXIMATE TUITION   ROOM AND BOARD

IN STATE $ 620 $1480
OUT-OF-STATE $1240 $1480

REQUIREMENTS FOR ADMISSIONS:
  ACT Scores required
  SAT Scores required
  Particular rank in class 33% (in state)
    50% (out of state)

ADDITIONAL SERVICES OFFERED:
  Learning Lab
  Learning Lab has a specialist with a masters degree
    or above in Learning Disabilities
  Diagnostic testing services on campus
  Remedial and/or tutorial help available
  Reader services for the blind available for LD
  Special Education department

MODIFICATIONS TO TRADITIONAL LEARNING ENVIRONMENT:
  Oral presentation in lieu of written exams
  Use of calculator for all math courses
  Tape recorders to record class lectures
  Someone else may take class notes
  Multiple choice exams only
  Essay exams only
  Student takes exams in separate rooms
  Students have exams read to them
  Students take typewritten exams
  Longer time allowed to complete exams
  Submit papers on cassette tape
  Take limited course load and graduate within time
    required
  Physical education may be waived

MAJORS OFFERED:

  AGRICULTURE
  ARCHITECTURE
  BIOLOGICAL SCIENCES

```
BUSINESS AND MANAGEMENT
COMMUNICATIONS
COMPUTER SCIENCES
EDUCATION
ENGINEERING TECHNOLOGIES
FINE AND APPLIED ARTS
FOREIGN LANGUAGES
HEALTH
HOME ECONOMICS
HUMANITIES
LAW
LIBRARY SCIENCE
MATHEMATICS
PHYSICAL SCIENCES
PSYCHOLOGY
PUBLIC SERVICES
SOCIAL SCIENCES
```

===

PARK COLLEGE
KANSAS CITY, MO 64152
816-741-2000

KEY CONTACT: Attn: Handicapped Student Services

SIZE OF SCHOOL: SMALL

APPLICATION DEADLINE: NONE

```
        APPROXIMATE TUITION    ROOM AND BOARD

IN STATE          $3740          $1950
OUT-OF-STATE      $3740          $1950
```

REQUIREMENTS FOR ADMISSIONS:
  High school equivalency diploma
  High school diploma
  21 years of age or older, with or without a
    high school diploma or equivalency
  ACT Scores required
  SAT Scores required
  High school grade point average (not specified)
  Admission requirements modified
  Personal interview
  Recommendations

ADDITIONAL SERVICES OFFERED:
  Learning Lab
  Learning Lab has a specialist with a masters degree
    or above in Learning Disabilities

Diagnostic testing services on campus
Diagnostic testing services off campus
Remedial and/or tutorial help available
Reader services for the blind available for LD

MODIFICATIONS TO TRADITIONAL LEARNING ENVIRONMENT:
Oral presentation in lieu of written exams
Use of calculator for all math courses
Tape recorders to record class lectures
Someone else may take class notes
Student takes exams in separate rooms
Students have exams read to them
Take limited course load and graduate within time
    required
Extended time limits for graduation
Physical education may be waived

MAJORS OFFERED:

AGRICULTURE
BIOLOGICAL SCIENCES
BUSINESS AND MANAGEMENT
COMMUNICATIONS
EDUCATION
FINE AND APPLIED ARTS
HEALTH
HUMANITIES
LAW
MATHEMATICS
PHYSICAL SCIENCES
PSYCHOLOGY
PUBLIC SERVICES
SOCIAL SCIENCES

==

ROCKHURST COLLEGE
5225 TROOST AVENUE
KANSAS CITY, MO 64110
816-926-4100

KEY CONTACT: Attn: Handicapped Student Services

SIZE OF SCHOOL: SMALL

APPLICATION DEADLINE: JUNE 30

	APPROXIMATE TUITION	ROOM AND BOARD
IN STATE	$4160	$2400
OUT-OF-STATE	$4160	$2400

REQUIREMENTS FOR ADMISSIONS:
  ACT Scores required
  Particular rank in class (not specified)
  Recommendations

ADDITIONAL SERVICES OFFERED:
  Learning Lab
  Learning Lab has a specialist with a masters degree
    or above in Learning Disabilities
  Remedial and/or tutorial help available

MODIFICATIONS TO TRADITIONAL LEARNING ENVIRONMENT:
  Oral presentation in lieu of written exams
  Tape recorders to record class lectures
  Someone else may take class notes
  Multiple choice exams only
  Essay exams only
  Student takes exams in separate rooms
  Students have exams read to them
  Students take typewritten exams
  Longer time allowed to complete exams
  Submit papers on cassette tape
  Extended time limits for graduation
  Physical education may be waived
  Modifications at the discretion of individual teacher

MAJORS OFFERED:

  BIOLOGICAL SCIENCES
  BUSINESS AND MANAGEMENT
  COMMUNICATIONS
  COMPUTER SCIENCES
  EDUCATION
  ENGINEERING TECHNOLOGIES
  FOREIGN LANGUAGES
  HEALTH
  HUMANITIES
  LAW
  MATHEMATICS
  PHYSICAL SCIENCES
  PSYCHOLOGY
  PUBLIC SERVICES
  SOCIAL SCIENCES
  THEOLOGY

==

WASHINGTON UNIVERSTIY
BOX 1089
ST. LOUIS, MO 63130

KEY CONTACT: Attn: Handicapped Student Services

SIZE OF SCHOOL: MEDIUM

APPLICATION DEADLINE: NONE

       APPROXIMATE TUITION   ROOM AND BOARD

IN STATE $7945 $3420
OUT-OF-STATE $7945 $3420

REQUIREMENTS FOR ADMISSIONS:
  High school diploma
  ACT Scores required
  Untimed or oral ACT Scores accepted
  SAT Scores required
  Untimed or oral SAT Scores accepted
  Essay

ADDITIONAL SERVICES OFFERED:
  Learning Lab
  Diagnostic testing services on campus
  Remedial and/or tutorial help available
  Handicapped student services works with LD

MODIFICATIONS TO TRADITIONAL LEARNING ENVIRONMENT:
  Oral presentation in lieu of written exams
  Use of calculator for all math courses
  Has an adaptive physical education program
  Tape recorders to record class lectures
  Someone else may take class notes
  Student takes exams in separate rooms
  Students have exams read to them
  Students take typewritten exams
  Longer time allowed to complete exams
  Submit papers on cassette tape
  All modifications are arranged with individual
    instructors

MAJORS OFFERED:

  ARCHITECTURE
  AREA STUDIES
  BIOLOGICAL SCIENCES
  BUSINESS AND MANAGEMENT
  COMPUTER SCIENCES
  EDUCATION
  ENGINEERING TECHNOLOGIES
  FINE AND APPLIED ARTS
  FOREIGN LANGUAGES
  HEALTH

```
HUMANITIES
MATHEMATICS
MILITARY SCIENCES
PHYSICAL SCIENCES
PSYCHOLOGY
PUBLIC SERVICES
SOCIAL SCIENCES
```

==

```
WESTMINSTER COLLEGE
7TH AND WESTMINSTER AVENUES
FULTON, MO 65251
314-642-3361
```

KEY CONTACT: Attn: HENRY OTTINGER, DIRECTOR
                    LEARNING DISABILITIES PROGRAM

SIZE OF SCHOOL: SMALL

APPLICATION DEADLINE: NONE

	APPROXIMATE TUITION	ROOM AND BOARD
IN STATE	$4600	$2300
OUT-OF-STATE	$4600	$2300

REQUIREMENTS FOR ADMISSIONS:
  High school equivalency diploma
  High school diploma
  ACT Scores required
  Untimed or oral ACT Scores accepted
  SAT Scores required
  Untimed or oral SAT Scores accepted
  WAIS scores required
  Admission requirements modified
  Personal interview
  Placement tests
  Recommendations
  Essay

ADDITIONAL SERVICES OFFERED:
  Learning Lab
  Learning Lab has a specialist with a masters degree
    or above in Learning Disabilities
  Diagnostic testing services on campus
  Remedial and/or tutorial help available
  Reader services for the blind available for LD

MODIFICATIONS TO TRADITIONAL LEARNING ENVIRONMENT:
  Oral presentation in lieu of written exams
  Use of calculator for all math courses
  Has an adaptive physical education program
  Tape recorders to record class lectures
  Someone else may take class notes
  Student takes exams in separate rooms
  Students have exams read to them
  Students take typewritten exams
  Longer time allowed to complete exams
  Submit papers on cassette tape
  Extended time limits for graduation

MAJORS OFFERED:

  BIOLOGICAL SCIENCES
  BUSINESS AND MANAGEMENT
  COMMUNICATIONS
  EDUCATION
  ENGINEERING TECHNOLOGIES
  FINE AND APPLIED ARTS
  FOREIGN LANGUAGES
  HEALTH
  HUMANITIES
  MATHEMATICS
  PHYSICAL SCIENCES
  PSYCHOLOGY
  SOCIAL SCIENCES

==

MONTANA STATE UNIVERSITY
MONTANA HALL
BOZEMAN, MT 59717
406-994-2452

KEY CONTACT: Attn: ROBERT FRAZIER, DIRECTOR
                    HANDICAPPED SERVICES

SIZE OF SCHOOL: MEDIUM

APPLICATION DEADLINE: NONE

        APPROXIMATE TUITION   ROOM AND BOARD

IN STATE $ 800 $2300
OUT-OF-STATE $2340 $2300

REQUIREMENTS FOR ADMISSIONS:
  High school equivalency diploma
  High school diploma

ACT Scores required
Untimed or oral ACT Scores accepted
SAT Scores required
Untimed or oral SAT Scores accepted
University or College sponsored tests
Particular rank in class   50%
High school grade point average   2.5
Placement tests
Recommendations
State/District residency

ADDITIONAL SERVICES OFFERED:
  Learning Lab
  Diagnostic testing services on campus
  Diagnostic testing services off campus
  Remedial and/or tutorial help available
  Reader services for the blind available for LD
  Handicapped student services works with LD

MODIFICATIONS TO TRADITIONAL LEARNING ENVIRONMENT:
  Oral presentation in lieu of written exams
  Use of calculator for all math courses
  Has an adaptive physical education program
  Tape recorders to record class lectures
  Someone else may take class notes
  Student takes exams in separate rooms
  Students have exams read to them
  Students take typewritten exams
  Longer time allowed to complete exams
  Submit papers on cassette tape
  Take limited course load and graduate within time
    required
  Extended time limits for graduation
  Physical education may be waived

MAJORS OFFERED:

  AGRICULTURE
  ARCHITECTURE
  BIOLOGICAL SCIENCES
  BUSINESS AND MANAGEMENT
  COMMUNICATIONS
  COMPUTER SCIENCES
  EDUCATION
  ENGINEERING TECHNOLOGIES
  FINE AND APPLIED ARTS
  FOREIGN LANGUAGES
  HEALTH
  HOME ECONOMICS
  HUMANITIES
  MATHEMATICS

PHYSICAL SCIENCES
PSYCHOLOGY
PUBLIC SERVICES
SOCIAL SCIENCES

===

NORTHERN MONTANA COLLEGE
HAVRE, MT 59501
406-265-7821

KEY CONTACT: Attn: Handicapped Student Services

SIZE OF SCHOOL: SMALL

APPLICATION DEADLINE: NONE

	APPROXIMATE TUITION	ROOM AND BOARD
IN STATE	$ 650	$2130
OUT-OF-STATE	$1840	$2130

REQUIREMENTS FOR ADMISSIONS:
  High school equivalency diploma
  High school diploma
  21 years of age or older, with or without a
    high school diploma or equivalency
  ACT Scores required
  University or College sponsored tests
  Placement tests
  Essay

ADDITIONAL SERVICES OFFERED:
  Learning Lab
  Diagnostic testing services on campus
  Remedial and/or tutorial help available

MODIFICATIONS TO TRADITIONAL LEARNING ENVIRONMENT:
  Oral presentation in lieu of written exams
  Has an adaptive physical education program
  Tape recorders to record class lectures
  Someone else may take class notes
  Student takes exams in separate rooms
  Students have exams read to them
  Longer time allowed to complete exams
  Take limited course load and graduate within time
    required
  Extended time limits for graduation
  Physical education may be waived

MAJORS OFFERED:

    ARCHITECTURE
    BUSINESS AND MANAGEMENT
    COMPUTER SCIENCES
    EDUCATION
    ENGINEERING TECHNOLOGIES
    FINE AND APPLIED ARTS
    HUMANITIES

===

COLLEGE OF ST. MARY
1901 SOUTH 72ND STREET
OMAHA, NE 68124
402-393-8800

KEY CONTACT: Attn: Handicapped Student Services

SIZE OF SCHOOL: SMALL

APPLICATION DEADLINE: NONE

         APPROXIMATE TUITION   ROOM AND BOARD

IN STATE $4870 $1900
OUT-OF-STATE $4870 $1900

REQUIREMENTS FOR ADMISSIONS:
  High school diploma
  ACT Scores required
  Particular rank in class   50%
  High school grade point average   2.0
  Admission requirements modified

ADDITIONAL SERVICES OFFERED:
  Reader services for the blind available for LD

MODIFICATIONS TO TRADITIONAL LEARNING ENVIRONMENT:
  Oral presentation in lieu of written exams
  Use of calculator for all math courses
  Tape recorders to record class lectures
  Someone else may take class notes
  Multiple choice exams only
  Essay exams only
  Student takes exams in separate rooms
  Students have exams read to them
  Students take typewritten exams
  Longer time allowed to complete exams
  Physical education may be waived

MAJORS OFFERED:

  BIOLOGICAL SCIENCES
  BUSINESS AND MANAGEMENT
  COMPUTER SCIENCES
  EDUCATION
  FINE AND APPLIED ARTS
  HEALTH
  HUMANITIES
  PHYSICAL SCIENCES
  PUBLIC SERVICES
  SOCIAL SCIENCES

==

PERU STATE COLLEGE
PERU, NE 68421
402-872-3815

KEY CONTACT: Attn: Handicapped Student Services

SIZE OF SCHOOL: SMALL

APPLICATION DEADLINE: NONE

         APPROXIMATE TUITION   ROOM AND BOARD

IN STATE $ 750 $1750
OUT-OF-STATE $1280 $1750

REQUIREMENTS FOR ADMISSIONS:
  High school equivalency diploma
  High school diploma
  ACT Scores required

ADDITIONAL SERVICES OFFERED:
  Learning Lab
  Learning Lab has a specialist with a masters degree
    or above in Learning Disabilities
  Diagnostic testing services off campus
  Remedial and/or tutorial help available
  Reader services for the blind available for LD

MODIFICATIONS TO TRADITIONAL LEARNING ENVIRONMENT:
  Use of calculator for all math courses
  Tape recorders to record class lectures
  Someone else may take class notes
  Multiple choice exams only
  Essay exams only
  Student takes exams in separate rooms
  Students have exams read to them

Students take typewritten exams
Longer time allowed to complete exams
Submit papers on cassette tape
Extended time limits for graduation
Physical education may be waived

MAJORS OFFERED:

AGRICULTURE
BIOLOGICAL SCIENCES
BUSINESS AND MANAGEMENT
COMMUNICATIONS
COMPUTER SCIENCES
EDUCATION
FINE AND APPLIED ARTS
HEALTH
HUMANITIES
MATHEMATICS
PHYSICAL SCIENCES
PSYCHOLOGY
PUBLIC SERVICES
SOCIAL SCIENCES

===

UNIVERSITY OF NEBRASKA - OMAHA
60TH AND DODGE STREETS
OMAHA, NE 68182
402-554-2393

KEY CONTACT: Attn: Handicapped Student Services

SIZE OF SCHOOL: LARGE

APPLICATION DEADLINE: AUGUST 1

	APPROXIMATE TUITION	ROOM AND BOARD
IN STATE	$1125	$NOT OFFERED
OUT-OF-STATE	$2900	$NOT OFFERED

REQUIREMENTS FOR ADMISSIONS:
  High school equivalency diploma
  High school diploma
  21 years of age or older, with or without a
    high school diploma or equivalency
  ACT Scores required
  SAT Scores required
  Admission requirements modified

ADDITIONAL SERVICES OFFERED:

Learning Lab
Learning Lab has a specialist with a masters degree
    or above in Learning Disabilities
Diagnostic testing services on campus
Diagnostic testing services off campus
Remedial and/or tutorial help available
Reader services for the blind available for LD
Special Education department
Handicapped student services works with LD

MODIFICATIONS TO TRADITIONAL LEARNING ENVIRONMENT:
Tape recorders to record class lectures
Someone else may take class notes
Multiple choice exams only
Essay exams only
Student takes exams in separate rooms
Students have exams read to them
Students take typewritten exams
Longer time allowed to complete exams
Take limited course load and graduate within time
    required
Extended time limits for graduation
Physical education may be waived

MAJORS OFFERED:

AREA STUDIES
BIOLOGICAL SCIENCES
BUSINESS AND MANAGEMENT
COMMUNICATIONS
COMPUTER SCIENCES
EDUCATION
ENGINEERING TECHNOLOGIES
FINE AND APPLIED ARTS
FOREIGN LANGUAGES
HEALTH
HOME ECONOMICS
HUMANITIES
LIBRARY SCIENCE
MATHEMATICS
MILITARY SCIENCES
PHYSICAL SCIENCES
PSYCHOLOGY
PUBLIC SERVICES
SOCIAL SCIENCES

==

```
UNIVERSITY OF NEVADA - LAS VEGAS
4505 MARYLAND PARKWAY
LAS VEGAS, NV 89154
702-739-3443
```

KEY CONTACT: Attn: Handicapped Student Services

SIZE OF SCHOOL: MEDIUM

APPLICATION DEADLINE: AUGUST 15

	APPROXIMATE TUITION	ROOM AND BOARD
IN STATE	$ 930	$2415
OUT-OF-STATE	$2930	$2415

REQUIREMENTS FOR ADMISSIONS:
  High school equivalency diploma
  High school diploma
  Untimed or oral ACT Scores accepted
  Untimed or oral SAT Scores accepted
  University or College sponsored tests
  High school grade point average 2.3
  Admission requirements modified
  Personal interview

ADDITIONAL SERVICES OFFERED:
  Learning Lab
  Learning Lab has a specialist with a masters degree
    or above in Learning Disabilities
  Diagnostic testing services on campus
  Diagnostic testing services off campus
  Remedial and/or tutorial help available
  Reader services for the blind available for LD
  Special Education department
  Handicapped student services works with LD

MODIFICATIONS TO TRADITIONAL LEARNING ENVIRONMENT:
  Oral presentation in lieu of written exams
  Use of calculator for all math courses
  Has an adaptive physical education program
  Tape recorders to record class lectures
  Someone else may take class notes
  Student takes exams in separate rooms
  Students have exams read to them
  Students take typewritten exams
  Longer time allowed to complete exams
  Extended time limits for graduation
  Physical education may be waived

MAJORS OFFERED:

  BIOLOGICAL SCIENCES
  BUSINESS AND MANAGEMENT
  COMMUNICATIONS
  COMPUTER SCIENCES
  EDUCATION
  ENGINEERING TECHNOLOGIES
  FINE AND APPLIED ARTS
  FOREIGN LANGUAGES
  HEALTH
  HUMANITIES
  MATHEMATICS
  PHYSICAL SCIENCES
  PSYCHOLOGY
  PUBLIC SERVICES
  SOCIAL SCIENCES

==

NOTRE DAME COLLEGE
2321 ELM STREET
MANCHESTER, NH 03104
603-669-4298

KEY CONTACT: Attn: DR. ROBERT CRAY ANDREWS
                    SPECIAL NEEDS ASSISTANCE PROGRAM

SIZE OF SCHOOL: SMALL

APPLICATION DEADLINE: NONE

        APPROXIMATE TUITION   ROOM AND BOARD

IN STATE $3700 $2420
OUT-OF-STATE $3700 $2420

REQUIREMENTS FOR ADMISSIONS:
  High school equivalency diploma
  High school diploma
  Untimed or oral SAT Scores accepted
  WAIS scores required
  University or College sponsored tests
  High school grade point average 2.0
  Personal interview
  Placement tests
  Recommendations
  SAT scores are required for enrollment at college,
    but not for admission

ADDITIONAL SERVICES OFFERED:
  Diagnostic testing services on campus
  Remedial and/or tutorial help available
  Special Education department

MODIFICATIONS TO TRADITIONAL LEARNING ENVIRONMENT:
  Oral presentation in lieu of written exams
  Tape recorders to record class lectures
  Someone else may take class notes
  Student takes exams in separate rooms
  Students have exams read to them
  Students take typewritten exams
  Longer time allowed to complete exams
  Submit papers on cassette tape
  Extended time limits for graduation
  All modifications are with the permission
    of instructor

MAJORS OFFERED:

  BIOLOGICAL SCIENCES
  BUSINESS AND MANAGEMENT
  EDUCATION
  FINE AND APPLIED ARTS
  FOREIGN LANGUAGES
  HEALTH
  HUMANITIES
  LAW
  SOCIAL SCIENCES

==

UNIVERSITY OF NEW HAMPSHIRE
DURHAM, NH 03824
603-862-1360

KEY CONTACT: Attn: SHARON KRAFT - LUND HANDICAPPED
                    SERVICES COORDINATOR

SIZE OF SCHOOL: MEDIUM

APPLICATION DEADLINE: FEBRUARY 1

        APPROXIMATE TUITION   ROOM AND BOARD

IN STATE $1750 $2275
OUT-OF-STATE $4850 $2275

REQUIREMENTS FOR ADMISSIONS:
  High school equivalency diploma
  High school diploma

Untimed or oral ACT Scores accepted
SAT Scores required
Untimed or oral SAT Scores accepted
Particular rank in class (not specified)
High school grade point average (not specified)
Personal interview (suggested)
Recommendations
Essay

ADDITIONAL SERVICES OFFERED:
    Learning Lab
    Diagnostic testing services on campus
    Diagnostic testing services off campus
    Remedial and/or tutorial help available
    Reader services for the blind available for LD
    Special Education department
    Handicapped student services works with LD

MODIFICATIONS TO TRADITIONAL LEARNING ENVIRONMENT:
    Oral presentation in lieu of written exams
    Has an adaptive physical education program
    Tape recorders to record class lectures
    Someone else may take class notes
    Student takes exams in separate rooms
    Students have exams read to them
    Students take typewritten exams
    Longer time allowed to complete exams
    Submit papers on cassette tape
    Extended time limits for graduation
    Physical education may be waived

MAJORS OFFERED:

    AGRICULTURE
    ARCHITECTURE
    BIOLOGICAL SCIENCES
    BUSINESS AND MANAGEMENT
    COMMUNICATIONS
    COMPUTER SCIENCES
    EDUCATION
    ENGINEERING TECHNOLOGIES
    FINE AND APPLIED ARTS
    FOREIGN LANGUAGES
    HEALTH
    HOME ECONOMICS
    HUMANITIES
    MATHEMATICS
    PHYSICAL SCIENCES
    PSYCHOLOGY
    PUBLIC SERVICES
    SOCIAL SCIENCES

```
JERSEY CITY STATE COLLEGE
2039 KENNEDY BOULEVARD
JERSEY CITY, NJ 07305
201-547-3234
```

KEY CONTACT: Attn: Handicapped Student Services

SIZE OF SCHOOL: MEDIUM

APPLICATION DEADLINE: JUNE 1

	APPROXIMATE TUITION	ROOM AND BOARD
IN STATE	$ 840	$1350
OUT-OF-STATE	$1300	$1350

REQUIREMENTS FOR ADMISSIONS:
  High school equivalency diploma
  High school diploma
  SAT Scores required

ADDITIONAL SERVICES OFFERED:
  Learning Lab
  Learning Lab has a specialist with a masters degree
    or above in Learning Disabilities
  Remedial and/or tutorial help available

MODIFICATIONS TO TRADITIONAL LEARNING ENVIRONMENT:
  Oral presentation in lieu of written exams
  Use of calculator for all math courses
  Tape recorders to record class lectures
  Someone else may take class notes
  Student takes exams in separate rooms
  Students have exams read to them
  Students take typewritten exams
  Longer time allowed to complete exams
  Take limited course load and graduate within time
    required
  Physical education may be waived

MAJORS OFFERED:

  BIOLOGICAL SCIENCES
  BUSINESS AND MANAGEMENT
  COMMUNICATIONS
  COMPUTER SCIENCES
  EDUCATION
  FINE AND APPLIED ARTS
  FOREIGN LANGUAGES
  HEALTH
  HUMANITIES

```
MATHEMATICS
PHYSICAL SCIENCES
PSYCHOLOGY
PUBLIC SERVICES
SOCIAL SCIENCES
```

===

TRENTON STATE COLLEGE
TRENTON, NJ 08625
609-771-2131

KEY CONTACT: Attn: Handicapped Student Services

SIZE OF SCHOOL: MEDIUM

APPLICATION DEADLINE: MARCH 15

	APPROXIMATE TUITION	ROOM AND BOARD
IN STATE	$1050	$2700
OUT-OF-STATE	$1850	$2700

REQUIREMENTS FOR ADMISSIONS:
  High school diploma
  SAT Scores required
  Untimed or oral SAT Scores accepted

ADDITIONAL SERVICES OFFERED:
  Learning Lab
  Diagnostic testing services off campus
  Diagnostic testing services on campus
  Remedial and/or tutorial help available
  Reader services for the blind available for LD
  Special Education department
  Handicapped student services works with LD

MODIFICATIONS TO TRADITIONAL LEARNING ENVIRONMENT:
  Has an adaptive physical education program
  Tape recorders to record class lectures
  Someone else may take class notes
  Student takes exams in separate rooms
  Students have exams read to them
  Students take typewritten exams
  Longer time allowed to complete exams
  Submit papers on cassette tape
  Take limited course load and graduate within time
    required
  Extended time limits for graduation
  All other modifications at the discretion of the
    instructor

MAJORS OFFERED:

    ARCHITECTURE
    BIOLOGICAL SCIENCES
    BUSINESS AND MANAGEMENT
    COMMUNICATIONS
    COMPUTER SCIENCES
    EDUCATION
    ENGINEERING TECHNOLOGIES
    FINE AND APPLIED ARTS
    HEALTH
    HUMANITIES
    LIBRARY SCIENCE
    MATHEMATICS
    PHYSICAL SCIENCES
    PSYCHOLOGY
    PUBLIC SERVICES
    SOCIAL SCIENCES

==

ADELPHI UNIVERSITY
SOUTH AVENUE
GARDEN CITY, NY 11530
516-663-1100

KEY CONTACT: Attn: Handicapped Student Services

SIZE OF SCHOOL: MEDIUM

APPLICATION DEADLINE: NONE

         APPROXIMATE TUITION   ROOM AND BOARD

IN STATE $5495 $3000
OUT-OF-STATE $5495 $3000

REQUIREMENTS FOR ADMISSIONS:
    High school diploma
    SAT Scores required
    WAIS scores required
    Admission requirements modified
    Personal interview
    Recommendations
    Essay

ADDITIONAL SERVICES OFFERED:
    Learning Lab has a specialist with a masters degree
        or above in Learning Disabilities
    Diagnostic testing services on campus
    Diagnostic testing services off campus

Remedial and/or tutorial help available
Pre admission orientation

MODIFICATIONS TO TRADITIONAL LEARNING ENVIRONMENT:
  Oral presentation in lieu of written exams
  Use of calculator for all math courses
  Tape recorders to record class lectures
  Student takes exams in separate rooms
  Students have exams read to them
  Longer time allowed to complete exams
  Submit papers on cassette tape
  Extended time limits for graduation
  Physical education may be waived

MAJORS OFFERED:

  AREA STUDIES
  BIOLOGICAL SCIENCES
  BUSINESS AND MANAGEMENT
  COMMUNICATIONS
  COMPUTER SCIENCES
  EDUCATION
  ENGINEERING TECHNOLOGIES
  FINE AND APPLIED ARTS
  FOREIGN LANGUAGES
  HEALTH
  HUMANITIES
  MATHEMATICS
  PHYSICAL SCIENCES
  PSYCHOLOGY
  PUBLIC SERVICES
  SOCIAL SCIENCES

===

CUNY - HUNTER COLLEGE
695 PARK AVENUE
NEW YORK, NY 10021
212-570-5483

KEY CONTACT: Attn: Handicapped Student Services

SIZE OF SCHOOL: MEDIUM

APPLICATION DEADLINE: NONE

         APPROXIMATE TUITION   ROOM AND BOARD

IN STATE $1250 $2500
OUT-OF-STATE $2650 $2500

ADDITIONAL SERVICES OFFERED:
  Learning Lab
  Learning Lab has a specialist with a masters degree
    or above in Learning Disabilities
  Diagnostic testing services off campus
  Remedial and/or tutorial help available
  Reader services for the blind available for LD
  Handicapped student services works with LD

MODIFICATIONS TO TRADITIONAL LEARNING ENVIRONMENT:
  Oral presentation in lieu of written exams
  Use of calculator for all math courses
  Has an adaptive physical education program
  Tape recorders to record class lectures
  Someone else may take class notes
  Student takes exams in separate rooms
  Students have exams read to them
  Students take typewritten exams
  Longer time allowed to complete exams
  Submit papers on cassette tape
  Extended time limits for graduation
  Physical education may be waived

MAJORS OFFERED:

  AREA STUDIES
  BIOLOGICAL SCIENCES
  BUSINESS AND MANAGEMENT
  COMMUNICATIONS
  COMPUTER SCIENCES
  EDUCATION
  FINE AND APPLIED ARTS
  FOREIGN LANGUAGES
  HEALTH
  HOME ECONOMICS
  HUMANITIES
  LAW
  MATHEMATICS
  PHYSICAL SCIENCES
  PSYCHOLOGY
  SOCIAL SCIENCES

===

COLLEGE OF NEW ROCHELLE
SCHOOL OF NEW RESOURCES
CASTLE PLACE
NEW ROCHELLE, NY 10801
914-632-5300

KEY CONTACT: Attn: Handicapped Student Services

SIZE OF SCHOOL: MEDIUM

APPLICATION DEADLINE: NONE

APPROXIMATE TUITION   ROOM AND BOARD

IN STATE $4800 $3000
OUT-OF-STATE $4800 $3000

REQUIREMENTS FOR ADMISSIONS:
  High school equivalency diploma
  High school diploma
  Personal interview

ADDITIONAL SERVICES OFFERED:
  Learning Lab
  Remedial and/or tutorial help available
  Reader services for the blind available for LD

MODIFICATIONS TO TRADITIONAL LEARNING ENVIRONMENT:
  Tape recorders to record class lectures
  Someone else may take class notes
  Student takes exams in separate rooms
  Students have exams read to them
  Students take typewritten exams
  Longer time allowed to complete exams
  Take limited course load and graduate within time
    required
  Extended time limits for graduation
  Physical education may be waived

MAJORS OFFERED:

  BIOLOGICAL SCIENCES
  BUSINESS AND MANAGEMENT
  COMMUNICATIONS
  EDUCATION
  FINE AND APPLIED ARTS
  FOREIGN LANGUAGES
  HUMANITIES
  MATHEMATICS
  PHYSICAL SCIENCES
  PSYCHOLOGY
  PUBLIC SERVICES
  SOCIAL SCIENCES

===

```
CORNELL UNIVERSITY
410 THURSTON AVENUE
ITHACA, NY 14853
607-256-5241
```

KEY CONTACT: Attn: Handicapped Student Services

SIZE OF SCHOOL: LARGE

APPLICATION DEADLINE: JANUARY 1

	APPROXIMATE TUITION	ROOM AND BOARD
IN STATE	$8900	$3250
OUT-OF-STATE	$8900	$3250

REQUIREMENTS FOR ADMISSIONS:
  High school diploma
  ACT Scores required
  Untimed or oral ACT Scores accepted
  SAT Scores required
  Untimed or oral SAT Scores accepted
  Particular rank in class Top 5-10%
  High school grade point average Honors
  Personal interview (sometimes)
  Placement tests (sometimes)
  Recommendations
  Essay
  Each college at Cornell sets its own admissions
    standards - there are seven colleges

ADDITIONAL SERVICES OFFERED:
  Diagnostic testing services off campus
  Remedial and/or tutorial help available
  Reader services for the blind available for LD
  Handicapped student services works with LD

MODIFICATIONS TO TRADITIONAL LEARNING ENVIRONMENT:
  Use of calculator for all math courses
  Has an adaptive physical education program
  Someone else may take class notes
  Physical education may be waived
  All students are required to take the courses
    required for their degree. There are no specific
    programs for LD students

MAJORS OFFERED:

  AGRICULTURE
  ARCHITECTURE
  AREA STUDIES

BIOLOGICAL SCIENCES
BUSINESS AND MANAGEMENT
COMMUNICATIONS
COMPUTER SCIENCES
EDUCATION
ENGINEERING TECHNOLOGIES
FINE AND APPLIED ARTS
FOREIGN LANGUAGES
HEALTH
HOME ECONOMICS
HUMANITIES
LAW
MATHEMATICS
PHYSICAL SCIENCES
PSYCHOLOGY
PUBLIC SERVICES
SOCIAL SCIENCES

==

HOFSTRA UNIVERSITY
FULTON AVENUE
HEMPSTEAD, NY 11550
516-560-6700

KEY CONTACT: Attn: IGNACIO L. GOTZ. DIRECTOR
                    HANDICAPPED STUDENT SERVICES

SIZE OF SCHOOL: MEDIUM

APPLICATION DEADLINE: NONE

        APPROXIMATE TUITION   ROOM AND BOARD

IN STATE $4950 $2500
OUT-OF-STATE $4950 $2500

REQUIREMENTS FOR ADMISSIONS:
  High school equivalency diploma
  High school diploma
  Untimed or oral ACT Scores accepted
  Untimed or oral SAT Scores accepted
  WAIS scores required
  Admission requirements modified
  Personal interview
  Essay

ADDITIONAL SERVICES OFFERED:
  Learning Lab
  Learning Lab has a specialist with a masters degree
    or above in Learning Disabilities

Diagnostic testing services on campus
Remedial and/or tutorial help available
Reader services for the blind available for LD
Special Education department
Handicapped student services works with LD

MODIFICATIONS TO TRADITIONAL LEARNING ENVIRONMENT:
Oral presentation in lieu of written exams
Use of calculator for all math courses
Has an adaptive physical education program
Tape recorders to record class lectures
Someone else may take class notes
Student takes exams in separate rooms
Students have exams read to them
Students take typewritten exams
Longer time allowed to complete exams
Submit papers on cassette tape
Extended time limits for graduation

MAJORS OFFERED:

AGRICULTURE
AREA STUDIES
BIOLOGICAL SCIENCES
BUSINESS AND MANAGEMENT
COMMUNICATIONS
COMPUTER SCIENCES
EDUCATION
ENGINEERING TECHNOLOGIES
FINE AND APPLIED ARTS
FOREIGN LANGUAGES
HEALTH
HUMANITIES
MATHEMATICS
MILITARY SCIENCES
PHYSICAL SCIENCES
PSYCHOLOGY
SOCIAL SCIENCES
THEOLOGY

==

HOUGHTON COLLEGE
HOUGHTON, NY 14744
716-567-2211

KEY CONTACT: Attn: DR. ANNE SCHROER, DIRECTOR
                     COUNSELING CENTER

SIZE OF SCHOOL: SMALL

APPLICATION DEADLINE: AUGUST 1

         APPROXIMATE TUITION   ROOM AND BOARD

IN STATE $4390 $2100
OUT-OF-STATE $4390 $2100

REQUIREMENTS FOR ADMISSIONS:
  High school equivalency diploma
  High school diploma
  ACT Scores required
  SAT Scores required
  Particular rank in class 40%
  Admission requirements modified
  Recommendations

ADDITIONAL SERVICES OFFERED:
  Learning Lab
  Learning Lab has a specialist with a masters degree
     or above in Learning Disabilities
  Diagnostic testing services on campus
  Diagnostic testing services off campus
  Remedial and/or tutorial help available
  Reader services for the blind available for LD

MODIFICATIONS TO TRADITIONAL LEARNING ENVIRONMENT:
  Oral presentation in lieu of written exams
  Use of calculator for all math courses
  Has an adaptive physical education program
  Tape recorders to record class lectures
  Someone else may take class notes
  Student takes exams in separate rooms
  Students have exams read to them
  Students take typewritten exams
  Longer time allowed to complete exams
  Submit papers on cassette tape
  Extended time limits for graduation
  Physical education may be waived

MAJORS OFFERED:

  BIOLOGICAL SCIENCES
  BUSINESS AND MANAGEMENT
  COMMUNICATIONS
  EDUCATION
  FINE AND APPLIED ARTS
  FOREIGN LANGUAGES
  HEALTH
  HUMANITIES
  LAW
  MATHEMATICS

```
PHYSICAL SCIENCES
PSYCHOLOGY
SOCIAL SCIENCES
```

==

```
LONG ISLAND UNIVERSITY - BROOKLYN
UNIVERSITY PLAZA
BROOKLYN, NY 11201
212-834-6049
```

KEY CONTACT: Attn: Handicapped Student Services

SIZE OF SCHOOL: MEDIUM

APPLICATION DEADLINE: NONE

	APPROXIMATE TUITION	ROOM AND BOARD
IN STATE	$4590	$3420
OUT-OF-STATE	$4590	$3420

REQUIREMENTS FOR ADMISSIONS:
  High school equivalency diploma
  High school diploma
  Admission requirements modified
  Placement tests

ADDITIONAL SERVICES OFFERED:
  Learning Lab
  Learning Lab has a specialist with a masters degree
    or above in Learning Disabilities
  Diagnostic testing services on campus
  Diagnostic testing services off campus
  Remedial and/or tutorial help available
  Reader services for the blind available for LD
  Special Education department
  Handicapped student services works with LD

MODIFICATIONS TO TRADITIONAL LEARNING ENVIRONMENT:
  Use of calculator for all math courses
  Tape recorders to record class lectures
  Someone else may take class notes
  Student takes exams in separate rooms
  Students have exams read to them
  Students take typewritten exams
  Longer time allowed to complete exams
  Submit papers on cassette tape
  Extended time limits for graduation
  Physical education may be waived

MAJORS OFFERED:

  BIOLOGICAL SCIENCES
  BUSINESS AND MANAGEMENT
  COMMUNICATIONS
  COMPUTER SCIENCES
  EDUCATION
  FINE AND APPLIED ARTS
  HEALTH
  HUMANITIES
  MATHEMATICS
  PHYSICAL SCIENCES
  PSYCHOLOGY
  SOCIAL SCIENCES

==

MARIST COLLEGE
NORTH ROAD
POUGHKEEPSIE, NY 12601
914-471-3240

KEY CONTACT: Attn: DIANE C. PERREIRA, DIRECTOR
                     SPECIAL SERVICES

SIZE OF SCHOOL: SMALL

APPLICATION DEADLINE: MARCH 1

         APPROXIMATE TUITION   ROOM AND BOARD

IN STATE $4430 $2860
OUT-OF-STATE $4430 $2860

REQUIREMENTS FOR ADMISSIONS:
  High school equivalency diploma
  High school diploma
  ACT Scores required
  Untimed or oral ACT Scores accepted
  SAT Scores required
  Untimed or oral SAT Scores accepted
  WAIS scores required
  Admission requirements modified
  Personal interview
  Placement tests
  Recommendations

ADDITIONAL SERVICES OFFERED:
  Learning Lab
  Learning Lab has a specialist with a masters degree
    or above in Learning Disabilities

Diagnostic testing services on campus
Remedial and/or tutorial help available
Reader services for the blind available for LD
Special Education department
Handicapped student services works with LD

MODIFICATIONS TO TRADITIONAL LEARNING ENVIRONMENT:
Oral presentation in lieu of written exams
Use of calculator for all math courses
Has an adaptive physical education program
Tape recorders to record class lectures
Someone else may take class notes
Student takes exams in separate rooms
Students have exams read to them
Students take typewritten exams
Longer time allowed to complete exams
Submit papers on cassette tape
Extended time limits for graduation

MAJORS OFFERED:

AREA STUDIES
BIOLOGICAL SCIENCES
BUSINESS AND MANAGEMENT
COMMUNICATIONS
COMPUTER SCIENCES
EDUCATION
ENGINEERING TECHNOLOGIES
FINE AND APPLIED ARTS
FOREIGN LANGUAGES
HEALTH
HOME ECONOMICS
HUMANITIES
LAW
MATHEMATICS
PHYSICAL SCIENCES
PSYCHOLOGY
PUBLIC SERVICES
SOCIAL SCIENCES

==

MOUNT SAINT MARY COLLEGE
POWELL AVENUE
NEWBURGH, NY 12550
914-561-0800

KEY CONTACT: Attn: Handicapped Student Services

SIZE OF SCHOOL: SMALL

APPLICATION DEADLINE: AUGUST 15

          APPROXIMATE TUITION   ROOM AND BOARD

IN STATE $3930 $2380
OUT-OF-STATE $3930 $2380

REQUIREMENTS FOR ADMISSIONS:
  High school equivalency diploma
  High school diploma
  ACT Scores required
  SAT Scores required
  Admission requirements modified

ADDITIONAL SERVICES OFFERED:
  Learning Lab
  Learning Lab has a specialist with a masters degree
    or above in Learning Disabilities
  Diagnostic testing services off campus
  Remedial and/or tutorial help available
  Handicapped student services works with LD

MODIFICATIONS TO TRADITIONAL LEARNING ENVIRONMENT:
  Oral presentation in lieu of written exams
  Use of calculator for all math courses
  Tape recorders to record class lectures
  Someone else may take class notes
  Multiple choice exams only
  Essay exams only
  Student takes exams in separate rooms
  Students have exams read to them
  Students take typewritten exams
  Longer time allowed to complete exams
  Submit papers on cassette tape
  Extended time limits for graduation
  Physical education may be waived

MAJORS OFFERED:

  AREA STUDIES
  BIOLOGICAL SCIENCES
  BUSINESS AND MANAGEMENT
  COMMUNICATIONS
  EDUCATION
  HEALTH
  HUMANITIES
  MATHEMATICS
  PHYSICAL SCIENCES
  PSYCHOLOGY
  SOCIAL SCIENCES

NIAGRA UNIVERSITY
NIAGRA UNIVERSITY, NY 14109
716-285-1212

KEY CONTACT: Attn: Handicapped Student Services

SIZE OF SCHOOL: SMALL

APPLICATION DEADLINE: AUGUST 1

         APPROXIMATE TUITION   ROOM AND BOARD

IN STATE $4790 $2800
OUT-OF-STATE $4790 $2800

REQUIREMENTS FOR ADMISSIONS:
  High school equivalency diploma
  High school diploma
  ACT Scores required
  SAT Scores required
  Particular rank in class 50%
  High school grade point average B
  Placement tests

ADDITIONAL SERVICES OFFERED:
  Learning Lab
  Diagnostic testing services off campus
  Remedial and/or tutorial help available
  Reader services for the blind available for LD
  Handicapped student services works with LD

MODIFICATIONS TO TRADITIONAL LEARNING ENVIRONMENT:
  Oral presentation in lieu of written exams
  Use of calculator for all math courses
  Tape recorders to record class lectures
  Someone else may take class notes
  Multiple choice exams only
  Student takes exams in separate rooms
  Students have exams read to them
  Students take typewritten exams
  Longer time allowed to complete exams
  Submit papers on cassette tape
  Extended time limits for graduation
  Physical education may be waived
  Modifications at the discretion of individual
    instructors

MAJORS OFFERED:

  BIOLOGICAL SCIENCES
  BUSINESS AND MANAGEMENT

```
COMMUNICATIONS
COMPUTER SCIENCES
EDUCATION
FINE AND APPLIED ARTS
FOREIGN LANGUAGES
HEALTH
HUMANITIES
MATHEMATICS
PHYSICAL SCIENCES
PSYCHOLOGY
PUBLIC SERVICES
SOCIAL SCIENCES
THEOLOGY
```

===

```
RENSSELAER POLYTECHNIC INSTITUTE
TROY, NY 12181
518-270-6216
```

KEY CONTACT: Attn: RITA STAR, SPECIALIST FOR
                     THE HANDICAPPED

SIZE OF SCHOOL: MEDIUM

APPLICATION DEADLINE: JANUARY 1

	APPROXIMATE TUITION	ROOM AND BOARD
IN STATE	$9600	$2900
OUT-OF-STATE	$9600	$2900

REQUIREMENTS FOR ADMISSIONS:
  High school diploma
  ACT Scores required
  Untimed or oral ACT Scores accepted
  SAT Scores required
  Untimed or oral SAT Scores accepted
  Particular rank in class   Top 10%
  High school grade point average   90
  Personal interview
  Recommendations
  Essay

ADDITIONAL SERVICES OFFERED:
  Learning Lab
  Learning Lab has a specialist with a masters degree
    or above in Learning Disabilities
  Diagnostic testing services on campus
  Remedial and/or tutorial help available
  Reader services for the blind available for LD

Handicapped student services works with LD

MODIFICATIONS TO TRADITIONAL LEARNING ENVIRONMENT:
  Oral presentation in lieu of written exams
  Has an adaptive physical education program
  Tape recorders to record class lectures
  Someone else may take class notes
  Student takes exams in separate rooms
  Students have exams read to them
  Students take typewritten exams
  Longer time allowed to complete exams
  Extended time limits for graduation
  Physical education may be waived
  Adaptations must be arranged and are possible

MAJORS OFFERED:

  ARCHITECTURE
  BIOLOGICAL SCIENCES
  BUSINESS AND MANAGEMENT
  COMMUNICATIONS
  COMPUTER SCIENCES
  ENGINEERING TECHNOLOGIES
  FOREIGN LANGUAGES
  HEALTH
  HUMANITIES
  LAW
  MATHEMATICS
  PHYSICAL SCIENCES
  PSYCHOLOGY
  SOCIAL SCIENCES

===

ROCHESTER INSTITUTE OF TECHNOLOGY
ONE LOMB MEMORIAL DRIVE
ROCHESTER, NY 14623
716-475-6631

KEY CONTACT: Attn: Handicapped Student Services

SIZE OF SCHOOL: MEDIUM

APPLICATION DEADLINE: NONE

        APPROXIMATE TUITION   ROOM AND BOARD

IN STATE $5560 $3165
OUT-OF-STATE $5560 $3165

REQUIREMENTS FOR ADMISSIONS:

ACT Scores required
Untimed or oral ACT Scores accepted
SAT Scores required
Untimed or oral SAT Scores accepted
Recommendations

ADDITIONAL SERVICES OFFERED:
  Learning Lab
  Learning Lab has a specialist with a masters degree
    or above in Learning Disabilities
  Diagnostic testing services on campus
  Diagnostic testing services off campus
  Remedial and/or tutorial help available
  Reader services for the blind available for LD
  Special Education department

MODIFICATIONS TO TRADITIONAL LEARNING ENVIRONMENT:
  Oral presentation in lieu of written exams
  Use of calculator for all math courses
  Has an adaptive physical education program
  Tape recorders to record class lectures
  Someone else may take class notes
  Student takes exams in separate rooms
  Students have exams read to them
  Students take typewritten exams
  Longer time allowed to complete exams
  Submit papers on cassette tape
  Extended time limits for graduation
  Physical education may be waived

MAJORS OFFERED:

  ARCHITECTURE
  BIOLOGICAL SCIENCES
  BUSINESS AND MANAGEMENT
  COMMUNICATIONS
  COMPUTER SCIENCES
  ENGINEERING TECHNOLOGIES
  FINE AND APPLIED ARTS
  HEALTH
  HOME ECONOMICS
  MATHEMATICS
  PHYSICAL SCIENCES
  PUBLIC SERVICES

===

SUNY - BINGHAMTON
VESTAL PARKWAY EAST
BINGHAMTON, NY 13901
607-798-2171

KEY CONTACT: Attn: B. JEAN FAIRBAIRN, COORDINATOR
                    PROGRAMS FOR STUDENTS WITH
                    DISABILITIES

SIZE OF SCHOOL: MEDIUM

APPLICATION DEADLINE: JANUARY 15

      APPROXIMATE TUITION   ROOM AND BOARD

IN STATE $1495 $2755
OUT-OF-STATE $2795 $2755

REQUIREMENTS FOR ADMISSIONS:
  High school equivalency diploma
  High school diploma
  Untimed or oral ACT Scores accepted
  Untimed or oral SAT Scores accepted
  Particular rank in class (not specified)
  High school grade point average Mid 80's or higher
  Personal interview (recommended)
  Recommendations (recommended)
  Essay (recommended)
  ACT or SAT required

ADDITIONAL SERVICES OFFERED:
  Diagnostic testing services off campus
  Remedial and/or tutorial help available
  Reader services for the blind available for LD
  Handicapped student services works with LD

MODIFICATIONS TO TRADITIONAL LEARNING ENVIRONMENT:
  Oral presentation in lieu of written exams
  Use of calculator for all math courses
  Tape recorders to record class lectures
  Someone else may take class notes
  Student takes exams in separate rooms
  Students have exams read to them
  Students take typewritten exams
  Longer time allowed to complete exams
  Extended time limits for graduation
  Physical education may be waived
  Modifications made when appropriate

MAJORS OFFERED:

  AREA STUDIES
  BIOLOGICAL SCIENCES
  BUSINESS AND MANAGEMENT
  COMPUTER SCIENCES
  ENGINEERING TECHNOLOGIES
  FINE AND APPLIED ARTS
  FOREIGN LANGUAGES
  HEALTH
  HUMANITIES
  LAW
  MATHEMATICS
  PHYSICAL SCIENCES
  PSYCHOLOGY
  SOCIAL SCIENCES

==

SUNY - COLLEGE AT PLATTSBURGH
PLATTSBURGH, NY 12901
518-564-2040

KEY CONTACT: Attn: JAN LABUDA, JAIMIE TRAUTMAN,
                   HANDICAPPED SERVICES

SIZE OF SCHOOL: MEDIUM

APPLICATION DEADLINE: NONE

	APPROXIMATE TUITION	ROOM AND BOARD
IN STATE	$1455	$2460
OUT-OF-STATE	$2255	$2460

REQUIREMENTS FOR ADMISSIONS:
  High school equivalency diploma
  High school diploma
  SAT or ACT Scores required
  High school grade point average 80 or above
  Admission requirements modified (may depend on
    individual case)
  Recommendations (incase of low high school grades,
    recommendations may be requested)

ADDITIONAL SERVICES OFFERED:
  Learning Lab
  Learning Lab has a specialist with a masters degree
    or above in Learning Disabilities
  Remedial and/or tutorial help available
  Handicapped student services works with LD

MODIFICATIONS TO TRADITIONAL LEARNING ENVIRONMENT:
  Extended time limits for graduation
  Physical education may be waived
  Any modifications would depend on the specific case/
    circumstance

MAJORS OFFERED:

  AGRICULTURE
  ARCHITECTURE
  AREA STUDIES
  BIOLOGICAL SCIENCES
  BUSINESS AND MANAGEMENT
  COMMUNICATIONS
  COMPUTER SCIENCES
  EDUCATION
  ENGINEERING TECHNOLOGIES
  FINE AND APPLIED ARTS
  FOREIGN LANGUAGES
  HEALTH
  HOME ECONOMICS
  HUMANITIES
  MATHEMATICS
  PHYSICAL SCIENCES
  PSYCHOLOGY
  PUBLIC SERVICES
  SOCIAL SCIENCES

==

SUNY - COLLEGE AT POTSDAM
PIERREPONT AVENUE
POTSDAM, NY 13676
315-267-2180

KEY CONTACT: Attn: Handicapped Student Services

SIZE OF SCHOOL: MEDIUM

APPLICATION DEADLINE: MARCH 1

        APPROXIMATE TUITION   ROOM AND BOARD

IN STATE $1465 $2435
OUT-OF-STATE $3265 $2435

REQUIREMENTS FOR ADMISSIONS:
  ACT Scores required
  SAT Scores required
  Personal interview

ADDITIONAL SERVICES OFFERED:
  Learning Lab
  Learning Lab has a specialist with a masters degree
    or above in Learning Disabilities
  Remedial and/or tutorial help available
  Reader services for the blind available for LD
  Handicapped student services works with LD

MODIFICATIONS TO TRADITIONAL LEARNING ENVIRONMENT:
  Oral presentation in lieu of written exams
  Use of calculator for all math courses
  Tape recorders to record class lectures
  Someone else may take class notes
  Multiple choice exams only
  Essay exams only
  Student takes exams in separate rooms
  Students have exams read to them
  Students take typewritten exams
  Longer time allowed to complete exams
  Submit papers on cassette tape
  Take limited course load and graduate within time
    required
  Extended time limits for graduation
  Physical education may be waived

MAJORS OFFERED:

  BIOLOGICAL SCIENCES
  BUSINESS AND MANAGEMENT
  COMPUTER SCIENCES
  EDUCATION
  ENGINEERING TECHNOLOGIES
  FINE AND APPLIED ARTS
  FOREIGN LANGUAGES
  HUMANITIES
  MATHEMATICS
  PHYSICAL SCIENCES
  PSYCHOLOGY
  SOCIAL SCIENCES

==

SUNY - EMPIRE STATE COLLEGE
2 UNION AVE
SARATOGA SPRINGS, NY 12866
518-587-2100

KEY CONTACT: Attn: Handicapped Student Services

SIZE OF SCHOOL: SMALL

APPLICATION DEADLINE: NONE

APPROXIMATE TUITION   ROOM AND BOARD

IN STATE	$2055	$NOT OFFERED
OUT-OF-STATE	$4000	$NOT OFFERED

REQUIREMENTS FOR ADMISSIONS:
  21 years of age or older, with or without a
    high school diploma or equivalency

ADDITIONAL SERVICES OFFERED:
  Diagnostic testing services off campus
  Remedial and/or tutorial help available

MODIFICATIONS TO TRADITIONAL LEARNING ENVIRONMENT:
  All modifications decided on individual needs
    assesment

MAJORS OFFERED:

  BUSINESS AND MANAGEMENT
  COMPUTER SCIENCES
  EDUCATION
  FINE AND APPLIED ARTS
  HEALTH
  HUMANITIES
  MATHEMATICS
  PHYSICAL SCIENCES
  PSYCHOLOGY
  PUBLIC SERVICES
  SOCIAL SCIENCES

==

SARAH LAWRENCE COLLEGE
MEADWAY
BRONXVILLE, NY 10708
914-793-4242

KEY CONTACT: Attn: Handicapped Student Services

SIZE OF SCHOOL: SMALL

APPLICATION DEADLINE: FEBRUARY 15

APPROXIMATE TUITION   ROOM AND BOARD

IN STATE	$9280	$3850
OUT-OF-STATE	$8150	$3850

REQUIREMENTS FOR ADMISSIONS:
  High school equivalency diploma
  High school diploma
  ACT Scores required
  SAT Scores required
  Untimed or oral SAT Scores accepted
  Particular rank in class 33%
  Admission requirements modified

MODIFICATIONS TO TRADITIONAL LEARNING ENVIRONMENT:
  Oral presentation in lieu of written exams
  Use of calculator for all math courses
  Tape recorders to record class lectures
  Someone else may take class notes
  Multiple choice exams only
  Essay exams only
  Student takes exams in separate rooms
  Students have exams read to them
  Students take typewritten exams
  Longer time allowed to complete exams
  Submit papers on cassette tape
  Physical education may be waived

MAJORS OFFERED:

  AREA STUDIES
  BIOLOGICAL SCIENCES
  FINE AND APPLIED ARTS
  FOREIGN LANGUAGES
  HUMANITIES
  MATHEMATICS
  PHYSICAL SCIENCES
  PSYCHOLOGY
  SOCIAL SCIENCES

===

ST. THOMAS AQUINAS COLLEGE
ROUTE 340
SPARKILL, NY 10968
914-359-9500

KEY CONTACT: Attn: DR. DOONAN, DIRECTOR
                    HANDICAPPED STUDENT SERVICES

SIZE OF SCHOOL: SMALL

APPLICATION DEADLINE: NONE

```
        APPROXIMATE TUITION    ROOM AND BOARD

IN STATE          $3300          $2200
OUT-OF-STATE      $3300          $2200
```

REQUIREMENTS FOR ADMISSIONS:
  High school equivalency diploma
  High school diploma
  SAT Scores required
  Untimed or oral SAT Scores accepted
  WAIS scores required
  High school grade point average (college prep
    courses weigh more heavily than G.P.A.)
  Personal interview
  Recommendations
  Essay

ADDITIONAL SERVICES OFFERED:
  Learning Lab (College Learning Center, available to
    all students)
  Diagnostic testing services off campus
  Remedial and/or tutorial help available through
    individual departments and Learning Center
  Books on tape
  Special Education department
  Handicapped student services works with LD

MODIFICATIONS TO TRADITIONAL LEARNING ENVIRONMENT:
  Oral presentation in lieu of written exams
  Use of calculator for all math courses
  Tape recorders to record class lectures
  Someone else may take class notes
  Student takes exams in separate rooms
  Students have exams read to them
  Students take typewritten exams
  Longer time allowed to complete exams
  Submit papers on cassette tape
  Extended time limits for graduation
  Modifications depend on individual faculty menber

MAJORS OFFERED:

  BIOLOGICAL SCIENCES
  BUSINESS AND MANAGEMENT
  COMMUNICATIONS
  EDUCATION
  ENGINEERING TECHNOLOGIES
  FINE AND APPLIED ARTS
  FOREIGN LANGUAGES
  HEALTH
  HUMANITIES

    MATHEMATICS
    PHYSICAL SCIENCES
    PSYCHOLOGY
    PUBLIC SERVICES
    SOCIAL SCIENCES

==

APPALACHIAN STATE UNIVERSITY
BOONE, NC 28608
704-262-2120

KEY CONTACT: Attn: BARBARA DAYE, ASSISTANT VICE
                     CHANCELLOR FOR STUDENT AFFAIRS

SIZE OF SCHOOL: MEDIUM

APPLICATION DEADLINE: NONE

        APPROXIMATE TUITION   ROOM AND BOARD

IN STATE $ 735 $1460
OUT-OF-STATE $2520 $1460

REQUIREMENTS FOR ADMISSIONS:
   High school equivalency diploma
   High school diploma
   SAT Scores required
   Untimed or oral SAT Scores accepted
   Particular rank in class (not specified)
   High school grade point average (not specified)

ADDITIONAL SERVICES OFFERED:
   Diagnostic testing services off campus
   Remedial and/or tutorial help available
   Reader services for the blind available for LD
   Special Education department
   Handicapped student services works with LD

MODIFICATIONS TO TRADITIONAL LEARNING ENVIRONMENT:
   All modifications depend on needs of student, course
      requirements, and agreement with teacher of course

MAJORS OFFERED:

   AGRICULTURE
   ARCHITECTURE
   AREA STUDIES
   BIOLOGICAL SCIENCES
   BUSINESS AND MANAGEMENT
   COMMUNICATIONS

```
COMPUTER SCIENCES
EDUCATION
ENGINEERING TECHNOLOGIES
FINE AND APPLIED ARTS
FOREIGN LANGUAGES
HEALTH
HOME ECONOMICS
HUMANITIES
LIBRARY SCIENCE
MATHEMATICS
PHYSICAL SCIENCES
PSYCHOLOGY
SOCIAL SCIENCES
```

===

```
ATLANTIC CHRISTIAN COLLEGE
LEE STREET
WILSON, NC 27893
919-237-3161

KEY CONTACT: Attn:   DR. F. MARK DAVIS,
                     ACADEMIC DEAN

SIZE OF SCHOOL: SMALL

APPLICATION DEADLINE: NONE

        APPROXIMATE TUITION    ROOM AND BOARD

IN STATE           $3260         $1600
OUT-OF-STATE       $3260         $1600

REQUIREMENTS FOR ADMISSIONS:
  High school equivalency diploma
  High school diploma
  21 years of age or older, with or without a
    high school diploma or equivalency
  Untimed or oral ACT Scores accepted
  SAT Scores required
  Untimed or oral SAT Scores accepted
  University or College sponsored tests
  High school grade point average  2.0
  Personal interview
  Placement tests
  Essay

ADDITIONAL SERVICES OFFERED:
  Learning Lab
  Diagnostic testing services on campus
  Remedial and/or tutorial help available
```

Handicapped student services works with LD

MODIFICATIONS TO TRADITIONAL LEARNING ENVIRONMENT:
Oral presentation in lieu of written exams
Has an adaptive physical education program
Tape recorders to record class lectures
Someone else may take class notes
Student takes exams in separate rooms
Students have exams read to them
Students take typewritten exams
Longer time allowed to complete exams
Extended time limits for graduation
Physical education may be waived

MAJORS OFFERED:

BIOLOGICAL SCIENCES
BUSINESS AND MANAGEMENT
EDUCATION
FINE AND APPLIED ARTS
FOREIGN LANGUAGES
HEALTH
HUMANITIES
LAW
MATHEMATICS
PHYSICAL SCIENCES
PSYCHOLOGY
SOCIAL SCIENCES

===

SACRED HEART COLLEGE
MAIN STREET
BELMONT, NC 28012
704-825-5146

KEY CONTACT: Attn: Handicapped Student Services

SIZE OF SCHOOL: SMALL

APPLICATION DEADLINE: AUGUST 1

        APPROXIMATE TUITION   ROOM AND BOARD

IN STATE $3270 $2030
OUT-OF-STATE $3270 $2030

REQUIREMENTS FOR ADMISSIONS:
High school equivalency diploma
High school diploma
ACT Scores required

```
    SAT Scores required
    Admission requirements modified
```

ADDITIONAL SERVICES OFFERED:
```
    Learning Lab
    Learning Lab has a specialist with a masters degree
        or above in Learning Disabilities
    Diagnostic testing services off campus
    Remedial and/or tutorial help available
    Reader services for the blind available for LD
    Special Education department
    Handicapped student services works with LD
```

MODIFICATIONS TO TRADITIONAL LEARNING ENVIRONMENT:
```
    Oral presentation in lieu of written exams
    Use of calculator for all math courses
    Has an adaptive physical education program
    Tape recorders to record class lectures
    Someone else may take class notes
    Multiple choice exams only
    Essay exams only
    Student takes exams in separate rooms
    Students have exams read to them
    Students take typewritten exams
    Longer time allowed to complete exams
    Submit papers on cassette tape
    Extended time limits for graduation
    Physical education may be waived
```

MAJORS OFFERED:

```
    BIOLOGICAL SCIENCES
    BUSINESS AND MANAGEMENT
    EDUCATION
    FINE AND APPLIED ARTS
    HEALTH
    HUMANITIES
    LAW
    MATHEMATICS
    PHYSICAL SCIENCES
    PSYCHOLOGY
    PUBLIC SERVICES
    SOCIAL SCIENCES
    THEOLOGY
```

===

```
WESTERN CAROLINA UNIVERSITY
CULLOWHEE, NC 28723
704-227-7317
```

KEY CONTACT: Attn: Handicapped Student Services

SIZE OF SCHOOL: MEDIUM

APPLICATION DEADLINE: AUGUST 15

      APPROXIMATE TUITION   ROOM AND BOARD

IN STATE $ 720 $1550
OUT-OF-STATE $2500 $1550

REQUIREMENTS FOR ADMISSIONS:
  High school equivalency diploma
  High school diploma
  SAT Scores required

ADDITIONAL SERVICES OFFERED:
  Learning Lab
  Learning Lab has a specialist with a masters degree
    or above in Learning Disabilities
  Diagnostic testing services on campus
  Remedial and/or tutorial help available
  Reader services for the blind available for LD
  Special Education department
  Handicapped student services works with LD

MODIFICATIONS TO TRADITIONAL LEARNING ENVIRONMENT:
  Oral presentation in lieu of written exams
  Use of calculator for all math courses
  Tape recorders to record class lectures
  Someone else may take class notes
  Multiple choice exams only
  Essay exams only
  Student takes exams in separate rooms
  Students have exams read to them
  Students take typewritten exams
  Longer time allowed to complete exams
  Submit papers on cassette tape
  Physical education may be waived

MAJORS OFFERED:

  BIOLOGICAL SCIENCES
  BUSINESS AND MANAGEMENT
  COMPUTER SCIENCES
  EDUCATION
  ENGINEERING TECHNOLOGIES
  FINE AND APPLIED ARTS
  FOREIGN LANGUAGES
  HEALTH
  HOME ECONOMICS

```
HUMANITIES
MATHEMATICS
PHYSICAL SCIENCES
PSYCHOLOGY
PUBLIC SERVICES
SOCIAL SCIENCES
```

==

```
CLEVELAND STATE UNIVERSITY
EAST 24TH AND EUCLID AVENUE
CLEVELAND, OH 44115
216-687-3755
```

KEY CONTACT: Attn: Handicapped Student Services

SIZE OF SCHOOL: MEDIUM

APPLICATION DEADLINE: NONE

	APPROXIMATE TUITION	ROOM AND BOARD
IN STATE	$1380	$2000
OUT-OF-STATE	$2755	$2000

REQUIREMENTS FOR ADMISSIONS:
  High school equivalency diploma
  High school diploma
  ACT Scores required
  SAT Scores required
  Diagnostic testing required

ADDITIONAL SERVICES OFFERED:
  Learning Lab
  Learning Lab has a specialist with a masters degree
    or above in Learning Disabilities
  Diagnostic testing services on campus
  Diagnostic testing services off campus
  Remedial and/or tutorial help available
  Reader services for the blind available for LD
  Special Education department
  Handicapped student services works with LD

MODIFICATIONS TO TRADITIONAL LEARNING ENVIRONMENT:
  Oral presentation in lieu of written exams
  Use of calculator for all math courses
  Tape recorders to record class lectures
  Someone else may take class notes
  Multiple choice exams only
  Student takes exams in separate rooms
  Students have exams read to them

Students take typewritten exams
Longer time allowed to complete exams
Submit papers on cassette tape
Take limited course load and graduate within time
    required
Physical education may be waived

MAJORS OFFERED:

BIOLOGICAL SCIENCES
BUSINESS AND MANAGEMENT
COMMUNICATIONS
COMPUTER SCIENCES
EDUCATION
ENGINEERING TECHNOLOGIES
FINE AND APPLIED ARTS
FOREIGN LANGUAGES
HEALTH
HUMANITIES
MATHEMATICS
PHYSICAL SCIENCES
PSYCHOLOGY
PUBLIC SERVICES
SOCIAL SCIENCES

===

COLLEGE OF MOUNT ST. JOSEPH ON THE OHIO
MOUNT ST. JOSEPH, OH 45051
513-244-4531

KEY CONTACT: Attn: CLARETTA CLAXTON
                    LEARNING DISABILITIES COORDINATOR

SIZE OF SCHOOL: SMALL

APPLICATION DEADLINE: NONE

        APPROXIMATE TUITION   ROOM AND BOARD

IN STATE $3935 $2440
OUT-OF-STATE $3935 $2440

REQUIREMENTS FOR ADMISSIONS:
  High school diploma
  ACT Scores required
  Untimed or oral ACT Scores accepted
  SAT Scores required
  Untimed or oral SAT Scores accepted
  WAIS scores required
  University or College sponsored tests

Admission requirements modified
Personal interview
Placement tests
Recommendations

ADDITIONAL SERVICES OFFERED:
Diagnostic testing services on campus
Remedial and/or tutorial help available
Reader services for the blind available for LD
Special Education department

MODIFICATIONS TO TRADITIONAL LEARNING ENVIRONMENT:
Oral presentation in lieu of written exams
Use of calculator for all math courses
Tape recorders to record class lectures
Someone else may take class notes
Essay exams only
Student takes exams in separate rooms
Students have exams read to them
Students take typewritten exams
Longer time allowed to complete exams
Extended time limits for graduation

MAJORS OFFERED:

AGRICULTURE
BIOLOGICAL SCIENCES
BUSINESS AND MANAGEMENT
COMMUNICATIONS
COMPUTER SCIENCES
EDUCATION
FINE AND APPLIED ARTS
HEALTH
HOME ECONOMICS
HUMANITIES
LAW
PSYCHOLOGY
PUBLIC SERVICES
SOCIAL SCIENCES
THEOLOGY

==

COLLEGE OF WOOSTER
WOOSTER, OH 44691
216-264-1234

KEY CONTACT: Attn: Handicapped Student Services

SIZE OF SCHOOL: SMALL

APPLICATION DEADLINE: MAY 1

```
        APPROXIMATE TUITION    ROOM AND BOARD

IN STATE              $7650        $2000
OUT-OF-STATE          $7650        $2000
```

REQUIREMENTS FOR ADMISSIONS:
  ACT Scores required
  SAT Scores required
  Recommendations

ADDITIONAL SERVICES OFFERED:
  Learning Lab
  Diagnostic testing services off campus
  Remedial and/or tutorial help available
  Reader services for the blind available for LD

MODIFICATIONS TO TRADITIONAL LEARNING ENVIRONMENT:
  Oral presentation in lieu of written exams
  Tape recorders to record class lectures
  Someone else may take class notes
  Student takes exams in separate rooms
  Students have exams read to them
  Students take typewritten exams
  Longer time allowed to complete exams
  Submit papers on cassette tape
  Extended time limits for graduation
  Physical education may be waived

MAJORS OFFERED:

  AREA STUDIES
  BIOLOGICAL SCIENCES
  BUSINESS AND MANAGEMENT
  COMMUNICATIONS
  COMPUTER SCIENCES
  EDUCATION
  FINE AND APPLIED ARTS
  FOREIGN LANGUAGES
  HEALTH
  HUMANITIES
  MATHEMATICS
  PHYSICAL SCIENCES
  PSYCHOLOGY
  PUBLIC SERVICES
  SOCIAL SCIENCES

===

```
DEFIANCE COLLEGE
701 NORTH CLINTON STREET
DEFIANCE, OH 43512
419-784-4010
```

KEY CONTACT: Attn: DR, ROBERT M. GAFFGA
                    ASSOCIATE ACADEMIC DEAN

SIZE OF SCHOOL: SMALL

APPLICATION DEADLINE: NONE

APPROXIMATE TUITION   ROOM AND BOARD

IN STATE	$4460	$2100
OUT-OF-STATE	$4460	$2100

REQUIREMENTS FOR ADMISSIONS:
  High school equivalency diploma
  High school diploma
  21 years of age or older, with or without a
    high school diploma or equivalency
  ACT Scores not required but preferred
  Untimed or oral ACT Scores accepted
  Untimed or oral SAT Scores accepted
  Admission requirements modified
  Placement tests
  Recommendations
  Essay

ADDITIONAL SERVICES OFFERED:
  Learning Lab
  Learning Lab has a specialist with a masters degree
    or above in Learning Disabilities
  Diagnostic testing services on campus
  Diagnostic testing services off campus
  Remedial and/or tutorial help available
  Reader services for the blind available for LD
  Special Education department

MODIFICATIONS TO TRADITIONAL LEARNING ENVIRONMENT:
  Use of calculator for all math courses
  Has an adaptive physical education program
  Tape recorders to record class lectures
  Someone else may take class notes
  Longer time allowed to complete exams
  Take limited course load and graduate within time
    required
  Extended time limits for graduation
  Physical education may be waived
  Other modifications on an individual basis

MAJORS OFFERED:

  BIOLOGICAL SCIENCES
  BUSINESS AND MANAGEMENT
  COMMUNICATIONS
  COMPUTER SCIENCES
  EDUCATION
  FINE AND APPLIED ARTS
  FOREIGN LANGUAGES
  HEALTH
  HUMANITIES
  LAW
  MATHEMATICS
  PHYSICAL SCIENCES
  PSYCHOLOGY
  PUBLIC SERVICES
  SOCIAL SCIENCES
  THEOLOGY

===

FRANKLIN UNIVERSITY
201 SOUTH GRANT AVENUE
COLUMBUS, OH 43215
614-224-6413

KEY CONTACT: Attn: JENNIFER C. KING, COORDINATOR
                    HANDICAPPED STUDENT SERVICES

SIZE OF SCHOOL: MEDIUM

APPLICATION DEADLINE: NONE

           APPROXIMATE TUITION   ROOM AND BOARD

IN STATE $2400 $NOT OFFERED
OUT-OF-STATE $2400 $NOT OFFERED

REQUIREMENTS FOR ADMISSIONS:
  High school equivalency diploma
  High school diploma
  Untimed or oral ACT Scores accepted
  Untimed or oral SAT Scores accepted
  University or College sponsored tests
  Personal interview
  Placement tests
  Recommendations

ADDITIONAL SERVICES OFFERED:
  Diagnostic testing services off campus
  Remedial and/or tutorial help available

Reader services for the blind available for LD
Handicapped student services works with LD

MODIFICATIONS TO TRADITIONAL LEARNING ENVIRONMENT:
  Oral presentation in lieu of written exams
  Tape recorders to record class lectures
  Someone else may take class notes
  Student takes exams in separate rooms
  Students have exams read to them
  Students take typewritten exams
  Longer time allowed to complete exams
  Submit papers on cassette tape
  Take limited course load and graduate within time
    required
  Extended time limits for graduation

MAJORS OFFERED:

  BUSINESS AND MANAGEMENT
  COMPUTER SCIENCES
  ENGINEERING TECHNOLOGIES
  HEALTH
  PUBLIC SERVICES

===

HIRAM COLLEGE
HIRAM, OH 44234
216-569-5169

KEY CONTACT: Attn: DOROTHY MACCANKEY, VICE PRESIDENT
                     DEAN

SIZE OF SCHOOL: SMALL

APPLICATION DEADLINE: AUGUST 1

        APPROXIMATE TUITION   ROOM AND BOARD

IN STATE $6660 $2020
OUT-OF-STATE $6660 $2020

REQUIREMENTS FOR ADMISSIONS:
  Careful determinations made based on students
diagnostic information and on personal interview.

ADDITIONAL SERVICES OFFERED:
  Although no campus wide programs exist that are
specifically tutorial help, remedial programs, learning
labs, and so forth, Hiram does individualize each
student's curriculum and augment his/her learning needs

as indicated.

MODIFICATIONS TO TRADITIONAL LEARNING ENVIRONMENT:
  All modifications are based individual needs of the
student.

MAJORS OFFERED:

  BIOLOGICAL SCIENCES
  BUSINESS AND MANAGEMENT
  COMMUNICATIONS
  COMPUTER SCIENCES
  EDUCATION
  FINE AND APPLIED ARTS
  FOREIGN LANGUAGES
  HEALTH
  HUMANITIES
  MATHEMATICS
  PHYSICAL SCIENCES
  PSYCHOLOGY
  SOCIAL SCIENCES

==

KENT STATE UNIVERSITY
145 ROCKWELL HALL
KENT, OH 44242
216-672-2444

KEY CONTACT: Attn: JOANNA GARTNER, COORDINATOR
                     HANDICAPPED STUDENT SERVICES

SIZE OF SCHOOL: LARGE

APPLICATION DEADLINE: JULY 1

       APPROXIMATE TUITION   ROOM AND BOARD

IN STATE $1710 $2070
OUT-OF-STATE $2910 $2070

REQUIREMENTS FOR ADMISSIONS:
  High school equivalency diploma
  High school diploma
  ACT Scores required
  Untimed or oral ACT Scores accepted
  Placement tests
  Open admissions to Ohio residents

ADDITIONAL SERVICES OFFERED:
  Diagnostic testing services on campus

Diagnostic testing services off campus
Remedial and/or tutorial help available
Reader services for the blind available for LD
Handicapped student services works with LD

MODIFICATIONS TO TRADITIONAL LEARNING ENVIRONMENT:
Oral presentation in lieu of written exams
Tape recorders to record class lectures
Someone else may take class notes
Students have exams read to them
Longer time allowed to complete exams
Take limited course load and graduate within time
    required
Extended time limits for graduation
Other modifications with the permission of instructor

MAJORS OFFERED:

AGRICULTURE
ARCHITECTURE
AREA STUDIES
BIOLOGICAL SCIENCES
BUSINESS AND MANAGEMENT
COMMUNICATIONS
COMPUTER SCIENCES
EDUCATION
ENGINEERING TECHNOLOGIES
FINE AND APPLIED ARTS
FOREIGN LANGUAGES
HEALTH
HOME ECONOMICS
HUMANITIES
LIBRARY SCIENCE
MATHEMATICS
MILITARY SCIENCES
PHYSICAL SCIENCES
PSYCHOLOGY
PUBLIC SERVICES
SOCIAL SCIENCES

==

MUSKINGUM COLLEGE
NEW CONCORD, OH 43762
614-826-8137

KEY CONTACT: Attn: Handicapped Student Services

SIZE OF SCHOOL: SMALL

APPLICATION DEADLINE: AUGUST 1

```
        APPROXIMATE TUITION    ROOM AND BOARD

IN STATE              $5830        $2260
OUT-OF-STATE          $5830        $2260
```

REQUIREMENTS FOR ADMISSIONS:
  Admission requirements modified
  Placement tests
  Recommendations

MODIFICATIONS TO TRADITIONAL LEARNING ENVIRONMENT:
  Oral presentation in lieu of written exams
  Use of calculator for all math courses
  Tape recorders to record class lectures
  Someone else may take class notes
  Multiple choice exams only
  Essay exams only
  Student takes exams in separate rooms
  Students have exams read to them
  Students take typewritten exams
  Longer time allowed to complete exams
  Submit papers on cassette tape
  Take limited course load and graduate within time
    required
  Extended time limits for graduation
  Physical education may be waived

MAJORS OFFERED:

  AREA STUDIES
  BIOLOGICAL SCIENCES
  BUSINESS AND MANAGEMENT
  COMMUNICATIONS
  COMPUTER SCIENCES
  EDUCATION
  FINE AND APPLIED ARTS
  FOREIGN LANGUAGES
  HEALTH
  HUMANITIES
  LAW
  MATHEMATICS
  PHYSICAL SCIENCES
  PSYCHOLOGY
  SOCIAL SCIENCES

==

OHIO DOMINICAN COLLEGE
1216 SANBURY ROAD
COLUMBUS, OH 43219
614-253-2741

KEY CONTACT: Attn: SISTER THOMAS ALBERT CORBETT,
                    DIRECTOR INSTITUTIONAL RESEARCH

SIZE OF SCHOOL: SMALL

APPLICATION DEADLINE: AUGUST 25

          APPROXIMATE TUITION   ROOM AND BOARD

IN STATE $4390 $2500
OUT-OF-STATE $4390 $2500

REQUIREMENTS FOR ADMISSIONS:
  High school equivalency diploma
  High school diploma
  ACT Scores required
  SAT Scores required
  Particular rank in class 50%
  High school grade point average C
  Admission requirements modified

ADDITIONAL SERVICES OFFERED:
  Learning Lab
  Learning Lab has a specialist with a masters degree
    or above in Learning Disabilities
  Diagnostic testing services on campus
  Diagnostic testing services off campus
  Remedial and/or tutorial help available
  Reader services for the blind available for LD

MODIFICATIONS TO TRADITIONAL LEARNING ENVIRONMENT:
  Oral presentation in lieu of written exams
  Use of calculator for all math courses
  Tape recorders to record class lectures
  Someone else may take class notes
  Student takes exams in separate rooms
  Students have exams read to them
  Students take typewritten exams
  Longer time allowed to complete exams
  Extended time limits for graduation
  Physical education may be waived

MAJORS OFFERED:

  BIOLOGICAL SCIENCES
  BUSINESS AND MANAGEMENT
  COMMUNICATIONS
  EDUCATION
  FINE AND APPLIED ARTS
  FOREIGN LANGUAGES
  HEALTH

```
HOME ECONOMICS
HUMANITIES
LIBRARY SCIENCE
MATHEMATICS
PHYSICAL SCIENCES
PSYCHOLOGY
PUBLIC SERVICES
SOCIAL SCIENCES
```

===

OHIO STATE UNIVERSITY
COLUMBUS, OH 43210
614-422-3980

KEY CONTACT: Attn: OFFICE OF PHYSICALLY IMPAIRED

SIZE OF SCHOOL: LARGE

APPLICATION DEADLINE: AUGUST 15

	APPROXIMATE TUITION	ROOM AND BOARD
IN STATE	$1460	$2515
OUT-OF-STATE	$3730	$2515

REQUIREMENTS FOR ADMISSIONS:
  High school diploma
  Admission requirements modified
  Placement tests

ADDITIONAL SERVICES OFFERED:
  Learning Lab
  Learning Lab has a specialist with a masters degree
    or above in Learning Disabilities
  Diagnostic testing services off campus
  Remedial and/or tutorial help available
  Reader services for the blind available for LD
  Handicapped student services works with LD

MODIFICATIONS TO TRADITIONAL LEARNING ENVIRONMENT:
  Oral presentation in lieu of written exams
  Use of calculator for all math courses
  Tape recorders to record class lectures
  Someone else may take class notes
  Multiple choice exams only
  Essay exams only
  Student takes exams in separate rooms
  Students have exams read to them
  Students take typewritten exams
  Longer time allowed to complete exams

```
     Submit papers on cassette tape
     Extended time limits for graduation
     Physical education may be waived
```

MAJORS OFFERED:

```
   AGRICULTURE
   ARCHITECTURE
   AREA STUDIES
   BIOLOGICAL SCIENCES
   BUSINESS AND MANAGEMENT
   COMMUNICATIONS
   COMPUTER SCIENCES
   EDUCATION
   ENGINEERING TECHNOLOGIES
   FINE AND APPLIED ARTS
   FOREIGN LANGUAGES
   HEALTH
   HOME ECONOMICS
   HUMANITIES
   MATHEMATICS
   PHYSICAL SCIENCES
   PUBLIC SERVICES
   SOCIAL SCIENCES
   THEOLOGY
```

==

```
OHIO STATE UNIVERSITY - MANSFIELD
1680 UNIVERSTIY DRIVE
MANSFIELD, OH 44906
419-755-4226
```

KEY CONTACT: Attn: GINNY CORSO, ACADEMIC ADVISOR

SIZE OF SCHOOL: SMALL

APPLICATION DEADLINE: AUGUST 15

	APPROXIMATE TUITION	ROOM AND BOARD
IN STATE	$1415	$NOT OFFERED
OUT-OF-STATE	$3680	$NOT OFFERED

REQUIREMENTS FOR ADMISSIONS:
  High school equivalency diploma
  High school diploma
  ACT Scores required
  SAT Scores required
  Placement tests

ADDITIONAL SERVICES OFFERED:
  Learning Lab
  Learning Lab has a specialist with a masters degree
    or above in Learning Disabilities
  Diagnostic testing services on campus
  Diagnostic testing services off campus
  Remedial and/or tutorial help available
  Reader services for the blind available for LD
  Handicapped student services works with LD

MODIFICATIONS TO TRADITIONAL LEARNING ENVIRONMENT:
  Oral presentation in lieu of written exams
  Use of calculator for all math courses
  Tape recorders to record class lectures
  Someone else may take class notes
  Student takes exams in separate rooms
  Students have exams read to them
  Students take typewritten exams
  Longer time allowed to complete exams
  Submit papers on cassette tape
  Students may take tests that are on tape and the
    student can also record test answers on tape
  Instructors have final say on modifications

MAJORS OFFERED:

  EDUCATION

===

UNIVERSITY IF CINCINNATI
CINCINNATI, OH 45221
513-475-3425

KEY CONTACT: Attn: Handicapped Student Services

SIZE OF SCHOOL: LARGE

APPLICATION DEADLINE: NONE

          APPROXIMATE TUITION   ROOM AND BOARD

IN STATE $1670 $2820
OUT-OF-STATE $4010 $2820

REQUIREMENTS FOR ADMISSIONS:
  High school equivalency diploma
  High school diploma

ADDITIONAL SERVICES OFFERED:
  Learning Lab

Learning Lab has a specialist with a masters degree
   or above in Learning Disabilities
Diagnostic testing services off campus
Remedial and/or tutorial help available
Reader services for the blind available for LD
Special Education department
Handicapped student services works with LD

MODIFICATIONS TO TRADITIONAL LEARNING ENVIRONMENT:
   Oral presentation in lieu of written exams
   Use of calculator for all math courses
   Tape recorders to record class lectures
   Someone else may take class notes
   Student takes exams in separate rooms
   Students have exams read to them
   Students take typewritten exams
   Longer time allowed to complete exams
   Extended time limits for graduation
   Physical education may be waived

MAJORS OFFERED:

   ARCHITECTURE
   AREA STUDIES
   BIOLOGICAL SCIENCES
   BUSINESS AND MANAGEMENT
   COMMUNICATIONS
   COMPUTER SCIENCES
   EDUCATION
   ENGINEERING TECHNOLOGIES
   FINE AND APPLIED ARTS
   FOREIGN LANGUAGES
   HEALTH
   HOME ECONOMICS
   HUMANITIES
   LAW
   LIBRARY SCIENCE
   MATHEMATICS
   MILITARY SCIENCES
   PHYSICAL SCIENCES
   PSYCHOLOGY
   PUBLIC SERVICES
   SOCIAL SCIENCES
   THEOLOGY

===

WRIGHT STATE UNIVERSITY
COLONEL GLENN HIGHWAY
DAYTON, OH 45435
513-873-2211

```
ENGINEERING TECHNOLOGIES
FINE AND APPLIED ARTS
FOREIGN LANGUAGES
HEALTH
HUMANITIES
LIBRARY SCIENCE
MATHEMATICS
PHYSICAL SCIENCES
PSYCHOLOGY
PUBLIC SERVICES
SOCIAL SCIENCES
```

===

UNIVERSITY OF OKLAHOMA - NORMAN
1000 ASP AVENUE
NORMAN, OK 73019
405-325-2251

KEY CONTACT: Attn: LINDA ZINNER, COORDINATOR
                     HANDICAPPED STUDENT SERVICES

SIZE OF SCHOOL: LARGE

APPLICATION DEADLINE: JUNE 1

        APPROXIMATE TUITION   ROOM AND BOARD

IN STATE $ 830 $2125
OUT-OF-STATE $2170 $2125

REQUIREMENTS FOR ADMISSIONS:
  High school equivalency diploma
  High school diploma
  21 years of age or older, with or without a
    high school diploma or equivalency
  ACT Scores required
  Untimed or oral ACT Scores accepted
  Untimed or oral SAT Scores accepted
  Particular rank in class 50%
  High school grade point average 3.0

ADDITIONAL SERVICES OFFERED:
  Diagnostic testing services on campus
  Handicapped student services works with LD

MODIFICATIONS TO TRADITIONAL LEARNING ENVIRONMENT:
  Oral presentation in lieu of written exams (with
    instructor's approval)
  Has an adaptive physical education program
  Student takes exams in separate rooms

```
ENGINEERING TECHNOLOGIES
FINE AND APPLIED ARTS
FOREIGN LANGUAGES
HEALTH
HUMANITIES
LIBRARY SCIENCE
MATHEMATICS
PHYSICAL SCIENCES
PSYCHOLOGY
PUBLIC SERVICES
SOCIAL SCIENCES
```

===

UNIVERSITY OF OKLAHOMA - NORMAN
1000 ASP AVENUE
NORMAN, OK 73019
405-325-2251

KEY CONTACT: Attn: LINDA ZINNER, COORDINATOR
                     HANDICAPPED STUDENT SERVICES

SIZE OF SCHOOL: LARGE

APPLICATION DEADLINE: JUNE 1

	APPROXIMATE TUITION	ROOM AND BOARD
IN STATE	$ 830	$2125
OUT-OF-STATE	$2170	$2125

REQUIREMENTS FOR ADMISSIONS:
  High school equivalency diploma
  High school diploma
  21 years of age or older, with or without a
    high school diploma or equivalency
  ACT Scores required
  Untimed or oral ACT Scores accepted
  Untimed or oral SAT Scores accepted
  Particular rank in class 50%
  High school grade point average 3.0

ADDITIONAL SERVICES OFFERED:
  Diagnostic testing services on campus
  Handicapped student services works with LD

MODIFICATIONS TO TRADITIONAL LEARNING ENVIRONMENT:
  Oral presentation in lieu of written exams (with
    instructor's approval)
  Has an adaptive physical education program
  Student takes exams in separate rooms

```
Students have exams read to them
Longer time allowed to complete exams
Submit papers on cassette tape
Office of Handicapped student services will type
  papers from cassette tape
Modifications made when requested and after
  diagnostic testing
```

MAJORS OFFERED:

```
ARCHITECTURE
AREA STUDIES
BIOLOGICAL SCIENCES
BUSINESS AND MANAGEMENT
COMMUNICATIONS
COMPUTER SCIENCES
EDUCATION
ENGINEERING TECHNOLOGIES
FINE AND APPLIED ARTS
FOREIGN LANGUAGES
HEALTH
HOME ECONOMICS
HUMANITIES
LAW
LIBRARY SCIENCE
MATHEMATICS
PHYSICAL SCIENCES
PSYCHOLOGY
PUBLIC SERVICES
SOCIAL SCIENCES
```

==

```
CONCORDIA COLLEGE
2811 NORTHEAST HOLMAN
PORTLAND, OR 97211
503-288-9371
```

KEY CONTACT: Attn: Handicapped Student Services

SIZE OF SCHOOL: SMALL

APPLICATION DEADLINE: SEPTEMBER 1

	APPROXIMATE TUITION	ROOM AND BOARD
IN STATE	$4090	$2490
OUT-OF-STATE	$4090	$2490

REQUIREMENTS FOR ADMISSIONS:
  High school equivalency diploma

High school diploma
Untimed or oral ACT Scores accepted
SAT Scores required
Untimed or oral SAT Scores accepted
High school grade point average (not specified)
Admission requirements modified
Personal interview
Placement tests
Recommendations

ADDITIONAL SERVICES OFFERED:
Learning Lab
Diagnostic testing services off campus
Remedial and/or tutorial help available
Handicapped student services works with LD

MODIFICATIONS TO TRADITIONAL LEARNING ENVIRONMENT:
Oral presentation in lieu of written exams
Use of calculator for all math courses
Has an adaptive physical education program
Tape recorders to record class lectures
Someone else may take class notes
Student takes exams in separate rooms
Students have exams read to them
Students take typewritten exams
Longer time allowed to complete exams
Submit papers on cassette tape
Extended time limits for graduation
Physical education may be waived

MAJORS OFFERED:

BIOLOGICAL SCIENCES
BUSINESS AND MANAGEMENT
EDUCATION
FINE AND APPLIED ARTS
HEALTH
HUMANITIES
LAW
PHYSICAL SCIENCES
PUBLIC SERVICES
SOCIAL SCIENCES
THEOLOGY

===

EASTERN OREGON STATE COLLEGE
8TH AND K AVENUES
LA GRANDE, OR 97850
503-963-2171

KEY CONTACT: Attn: Handicapped Student Services

SIZE OF SCHOOL: SMALL

APPLICATION DEADLINE: NONE

     APPROXIMATE TUITION   ROOM AND BOARD

IN STATE $1340 $2200
OUT-OF-STATE $1340 $2200

REQUIREMENTS FOR ADMISSIONS:
  High school equivalency diploma
  High school diploma
  21 years of age or older, with or without a
    high school diploma or equivalency
  ACT Scores required
  SAT Scores required
  Admission requirements modified

ADDITIONAL SERVICES OFFERED:
  Remedial and/or tutorial help available

MODIFICATIONS TO TRADITIONAL LEARNING ENVIRONMENT:
  Oral presentation in lieu of written exams
  Use of calculator for all math courses
  Tape recorders to record class lectures
  Someone else may take class notes
  Multiple choice exams only
  Essay exams only
  Student takes exams in separate rooms
  Students have exams read to them
  Students take typewritten exams
  Longer time allowed to complete exams
  Submit papers on cassette tape
  Take limited course load and graduate within time
    required
  Extended time limits for graduation
  Physical education may be waived

MAJORS OFFERED:

  AGRICULTURE
  BIOLOGICAL SCIENCES
  BUSINESS AND MANAGEMENT
  EDUCATION
  FINE AND APPLIED ARTS
  HEALTH
  HUMANITIES
  MATHEMATICS
  PHYSICAL SCIENCES

```
PSYCHOLOGY
PUBLIC SERVICES
SOCIAL SCIENCES
```

==

```
OREGON STATE UNIVERSITY
CERVALLIS, OR 97331
503-754-4411
```

KEY CONTACT: Attn: SALLY WONG, PROGRAM DIRECTOR
                    HANDICAPPED STUDENT SERVICES

SIZE OF SCHOOL: LARGE

APPLICATION DEADLINE: NONE

	APPROXIMATE TUITION	ROOM AND BOARD
IN STATE	$1355	$2260
OUT-OF-STATE	$3980	$2260

REQUIREMENTS FOR ADMISSIONS:
  High school equivalency diploma
  High school diploma
  ACT Scores required
  Untimed or oral ACT Scores accepted
  SAT Scores required
  Untimed or oral SAT Scores accepted
  High school grade point average 2.5
  Admission requirements modified
  Placement tests

ADDITIONAL SERVICES OFFERED:
  Diagnostic testing services on campus
  Diagnostic testing services off campus
  Remedial and/or tutorial help available
  Reader services for the blind available for LD
  Special Education department
  Handicapped student services works with LD

MODIFICATIONS TO TRADITIONAL LEARNING ENVIRONMENT:
  Oral presentation in lieu of written exams
  Use of calculator for all math courses
  Has an adaptive physical education program
  Tape recorders to record class lectures
  Someone else may take class notes
  Multiple choice exams only
  Essay exams only
  Student takes exams in separate rooms
  Students have exams read to them

Students take typewritten exams
Longer time allowed to complete exams
Submit papers on cassette tape
Take limited course load and graduate within time
  required
Extended time limits for graduation
Physical education may be waived

MAJORS OFFERED:

AGRICULTURE
AREA STUDIES
BIOLOGICAL SCIENCES
BUSINESS AND MANAGEMENT
COMMUNICATIONS
COMPUTER SCIENCES
EDUCATION
ENGINEERING TECHNOLOGIES
FINE AND APPLIED ARTS
FOREIGN LANGUAGES
HEALTH
HOME ECONOMICS
HUMANITIES
MATHEMATICS
PHYSICAL SCIENCES
PSYCHOLOGY
PUBLIC SERVICES
SOCIAL SCIENCES

===

PORTLAND STATE UNIVERSITY
PORTLAND, OR 97207
503-229-3511

KEY CONTACT: Attn: CINDY CALLIS, DIRECTOR
                    HANDICAPPED STUDENT SERVICES

SIZE OF SCHOOL: MEDIUM

APPLICATION DEADLINE: SEPTEMBER 15

       APPROXIMATE TUITION   ROOM AND BOARD

IN STATE $1375 $NOT OFFERED
OUT-OF-STATE $4000 $NOT OFFERED

REQUIREMENTS FOR ADMISSIONS:
  High school equivalency diploma
  High school diploma
  SAT Scores required

    Untimed or oral SAT Scores accepted
    Admission requirements modified
    Perspective student must meet regular college
      requirements with testing modifications

ADDITIONAL SERVICES OFFERED:
    Remedial and/or tutorial help available
    Reader services for the blind available for LD
    Handicapped student services works with LD

MODIFICATIONS TO TRADITIONAL LEARNING ENVIRONMENT:
    Oral presentation in lieu of written exams
    Has an adaptive physical education program
    Tape recorders to record class lectures
    Someone else may take class notes
    Student takes exams in separate rooms
    Students have exams read to them
    Students take typewritten exams
    Longer time allowed to complete exams
    Submit papers on cassette tape
    Extended time limits for graduation
    Physical education may be waived

MAJORS OFFERED:

    BIOLOGICAL SCIENCES
    BUSINESS AND MANAGEMENT
    COMPUTER SCIENCES
    EDUCATION
    ENGINEERING TECHNOLOGIES
    FINE AND APPLIED ARTS
    FOREIGN LANGUAGES
    HUMANITIES
    MATHEMATICS
    PHYSICAL SCIENCES
    PSYCHOLOGY
    PUBLIC SERVICES
    SOCIAL SCIENCES

==

SOUTHERN OREGON STATE COLLEGE
1200 SISKIYOU BOULEVARD
ASHLAND, OR 97520
503-482-6411

KEY CONTACT: Attn: Handicapped Student Services

SIZE OF SCHOOL: MEDIUM

APPLICATION DEADLINE: NONE

```
       APPROXIMATE TUITION    ROOM AND BOARD

IN STATE           $1375        $2350
OUT-OF-STATE       $3620        $2350
```

REQUIREMENTS FOR ADMISSIONS:
  ACT Scores required (composite 20)
  SAT Scores required (total 880)
  High school grade point average   C
  Admission requirements modified

ADDITIONAL SERVICES OFFERED:
  Learning Lab
  Learning Lab has a specialist with a masters degree
    or above in Learning Disabilities
  Diagnostic testing services on campus
  Diagnostic testing services off campus
  Remedial and/or tutorial help available
  Handicapped student services works with LD

MODIFICATIONS TO TRADITIONAL LEARNING ENVIRONMENT:
  Oral presentation in lieu of written exams
  Use of calculator for all math courses
  Tape recorders to record class lectures
  Someone else may take class notes
  Multiple choice exams only
  Student takes exams in separate rooms
  Students have exams read to them
  Students take typewritten exams
  Longer time allowed to complete exams
  Submit papers on cassette tape
  Extended time limits for graduation
  Physical education may be waived

MAJORS OFFERED:

  BIOLOGICAL SCIENCES
  BUSINESS AND MANAGEMENT
  COMMUNICATIONS
  COMPUTER SCIENCES
  EDUCATION
  FINE AND APPLIED ARTS
  FOREIGN LANGUAGES
  HEALTH
  HUMANITIES
  LAW
  MATHEMATICS
  PHYSICAL SCIENCES
  PSYCHOLOGY
  PUBLIC SERVICES
  SOCIAL SCIENCES

UNIVERSITY OF OREGON
270 OREGON HALL
EUGENE, OR 97403
503-686-4091

KEY CONTACT: Attn: Handicapped Student Services

SIZE OF SCHOOL: LARGE

APPLICATION DEADLINE: NONE

	APPROXIMATE TUITION	ROOM AND BOARD
IN STATE	$1380	$2200
OUT-OF-STATE	$4000	$2200

REQUIREMENTS FOR ADMISSIONS:
  High school equivalency diploma
  High school diploma
  Student must meet school standards

ADDITIONAL SERVICES OFFERED:
  Diagnostic testing services on campus
  Remedial and/or tutorial help available
  Reader services for the blind available for LD
  Special Education department
  Handicapped student services works with LD

MODIFICATIONS TO TRADITIONAL LEARNING ENVIRONMENT:
  Use of calculator for all math courses
  Has an adaptive physical education program
  Tape recorders to record class lectures
  Someone else may take class notes
  Student takes exams in separate rooms
  Students have exams read to them
  Students take typewritten exams
  Physical education may be waived

MAJORS OFFERED:

  ARCHITECTURE
  AREA STUDIES
  BIOLOGICAL SCIENCES
  BUSINESS AND MANAGEMENT
  COMMUNICATIONS
  COMPUTER SCIENCES
  EDUCATION
  FINE AND APPLIED ARTS
  FOREIGN LANGUAGES
  HEALTH
  HUMANITIES

```
MATHEMATICS
PHYSICAL SCIENCES
PSYCHOLOGY
PUBLIC SERVICES
SOCIAL SCIENCES
```

==

```
BLOOMSBURG UNIVERSITY OF PENNSYLVANIA
BLOOMSBURG, PA 17815
717-389-4316
```

KEY CONTACT: Attn: DR. JESSIE BRYAN, DIRECTOR
                    CENTER FOR ACADEMIC DEVELOPMENT

SIZE OF SCHOOL: MEDIUM

APPLICATION DEADLINE: NONE

	APPROXIMATE TUITION	ROOM AND BOARD
IN STATE	$1480	$1475
OUT-OF-STATE	$2590	$1475

REQUIREMENTS FOR ADMISSIONS:
  High school equivalency diploma
  High school diploma
  SAT Scores required
  Untimed or oral SAT Scores accepted
  Particular rank in class Upper 50%
  High school grade point average 2.5
  Admission requirements modified
  Placement tests
  Recommendations

ADDITIONAL SERVICES OFFERED:
  Learning Lab
  Learning Lab has a specialist with a masters degree
    or above in Learning Disabilities
  Diagnostic testing services on campus
  Remedial and/or tutorial help available
  Special Education department
  Handicapped student services works with LD

MODIFICATIONS TO TRADITIONAL LEARNING ENVIRONMENT:
  No institution policy
  Arrangements are made on an individual student basis
    and professor basis

MAJORS OFFERED:

   BIOLOGICAL SCIENCES
   BUSINESS AND MANAGEMENT
   COMMUNICATIONS
   COMPUTER SCIENCES
   EDUCATION
   FINE AND APPLIED ARTS
   FOREIGN LANGUAGES
   HEALTH
   HUMANITIES
   MATHEMATICS
   PHYSICAL SCIENCES
   PSYCHOLOGY
   SOCIAL SCIENCES

==

CLARION UNIVERSITY OF PENNSYLVANIA
CLARION, PA 16214
814-226-2306

KEY CONTACT: Attn: Handicapped Student Services

SIZE OF SCHOOL: MEDIUM

APPLICATION DEADLINE: NONE

	APPROXIMATE TUITION	ROOM AND BOARD
IN STATE	$1600	$1700
OUT-OF-STATE	$2500	$1700

REQUIREMENTS FOR ADMISSIONS:
  SAT Scores required
  Particular rank in class (not specified)
  Recommendations

ADDITIONAL SERVICES OFFERED:
  Diagnostic testing services on campus
  Remedial and/or tutorial help available
  Special Education department

MODIFICATIONS TO TRADITIONAL LEARNING ENVIRONMENT:
  Oral presentation in lieu of written exams
  Use of calculator for all math courses
  Tape recorders to record class lectures
  Someone else may take class notes
  Multiple choice exams only
  Essay exams only
  Student takes exams in separate rooms

```
Students have exams read to them
Students take typewritten exams
Longer time allowed to complete exams
Submit papers on cassette tape
Physical education may be waived
```

MAJORS OFFERED:

```
BIOLOGICAL SCIENCES
BUSINESS AND MANAGEMENT
COMMUNICATIONS
COMPUTER SCIENCES
EDUCATION
ENGINEERING TECHNOLOGIES
FINE AND APPLIED ARTS
FOREIGN LANGUAGES
HEALTH
HUMANITIES
LIBRARY SCIENCE
MATHEMATICS
PHYSICAL SCIENCES
PSYCHOLOGY
SOCIAL SCIENCES
```

==

```
LA ROCHE COLLEGE
9000 BABCOCK BOULEVARD
PITTSBURGH, PA 15237
412-367-1501
```

KEY CONTACT: Attn: Handicapped Student Services

SIZE OF SCHOOL: SMALL

APPLICATION DEADLINE: NONE

	APPROXIMATE TUITION	ROOM AND BOARD
IN STATE	$3425	$2510
OUT-OF-STATE	$3425	$2510

ADDITIONAL SERVICES OFFERED:
  Learning Lab

MODIFICATIONS TO TRADITIONAL LEARNING ENVIRONMENT:
  Oral presentation in lieu of written exams
  Use of calculator for all math courses
  Tape recorders to record class lectures
  Someone else may take class notes
  No special or specific program for disabled students

MAJORS OFFERED:

```
AGRICULTURE
BIOLOGICAL SCIENCES
BUSINESS AND MANAGEMENT
COMMUNICATIONS
COMPUTER SCIENCES
FINE AND APPLIED ARTS
HEALTH
HUMANITIES
PHYSICAL SCIENCES
PSYCHOLOGY
SOCIAL SCIENCES
THEOLOGY
```

==

PHILADELPHIA COLLEGE OF ART
BROAD AND SPRUCE STREETS
PHILADELPHIA, PA 19102
215-893-3174

KEY CONTACT: Attn: DR. EVE ORLOW, DIRECTOR
                     LEARNING SKILLS CENTER

SIZE OF SCHOOL: SMALL

APPLICATION DEADLINE: NONE

	APPROXIMATE TUITION	ROOM AND BOARD
IN STATE	$6375	$2000
OUT-OF-STATE	$6375	$2000

REQUIREMENTS FOR ADMISSIONS:
  High school equivalency diploma
  High school diploma
  ACT Scores required
  Untimed or oral ACT Scores accepted
  SAT Scores required
  Untimed or oral SAT Scores accepted
  Admission requirements modified
  Personal interview
  Placement tests
  Recommendations
  Essay

ADDITIONAL SERVICES OFFERED:
  Learning Lab
  Learning Lab has a specialist with a masters degree
    or above in Learning Disabilities

Diagnostic testing services off campus
Remedial and/or tutorial help available
Reader services for the blind available for LD

MODIFICATIONS TO TRADITIONAL LEARNING ENVIRONMENT:
Oral presentation in lieu of written exams
Tape recorders to record class lectures
Student takes exams in separate rooms
Longer time allowed to complete exams
Submit papers on cassette tape
Extended time limits for graduation

MAJORS OFFERED:

ARCHITECTURE
EDUCATION
FINE AND APPLIED ARTS

===

POINT PARK COLLEGE
201 WOOD STREET
PITTSBURGH, PA 15222
412-391-4100

KEY CONTACT: Attn: MARK BOSCARDIN

SIZE OF SCHOOL: SMALL

APPLICATION DEADLINE: NONE

	APPROXIMATE TUITION	ROOM AND BOARD
IN STATE	$4335	$2620
OUT-OF-STATE	$4335	$2620

REQUIREMENTS FOR ADMISSIONS:
High school equivalency diploma
ACT Scores required
SAT Scores required
Admission requirements modified

ADDITIONAL SERVICES OFFERED:
Learning Lab
Learning Lab has a specialist with a masters degree
or above in Learning Disabilities
Diagnostic testing services on campus
Diagnostic testing services off campus
Remedial and/or tutorial help available
Reader services for the blind available for LD
Handicapped student services works with LD

MODIFICATIONS TO TRADITIONAL LEARNING ENVIRONMENT:
  Oral presentation in lieu of written exams
  Use of calculator for all math courses
  Tape recorders to record class lectures
  Someone else may take class notes
  Multiple choice exams only
  Student takes exams in separate rooms
  Students have exams read to them
  Students take typewritten exams
  Longer time allowed to complete exams
  Submit papers on cassette tape
  Extended time limits for graduation
  Physical education may be waived
  Modifications at the instructors discretion

MAJORS OFFERED:

  BIOLOGICAL SCIENCES
  BUSINESS AND MANAGEMENT
  COMMUNICATIONS
  COMPUTER SCIENCES
  EDUCATION
  ENGINEERING TECHNOLOGIES
  FINE AND APPLIED ARTS
  FOREIGN LANGUAGES
  HEALTH
  HUMANITIES
  MATHEMATICS
  PSYCHOLOGY
  PUBLIC SERVICES
  SOCIAL SCIENCES

==

SLIPPERY ROCK UNIVERSITY OF PENNSYLVANIA
SLIPPERY ROCK, PA 16057
412-794-7203

KEY CONTACT: Attn: ELIOT BAKER
                    DIRECTOR OF ADMISSIONS

SIZE OF SCHOOL: MEDIUM

APPLICATION DEADLINE: AUGUST 15

        APPROXIMATE TUITION   ROOM AND BOARD

IN STATE $1680 $1705
OUT-OF-STATE $2790 $1705

REQUIREMENTS FOR ADMISSIONS:
  High school equivalency diploma
  High school diploma
  21 years of age or older, with or without a
    high school diploma or equivalency
  ACT Scores required
  Untimed or oral ACT Scores accepted
  SAT Scores required
  Untimed or oral SAT Scores accepted
  WAIS scores required
  High school grade point average 2.3 or above
  Personal interview
  Recommendations
  Essay
  Wide Range Achievment test required (WRAT)

ADDITIONAL SERVICES OFFERED:
  Diagnostic testing services on campus
  Remedial and/or tutorial help available
  Reader services for the blind available for LD
  Special Education department
  Handicapped student services works with LD

MODIFICATIONS TO TRADITIONAL LEARNING ENVIRONMENT:
  Oral presentation in lieu of written exams
  Has an adaptive physical education program
  Tape recorders to record class lectures
  Someone else may take class notes
  Student takes exams in separate rooms
  Students have exams read to them
  Longer time allowed to complete exams
  Extended time limits for graduation
  Physical education may be waived

MAJORS OFFERED:

  BIOLOGICAL SCIENCES
  BUSINESS AND MANAGEMENT
  COMMUNICATIONS
  COMPUTER SCIENCES
  EDUCATION
  ENGINEERING TECHNOLOGIES
  FINE AND APPLIED ARTS
  FOREIGN LANGUAGES
  HEALTH
  HUMANITIES
  LIBRARY SCIENCE
  MATHEMATICS
  MILITARY SCIENCES
  PHYSICAL SCIENCES
  PSYCHOLOGY

```
PUBLIC SERVICES
SOCIAL SCIENCES
```

===

```
ST. JOSEPH'S UNIVERSITY
5600 CITY LINE AVENUE
PHILADELPHIA, PA 19131
215-879-7400
```

KEY CONTACT: Attn: Handicapped Student Services

SIZE OF SCHOOL: SMALL

APPLICATION DEADLINE: MARCH 1

	APPROXIMATE TUITION	ROOM AND BOARD
IN STATE	$4510	$2960
OUT-OF-STATE	$4510	$2960

REQUIREMENTS FOR ADMISSIONS:
  High school equivalency diploma
  SAT Scores required
  Particular rank in class 40%
  Admission requirements modified

MODIFICATIONS TO TRADITIONAL LEARNING ENVIRONMENT:
  Tape recorders to record class lectures
  Someone else may take class notes
  Student takes exams in separate rooms
  Students have exams read to them
  Students take typewritten exams
  Longer time allowed to complete exams
  Submit papers on cassette tape
  Take limited course load and graduate within time
    required
  Physical education may be waived

MAJORS OFFERED:

  BIOLOGICAL SCIENCES
  BUSINESS AND MANAGEMENT
  COMPUTER SCIENCES
  EDUCATION
  ENGINEERING TECHNOLOGIES
  FINE AND APPLIED ARTS
  HUMANITIES
  MATHEMATICS
  PHYSICAL SCIENCES
  PSYCHOLOGY

PUBLIC SERVICES
SOCIAL SCIENCES

==

UNIVERSITY OF PITTSBURGH
4200 FIFTH AVENUE
PITTSBURGH, PA 15260
412-624-5761

KEY CONTACT: Attn: TOM GALANTE, COORDINATOR
                    DISABLED STUDENT SERVICES

SIZE OF SCHOOL: LARGE

APPLICATION DEADLINE: NONE

          APPROXIMATE TUITION   ROOM AND BOARD

IN STATE $2210 $2450
OUT-OF-STATE $4420 $2450

REQUIREMENTS FOR ADMISSIONS:
  High school diploma
  Untimed or oral ACT Scores accepted
  SAT Scores required
  Untimed or oral SAT Scores accepted
  University or College sponsored tests
  Particular rank in class upper 50%
  High school grade point average 2.0
  Admission requirements modified
  Personal interview
  Placement tests
  Recommendations
  Essay

ADDITIONAL SERVICES OFFERED:
  Diagnostic testing services off campus
  Remedial and/or tutorial help available
  Reader services for the blind available for LD
  Special Education department
  Handicapped student services works with LD

MODIFICATIONS TO TRADITIONAL LEARNING ENVIRONMENT:
  Use of calculator for all math courses
  Has an adaptive physical education program
  Tape recorders to record class lectures
  Someone else may take class notes
  Student takes exams in separate rooms
  Students have exams read to them
  Students take typewritten exams

Longer time allowed to complete exams
Take limited course load and graduate within time
   required
Extended time limits for graduation

MAJORS OFFERED:

ARCHITECTURE
BIOLOGICAL SCIENCES
BUSINESS AND MANAGEMENT
COMMUNICATIONS
COMPUTER SCIENCES
EDUCATION
FINE AND APPLIED ARTS
FOREIGN LANGUAGES
HEALTH
HOME ECONOMICS
HUMANITIES
LAW
MATHEMATICS
PHYSICAL SCIENCES
PSYCHOLOGY
PUBLIC SERVICES
SOCIAL SCIENCES

==

BARRINGTON COLLEGE
MIDDLE HIGHWAY
BARRINGTON, RI 02806
401-246-1200

KEY CONTACT: Attn: Handicapped Student Services

SIZE OF SCHOOL: SMALL

APPLICATION DEADLINE: SEPTEMBER 1

        APPROXIMATE TUITION   ROOM AND BOARD

IN STATE $5715 $2475
OUT-OF-STATE $5715 $2475

REQUIREMENTS FOR ADMISSIONS:
   Particular rank in class 60%
   High school grade point average 2.0
   Admission requirements modified

ADDITIONAL SERVICES OFFERED:
   Learning Lab
   Remedial and/or tutorial help available

Reader services for the blind available for LD
Handicapped student services works with LD

MODIFICATIONS TO TRADITIONAL LEARNING ENVIRONMENT:
  Oral presentation in lieu of written exams
  Tape recorders to record class lectures
  Someone else may take class notes
  Student takes exams in separate rooms
  Students have exams read to them
  Students take typewritten exams
  Longer time allowed to complete exams
  Extended time limits for graduation
  Physical education may be waived

MAJORS OFFERED:

  AREA STUDIES
  BIOLOGICAL SCIENCES
  BUSINESS AND MANAGEMENT
  COMPUTER SCIENCES
  EDUCATION
  ENGINEERING TECHNOLOGIES
  FINE AND APPLIED ARTS
  HEALTH
  HUMANITIES
  PHYSICAL SCIENCES
  PSYCHOLOGY
  PUBLIC SERVICES
  THEOLOGY

==

ROGER WILLIAMS COLLEGE
BRISTOL, RI 02809
401-255-2151

KEY CONTACT: Attn: Handicapped Student Services

SIZE OF SCHOOL: SMALL

APPLICATION DEADLINE: NONE

        APPROXIMATE TUITION   ROOM AND BOARD

IN STATE $4420 $2800
OUT-OF-STATE $4420 $2800

REQUIREMENTS FOR ADMISSIONS:
  Requirements vary by major

ADDITIONAL SERVICES OFFERED:
  Handicapped student services works with LD

MODIFICATIONS TO TRADITIONAL LEARNING ENVIRONMENT:
  Oral presentation in lieu of written exams
  Use of calculator for all math courses
  Tape recorders to record class lectures
  Someone else may take class notes
  Student takes exams in separate rooms
  Students have exams read to them
  Longer time allowed to complete exams
  Submit papers on cassette tape
  Extended time limits for graduation
  Physical education may be waived

MAJORS OFFERED:

  AGRICULTURE
  ARCHITECTURE
  AREA STUDIES
  BIOLOGICAL SCIENCES
  BUSINESS AND MANAGEMENT
  COMMUNICATIONS
  COMPUTER SCIENCES
  EDUCATION
  ENGINEERING TECHNOLOGIES
  FINE AND APPLIED ARTS
  HEALTH
  HUMANITIES
  LAW
  MATHEMATICS
  PHYSICAL SCIENCES
  PSYCHOLOGY
  PUBLIC SERVICES
  SOCIAL SCIENCES

==

UNIVERSITY OF RHODE ISLAND
KINGSTON, RI 02881
401-792-2164

KEY CONTACT: Attn: JANE THEIRFELD, COORDINATOR
                    HANDICAPPED STUDENT SERVICES

SIZE OF SCHOOL: MEDIUM

APPLICATION DEADLINE: MARCH 1

```
        APPROXIMATE TUITION    ROOM AND BOARD

IN STATE              $1725        $2855
OUT-OF-STATE          $4500        $2855
```

REQUIREMENTS FOR ADMISSIONS:
  High school equivalency diploma
  High school diploma
  Untimed or oral ACT Scores accepted
  SAT Scores required
  Untimed or oral SAT Scores accepted
  Particular rank in class (not specified)
  High school grade point average (not specified)

ADDITIONAL SERVICES OFFERED:
  Diagnostic testing services on campus
  Diagnostic testing services off campus
  Reader services for the blind available for LD
  Special Education department
  Handicapped student services works with LD

MODIFICATIONS TO TRADITIONAL LEARNING ENVIRONMENT:
  Has an adaptive physical education program
  Tape recorders to record class lectures
  Someone else may take class notes
  All modifications depend on professor

MAJORS OFFERED:

  AGRICULTURE
  AREA STUDIES
  BIOLOGICAL SCIENCES
  BUSINESS AND MANAGEMENT
  COMMUNICATIONS
  COMPUTER SCIENCES
  EDUCATION
  ENGINEERING TECHNOLOGIES
  FINE AND APPLIED ARTS
  FOREIGN LANGUAGES
  HEALTH
  HOME ECONOMICS
  HUMANITIES
  MATHEMATICS
  PHYSICAL SCIENCES
  PSYCHOLOGY
  SOCIAL SCIENCES

===

CITADEL - THE MILITARY COLLEGE OF SOUTH CAROLINA
CITADEL STATION
CHARLESTON, SC 29409
803-792-5230

KEY CONTACT: Attn: Handicapped Student Services

SIZE OF SCHOOL: SMALL

APPLICATION DEADLINE: MARCH 15

        APPROXIMATE TUITION   ROOM AND BOARD

IN STATE $3840 $1530
OUT-OF-STATE $5790 $1530

REQUIREMENTS FOR ADMISSIONS:
  High school equivalency diploma
  High school diploma
  SAT Scores required
  Recommendations

ADDITIONAL SERVICES OFFERED:
  Learning Lab
  Learning Lab has a specialist with a masters degree
    or above in Learning Disabilities
  Diagnostic testing services off campus
  Special Education department

MODIFICATIONS TO TRADITIONAL LEARNING ENVIRONMENT:
  Extended time limits for graduation

MAJORS OFFERED:

  BIOLOGICAL SCIENCES
  BUSINESS AND MANAGEMENT
  COMPUTER SCIENCES
  EDUCATION
  ENGINEERING TECHNOLOGIES
  FOREIGN LANGUAGES
  HEALTH
  HUMANITIES
  LAW
  MATHEMATICS
  MILITARY SCIENCES
  PHYSICAL SCIENCES
  PSYCHOLOGY
  SOCIAL SCIENCES

==

COKER COLLEGE
COLLEGE AVENUE
HARTSVILLE, SC 29550
803-332-1381

KEY CONTACT: Attn: Handicapped Student Services

SIZE OF SCHOOL: SMALL

APPLICATION DEADLINE: NONE

	APPROXIMATE TUITION	ROOM AND BOARD
IN STATE	$4235	$2220
OUT-OF-STATE	$4235	$2220

REQUIREMENTS FOR ADMISSIONS:
  High school equivalency diploma
  High school diploma
  21 years of age or older, with or without a
    high school diploma or equivalency
  SAT Scores required
  High school grade point average 2.0
  Applicants considered on an individual basis

MODIFICATIONS TO TRADITIONAL LEARNING ENVIRONMENT:
  Oral presentation in lieu of written exams
  Use of calculator for all math courses
  Tape recorders to record class lectures
  Someone else may take class notes
  Multiple choice exams only
  Essay exams only
  Student takes exams in separate rooms
  Students have exams read to them
  Students take typewritten exams
  Longer time allowed to complete exams
  Submit papers on cassette tape
  Physical education may be waived

MAJORS OFFERED:

  BIOLOGICAL SCIENCES
  BUSINESS AND MANAGEMENT
  COMMUNICATIONS
  EDUCATION
  FINE AND APPLIED ARTS
  HEALTH
  HUMANITIES
  PHYSICAL SCIENCES
  PSYCHOLOGY
  SOCIAL SCIENCES

```
CONVERSE COLLEGE
580 EAST MAIN STREET
SPARTANBURG, SC 29301
803-585-6421
```

KEY CONTACT: Attn: THOMAS REEVES, VICE PRESIDENT
                     STUDENT AFFAIRS

SIZE OF SCHOOL: SMALL

APPLICATION DEADLINE: NONE

	APPROXIMATE TUITION	ROOM AND BOARD
IN STATE	$4575	$2875
OUT-OF-STATE	$4575	$2875

REQUIREMENTS FOR ADMISSIONS:
  High school diploma
  ACT Scores required
  Untimed or oral ACT Scores accepted
  SAT Scores required
  Untimed or oral SAT Scores accepted
  High school grade point average (not specified)
  Personal interview recommended
  Recommendations recommended

ADDITIONAL SERVICES OFFERED:
  Learning Lab
  Diagnostic testing services off campus
  Remedial and/or tutorial help available
  Special Education department

MODIFICATIONS TO TRADITIONAL LEARNING ENVIRONMENT:
  Oral presentation in lieu of written exams
  Has an adaptive physical education program
  Tape recorders to record class lectures
  Someone else may take class notes
  Multiple choice exams only
  Essay exams only
  Longer time allowed to complete exams
  Extended time limits for graduation
  Physical education may be waived
  Each case handled independently by committee

MAJORS OFFERED:

  ARCHITECTURE
  BIOLOGICAL SCIENCES
  BUSINESS AND MANAGEMENT
  COMPUTER SCIENCES

```
EDUCATION
FINE AND APPLIED ARTS
FOREIGN LANGUAGES
HEALTH
HUMANITIES
MATHEMATICS
PHYSICAL SCIENCES
PSYCHOLOGY
SOCIAL SCIENCES
```

==

```
ERSKINE COLLEGE
DUE WEST, SC 29639
803-379-8838
```

KEY CONTACT: Attn: KATHERINE B. CHANDLER
                     LEARNING DISABILITY PROGRAM

SIZE OF SCHOOL: SMALL

APPLICATION DEADLINE: NONE

           APPROXIMATE TUITION   ROOM AND BOARD

IN STATE $4480 $2150
OUT-OF-STATE $4480 $2150

REQUIREMENTS FOR ADMISSIONS:
  High school equivalency diploma
  High school diploma
  SAT Scores required
  Untimed or oral SAT Scores accepted
  Admission requirements modified
  Personal interview

ADDITIONAL SERVICES OFFERED:
  Learning Lab
  Diagnostic testing services off campus
  Remedial and/or tutorial help available
  Reader services for the blind available for LD
  Handicapped student services works with LD

MODIFICATIONS TO TRADITIONAL LEARNING ENVIRONMENT:
  Oral presentation in lieu of written exams
  Use of calculator for all math courses
  Tape recorders to record class lectures
  Someone else may take class notes
  Multiple choice exams only
  Essay exams only
  Student takes exams in separate rooms

```
Students have exams read to them
Students take typewritten exams
Longer time allowed to complete exams
Submit papers on cassette tape
Extended time limits for graduation
Physical education may be waived
```

MAJORS OFFERED:

```
AREA STUDIES
BIOLOGICAL SCIENCES
BUSINESS AND MANAGEMENT
EDUCATION
FINE AND APPLIED ARTS
FOREIGN LANGUAGES
HEALTH
HUMANITIES
MATHEMATICS
PHYSICAL SCIENCES
PSYCHOLOGY
PUBLIC SERVICES
SOCIAL SCIENCES
THEOLOGY
```

==

MOUNT MARTY COLLEGE
1100 WEST 5TH
YANKTON, SD 57078
605-668-1524

KEY CONTACT: Attn: Handicapped Student Services

SIZE OF SCHOOL: SMALL

APPLICATION DEADLINE: SEPTEMBER 1

```
        APPROXIMATE TUITION    ROOM AND BOARD

IN STATE          $3945           $1860
OUT-OF-STATE      $3945           $1860
```

REQUIREMENTS FOR ADMISSIONS:
  High school equivalency diploma
  High school diploma
  ACT Scores required
  Particular rank in class 50%
  Admission requirements modified

ADDITIONAL SERVICES OFFERED:
  Learning Lab
  Diagnostic testing services off campus
  Remedial and/or tutorial help available

MODIFICATIONS TO TRADITIONAL LEARNING ENVIRONMENT:
  Oral presentation in lieu of written exams
  Use of calculator for all math courses
  Tape recorders to record class lectures
  Someone else may take class notes
  Student takes exams in separate rooms
  Students have exams read to them
  Students take typewritten exams
  Longer time allowed to complete exams
  Submit papers on cassette tape
  Take limited course load and graduate within time
    required
  Extended time limits for graduation
  Physical education may be waived

MAJORS OFFERED:

  BIOLOGICAL SCIENCES
  BUSINESS AND MANAGEMENT
  COMMUNICATIONS
  EDUCATION
  ENGINEERING TECHNOLOGIES
  FINE AND APPLIED ARTS
  HEALTH
  HOME ECONOMICS
  HUMANITIES
  LAW
  MATHEMATICS
  PHYSICAL SCIENCES
  PUBLIC SERVICES
  SOCIAL SCIENCES
  THEOLOGY

===

MOUNT MARTY COLLEGE
1100 WEST 5TH
YANKTON, SD 57078
605-668-1524

KEY CONTACT: Attn: Handicapped Student Services

SIZE OF SCHOOL: SMALL

APPLICATION DEADLINE: SEPTEMBER 1

```
          APPROXIMATE TUITION    ROOM AND BOARD

IN STATE           $3945         $1860
OUT-OF-STATE       $3945         $1860
```

REQUIREMENTS FOR ADMISSIONS:
  High school equivalency diploma
  High school diploma
  ACT Scores required
  Particular rank in class 50%
  Admission requirements modified

ADDITIONAL SERVICES OFFERED:
  Learning Lab
  Diagnostic testing services off campus
  Remedial and/or tutorial help available

MODIFICATIONS TO TRADITIONAL LEARNING ENVIRONMENT:
  Oral presentation in lieu of written exams
  Use of calculator for all math courses
  Tape recorders to record class lectures
  Someone else may take class notes
  Student takes exams in separate rooms
  Students have exams read to them
  Students take typewritten exams
  Longer time allowed to complete exams
  Submit papers on cassette tape
  Take limited course load and graduate within time
    required
  Extended time limits for graduation
  Physical education may be waived

MAJORS OFFERED:

  BIOLOGICAL SCIENCES
  BUSINESS AND MANAGEMENT
  COMMUNICATIONS
  EDUCATION
  ENGINEERING TECHNOLOGIES
  FINE AND APPLIED ARTS
  HEALTH
  HOME ECONOMICS
  HUMANITIES
  LAW
  MATHEMATICS
  PHYSICAL SCIENCES
  PUBLIC SERVICES
  SOCIAL SCIENCES
  THEOLOGY

==

NORTHERN STATE COLLEGE
ABERDENE, SD 57401
605-622-2544

KEY CONTACT: Attn: Handicapped Student Services

SIZE OF SCHOOL: SMALL

APPLICATION DEADLINE: AUGUST 15

        APPROXIMATE TUITION   ROOM AND BOARD

IN STATE $1065 $1400
OUT-OF-STATE $1725 $1400

REQUIREMENTS FOR ADMISSIONS:
  High school equivalency diploma
  High school diploma
  ACT Scores required
  Particular rank in class 66% (resident)
    50% (non-resident)
  Admission requirements modified

ADDITIONAL SERVICES OFFERED:
  Has a specialist with a masters degree
    or above in Learning Disabilities
  Diagnostic testing services off campus
  Remedial and/or tutorial help available
  Reader services for the blind available for LD
  Special Education department

MODIFICATIONS TO TRADITIONAL LEARNING ENVIRONMENT:
  Oral presentation in lieu of written exams
  Use of calculator for all math courses
  Has an adaptive physical education program
  Tape recorders to record class lectures
  Someone else may take class notes
  Student takes exams in separate rooms
  Students have exams read to them
  Students take typewritten exams
  Longer time allowed to complete exams
  Submit papers on cassette tape
  Extended time limits for graduation
  Physical education may be waived
  All modifications arranged individually

MAJORS OFFERED:

  BIOLOGICAL SCIENCES
  BUSINESS AND MANAGEMENT
  EDUCATION

```
FINE AND APPLIED ARTS
HEALTH
HUMANITIES
LIBRARY SCIENCE
MATHEMATICS
PHYSICAL SCIENCES
PSYCHOLOGY
PUBLIC SERVICES
SOCIAL SCIENCES
```

===

LINCOLN MEMORIAL UNIVERSITY
HARROGATE, TN 37752
615-869-3611

KEY CONTACT: Attn: CAROL DANIELS
                    DIRECTOR OF ADMISSIONS

SIZE OF SCHOOL: SMALL

APPLICATION DEADLINE: NONE

        APPROXIMATE TUITION   ROOM AND BOARD

IN STATE $2250 $1800
OUT-OF-STATE $2250 $1800

REQUIREMENTS FOR ADMISSIONS:
  High school equivalency diploma
  High school diploma
  University or College sponsored tests
  Placement tests
  Recommendations

ADDITIONAL SERVICES OFFERED:
  Learning Lab
  Remedial and/or tutorial help available

MODIFICATIONS TO TRADITIONAL LEARNING ENVIRONMENT:
  Oral presentation in lieu of written exams
  Tape recorders to record class lectures
  Someone else may take class notes
  Student takes exams in separate rooms
  Students have exams read to them
  Longer time allowed to complete exams
  Extended time limits for graduation
  Physical education may be waived

MAJORS OFFERED:

  AGRICULTURE
  BIOLOGICAL SCIENCES
  BUSINESS AND MANAGEMENT
  COMPUTER SCIENCES
  EDUCATION
  ENGINEERING TECHNOLOGIES
  FINE AND APPLIED ARTS
  HEALTH
  HUMANITIES
  LAW
  MILITARY SCIENCES
  PHYSICAL SCIENCES
  PSYCHOLOGY
  PUBLIC SERVICES
  SOCIAL SCIENCES

===

MEMPHIS STATE UNIVERSITY
MEMPHIS, TN 38152
901-454-2101

KEY CONTACT: Attn: DONA SPARGER, DIRECTOR
                    HANDICAPPED STUDENT SERVICES

SIZE OF SCHOOL: LARGE

APPLICATION DEADLINE: AUGUST 1

      APPROXIMATE TUITION   ROOM AND BOARD

IN STATE $ 835 $1875
OUT-OF-STATE $2595 $1875

REQUIREMENTS FOR ADMISSIONS:
  High school equivalency diploma
  High school diploma
  21 years of age or older, with or without a
    high school diploma or equivalency
  ACT Scores required
  Untimed or oral ACT Scores accepted
  University or College sponsored tests
  Admission requirements modified
  Placement tests
  Special committee review is available/possible for
    those who don't meet published requirements

ADDITIONAL SERVICES OFFERED:
  Learning Lab
  Remedial and/or tutorial help available
  Reader services for the blind available for LD
  Special Education department
  Handicapped student services works with LD

MODIFICATIONS TO TRADITIONAL LEARNING ENVIRONMENT:
  Oral presentation in lieu of written exams
    (sometimes)
  Has an adaptive physical education program
  Tape recorders to record class lectures
  Someone else may take class notes
  Student takes exams in separate rooms
  Students have exams read to them
  Students take typewritten exams
  Longer time allowed to complete exams
  Take limited course load and graduate within time
    required
  Extended time limits for graduation possible

MAJORS OFFERED:

  AREA STUDIES
  BIOLOGICAL SCIENCES
  BUSINESS AND MANAGEMENT
  COMMUNICATIONS
  COMPUTER SCIENCES
  EDUCATION
  ENGINEERING TECHNOLOGIES
  FINE AND APPLIED ARTS
  FOREIGN LANGUAGES
  HEALTH
  HOME ECONOMICS
  HUMANITIES
  MATHEMATICS
  MILITARY SCIENCES
  PHYSICAL SCIENCES
  PUBLIC SERVICES
  SOCIAL SCIENCES

==

EAST TEXAS STATE UNIVERSITY
EAST TEXAS STATION
COMMERCE, TX 75428
214-886-5081

KEY CONTACT: Attn: JOHN R. MOSS, PROFESSOR

SIZE OF SCHOOL: MEDIUM

APPLICATION DEADLINE: AUGUST 1

    APPROXIMATE TUITION   ROOM AND BOARD

	APPROXIMATE TUITION	ROOM AND BOARD
IN STATE	$ 440	$2190
OUT-OF-STATE	$1540	$2190

REQUIREMENTS FOR ADMISSIONS:
  High school equivalency diploma
  High school diploma
  ACT Scores required
  Untimed or oral ACT Scores accepted
  SAT Scores required
  Untimed or oral SAT Scores accepted
  Placement tests

ADDITIONAL SERVICES OFFERED:
  Learning Lab
  Learning Lab has a specialist with a masters degree
    or above in Learning Disabilities
  Diagnostic testing services off campus
  Remedial and/or tutorial help available
  Reader services for the blind available for LD
  Special Education department
  Handicapped student services works with LD

MODIFICATIONS TO TRADITIONAL LEARNING ENVIRONMENT:
  Oral presentation in lieu of written exams
  Tape recorders to record class lectures
  Someone else may take class notes
  Student takes exams in separate rooms
  Students have exams read to them
  Students take typewritten exams
  Longer time allowed to complete exams
  Submit papers on cassette tape
  Extended time limits for graduation

MAJORS OFFERED:

  AGRICULTURE
  BIOLOGICAL SCIENCES
  BUSINESS AND MANAGEMENT
  COMMUNICATIONS
  COMPUTER SCIENCES
  EDUCATION
  FINE AND APPLIED ARTS
  FOREIGN LANGUAGES
  HEALTH
  HOME ECONOMICS
  HUMANITIES
  MATHEMATICS

```
      PHYSICAL SCIENCES
      PSYCHOLOGY
      PUBLIC SERVICES
      SOCIAL SCIENCES
```

==

```
NORTH TEXAS STATE UNIVERSITY
DENTON, TX 76203
817-788-2681
```

KEY CONTACT: Attn: Handicapped Student Services

SIZE OF SCHOOL: LARGE

APPLICATION DEADLINE: AUGUST 1

```
      APPROXIMATE TUITION    ROOM AND BOARD

IN STATE          $ 465        $2455
OUT-OF-STATE      $1545        $2455
```

REQUIREMENTS FOR ADMISSIONS:
  High school diploma
  ACT Scores required (can be waived)
  SAT Scores required (can be waived)
  Particular rank in class 25%
  Admission requirements modified

ADDITIONAL SERVICES OFFERED:
  Learning Lab has a specialist with a masters degree
    or above in Learning Disabilities
  Diagnostic testing services on campus
  Reader services for the blind available for LD
  Special Education department
  Handicapped student services works with LD

MODIFICATIONS TO TRADITIONAL LEARNING ENVIRONMENT:
  Oral presentation in lieu of written exams
  Use of calculator for all math courses
  Has an adaptive physical education program
  Tape recorders to record class lectures
  Someone else may take class notes
  Student takes exams in separate rooms
  Students have exams read to them
  Students take typewritten exams
  Longer time allowed to complete exams
  Submit papers on cassette tape
  Take limited course load and graduate within time
    required
  Physical education may be waived

MAJORS OFFERED:

  ARCHITECTURE
  BIOLOGICAL SCIENCES
  BUSINESS AND MANAGEMENT
  COMMUNICATIONS
  COMPUTER SCIENCES
  EDUCATION
  FINE AND APPLIED ARTS
  FOREIGN LANGUAGES
  HEALTH
  HOME ECONOMICS
  HUMANITIES
  LIBRARY SCIENCE
  MATHEMATICS
  PHYSICAL SCIENCES
  PSYCHOLOGY
  PUBLIC SERVICES
  SOCIAL SCIENCES

==

SCHREINER COLLEGE
KERRVILLE, TX 78028
512-896-5411

KEY CONTACT: Attn: KAREN DOOLEY, DIRECTOR
                    LEARNING SUPPORT SERVICES

SIZE OF SCHOOL: SMALL

APPLICATION DEADLINE: NONE

	APPROXIMATE TUITION	ROOM AND BOARD
IN STATE	$3690	$2525
OUT-OF-STATE	$3690	$2525

REQUIREMENTS FOR ADMISSIONS:
  High school equivalency diploma
  High school diploma
  Untimed or oral ACT Scores accepted
  Untimed or oral SAT Scores accepted
  WAIS scores required
  Admission requirements modified
  Personal interview
  Placement tests
  Recommendations

ADDITIONAL SERVICES OFFERED:
  Learning Lab
  Diagnostic testing services on campus
  Diagnostic testing services off campus
  Remedial and/or tutorial help available
  Reader services for the blind available for LD

MODIFICATIONS TO TRADITIONAL LEARNING ENVIRONMENT:
  Oral presentation in lieu of written exams
  Use of calculator for all math courses
  Has an adaptive physical education program
  Tape recorders to record class lectures
  Students have exams read to them
  Students take typewritten exams
  Longer time allowed to complete exams
  Submit papers on cassette tape
  Take limited course load and graduate within time
    required
  Extended time limits for graduation

MAJORS OFFERED:

  BUSINESS AND MANAGEMENT
  COMPUTER SCIENCES
  FINE AND APPLIED ARTS
  FOREIGN LANGUAGES
  HUMANITIES
  MATHEMATICS
  SOCIAL SCIENCES

==

UNIVERSITY OF TEXAS - EL PASO
EL PASO, TX 79968
915-747-5576

KEY CONTACT: Attn: Handicapped Student Services

SIZE OF SCHOOL: LARGE

APPLICATION DEADLINE: JULY 1

        APPROXIMATE TUITION   ROOM AND BOARD

IN STATE $ 400 $2000
OUT-OF-STATE $1475 $2000

REQUIREMENTS FOR ADMISSIONS:
  High school equivalency diploma
  High school diploma
  Admission requirements modified

ADDITIONAL SERVICES OFFERED:
  Learning Lab
  Learning Lab has a specialist with a masters degree
    or above in Learning Disabilities
  Diagnostic testing services on campus
  Diagnostic testing services off campus
  Reader services for the blind available for LD
  Handicapped student services works with LD

MODIFICATIONS TO TRADITIONAL LEARNING ENVIRONMENT:
  Oral presentation in lieu of written exams
  Use of calculator for all math courses
  Tape recorders to record class lectures
  Someone else may take class notes
  Multiple choice exams only
  Essay exams only
  Student takes exams in separate rooms
  Students have exams read to them
  Students take typewritten exams
  Longer time allowed to complete exams
  Submit papers on cassette tape
  Take limited course load and graduate within time
    required
  Extended time limits for graduation
  Physical education may be waived

MAJORS OFFERED:

  AREA STUDIES
  BIOLOGICAL SCIENCES
  BUSINESS AND MANAGEMENT
  COMMUNICATIONS
  COMPUTER SCIENCES
  EDUCATION
  ENGINEERING TECHNOLOGIES
  FINE AND APPLIED ARTS
  FOREIGN LANGUAGES
  HEALTH
  HUMANITIES
  MATHEMATICS
  PHYSICAL SCIENCES
  PSYCHOLOGY
  PUBLIC SERVICES
  SOCIAL SCIENCES

===

UTAH STATE UNIVERSITY
LOGAN, UT 84322
801-750-1107

KEY CONTACT: Attn: Handicapped Student Services

SIZE OF SCHOOL: MEDIUM

APPLICATION DEADLINE: NONE

APPROXIMATE TUITION   ROOM AND BOARD

IN STATE	$ 855	$1990
OUT-OF-STATE	$2415	$1990

REQUIREMENTS FOR ADMISSIONS:
  High school equivalency diploma
  High school diploma
  21 years of age or older, with or without a
    high school diploma or equivalency
  ACT Scores required
  Admission requirements modified

ADDITIONAL SERVICES OFFERED:
  Learning Lab
  Learning Lab has a specialist with a masters degree
    or above in Learning Disabilities
  Diagnostic testing services on campus
  Diagnostic testing services off campus
  Remedial and/or tutorial help available
  Reader services for the blind available for LD
  Special Education department
  Handicapped student services works with LD

MODIFICATIONS TO TRADITIONAL LEARNING ENVIRONMENT:
  Tape recorders to record class lectures
  Someone else may take class notes
  Student takes exams in separate rooms
  Students have exams read to them
  Students take typewritten exams
  Longer time allowed to complete exams
  Take limited course load and graduate within time
    required
  Extended time limits for graduation
  Physical education may be waived
  All modifications determined by Teachers and Deans

MAJORS OFFERED:

  AGRICULTURE
  ARCHITECTURE
  AREA STUDIES
  BIOLOGICAL SCIENCES
  BUSINESS AND MANAGEMENT
  COMMUNICATIONS

```
COMPUTER SCIENCES
EDUCATION
ENGINEERING TECHNOLOGIES
FINE AND APPLIED ARTS
FOREIGN LANGUAGES
HEALTH
HOME ECONOMICS
HUMANITIES
LAW
MATHEMATICS
MILITARY SCIENCES
PHYSICAL SCIENCES
PSYCHOLOGY
PUBLIC SERVICES
SOCIAL SCIENCES
```

===

```
WEBER STATE COLLEGE
3750 HARRISON BOULEVARD
OGDEN, UT 84408
801-626-6043
```

KEY CONTACT: Attn: LAMAR C. KAP, DIRECTOR
                    HANDICAPPED STUDENT SERVICES

SIZE OF SCHOOL: MEDIUM

APPLICATION DEADLINE: AUGUST 1

	APPROXIMATE TUITION	ROOM AND BOARD
IN STATE	$ 810	$2025
OUT-OF-STATE	$2190	$2025

REQUIREMENTS FOR ADMISSIONS:
  High school equivalency diploma
  High school diploma
  ACT Scores required
  Admission requirements modified

ADDITIONAL SERVICES OFFERED:
  Learning Lab
  Diagnostic testing services on campus
  Diagnostic testing services off campus
  Remedial and/or tutorial help available
  Reader services for the blind available for LD
  Handicapped student services works with LD

MODIFICATIONS TO TRADITIONAL LEARNING ENVIRONMENT:
  Oral presentation in lieu of written exams

Use of calculator for all math courses
Has an adaptive physical education program
Tape recorders to record class lectures
Someone else may take class notes
Multiple choice exams only
Student takes exams in separate rooms
Students have exams read to them
Longer time allowed to complete exams
Take limited course load and graduate within time
    required
Extended time limits for graduation
Physical education may be waived

MAJORS OFFERED:

ARCHITECTURE
AREA STUDIES
BIOLOGICAL SCIENCES
BUSINESS AND MANAGEMENT
COMMUNICATIONS
COMPUTER SCIENCES
EDUCATION
ENGINEERING TECHNOLOGIES
FINE AND APPLIED ARTS
FOREIGN LANGUAGES
HEALTH
HOME ECONOMICS
HUMANITIES
LAW
PHYSICAL SCIENCES
PSYCHOLOGY
PUBLIC SERVICES
SOCIAL SCIENCES

==

WEBER STATE COLLEGE
OGDEN, UT 84408
801-626-6043

KEY CONTACT: Attn: LAMAR C. KAP, DIRECTOR
                    HANDICAPPED STUDENT SERVICES

SIZE OF SCHOOL: MEDIUM

APPLICATION DEADLINE: AUGUST 1

        APPROXIMATE TUITION   ROOM AND BOARD

IN STATE $ 810 $2025
OUT-OF-STATE $2190 $2025

REQUIREMENTS FOR ADMISSIONS:
  High school equivalency diploma
  High school diploma
  ACT Scores required
  Admission requirements modified

ADDITIONAL SERVICES OFFERED:
  Learning Lab
  Diagnostic testing services on campus
  Diagnostic testing services off campus
  Remedial and/or tutorial help available
  Reader services for the blind available for LD
  Handicapped student services works with LD

MODIFICATIONS TO TRADITIONAL LEARNING ENVIRONMENT:
  Oral presentation in lieu of written exams
  Use of calculator for all math courses
  Has an adaptive physical education program
  Tape recorders to record class lectures
  Someone else may take class notes
  Multiple choice exams only
  Student takes exams in separate rooms
  Students have exams read to them
  Longer time allowed to complete exams
  Take limited course load and graduate within time
    required
  Extended time limits for graduation
  Physical education may be waived

MAJORS OFFERED:

  ARCHITECTURE
  AREA STUDIES
  BIOLOGICAL SCIENCES
  BUSINESS AND MANAGEMENT
  COMMUNICATIONS
  COMPUTER SCIENCES
  EDUCATION
  ENGINEERING TECHNOLOGIES
  FINE AND APPLIED ARTS
  FOREIGN LANGUAGES
  HEALTH
  HOME ECONOMICS
  HUMANITIES
  LAW
  PHYSICAL SCIENCES
  PSYCHOLOGY
  PUBLIC SERVICES
  SOCIAL SCIENCES

==

WESTMINSTER COLLEGE
1840 SOUTH 13TH EAST
SALT LAKE CITY, UT 84105
801-484-7651

KEY CONTACT: Attn: Handicapped Student Services

SIZE OF SCHOOL: SMALL

APPLICATION DEADLINE: NONE

          APPROXIMATE TUITION   ROOM AND BOARD

IN STATE $3660 $2600
OUT-OF-STATE $3660 $2600

REQUIREMENTS FOR ADMISSIONS:
  High school equivalency diploma
  High school diploma
  High school grade point average 2.0

ADDITIONAL SERVICES OFFERED:
  Reader services for the blind available for LD

MODIFICATIONS TO TRADITIONAL LEARNING ENVIRONMENT:
  Oral presentation in lieu of written exams
  Use of calculator for all math courses
  Tape recorders to record class lectures
  Someone else may take class notes
  Multiple choice exams only
  Student takes exams in separate rooms
  Students have exams read to them
  Students take typewritten exams
  Longer time allowed to complete exams
  Submit papers on cassette tape
  Extended time limits for graduation
  Physical education may be waived
  Modifications at the discretion of instructors

MAJORS OFFERED:

  BIOLOGICAL SCIENCES
  BUSINESS AND MANAGEMENT
  COMMUNICATIONS
  COMPUTER SCIENCES
  EDUCATION
  FINE AND APPLIED ARTS
  HEALTH
  HUMANITIES
  MATHEMATICS
  PHYSICAL SCIENCES

```
PSYCHOLOGY
SOCIAL SCIENCES
```

==

```
GODDARD COLLEGE
PLAINFIELD, VT 05667
802-454-8311
```

KEY CONTACT: Attn: DEBRA CRESPIN, ASSISTANT TO THE
                    PRESIDENT

SIZE OF SCHOOL: SMALL

APPLICATION DEADLINE: NONE

	APPROXIMATE TUITION	ROOM AND BOARD
IN STATE	$6500	$2200
OUT-OF-STATE	$6500	$2200

REQUIREMENTS FOR ADMISSIONS:
  High school equivalency diploma
  High school diploma
  Untimed or oral ACT Scores accepted
  Untimed or oral SAT Scores accepted
  Admission requirements modified
  Personal interview
  Recommendations
  Essay

ADDITIONAL SERVICES OFFERED:
  Remedial and/or tutorial help available
  Special Education department
  Handicapped student services works with LD

MODIFICATIONS TO TRADITIONAL LEARNING ENVIRONMENT:
  Oral presentation in lieu of written exams
  Use of calculator for all math courses
  Tape recorders to record class lectures
  Someone else may take class notes
  Submit papers on cassette tape
  Take limited course load and graduate within time
    required
  Extended time limits for graduation

MAJORS OFFERED:

  AGRICULTURE
  AREA STUDIES
  BIOLOGICAL SCIENCES

```
BUSINESS AND MANAGEMENT
COMMUNICATIONS
COMPUTER SCIENCES
EDUCATION
FINE AND APPLIED ARTS
HUMANITIES
MATHEMATICS
PHYSICAL SCIENCES
PSYCHOLOGY
PUBLIC SERVICES
SOCIAL SCIENCES
```

==

```
SOUTHERN VERMONT COLLEGE
MONUMENT ROAD
BENNINGTON, VT 05201
802-442-5427
```

KEY CONTACT: Attn: LISA SCHELL, COORDINATOR
                     LEARNING DISABILITES PROGRAM

SIZE OF SCHOOL: SMALL

APPLICATION DEADLINE: NONE

	APPROXIMATE TUITION	ROOM AND BOARD
IN STATE	$3400	$2800
OUT-OF-STATE	$3400	$2800

REQUIREMENTS FOR ADMISSIONS:
  High school equivalency diploma
  High school diploma
  Untimed or oral ACT Scores accepted
  Untimed or oral SAT Scores accepted
  WAIS scores required
  University or College sponsored tests
  Admission requirements modified
  Personal interview
  Placement tests
  Recommendations

ADDITIONAL SERVICES OFFERED:
  Learning Lab
  Learning Lab has a specialist with a masters degree
    or above in Learning Disabilities
  Diagnostic testing services on campus
  Diagnostic testing services off campus
  Remedial and/or tutorial help available

MODIFICATIONS TO TRADITIONAL LEARNING ENVIRONMENT:
  Oral presentation in lieu of written exams
  Tape recorders to record class lectures
  Someone else may take class notes
  Extended time limits for graduation
  Each students needs are considered individually

MAJORS OFFERED:

  BIOLOGICAL SCIENCES
  BUSINESS AND MANAGEMENT
  COMMUNICATIONS
  HEALTH
  HUMANITIES
  PUBLIC SERVICES

===

UNIVERSITY OF VERMONT
194 SOUTH PROSPECT STREET
BURLINGTON, VT 05401
802-656-3370

KEY CONTACT: Attn: NANCY OLIKER, COORDINATOR
                    HANDICAPPED STUDENT SERVICES

SIZE OF SCHOOL: MEDIUM

APPLICATION DEADLINE: FEBRUARY 1

        APPROXIMATE TUITION   ROOM AND BOARD

IN STATE $2355 $2610
OUT-OF-STATE $5990 $2610

REQUIREMENTS FOR ADMISSIONS:
  High school equivalency diploma
  High school diploma
  SAT Scores required
  Untimed or oral SAT Scores accepted
  Particular rank in class (out of state - top 20%)
    (in state - top 30%)
  Recommendations
  Essay

ADDITIONAL SERVICES OFFERED:
  Learning Lab has a specialist with a masters degree
    or above in Learning Disabilities
  Diagnostic testing services on campus
  Diagnostic testing services off campus
  Remedial and/or tutorial help available

Reader services for the blind available for LD
Special Education department
Handicapped student services works with LD

MODIFICATIONS TO TRADITIONAL LEARNING ENVIRONMENT:
  Oral presentation in lieu of written exams
  Use of calculator for all math courses
  Has an adaptive physical education program
  Tape recorders to record class lectures
  Someone else may take class notes
  Student takes exams in separate rooms (possible)
  Students have exams read to them
  Students take typewritten exams (possible)
  Longer time allowed to complete exams
  Submit papers on cassette tape (possible)
  Extended time limits for graduation
  Physical education may be waived
  Arrangements negotiated with professor with
    assistance of staff of LD program

MAJORS OFFERED:

  AGRICULTURE
  ARCHITECTURE
  AREA STUDIES
  BIOLOGICAL SCIENCES
  BUSINESS AND MANAGEMENT
  COMPUTER SCIENCES
  EDUCATION
  ENGINEERING TECHNOLOGIES
  FINE AND APPLIED ARTS
  FOREIGN LANGUAGES
  HEALTH
  HOME ECONOMICS
  HUMANITIES
  MATHEMATICS
  PHYSICAL SCIENCES
  PSYCHOLOGY
  PUBLIC SERVICES
  SOCIAL SCIENCES

==

AVERETT COLLEGE
WEST MAIN STREET
DANVILLE, VA 24541
804-793-7811

KEY CONTACT: Attn: C. KUSHNER

SIZE OF SCHOOL: SMALL

APPLICATION DEADLINE: AUGUST 15

         APPROXIMATE TUITION   ROOM AND BOARD

	APPROXIMATE TUITION	ROOM AND BOARD
IN STATE	$3450	$2500
OUT-OF-STATE	$3450	$2500

REQUIREMENTS FOR ADMISSIONS:
  High school equivalency diploma
  High school diploma
  ACT Scores required
  SAT Scores required
  Admission requirements modified

ADDITIONAL SERVICES OFFERED:
  Learning Lab
  Learning Lab has a specialist with a masters degree
    or above in Learning Disabilities
  Diagnostic testing services off campus
  Remedial and/or tutorial help available
  Reader services for the blind available for LD
  Special Education department

MODIFICATIONS TO TRADITIONAL LEARNING ENVIRONMENT:
  Oral presentation in lieu of written exams
  Use of calculator for all math courses
  Tape recorders to record class lectures
  Someone else may take class notes
  Multiple choice exams only
  Student takes exams in separate rooms
  Students have exams read to them
  Students take typewritten exams
  Longer time allowed to complete exams
  Submit papers on cassette tape
  Take limited course load and graduate within time
    required
  Extended time limits for graduation
  Physical education may be waived

MAJORS OFFERED:

  AGRICULTURE
  BIOLOGICAL SCIENCES
  BUSINESS AND MANAGEMENT
  COMMUNICATIONS
  EDUCATION
  FINE AND APPLIED ARTS
  HEALTH
  HUMANITIES
  MATHEMATICS
  PHYSICAL SCIENCES

```
PSYCHOLOGY
PUBLIC SERVICES
SOCIAL SCIENCES
THEOLOGY
```

==

```
GEORGE MASON UNIVERSITY /
4400 UNIVERSITY DRIVE
FAIRFAX, VA 22030
703-323-2100
```

KEY CONTACT: Attn: Handicapped Student Services

SIZE OF SCHOOL: LARGE

APPLICATION DEADLINE: MARCH 1

	APPROXIMATE TUITION	ROOM AND BOARD
IN STATE	$1380	$3265
OUT-OF-STATE	$2665	$3265

REQUIREMENTS FOR ADMISSIONS:
  SAT Scores required
  Admission requirements modified

ADDITIONAL SERVICES OFFERED:
  Learning Lab
  Learning Lab has a specialist with a masters degree
    or above in Learning Disabilities
  Diagnostic testing services off campus
  Reader services for the blind available for LD
  Handicapped student services works with LD

MODIFICATIONS TO TRADITIONAL LEARNING ENVIRONMENT:
  Use of calculator for all math courses
  Tape recorders to record class lectures
  Someone else may take class notes
  Multiple choice exams only
  Essay exams only
  Student takes exams in separate rooms
  Students have exams read to them
  Longer time allowed to complete exams
  Submit papers on cassette tape
  Extended time limits for graduation
  Physical education may be waived
  Some modifications at the discretion of individual
    instructor

MAJORS OFFERED:

    AREA STUDIES
    BIOLOGICAL SCIENCES
    BUSINESS AND MANAGEMENT
    COMMUNICATIONS
    COMPUTER SCIENCES
    EDUCATION
    ENGINEERING TECHNOLOGIES
    FINE AND APPLIED ARTS
    FOREIGN LANGUAGES
    HEALTH
    HUMANITIES
    MATHEMATICS
    PHYSICAL SCIENCES
    PSYCHOLOGY
    PUBLIC SERVICES
    SOCIAL SCIENCES

===

HOLLINS COLLEGE
HOLLINS COLLEGE, VA 24020
703-362-6401

KEY CONTACT: Attn: Handicapped Student Services

SIZE OF SCHOOL: SMALL

APPLICATION DEADLINE: MARCH 1

	APPROXIMATE TUITION	ROOM AND BOARD
IN STATE	$6500	$3150
OUT-OF-STATE	$6500	$3150

REQUIREMENTS FOR ADMISSIONS:
    SAT Scores required
    Personal interview
    Recommendations

ADDITIONAL SERVICES OFFERED:
    Reader services for the blind available for LD

MODIFICATIONS TO TRADITIONAL LEARNING ENVIRONMENT:
    Oral presentation in lieu of written exams
    Use of calculator for all math courses
    Tape recorders to record class lectures
    Someone else may take class notes
    Multiple choice exams only
    Student takes exams in separate rooms

Students have exams read to them
Students take typewritten exams
Longer time allowed to complete exams
Submit papers on cassette tape
Extended time limits for graduation
Physical education may be waived
Modifications at the discretion of individual
  instructors

MAJORS OFFERED:

AREA STUDIES
BIOLOGICAL SCIENCES
COMPUTER SCIENCES
EDUCATION
FINE AND APPLIED ARTS
FOREIGN LANGUAGES
HUMANITIES
MATHEMATICS
PHYSICAL SCIENCES
PSYCHOLOGY
SOCIAL SCIENCES

===

UNIVERSITY OF VIRGINIA
CHARLOTTESVILLE, VA 22904
804-924-7751

KEY CONTACT: Attn: Handicapped Student Services

SIZE OF SCHOOL: LARGE

APPLICATION DEADLINE: FEBRUARY 1

        APPROXIMATE TUITION   ROOM AND BOARD

IN STATE $1570 $2570
OUT-OF-STATE $3750 $2570

REQUIREMENTS FOR ADMISSIONS:
  SAT Scores required
  Particular rank in class Top 10%
  Admission requirements modified

ADDITIONAL SERVICES OFFERED:
  Learning Lab
  Learning Lab has a specialist with a masters degree
    or above in Learning Disabilities
  Diagnostic testing services on campus
  Diagnostic testing services off campus

SIZE OF SCHOOL: MEDIUM

APPLICATION DEADLINE: NONE

          APPROXIMATE TUITION   ROOM AND BOARD

IN STATE $4800 $3060
OUT-OF-STATE $4800 $3060

REQUIREMENTS FOR ADMISSIONS:
  High school equivalency diploma
  High school diploma
  21 years of age or older, with or without a
    high school diploma or equivalency
  ACT or SAT Scores required
  Untimed or oral ACT Scores accepted
  Untimed or oral SAT Scores accepted
  Particular rank in class (not specified)
  Admission requirements modified upon request if
    acceptable

ADDITIONAL SERVICES OFFERED:
  Remedial and/or tutorial help available
  Reader services for the blind available for LD
  Handicapped student services works with LD

MODIFICATIONS TO TRADITIONAL LEARNING ENVIRONMENT:
  All modifications are possible but have never been
    utilized as yet

MAJORS OFFERED:

  BIOLOGICAL SCIENCES
  BUSINESS AND MANAGEMENT
  COMMUNICATIONS
  COMPUTER SCIENCES
  EDUCATION
  ENGINEERING TECHNOLOGIES
  FINE AND APPLIED ARTS
  FOREIGN LANGUAGES
  HEALTH
  HUMANITIES
  MATHEMATICS
  MILITARY SCIENCES
  PHYSICAL SCIENCES
  PSYCHOLOGY
  PUBLIC SERVICES
  SOCIAL SCIENCES

===

```
              APPROXIMATE TUITION    ROOM AND BOARD

IN STATE              $1470          $2290
OUT-OF-STATE          $2990          $2290
```

REQUIREMENTS FOR ADMISSIONS:
   SAT Scores required
   High school grade point average (not specified)

ADDITIONAL SERVICES OFFERED:
   Learning Lab
   Learning Lab has a specialist with a masters degree
      or above in Learning Disabilities
   Diagnostic testing services on campus
   Remedial and/or tutorial help available
   Reader services for the blind available for LD
   Special Education department
   Handicapped student services works with LD

MODIFICATIONS TO TRADITIONAL LEARNING ENVIRONMENT:
   Use of calculator for all math courses
   Tape recorders to record class lectures
   Someone else may take class notes
   Student takes exams in separate rooms
   Students have exams read to them
   Students take typewritten exams
   Longer time allowed to complete exams
   Submit papers on cassette tape
   Extended time limits for graduation
   Physical education may be waived

MAJORS OFFERED:

   ARCHITECTURE
   BIOLOGICAL SCIENCES
   BUSINESS AND MANAGEMENT
   COMMUNICATIONS
   COMPUTER SCIENCES
   EDUCATION
   ENGINEERING TECHNOLOGIES
   FINE AND APPLIED ARTS
   FOREIGN LANGUAGES
   HEALTH
   HUMANITIES
   MATHEMATICS
   PHYSICAL SCIENCES
   PSYCHOLOGY
   PUBLIC SERVICES
   SOCIAL SCIENCES
   THEOLOGY

```
VIRGINIA INTERMONT COLLEGE
MOORE STREET
BRISTOL, VA 24201
703-669-6101
```

KEY CONTACT: Attn: CHARLES H. FADDIS, DIRECTOR
                     SPECIAL SERVICES

SIZE OF SCHOOL: SMALL

APPLICATION DEADLINE: NONE

	APPROXIMATE TUITION	ROOM AND BOARD
IN STATE	$3525	$2200
OUT-OF-STATE	$3525	$2200

REQUIREMENTS FOR ADMISSIONS:
  High school equivalency diploma
  High school diploma
  Untimed or oral ACT Scores accepted
  Untimed or oral SAT Scores accepted
  High school grade point average 2.0
  Admission requirements modified
  Personal interview
  Recommendations

ADDITIONAL SERVICES OFFERED:
  Diagnostic testing services on campus
  Diagnostic testing services off campus
  Remedial and/or tutorial help available
  Reader services for the blind available for LD
  Special services for disadvantaged students works
    with LD students

MODIFICATIONS TO TRADITIONAL LEARNING ENVIRONMENT:
  Oral presentation in lieu of written exams
  Has an adaptive physical education program
  Tape recorders to record class lectures
  Someone else may take class notes
  Student takes exams in separate rooms
  Students have exams read to them
  Students take typewritten exams
  Longer time allowed to complete exams
  Submit papers on cassette tape
  Take limited course load and graduate within time
    required
  Physical education may be waived

MAJORS OFFERED:

    AGRICULTURE
    BIOLOGICAL SCIENCES
    BUSINESS AND MANAGEMENT
    COMMUNICATIONS
    EDUCATION
    FINE AND APPLIED ARTS
    HEALTH
    HOME ECONOMICS
    HUMANITIES
    PSYCHOLOGY
    PUBLIC SERVICES
    SOCIAL SCIENCES
    THEOLOGY

==

VIRGINIA POLYTECHNIC INSTITUTE AND STATE UNIVERSITY
BLAKSBURG, VA 24061
703-961-6267

KEY CONTACT: Attn: Handicapped Student Services

SIZE OF SCHOOL: LARGE

APPLICATION DEADLINE: JANUARY 1

	APPROXIMATE TUITION	ROOM AND BOARD
IN STATE	$1400	$1500
OUT-OF-STATE	$2800	$1500

REQUIREMENTS FOR ADMISSIONS:
  High school equivalency diploma
  High school diploma
  SAT Scores required
  Untimed or oral SAT Scores accepted

ADDITIONAL SERVICES OFFERED:
  Remedial and/or tutorial help available
  Reader services for the blind available for LD
  Special Education department
  Handicapped student services works with LD

MODIFICATIONS TO TRADITIONAL LEARNING ENVIRONMENT:
  Oral presentation in lieu of written exams
  Tape recorders to record class lectures
  Someone else may take class notes
  Student takes exams in separate rooms
  Students have exams read to them

    Students take typewritten exams
    Longer time allowed to complete exams
    Submit papers on cassette tape
    Physical education may be waived
    Modifications vary person to person

MAJORS OFFERED:

    AGRICULTURE
    ARCHITECTURE
    BIOLOGICAL SCIENCES
    BUSINESS AND MANAGEMENT
    COMMUNICATIONS
    COMPUTER SCIENCES
    EDUCATION
    ENGINEERING TECHNOLOGIES
    FINE AND APPLIED ARTS
    FOREIGN LANGUAGES
    HEALTH
    HOME ECONOMICS
    HUMANITIES
    LAW
    MATHEMATICS
    PHYSICAL SCIENCES
    PSYCHOLOGY
    PUBLIC SERVICES
    SOCIAL SCIENCES

==

UNIVERSITY OF WASHINGTON
SEATTLE, WA 98105
206-543-9686

KEY CONTACT: Attn: Handicapped Student Services

SIZE OF SCHOOL: LARGE

APPLICATION DEADLINE: MAY 1

        APPROXIMATE TUITION   ROOM AND BOARD

IN STATE $1175 $2500
OUT-OF-STATE $3255 $2500

REQUIREMENTS FOR ADMISSIONS:
    ACT Scores required
    SAT Scores required
    High school grade point average (not specified)
    Admission requirements modified

ADDITIONAL SERVICES OFFERED:
  Learning Lab
  Learning Lab has a specialist with a masters degree
    or above in Learning Disabilities
  Remedial and/or tutorial help available
  Reader services for the blind available for LD
  Special Education department
  Handicapped student services works with LD

MODIFICATIONS TO TRADITIONAL LEARNING ENVIRONMENT:
  Oral presentation in lieu of written exams
  Use of calculator for all math courses
  Tape recorders to record class lectures
  Someone else may take class notes
  Multiple choice exams only
  Essay exams only
  Student takes exams in separate rooms
  Students have exams read to them
  Students take typewritten exams
  Longer time allowed to complete exams
  Submit papers on cassette tape
  Extended time limits for graduation
  Physical education may be waived

MAJORS OFFERED:

  AGRICULTURE
  ARCHITECTURE
  AREA STUDIES
  BIOLOGICAL SCIENCES
  BUSINESS AND MANAGEMENT
  COMMUNICATIONS
  COMPUTER SCIENCES
  EDUCATION
  ENGINEERING TECHNOLOGIES
  FINE AND APPLIED ARTS
  FOREIGN LANGUAGES
  HEALTH
  HUMANITIES
  LIBRARY SCIENCE
  MATHEMATICS
  PHYSICAL SCIENCES
  PSYCHOLOGY
  PUBLIC SERVICES
  SOCIAL SCIENCES

==

WASHINGTON STATE UNIVERSITY
PULLMAN, WA 99164
509-335-5586

KEY CONTACT: Attn: Handicapped Student Services

SIZE OF SCHOOL: LARGE

APPLICATION DEADLINE: MAY 1

	APPROXIMATE TUITION	ROOM AND BOARD
IN STATE	$1175	$2300
OUT-OF-STATE	$3255	$2300

REQUIREMENTS FOR ADMISSIONS:
  High school diploma
  High school grade point average   2.5
  Admission requirements modified

ADDITIONAL SERVICES OFFERED:
  Learning Lab
  Learning Lab has a specialist with a masters degree
    or above in Learning Disabilities
  Diagnostic testing services on campus
  Diagnostic testing services off campus
  Remedial and/or tutorial help available
  Reader services for the blind available for LD
  Handicapped student services works with LD

MODIFICATIONS TO TRADITIONAL LEARNING ENVIRONMENT:
  Oral presentation in lieu of written exams
  Use of calculator for all math courses
  Tape recorders to record class lectures
  Someone else may take class notes
  Multiple choice exams only
  Essay exams only
  Student takes exams in separate rooms
  Students have exams read to them
  Students take typewritten exams
  Longer time allowed to complete exams
  Submit papers on cassette tape
  Extended time limits for graduation
  Physical education may be waived

MAJORS OFFERED:

  AGRICULTURE
  ARCHITECTURE
  AREA STUDIES
  BIOLOGICAL SCIENCES
  BUSINESS AND MANAGEMENT
  COMMUNICATIONS
  COMPUTER SCIENCES
  EDUCATION

```
ENGINEERING TECHNOLOGIES
FINE AND APPLIED ARTS
FOREIGN LANGUAGES
HEALTH
HOME ECONOMICS
HUMANITIES
LAW
MATHEMATICS
MILITARY SCIENCES
PHYSICAL SCIENCES
PSYCHOLOGY
PUBLIC SERVICES
SOCIAL SCIENCES
```

==

```
WESTERN WASHINGTON UNIVERSITY
BELLINGHAM, WA 98225
206-676-3440
```

KEY CONTACT: Attn: OFFICE OF STUDENT LIFE SUPPORT
                     PROGRAMS AND SERVICES

SIZE OF SCHOOL: MEDIUM

APPLICATION DEADLINE: SEPTEMBER 1

	APPROXIMATE TUITION	ROOM AND BOARD
IN STATE	$ 940	$2175
OUT-OF-STATE	$3210	$2175

REQUIREMENTS FOR ADMISSIONS:
  High school equivalency diploma
  High school diploma
  ACT Scores required (out of state only)
  Untimed or oral ACT Scores accepted
  SAT Scores required (out of state only)
  Untimed or oral SAT Scores accepted
  University or College sponsored tests (for placement
    only)
  Particular rank in class 50%
  High school grade point average 2.5

ADDITIONAL SERVICES OFFERED:
  Diagnostic testing services on campus
  Diagnostic testing services off campus
  Remedial and/or tutorial help available
  Reader services for the blind available for LD
  Special Education department
  Handicapped student services works with LD

MODIFICATIONS TO TRADITIONAL LEARNING ENVIRONMENT:
  Has an adaptive physical education program
  Tape recorders to record class lectures
  Someone else may take class notes
  Student takes exams in separate rooms
  Students have exams read to them
  Students take typewritten exams
  Longer time allowed to complete exams
  Modifications depend on instructor

MAJORS OFFERED:

  ARCHITECTURE
  AREA STUDIES
  BIOLOGICAL SCIENCES
  BUSINESS AND MANAGEMENT
  COMMUNICATIONS
  COMPUTER SCIENCES
  EDUCATION
  ENGINEERING TECHNOLOGIES
  FINE AND APPLIED ARTS
  FOREIGN LANGUAGES
  HEALTH
  HOME ECONOMICS
  HUMANITIES
  MATHEMATICS
  PHYSICAL SCIENCES
  PSYCHOLOGY
  PUBLIC SERVICES
  SOCIAL SCIENCES

==

SALEM COLLEGE
SALEM, WV 26426
304-782-5336

KEY CONTACT: Attn: JIM GLESEY

SIZE OF SCHOOL: SMALL

APPLICATION DEADLINE: AUGUST 15

       APPROXIMATE TUITION   ROOM AND BOARD

IN STATE $3810 $2115
OUT-OF-STATE $3810 $2115

REQUIREMENTS FOR ADMISSIONS:
  High school equivalency diploma
  High school diploma

Untimed or oral ACT Scores accepted
Untimed or oral SAT Scores accepted
High school grade point average (not specified)
Admission requirements modified
Personal interview
Recommendations

ADDITIONAL SERVICES OFFERED:
Learning Lab
Diagnostic testing services on campus
Diagnostic testing services off campus
Remedial and/or tutorial help available
Reader services for the blind available for LD

MODIFICATIONS TO TRADITIONAL LEARNING ENVIRONMENT:
Oral presentation in lieu of written exams
Tape recorders to record class lectures
Someone else may take class notes
Student takes exams in separate rooms
Students have exams read to them
Students take typewritten exams
Longer time allowed to complete exams
Submit papers on cassette tape
Extended time limits for graduation
Physical education may be waived

MAJORS OFFERED:

AGRICULTURE
BIOLOGICAL SCIENCES
BUSINESS AND MANAGEMENT
COMMUNICATIONS
COMPUTER SCIENCES
EDUCATION
ENGINEERING TECHNOLOGIES
FINE AND APPLIED ARTS
HEALTH
MATHEMATICS
PSYCHOLOGY
PUBLIC SERVICES
SOCIAL SCIENCES

===

MARQUETTE UNIVERSITY
1217 WEST WISCONSIN AVENUE
MILWAUKEE, WI 53233
414-224-7302

KEY CONTACT: Attn: PATRICIA ALMAN, COORDINATOR
                    HANDICAPPED STUDENT SERVICES

SIZE OF SCHOOL: MEDIUM

APPLICATION DEADLINE: NONE

APPROXIMATE TUITION   ROOM AND BOARD

	APPROXIMATE TUITION	ROOM AND BOARD
IN STATE	$4800	$3060
OUT-OF-STATE	$4800	$3060

REQUIREMENTS FOR ADMISSIONS:
  High school equivalency diploma
  High school diploma
  21 years of age or older, with or without a
    high school diploma or equivalency
  ACT or SAT Scores required
  Untimed or oral ACT Scores accepted
  Untimed or oral SAT Scores accepted
  Particular rank in class (not specified)
  Admission requirements modified upon request if
    acceptable

ADDITIONAL SERVICES OFFERED:
  Remedial and/or tutorial help available
  Reader services for the blind available for LD
  Handicapped student services works with LD

MODIFICATIONS TO TRADITIONAL LEARNING ENVIRONMENT:
  All modifications are possible but have never been
    utilized as yet

MAJORS OFFERED:

  BIOLOGICAL SCIENCES
  BUSINESS AND MANAGEMENT
  COMMUNICATIONS
  COMPUTER SCIENCES
  EDUCATION
  ENGINEERING TECHNOLOGIES
  FINE AND APPLIED ARTS
  FOREIGN LANGUAGES
  HEALTH
  HUMANITIES
  MATHEMATICS
  MILITARY SCIENCES
  PHYSICAL SCIENCES
  PSYCHOLOGY
  PUBLIC SERVICES
  SOCIAL SCIENCES

===

UNIVERSITY OF WISCONSIN - LA CROSSE
LA CROSSE, WI 54601
608-785-8067

KEY CONTACT: Attn: Handicapped Student Services

SIZE OF SCHOOL: MEDIUM

APPLICATION DEADLINE: NONE

	APPROXIMATE TUITION	ROOM AND BOARD
IN STATE	$1070	$1660
OUT-OF-STATE	$3400	$1660

REQUIREMENTS FOR ADMISSIONS:
  High school equivalency diploma
  High school diploma
  21 years of age or older, with or without a
    high school diploma or equivalency
  Admission requirements modified

ADDITIONAL SERVICES OFFERED:
  Learning Lab
  Learning Lab has a specialist with a masters degree
    or above in Learning Disabilities
  Diagnostic testing services on campus
  Diagnostic testing services off campus
  Remedial and/or tutorial help available
  Reader services for the blind available for LD
  Handicapped student services works with LD

MODIFICATIONS TO TRADITIONAL LEARNING ENVIRONMENT:
  Has an adaptive physical education program
  Tape recorders to record class lectures
  Someone else may take class notes
  Student takes exams in separate rooms
  Students have exams read to them
  Students take typewritten exams
  Longer time allowed to complete exams
  Extended time limits for graduation
  Physical education may be waived

MAJORS OFFERED:

  AREA STUDIES
  BIOLOGICAL SCIENCES
  BUSINESS AND MANAGEMENT
  COMMUNICATIONS
  COMPUTER SCIENCES
  EDUCATION

```
FINE AND APPLIED ARTS
FOREIGN LANGUAGES
HEALTH
HUMANITIES
LAW
MATHEMATICS
MILITARY SCIENCES
PHYSICAL SCIENCES
PSYCHOLOGY
PUBLIC SERVICES
SOCIAL SCIENCES
```

===

UNIVERSITY OF WISCONSIN - MADISON
750 UNIVERSITY AVENUE
MADISON, WI 53706
608-262-3961

KEY CONTACT: Attn: NANCY SMITH, COORDINATOR
                    MCBURNEY RESOURCE CENTER

SIZE OF SCHOOL: LARGE

APPLICATION DEADLINE: MARCH 1

           APPROXIMATE TUITION   ROOM AND BOARD

	APPROXIMATE TUITION	ROOM AND BOARD
IN STATE	$1240	$2200
OUT-OF-STATE	$4180	$2200

REQUIREMENTS FOR ADMISSIONS:
  High school equivalency diploma
  High school diploma
  Particular rank in class Top 50%

ADDITIONAL SERVICES OFFERED:
  Has a specialist with a masters degree
    or above in Learning Disabilities
  Diagnostic testing services off campus
  Remedial and/or tutorial help available
  Reader services for the blind available for LD
  Handicapped student services works with LD

MODIFICATIONS TO TRADITIONAL LEARNING ENVIRONMENT:
  Oral presentation in lieu of written exams
  Use of calculator for all math courses
  Has an adaptive physical education program
  Tape recorders to record class lectures
  Someone else may take class notes
  Multiple choice exams only

```
Essay exams only
Student takes exams in separate rooms
Students have exams read to them
Longer time allowed to complete exams
```

MAJORS OFFERED:

```
AGRICULTURE
ARCHITECTURE
AREA STUDIES
BIOLOGICAL SCIENCES
BUSINESS AND MANAGEMENT
COMMUNICATIONS
COMPUTER SCIENCES
EDUCATION
ENGINEERING TECHNOLOGIES
FINE AND APPLIED ARTS
FOREIGN LANGUAGES
HEALTH
HOME ECONOMICS
HUMANITIES
LAW
MATHEMATICS
MILITARY SCIENCES
PHYSICAL SCIENCES
PSYCHOLOGY
PUBLIC SERVICES
SOCIAL SCIENCES
```

===

```
UNIVERSITY OF WISCONSIN - OSHKOSH
135 DEMPSEY HALL
OSHKOSH, WI 54901
414-424-0202
```

KEY CONTACT: Attn: Handicapped Student Services

SIZE OF SCHOOL: MEDIUM

APPLICATION DEADLINE: NONE

	APPROXIMATE TUITION	ROOM AND BOARD
IN STATE	$1075	$1840
OUT-OF-STATE	$3475	$1840

REQUIREMENTS FOR ADMISSIONS:
  High school equivalency diploma
  High school diploma
  Admission requirements modified

ADDITIONAL SERVICES OFFERED:
  Learning Lab
  Learning Lab has a specialist with a masters degree
    or above in Learning Disabilities
  Diagnostic testing services on campus
  Remedial and/or tutorial help available
  Reader services for the blind available for LD
  Special Education department
  Handicapped student services works with LD

MODIFICATIONS TO TRADITIONAL LEARNING ENVIRONMENT:
  Oral presentation in lieu of written exams
  Has an adaptive physical education program
  Tape recorders to record class lectures
  Someone else may take class notes
  Student takes exams in separate rooms
  Students have exams read to them
  Students take typewritten exams
  Longer time allowed to complete exams
  Physical education may be waived

MAJORS OFFERED:

  AREA STUDIES
  BIOLOGICAL SCIENCES
  BUSINESS AND MANAGEMENT
  COMMUNICATIONS
  COMPUTER SCIENCES
  EDUCATION
  FINE AND APPLIED ARTS
  FOREIGN LANGUAGES
  HEALTH
  HUMANITIES
  LAW
  LIBRARY SCIENCE
  MATHEMATICS
  PHYSICAL SCIENCES
  PSYCHOLOGY
  PUBLIC SERVICES
  SOCIAL SCIENCES

==

UNIVERSITY OF WYOMING
LARAMIE, WY 82071
307-766-5160

KEY CONTACT: Attn: Handicapped Student Services

SIZE OF SCHOOL: MEDIUM

APPLICATION DEADLINE: JULY 15

         APPROXIMATE TUITION   ROOM AND BOARD

IN STATE $ 620 $2400
OUT-OF-STATE $2075 $2400

REQUIREMENTS FOR ADMISSIONS:
  High school equivalency diploma
  High school diploma
  ACT Scores required
  Admission requirements modified

ADDITIONAL SERVICES OFFERED:
  Learning Lab
  Learning Lab has a specialist with a masters degree
     or above in Learning Disabilities
  Diagnostic testing services on campus
  Diagnostic testing services off campus
  Remedial and/or tutorial help available
  Reader services for the blind available for LD
  Handicapped student services works with LD

MODIFICATIONS TO TRADITIONAL LEARNING ENVIRONMENT:
  Use of calculator for all math courses
  Has an adaptive physical education program
  Tape recorders to record class lectures
  Someone else may take class notes
  Student takes exams in separate rooms
  Students have exams read to them
  Students take typewritten exams
  Longer time allowed to complete exams
  Submit papers on cassette tape
  Extended time limits for graduation
  Physical education may be waived

MAJORS OFFERED:

  AGRICULTURE
  ARCHITECTURE
  AREA STUDIES
  BIOLOGICAL SCIENCES
  BUSINESS AND MANAGEMENT
  COMMUNICATIONS
  COMPUTER SCIENCES
  EDUCATION
  ENGINEERING TECHNOLOGIES
  FINE AND APPLIED ARTS
  FOREIGN LANGUAGES
  HEALTH
  HOME ECONOMICS

```
HUMANITIES
LAW
MATHEMATICS
PHYSICAL SCIENCES
PSYCHOLOGY
PUBLIC SERVICES
SOCIAL SCIENCES
```

==